INTERNATIONAL TERRORISM AND
WORLD SECURITY

INTERNATIONAL TERRORISM AND WORLD SECURITY

A HALSTED PRESS BOOK

JOHN WILEY & SONS

New York   Toronto

Published in the U.S.A. and
Canada by Halsted Press, a
Division of John Wiley & Sons, Inc.,

© 1975 International School on Disarmament and
Research on Conflicts Fifth Course

Library of Congress Cataloging in Publication Data
International Schools on Disarmament and Research on
    Conflicts, 5th, Urbino, Italy, 1974.
    International terrorism and world security.

    "A Halsted Press book."
    1. Terrorism. 2. Atomic Weapons and disarmament.
3. Security, International. I. Carlton, David, 1938-
II. Schaerf, Carlo. III. Title.
JX6731.T4154 1974   327'.116   75-16273
ISBN 0-470-13503-4

Printed in Great Britain

JX
6731
.T4
I 54
1974

CONTENTS

Preface

ALMA COLLEGE
MONTEITH LIBRARY
ALMA, MICHIGAN

PREFACE

The papers in this volume were presented to the Fifth Course of the International School on Disarmament and Research on Conflicts, held in Urbino, Italy, between 12 and 24 August 1974.

The organisation of the course was made possible by the generous collaboration and financial contributions of different organisations and individuals.

For their financial contributions we wish to express our gratitude to:
UNESCO, in particular Prof. M. Paronetto-Valier;
The Ford Foundation, in particular Mr William B. Bader;
The Italian Ministry of Public Education;
The Italian National Research Council.

For hospitality in the City of Urbino and in Collegio Universitario we are indebted to:
The University of Urbino and its Rector, Prof. Carlo Bo;
The Collegio Universitario and the University of Urbino, its Director Prof. Giorgio Baiardi and Miss Giulia Zannini.
Dr Smeralda Bozzo and Mr Fernando Pacciano collaborated in the preparatory work in Frascati.

We would also like to acknowledge the dedicated collaboration of Miss Virginia Panaccia, Anna Centamore, Laura Matriolia and the staff of the Collegio Universitario.

The editors are grateful for help with translation to Mr. Hugh Collingham; and for advice on some international legal passages to Dr Peter Slinn.

The editors wish to thank Dr Christophe Bertram and the International Institute for Strategic Studies for giving permission to General Pasti to reproduce major sections from its annual publication, *The Military Balance*. Thanks are also due to Dr Ciro Zoppo and the California Arms Control and Foreign Policy Seminar under whose auspices three papers in this volume were originally prepared.

All opinions expressed during the formal lectures as well as during the ensuing discussions are of a purely private nature and do not necessarily represent the official opinion either of the organisers of the School or of the organisations to which the speakers belong.

SUMMARY OF PROCEEDINGS: OUR VIOLENT FUTURE

J. Henk Leurdijk

Introduction

One conclusion which relates to all subjects treated during the two
weeks of the ISODARCO discussions is that our future is going to be
violent. Two types of violence which we are experiencing already and
on which the major part of our discussions focused were nuclear deterrence and international terrorism. Although they are very different in
character and magnitude, there are nevertheless more similarities than
just the semantic similarity of deterrence and terror.

The broader perspective in which the discussions took place was the
recognition of the need for a new kind of world order which is still far
away but to which many references were made. And within this perspective I will touch only on those paradoxes and inconsistencies which
are inevitably part of any discussion on violence in our system.

Consideration was given to how political violence manifests itself in
the present international system which is generally regarded as having
three important features: the almost complete decolonisation except
for the colonial systems in Southern Africa; the pre-eminence of the
Soviet Union and the United States as the two superpowers whose relations have developed from the dangerous Cold War confrontation into
an alleged superpower bilateralism; and the existence of and race in
nuclear armaments.

Among those states which in the past played the power game of
war and alliances, open violence has lost its attractiveness as a result of
the existence of nuclear weapons. It is often said that the world has
experienced a generation of peace among the major powers because the
existence of these weapons has had a stabilising effect in an atmosphere
of Cold War antagonism, which might have easily erupted into open
violence. This is an attractive proposition to those second-rank powers
that consider themselves also to be involved in major antagonisms and,
rightly or wrongly, makes them regard nuclear weapons as perfectly
legitimate instruments of deterrence — which is their main justification
for trying to acquire them. How, then, can we prevent the proliferation
of nuclear weapons to minor powers when the major powers justify
nuclear weapons as a factor promoting peace, which is defined as the

1

absence of open war? This was the first paradox or inconsistency to emerge from the discussions.

There can be no doubt that — outside the deterrence relationships — there is an enormous potential for open violence in the international system, but it has mainly taken one of two forms. First, many of the developing countries are going through a period of withdrawing from the dominance of their one-time colonial masters and building up viable political institutions. Civil wars and *coup d'états* often provide occasions for the major powers to intervene in the internal affairs of these countries — in fact military interventions have been the main form of open violence since the Second World War. Secondly, at the same time many people in the developing world are beginning to fight back with revolutionary violence in one of its various manifestations. The 1960s saw two kinds of revolutionary violence in particular: first, 'national liberation' movements — each of which was unique — in every case the main target being the foreign countries which dominated their territory or were at least seen as dominating them; secondly, 'guerrilla movements' which erupted mostly in the Latin American countries and whose main targets were originally their oppressive domestic governments.

The distinction between the two types is sometimes difficult to make, but it certainly is true that in recent years we have seen a dramatic increase in international terrorism as a result of the failure of both types of warfare to achieve their desired goals. The unifying idea of the various types of international terrorism is to put their cause before the world audience and their means of doing that is to engage in dramatic acts of transnational violence, mainly directed against those whom they consider to be especially responsible for their ill-fortune. Acts of individual physical violence are often carried out against innocent persons; but in a broader context they may be regarded as small-scale reprisals for the acts of some Western governments, which, in resisting revolutionary warfare in the Third World, have allegedly engaged in the deliberate killing of whole villages of innocent civilians — acts which Western governments have for the most part not condemned. Some participants asked how one can persuade Third World international terrorists, who have practically no other means at their disposal, to agree to the outlawing of acts of small-scale terrorism while some Western governments, controlling an enormous potential for violence, perpetrate acts of terrorism on a much larger scale. This is a second paradox which was advanced in the discussions.

A third paradox can be found in the area of peace teaching. As one of the newer, not yet fully established, fields of university education, it attracted a great deal of attention especially among the younger participants. Although the concept of peace, as all agreed, is a rather vague one, it was felt that peace is something to be desired and ought to be taught in universities and schools. And so we urged in principle that peace teaching be included in the regular curriculum of our universities. Yet we did not know exactly what it is and, in particular, how to achieve it.

International Terrorism

Discussions on international terrorism concentrated on three themes: international terrorism in its historical context; the problem of definition; and how to deal with terrorism.

Acts of individual or collective terrorism have been known throughout history and have been used by those who felt themselves to be outside the established political system, but hitherto they always had a clearly visible political and local objective. Even now, terrorism is statistically — in terms of the number of victims — unimportant and a secondary problem as compared to other forms of political warfare. But today it attracts a good deal of attention which is out of proportion to its direct political effectiveness due to the nature of the acts involved. First, political terrorism seems at first sight so senseless, because more often than not innocent civilians, far away and with no relationship to the issues in dispute, are victims, which adds to the drama of the situation. But it was recognised that terrorists *do* have a rational political objective, which is to draw world attention to their problems. Secondly, world attention is attracted because terrorist acts are directed against airlines, foreign diplomats and businessmen in the metropolitan areas of the world and thus easily draw the attention of the news media in contrast to many of the actions of guerillas in rural and remote areas of the world.

In a sense, international terrorism as a type of warfare has grown out of the failure of national liberation movements and urban and rural guerrilla warfare during the 1960s to achieve meaningful results. Its acts are carried out across international borders, because the terrorists feel that the solution of their problems is not to be found in their immediate political environment, but rather in the capitals of the Western world. By contrast, it was pointed out that the so-called national liberation movements in Southern Africa which have successfully confronted a foreign power within their own country have not engaged in acts of international terrorism.

The definitional problem also attracted much attention. There may be confusion about a precise concept of international terrorism, but it is an important problem in terms of the means we choose to deal with it. For instance, we may try legalistically to differentiate between legitimate and illegitimate causes, although conceptions of what is a legitimate

3

cause are diverse. Certainly the views of the Western and developing countries are far apart on whether or not the definition should include a reference to colonialism. This points to a major element of contention: terrorism is often regarded as an outgrowth of Western domination and one should — according to this view — not confuse cause and effect. One should also distinguish between acts of terrorism for selfish reasons and those for political reasons, the first being a case for criminal law but the latter category being more a political than a legal problem.

A second definitional problem concerns the relationship between means and ends: what end justifies what means? If the cause is legitimate, and the means are efficient, where does one draw the line on acceptable means? Most would regard the killing of innocent civilians as an unacceptable means, but as soon as it has to be codified one is confronted with the problems of the double standard: how does one outlaw certain means as illegitimate and yet admit some exceptions? Moreover, international terrorism is often inefficient in terms of reaching an immediate solution to problems and in this context it was pointed out that the killing of innocent victims can be regarded as inefficient and therefore immoral and illegitimate. But, on the other hand, the main objective of the terrorists is to create fear and terror and to draw attention to their cause. If this assumption is accepted, then their present means may be regarded as more efficient than the more traditional ones, because they are acting from a position of inferiority.

A third major problem is how to deal with terrorism. A number of dilemmas emerged clearly from the discussions.

First, terrorists are outside the political system and working against it. What rules shall we apply to them? It was pointed out that if we accept that a good cause justifies bad means, we also have to recognise that the established system — in defending its good cause against terrorist attacks — has a wide superiority of means at its disposal. Yet, as was mentioned, the victims of international terrorist attacks are mainly to be found among Western democratic countries and they are — at least in principle — at a disadvantage in fighting terrorism: if they want to take away the main source of strength of international terrorism — its publicity — they have at the same time to violate one of the basic principles of their political system, the freedom of the press.

Secondly, there is the dilemma of what some participants called the double standard: how are we to condemn international terrorism and yet condone those actions Western countries execute on a much larger scale? In fighting national liberation movements in Third World countries some Western — and other — countries, it was alleged, have been engaged in large-scale terror and indiscriminate killing of the civilian population of these countries. And even if one does not recognise this problem of the double standard, it must still be admitted that where to draw the line is often dependent upon the culture of the political system.

Thirdly, we tend to search for solutions which are applicable to all cases and in doing this run into the difficulty that each case is unique despite superficial similarities in tactics. Each problem, it was said, is more unique than similar and we are often led to delude ourselves that as the tactics of international terrorists are superficially very similar, the solutions must also be so.

Finally, in dealing with international terrorism, we are often confronted with a variety of conflicting attitudes and interests. As mainly Western countries are the target of terrorist attacks, many countries, especially in the Third World, are unwilling to go along with Western proposals because of their ideological sympathies. But it was suggested that this might change in the future if terrorism spreads and developing countries themselves have unpleasant experiences. The Cuban-American agreement concerning hijacking was mentioned as an example of how attitudes can change. It was also recognised that many Western countries may be afraid of taking too strong measures for fear of reprisals and commercial sanctions. Another difficulty arises out of the fact that many treaties of extradition contain a clause stating exceptions for 'political offences'. This is why it may continue to be difficult to deny the terrorists 'sanctuaries' and 'safe havens'.

In coping with the problem of international terorism, three categories of measure were mentioned: recourse to the International Court of Justice; negotiating international treaties and adjusting the law of warfare to deal with these acts of international terrorism; and applying economic sanctions against those countries which condone acts of terrorism, although it was recognised that this may not be feasible. In this context it was suggested that the prosecution of terrorists should be decoupled from their underlying motives. But most participants agreed that without resolving the political causes of international terrorism, legal solutions might not offer much prospect of eliminating such behaviour. Nevertheless, there was broad agreement that international rules are necessary and that even if there are grey areas in which it is difficult to apply them, this should not be seen as a sufficient reason not to make the attempt.

The Arms Race and the Quest for Security in Europe and the Middle East

The second main focus of the discussions was nuclear weapons and related issues such as the diffusion of nuclear technology, European security and the Middle East question. Here mention can only be made of a few of the major themes in the debate, such as deterrence and how it may continue to work, proliferation and how to prevent it and the relationship between 'major power deterrence' and 'minor power proliferation'.

The discussion on 'major power deterrence' concentrated on two aspects in particular: the meaning and impact of the new American doctrine of 'flexible options' and how to make deterrence work best. As to the first point, it was emphasised that a distinction should be made between James Schlesinger's strategy of flexible options as a new targeting doctrine and as a new strategic doctrine. It was generally agreed that as far as the issue of targeting is concerned, the concept was not new. References were made to earlier efforts to enunciate such a policy – for example, Robert McNamara's Ann Arbor speech of 1962. But the main point was that the United States had built up such an enormous stock of nuclear weapons that military facilities must always have been targeted, simply because there were not enough civilian targets available. On the other hand, it was said that the new targeting doctrine was a defensive reaction to counter certain Soviet moves. There was, however, a strong consensus that it was not really a new strategy and that the objective of stating openly what always had been the policy of the United States was rather political. The political objectives were viewed in different ways. According to some, it was an attempt to deal with certain deficiencies in the concept of 'assured destruction' which, in an age of nuclear parity, meant in fact mutual annihilation. It was thus considered as an attempt 'to shore up deterrence'. It was pointed out, however, that the proposals for more options tended to strengthen the belief that it is possible to fight a limited and controlled war. And in these terms, what is important in this new strategy is not what it really means but 'whom one is trying to fool'.

Still, it may be necessary to analyse the impact of various strategic doctrines or targeting options on those areas in which the use of nuclear weapons is most likely, Central Europe and the Middle East. The military situation in Central Europe is highly ambiguous and – as the discussions proved – one's view of it is very much dependent on whether one concentrates on quantifiable factors (such as the number of divisions, men and tanks) or whether one also takes into account non-quantifiable factors (such as the quality of the weapons and the implications of the different strategic positions of the United States and the Soviet Union). Nobody, however, denied the close relationship between the American military presence and European security and that the one area in which the use of nuclear weapons is most often considered is Central Europe. Two views emerged with regard to the question of targeting options in Europe: on the one hand, it was emphasised that because either in a conventional war or a limited nuclear

6

war Europe would be destroyed, Western Europeans should stress the deterrent function of tactical nuclear weapons rather than their battle-field functions and that the strategy of flexible options was not compatible with this approach. On the other hand, some argued that this new strategy for American nuclear weapons implied a reduced belief in the option of a tactical nuclear war in Europe and should therefore be welcomed by Europeans. A related development, whose implications were made clear in the Yom Kippur War, is the fact that new defensive technologies are gaining the upper hand over offensive weapons. Both developments might reduce the emphasis on tactical nuclear weapons in Central Europe, their function either being taken over by new conventional defensive weapons or by strategic nuclear weapons. This might open up possibilities for certain arms control measures such as the reduction of so-called tactical nuclear weapons and manpower reductions.

In contrast to the situation in Europe, the situation in the Middle East is very unstable, not only as a result of local antagonisms, but also as a result of superpower actions. It was pointed out that — as in the Yom Kippur War — there is a danger that the United States and the Soviet Union might become involved in a direct nuclear confrontation because of local commitments. The Soviet Union considers the Mediterranean as one of those areas where she has to prove to be equal to the United States. Prospects for substantial reductions of forces were, therefore, regarded as small, but to avoid unintentional war as a result of the constant harassing that goes on between the Soviet and American fleets, prudential arms control measures might be feasible. The recent American offers of peaceful nuclear facilities to Egypt and Israel were considered to be potentially destabilising because this might add nuclear fuel to an already ongoing arms race.

The shift to a flexible options targeting doctrine is closely con-nected with the more general problem of how to make deterrence work best. We always have to choose between two conceptions: either we build up confidence that deterrence will work by stressing that escala-tion is inevitable, or we recognise that deterrence may fail and that we have to provide for various options to prevent a situation arising in which massive retaliation is the only possibility. Both views were ex-pressed. The conflict between the two conceptions in a certain sense cannot be solved: all understandings of nuclear war are imaginary because we have no experience of such a war. Given the existence of nuclear weapons (even their destruction would not eliminate human intelligence and know-how to produce them), one can only hope that no madman, and they are not unknown in history, will ever get access to nuclear weapons. Fortunately, the historical record is that since 1945 both the United States and the Soviet Union have practised considerable restraint.

But the possibilities of the rise of a madman is not the only cause for fear. Unintentional warfare cannot be excluded as a result of accidents, diplomatic misunderstandings in crisis situations, problems of inventory control and the widening gap between offensive and defensive nuclear weapons. It was said, however, that this problem has been given a great deal of attention and that the situation has been improved. According to some participants, assured destruction as posture plus arms control aiming at preventing unintentional warfare will provide a stable deterrent. Supporters of this view maintained that nuclear disarmament is not a viable option because it will destabilise the deterrent relationship and, in any case, one has to differentiate between what is desirable and what is feasible. As a kind of compromise solution, some attention was given to the concept of minimum deterrence. Although the concept is in itself a rather vague one, it was suggested that it might imply substantial disarmament, considering the huge capabilities that actually exist.

Participants also concentrated on minor power nuclear proliferation. A general impression from the debate was that we simply cannot stop the spread of nuclear weapons which now is really on the way since India became the sixth nuclear power. The discussion, however, touched more on the economic incentives for acquiring nuclear facilities than on the political incentives of nuclear proliferation, although motives may well be mixed. There were different views about the use of nuclear technology for peaceful purposes. On the other hand, it was emphasised that in many, especially less-developed countries, there is a rather mistaken impression about the importance of nuclear energy. First, it is often regarded as a way of acquiring a high technology with the implicit understanding that all progress in technology is in itself a good thing, and secondly, it is often regarded as the main, if not the only road to economic progress. Many participants emphasised that the benefits of nuclear technology were often over-stressed and this applied especially to test explosions for peaceful purposes and fast-breeder reactors. On the other hand, it was pointed out that nuclear energy *is* the cheapest way of generating energy and that nuclear energy may indeed be the only feasible way to economic development as alternative technologies may take a long time to develop.

Whatever solution one favours for dealing with the situation of underdevelopment, there is no doubt that nuclear facilities such as reactors, reprocessing plants and nuclear know-how will rapidly spread over the world and with it the danger of nuclear weapons proliferation. The nuclear Non-Proliferation Treaty (NPT), which was negotiated to stop the spread of nuclear weapons, has not done so and mainly for two reasons. First, the major nuclear powers did not live up to their obligations under the articles of the NPT and most of all they did not — by failing to stop the ever-spiralling arms race — create an international environment in which the importance of nuclear weapons was de-emphasised. But, of course, this is usually more of an excuse than a reason for states going nuclear. Secondly, whatever the political incentives may be, it is almost impossible to stop the spread of nuclear technology, which provides potential nuclear weapon countries with the necessary materials. There are a number of dangers which inevitably go with the spread of nuclear technology: the dangers of clandestine production and diversion of fissile material. Although a safeguards system works as a disincentive, in view of the enormous amounts of fissile material that will be available in nuclear reactors in the near future, the small fraction that can be diverted under a safeguard system will be enough for many states to produce nuclear weapons. A further danger is that of terrorist attacks following the theft of fissile material. As was pointed out, one of the main weaknesses of any safeguards system is when nuclear material is being transported.

A number of approaches were suggested to deal with these problems such as de-emphasising the importance of nuclear weapons in international politics and, at the other extreme, 'a new kind of nuclear imperialism' in order to deny the majority of countries nuclear technology and even to stop any kind of research and development in nuclear technology. It was pointed out that the uses of nuclear energy are often so much emphasised that the availability of conventional solutions tends to be forgotten. But it was argued that the use of nuclear energy is mainly seen in the developed world as a problem of how to change a situation from one of dependence on a small group of oil-producing countries to one where there are independent supplies of energy, in which case the fast-breeder reactor may be a solution.

A third problem concerning nuclear weapons is the inter-relationship between 'major power deterrence' and 'minor power proliferation'. It is sometimes suggested that to embrace deterrence and reject nuclear proliferation is at least logically inconsistent because one cannot reserve whatever benefits can be derived from the deterrent function of nuclear weapons to only a small group of countries, particularly as they are mainly developed countries. Against this thesis, linking the two concepts of 'major power deterrence' and 'minor power proliferation', a number of objections were raised. In the first place, in many smaller countries the reasons for going nuclear can be found in internal discussions and the interests of local bureaucracies, or in regional confrontations, but not in the logic or lack of logic in the broader international system. Secondly, it was emphasised that major powers *do* constitute a distinct category and that both in terms of prestige and status nuclear weapons are not going to improve the international position of smaller powers. Finally, nuclear guarantees and commitments to local powers might provide a better shield for smaller countries than having their own nuclear weapons which they might not be able to control sufficiently. It is, moreover, not the possession of nuclear weapons but their mutual unvulnerability which stabilises a relationship between the major powers and this additional requirement may be lacking in smaller nuclear countries.

Peace Teaching

An important part of the discussion related to the subject of peace teaching. Very often the discussions on peace research and peace teaching revolve around a few basic issues to which it is impossible to give a definite answer. Among these issues are the meaning of the concept of peace, the scope of the field of peace research, how to organise peace research and peace teaching in terms of intellectual approach, how to achieve peace and, finally, how and to whom to teach peace.

As is well-known, the concept of peace has many meanings. The two best-known are the definitions of peace in a negative and in a positive sense. The term 'positive peace', meaning peace with social justice, always brings us into an age-old philosophical discussion because it depends on the values one holds. But many would recognise that there is still a long way to go to achieve even very modest conditions of positive peace and thus in this sense peace *is* a revolutionary concept. On the other hand, peace in its negative meaning, implying the absence of open violence, is generally regarded as too narrow, because it does not refer to those non-peaceful, yet not openly violent situations which might at any time erupt into open violence. Peace is thus more than the absence of violence and less than an abstract definition of social justice.

As the concept of peace in itself is difficult to define, so is the field of peace research. Depending on how one defines peace, one may take a broad view of its scope which tends to widen the field far beyond that of political science and international relations and including a wide variety of other disciplines. Those who take a narrower view would tend to restrict its scope to the more traditional field of conflict analysis, which still covers a wider area than the traditional study of international relations.

As regards researching and teaching peace, it was said that often the field is tolerated in the curriculum of our universities because of the interest the younger students have in it. But it has not achieved a strong academic base both in terms of its inclusion in the curriculum and in terms of academic achievements. Peace research and peace teaching are interdisciplinary which means that practical difficulties are often considerable. Peace is in the first place a value and peace research and teaching are thus value orientated; it is therefore not a discipline in itself but a field of interest and as such interdisciplinary.

How can we achieve peace if we cannot agree on a concept of peace and if we do not even know what peace is? If, as was claimed by some participants, peace research has led to less than striking intellectual achievements, how can we provide the tools to work for a better world? But human behaviour is not altogether unpredictable and what is important is to channel the future in the directions we deem good.

A further problem is to whom are we going to teach peace. As it concerns a value-orientated field, peace teaching is often seen in terms of indoctrination and, in any case, it was felt that many people after a while turn their backs on it. Moreover, many students may be put off by the relative absence of a wide range of job opportunities. This general attitude of indifference is thus a major obstacle to be overcome in peace teaching. A good tactic might be to recognise various dimensions of peace teaching and approach the various constituents — such as students, decision-makers, and the general public — in the light of what they need most. However that may be, all agreed that we simply are not doing enough to prepare the younger generation to learn to cope with the problems they are going to face in this century.

The dilemmas that confront those involved in peace teaching are especially acute in an age of nuclear weapons. In the face of the possibilities of a nuclear war — accidental or intentional — how can one convince the people of the disastrous consequences of such a war? For it may be that one cannot prove to the people the horrors of a nuclear war without blowing up the world. If that is true, we may all be doomed. But it was felt that the peace teacher should face this possibility and yet still be convinced that a better world can be achieved.

Conclusion

Summarising the two weeks' discussion of ISODARCO and putting it in a broader perspective, we may say that the future modes of conflict will not be easily recognisable as problems with which countries can deal on the basis of their own narrow national interest. The future of the whole international system is at stake. We have to see what we still tend to call the international system of nation states as a world political system, in which individuals, groups and international and transnational organisations are going to have a large potential for violence, either in the form of open terrorism or in that of disguised terror. We may have reached the point where the human capacity for violence is too great for the world in which we live. Recognising this, we must try to change our perspective on the world, human nature notwithstanding.

PART I

INTERNATIONAL TERRORISM

1. INTERNATIONAL TERRORISM: A NEW MODE OF CONFLICT

Brian M. Jenkins

Introduction[1]

Terrorism appears to have increased markedly in the past few years. Political and criminal extremists in various parts of the world have attacked passengers in airline terminals and railway stations; planted bombs in government buildings, the offices of multinational corporations, pubs, and theatres; hijacked airliners and ships, even ferryboats in Singapore; held hundreds of passengers hostage; seized embassies; and kidnapped government officials, diplomats, and business executives. We read of new incidents almost daily. Terrorists may strike citizens of another country while they are living overseas, in transit from one country to another, or at home in their own country. Terrorism has become a new element in international relations.

Defining Terrorism

When we talk about terrorism, what exactly are we talking about? The word has no precise or widely accepted definition. One noted lawyer has defined terrorism as acts which in themselves may be classic forms of crime — murder, arson, the use of explosives — but which differ from classic criminal acts in that they are executed 'with the deliberate intention of causing panic, disorder, and terror within an organised society, in order to destroy social discipline, paralyse the forces of reaction of a society, and increase the misery and suffering of the community'.[2] Two scholars in the United States have provided a somewhat broader definition of terrorism:

> 'murder, assassination, sabotage and subversion, the destruction of public records, the spreading of rumor, the closing of churches, the sequestration of property, the breakdown of criminal law enforcement, the prostitution of the courts, the narcosis of the press — all these, as they contribute to a common end, constitute terror'.[3]

Without attempting to define terrorism in a way that will satisfy all lawyers and scholars, we may for the moment satisfy ourselves with the following description: the threat of violence, individual acts of violence, or a campaign of violence designed primarily to instil fear — to terrorise — may be called terrorism. Terrorism is violence for effect, not only, and sometimes not at all, for the effect on the actual victims of the terrorists. In fact, the victim may be totally unrelated to the terrorist's cause. Terrorism is violence aimed at the people watching. Fear is the intended effect, not the by-product of terrorism. That, at least, distinguishes terrorist tactics from mugging and other common forms of violent crime that may terrify but are not terrorism.

Those we call terrorists may include revolutionaries and other political extremists, criminals professing political aims, and a few authentic lunatics. Terrorists may operate alone or may be members of a large and well-organised group. Terrorists may even be government agents. Their cause may have extreme goals, such as the destruction of all government — in itself not a new idea — or their cause may be one that is comparatively reasonable and understandable — self-rule for a particular ethnic group. Or their motive may be purely personal — money or revenge. The ambition of terrorists may be limited and local — the overthrow of a particular regime — or they may be global — a simultaneous worldwide revolution.

Promiscuous Use of the Term 'Terrorism'

The problem of defining terrorism is compounded by the fact that terrorism has recently become a fad word which is used promiscuously and is often applied to a variety of acts of violence which are not strictly terrorism by definition. It is generally a pejorative. Some governments are prone to label as terrorism all violent acts committed by their political opponents, while anti-government extremists frequently claim to be the victims of government terror. What is called terrorism thus seems to depend on point of view. Use of the term implies a moral judgement, and if one party can successfully attach the label 'terrorist' to its opponent, then it has indirectly persuaded others to adopt its moral viewpoint. Terrorism is what the bad guys do.

The term 'terrorism' is also an attention-getting word and therefore tends to be used, especially in the news media, to heighten the drama surrounding any act of violence. What we have, in sum, is the sloppy use of a word that is rather imprecisely defined to begin with. Terrorism may properly refer to a specific set of actions the primary intent of which is to produce fear and alarm for a variety of purposes, which we shall discuss. But terrorism in general usage frequently is also applied to similar acts of violence — *all* ransom kidnappings, *all* hijackings, thrill killings, which are not intended by their perpetrators to be primarily terror producing. Once a group carries out a terrorist act, it acquires the label 'terrorist', a label that tends to stick, and from that point on, everything this group does, whether intended to produce terror or not, is also henceforth called terrorism. If it robs a bank or steals arms from an arsenal, not necessarily acts of terrorism but common urban guerrilla tactics, these too are described as terrorism. Eventually *all* similar acts by other gangs or groups also come to be called terrorism. At some point in this expanding use of the term, terrorism can mean just what those who use the term (not the terrorists) want it to mean — almost any violent act by any opponent.

The Theory of Terrorism

Terrorism is often described as *mindless* violence, *senseless* violence, or *irrational* violence. If we put aside the actions of a few authentic lunatics, terrorism is seldom mindless or irrational. There is a theory of terrorism, and it often works. To understand the theory, it must first be understood that terrorism is a means to an end, not an end in itself. In other words, terrorism has objectives, although those who carry out acts of terrorism may be so dedicated to violent action that even they sometimes seem to miss this point.

Unless we try to think like terrorists, we are also liable to miss the point, for the objectives of terrorism are often obscured by the fact that specific terrorist attacks may appear to be random, directed against targets whose death or destruction does not appear directly to benefit the terrorist's cause. It is hard for us to understand how the killing of Olympic athletes in Munich or the hijacking of a Lufthansa airliner in Rome will ease the plight of Palestinians in the Middle East, or how blowing up an office in Manhattan will help topple a dictator in Latin America. But the objectives of terrorism are not those of conventional combat. Terrorists do not try to take and hold ground or physically destroy their opponents' forces. Terrorists usually lack that kind of power, or having it, are constrained from applying it. We must be able to see beyond the apparent meaninglessness, sometimes even the tragic absurdity, of a single terrorist act to determine the objectives and the logic of terrorism.

While terrorists may kill, by our standards sometimes wantonly, and while they may threaten a lot of people, the objective of terrorism is *not* mass murder. Terrorists want a lot of people watching and a lot of people listening, and not a lot of people dead. A credible threat, a demonstration of the capacity to strike, may be from the terrorists' point of view often preferable to actually carrying out the threatened deed, which may explain why, apart from the technical difficulties involved, terrorists have not done some of the terribly damaging and terrifying things they could do, such as poisoning a city's water supply

15

spreading chemical or biological agents, or other things that could produce mass casualties.

The Purposes of Terror

Terrorists attempt to inspire and manipulate fear to achieve a variety of purposes. Terrorism may be aimed simultaneously at several objectives: specific tactical objectives, made explicit by the terrorists, and broader strategic objectives, which may be implicit in the choice of tactics or targets. First, individual acts of terrorism may be aimed at wringing specific concessions, such as the payment of ransom, the release of prisoners, or the publication of a terrorist message, under threat of death or destruction. Terrorists may seek to improve their bargaining power by creating a dramatic hostage situation and thereby coerce a government into fulfilling certain demands.

Secondly, terrorism may also be aimed at gaining publicity. Through terrorism, the terrorists hope to attract attention to their cause and project themselves as a force that merits recognition and that must be reckoned with. The publicity gained by frightening acts of violence and the atmosphere of fear and alarm created cause people to exaggerate the importance and strength of the terrorists and their movement. Since most terrorist groups are actually small and weak, the violence they carry out must be all the more dramatic and deliberately shocking.

Terrorist attacks are often carefully choreographed to attract the attention of the electronic media and the international press. Taking and holding hostages increases the drama. If certain demands are not satisfied, the hostages may be killed. The hostages as individuals often mean nothing to the terrorists. Terrorism is aimed at the people watching, not at the actual victims. Terrorism is theatre.

To illustrate this point, let us take a recent example from the United States with which most people are familiar — the Symbionese Liberation Army (SLA). There seem to be two SLAs. One of them appeared on television or in the newspapers almost daily. Everyone has seen the seven-headed cobra symbol; thousands have listened to SLA tapes. An enormous number of police and FBI agents were mobilised to try to find it; it excited and entertained, if not terrified, the people of California. Then there is the other SLA — the *real* SLA. It once had a dozen or so members, now perhaps three. It has to its credit one murder, one kidnapping, a food distribution financed by and extorted from the family of a hostage, one bank robbery, and a few stolen cars — hardly a crime wave. The difference between the two SLAs is the difference between the actual amount of violence and the greatly amplified effects of that violence.

There are other examples in which terrorism has been used to

16

magnify the importance of the cause and the stature of the group. Insurgents fought in Angola, Mozambique, and Portuguese Guinea for fourteen years using the standard tactics of rural guerrilla warfare. The world hardly noticed their struggle, while an approximately equal number of Palestinian commandos employing terrorist tactics have in a few years become a primary concern to the world.

Publicity may sometimes even exceed fear as the leading effect of a terrorist incident. The bombing of a bank or consulate at midnight, for example, may be a totally symbolic act that threatens no lives and produces little real damage. In a way, it is a violent form of graffiti, a declaration of existence, solidarity, or opposition; but since it is also a demonstration that the perpetrators are willing to resort to violence, and a warning of future violence, it does produce fear, though perhaps not terror, and, therefore, can be called terrorism.

Thirdly, terrorism may be aimed at causing widespread disorder, at demoralising society, and at breaking down the social order. This objective is typical of revolutionary, nihilistic, or anarchistic terrorists. Impatient at the reluctance of the 'people' — on whose behalf the revolution is to be carried out — to join them, terrorists may reject society's normal rules and relationships as intolerable complacency. If the benefits of political obedience are destroyed; if the complacency of uninvolvement is not allowed; if the government's ability to protect its citizens (which is after all the origin and most basic reason for the existence of government) is demonstrated to be ineffectual; if the government can be made to strike back brutally but blindly; and if there is no place to hide in the ensuing battle, then, it is presumed, the 'people' will join the opponents of that government and a revolution will be carried out. Such a strategy often backfires. With no immunity from random terrorist violence, even sympathisers may turn against the terrorist violence, and the terrorists, and support the government's moves to destroy them.

Fourthly, terrorism may be aimed at deliberately provoking repressions, reprisals, and counter-terrorism, which may ultimately lead to the collapse of an unpopular government. In the past, such terrorism has frequently been directed against government security and law enforcement personnel, but there are also examples of deliberately outrageous acts, the kidnapping of a foreign diplomat for example, or random violence against civilians designed to embarass a government and compel it to react with a heavy hand. The government may thus be induced by the terrorists into a course leading to self-destruction.

Fifthly, terrorism may also be used to enforce obedience and cooperation. This is the usual purpose of state or official terrorism, or what is frequently called 'institutional violence', but terrorists themselves may also employ institutional violence against their own members to ensure their loyalty. The outcome desired by the terrorists in this case is a prescribed pattern of behaviour: obedience to the state or to the cause, and full cooperation in identifying and rooting out infiltrators or enemies. The success of such terrorism again depends on the creation of an atmosphere of fear, reinforced by the seeming omnipresence of the internal security apparatus. As in other forms of terrorism, terrorism which is aimed at enforcing obedience contains elements of deliberate drama: defectors are abducted or mysteriously assassinated; dissidents are arrested at midnight; people disappear; and stories (often real) spread of dungeons, concentration camps, and torture. And as in other forms of terrorism, the objective is the effect all this has on the target audience. However, enforcement terrorism seldom chooses victims at random and does not seek widespread publicity, especially at the international level.

Sixthly, terrorism is frequently meant to punish. Terrorists often declare that the victim of their attack, whether person or object, is somehow guilty, or is the symbol of something the terrorists consider guilty. A person may be judged guilty because he has committed some crime himself — actively opposed, disobeyed, or informed upon the terrorists — or because he has tacitly cooperated with a guilty party. 'Cooperated' is often interpreted rather broadly to mean that the individual worked for, tacitly supported, accepted a visa from, or travelled on the national carrier of an enemy government. Victims of terrorists also have been chosen because their success in business of their life-style represented a system despised by the terrorists. Objects or buildings have been destroyed because they were symbols of a despised government, institution, or system.

There is, in terrorism, a stronger connotation of guilt and punishment than in other forms of warfare or politics, and a narrower definition of 'innocent' bystanders. To terrorists, there are few innocent bystanders. Even the victims of the Lod Airport massacre in 1972, many of whom happened to be Christian pilgrims from Puerto Rico, were said by the organisation responsible for the attack to be 'guilty' because they had arrived in Israel on Israeli visas and thereby had tacitly recognised the state that was the declared enemy of the Palestinians, and because by coming to Israel they had also entered what was in effect a war zone. One terrorist leader put it succinctly: 'There are no innocent tourists in Israel'. This rationalisation for the Lod killings is an interesting example, not atypical of terrorists declaring their victims guilty after the fact. The Popular Front for the Liberation of Palestine, which was responsible for the attack, was not saying the victims were innocent bystanders unfortunately caught in a cross-fire. neither was it saying that it would seek and kill all those holding visas from the State of Israel. The organisation *was* saying that those who happened to get shot — simply because they happened to be there at the wrong moment — were nevertheless guilty or they would not have been shot. In other words, they did not become victims because they were enemies, but rather they became enemies because they happened to be victims.

It is through the assignment of guilt, and the often matching claim of the administration of justice, that the terrorists not only rationalise their acts of violence but also seek to establish their moral superiority. Most political terrorists are imbued with a strong sense of moral outrage and an absolute conviction in the righteousness of their cause. By their acts, terrorists attempt to arouse the same sense of moral outrage which may be latent in the minds of the target audience, while at the same time reinforcing their own moral convictions.

Thus, while the leading effect of terrorism is fear and alarm, terrorism may be employed to accomplish a variety of objectives: specific concessions, widespread publicity for the terrorists and their cause, the dissolution of social norms, the provoking of repression, obedience to an organisation or its cause, and the punishment of those considered guilty by the terrorists. A single episode may be aimed at accomplishing several of these objectives simultaneously. Terrorism may be an instrument of government as well as a tactic of revolutionary and other anti-government forces.

Indiscriminate or Selective Violence

Terrorism may appear to be either indiscriminate or highly selective. Violence that appears totally and deliberately indiscriminate — that is, attacks which appear to be directed at random against civilian bystanders innocent of any involvement on either side of the struggle being carried on by the terrorists — is frequently called *pure terrorism*. The massacre of passengers at the Lod Airport in Israel, whatever the terrorists said later about their being guilty by simply being there, and the bombing of the Tower of London in which a number of tourists were killed or injured, closely approached pure terrorism. Pure terrorism is a cynical but rather effective means of attracting attention and of creating alarm. It is also difficult to protect against.

Very few acts of terrorism, however, are meant by the terrorists to appear indiscriminate. Terrorists normally want to appear selective. They may assassinate particular leaders, perhaps even forewarning their victims or potential victims with the publication of a death list, thus instilling terror among those named but still living. Or terrorists may strike only the members of a selected group, policemen for example, or village chiefs.

While indiscriminate violence may produce greater fear and alarm among the general population, selective but unpredictable attacks may

19

cause greater alarm within the selected group. Sometimes terrorists may be selective in choosing actual physical targets — government buildings or the airliners of a specific national carrier, for example — but they are not particularly concerned about who may be killed during the actual attack or bombing, and thus their violence appears indiscriminate.

Defining International Terrorism

The problem of defining international terrorism is complicated by international politics. Apart from a few categories of incidents that most nations have agreed to call international terrorism — airliner hijacking or the kidnapping of diplomats, for example — few nations agree on what international terrorism is. The most simple definition of international terrorism comprises acts of terrorism that have clear international consequences: incidents in which terrorists go abroad to strike their targets, select victims or targets because of their connecttions to a foreign state (diplomats, local executives of officers of foreign corporations), attack airliners in international flights, or force airliners to fly to another country. International terrorism would not include the local activities of dissident groups when carried out against a local government or citizens in their own country if no foreign connection is involved.

International terrorism may also be defined as acts of violence or campaigns of violence waged outside the accepted rules and procedures of international diplomacy and war. Breaking the rules may include attacking diplomats and other internationally protected persons, attacking international travel and commerce, or exporting violence by various means to nations that normally would not, under the traditional rules, be considered participants in the local conflict.

International terrorism in this sense is violence against the 'system', waged outside the 'system'. Therefore, the rules of the 'system' do not apply. For example, most other forms of warfare, at least in theory, recognise categories of civilians who are not directly engaged in the struggle — women and children, for example — and who therefore are not targets of violence. Terrorists recognise far fewer immune civilians. Terrorists may regard a person as an enemy, and therefore a target, solely on the basis of nationality, ethnicity, or religion. Or a person can become a target by mere chance — by watching a movie in a theatre when a bomb goes off, or by passing through an airport waiting room when passengers are machine-gunned. This is not to say that people we call terrorists are always indiscriminate killers, or that groups we call armies are always scrupulously discriminating; but exceptions do not invalidate our definition — they simply compel us to recognise that

20

soldiers may sometimes be terrorists. Indeed, a number of bombing campaigns undertaken by both sides during the Second World War and in subsequent wars — for example, the bombing of targets that in themselves had little military value to the enemy but were struck primarily to punish, to shock, to cause alarm, and to create disorder among the population of the enemy state — could qualify as terrorism under our definition of that term.

According to this definition, we could say that international terrorism, as employed recently by revolutionary and other dissident groups, is a new kind of warfare. It is warfare without territory, waged without armies as we know them. It is warfare that is not limited territorially: sporadic 'battles' may take place worldwide. It is warfare without neutrals, and with few or no civilian innocent bystanders.

We may disapprove of terrorism and deplore its use internationally, but terrorists can muster some cogent arguments in defence of their actions. Why, they will ask, should terrorists play by the established rules when these rules were contrived by a small group of primarily Western nations for their own advantage; and when these same rules deprive some groups without recognised governments, territory, or armies from exercising their 'right' to resort to violent means? Besides, playing by the rules does not necessarily command the world's attention. Breaking them does.

Thus far, we have been talking about two broad definitions of international terrorism — as acts of terrorism with international repercussions, and as violence outside the accepted norms of diplomacy and war. Such definitions fail to meet the more rigorous requirements of international law. Certain acts of violence which affect the international community have been defined as acts of international terrorism and outlawed by various agreements and conventions. However, international agreements cover only a few of the more prevalent tactics of terrorists, such as attacks on civilian aircraft or attacks on diplomats, and do not address the total spectrum of international terrorism.

There have been several attempts in various international forums, such as the United Nations, to define legally and thereby outlaw international terrorism. With the few exceptions already mentioned — hijacking and the kidnapping of diplomats — the effort has not gone beyond the prerequisite definition. All nations want to outlaw international terrorism — no one at least speaks out on behalf of terrorism — but each nation has a different idea as to what international terrorism is. After all, those who are terrorists to one nation may be 'freedom fighters' to another.

Each nation wants to proscribe, and therefore define international terrorism in a way that will include those acts which *it* considers terrorism — particularly those for which it may be a likely target. Some nations may also want to proscribe (and therefore will include in their definition) certain additional, potential acts by foreign adversaries, domestic dissidents, or dissident exiles, acts which may not exactly be international terrorism in the strictest sense but that it would be advantageous for the national government to have branded as international terrorism and outlawed by international law. Such definitions, if accepted, have the effect of endorsing the *status quo*. At the same time, most nations are careful to avoid definitions that might lead to laws which in any way could impinge upon their sovereignty. Being able to brand one's opponents as international criminals is desirable providing this in no way interferes with one's handling of one's own affairs. Finally, some nations, particularly those lacking the tools of modern conventional war, do not want to proscribe and therefore deliberately exclude from their definitions of terrorism other means of struggle — national wars of liberation or guerrilla warfare — which they may wish to employ, or which are being employed on behalf of causes which they support. The result is not one definition of international terrorism, but rather many competing definitions each written to encompass, and to exclude, specific actualities and potentialities. Such definitions strongly reflect political points of view.

This was clearly the case in recent discussions held by a special UN *ad hoc* committee on international terrorism. For example, the Government of Haiti proposed to define terrorism as 'any threat or act of violence committed by a person or group of persons on foreign territory or in any other place under international jurisdiction against *any* person with a view to achieving a political objective'.[4] This is also a fair definition of war.

The Government of France proposed to define international terrorism more narrowly as any 'heinous act of barbarism committed in the territory of a third state by a foreigner against a person possessing a nationality other than that of the offender for the purpose of exerting pressure in a conflict not strictly internal in nature'.[5] Curiously the definition possibly could exclude a hypothetical kidnapping of the French Ambassador in Washington, D.C., by French Guianese separatists. Possibly, the Government of France would prefer to deal with such a case as an internal affair. And reversing the situation, that is, if an Arab embassy in France were to be seized by Arab terrorists of the same nationality, the Government of France would have the option of calling it an internal affair of the Arabs, thereby avoiding direct involvement and responsibility.

A group of non-aligned nations (Algeria, Congo, Guinea, India, Mauritania, Nigeria, Southern Yemen, Syria, Tanzania, Tunisia, Yemen, Yugoslavia, Zaire, and Zambia) included in their proposed definition of international terrorism:

'acts of violence and other repressive acts by colonial, racist, and alien regimes against peoples struggling for their liberation . . . ; tolerating or assisting by a State the organization of the remnants of fascists or mercenary groups whose terrorist activity is directed against other sovereign countries; acts of violence committed by individuals or groups of individuals which endanger or take innocent human lives or jeopardize fundamental freedoms [providing this definition does] not affect the inalienable right to self-determination and independence of all peoples under colonial and racist regimes and other forms of alien domination . . . ; acts of violence committed by individuals or groups of individuals for private gain, the effects of which are not confined to one State.[6]

This definition is clearly very much affected by the unique history and problems of its primarily African and Asian authors.

Needless to say, the Ad Hoc Committee on International Terrorism failed to reach a conclusion as to just what international terrorism is. Several members of the committee suggested compiling a list of acts that most of the members considered to be examples of international terrorism and then determining their common characteristics. That idea is reminiscent of US Supreme Court of Justice Potter Stewart's famous remark on obscenity, 'I know it when I see it!'.

In sum, what is called international terrorism may refer broadly to any terrorist violence that has international repercussions; or to acts of violence which are outside the accepted norms of international diplomacy and rules of war. It may refer to a narrow set of acts which have been specifically identified and outlawed by international agreements; or, finally, it may refer to a collection of different definitions proposed by various national governments.

The Actual Effects of Terrorism

The actual amount of violence caused by international terrorism has been greatly exaggerated. Compared with the world volume of violence or with national crime rates, the toll has been small. There were 507 incidents of international terrorism between January 1968 and April 1974.[7] To repeat, these are incidents of *international* terrorism — that is, where terrorists have attacked foreign officials, or have gone abroad to strike their targets, or have hijacked international airliners. The actions of the Irish Republican Army (IRA) in Northern Ireland or those of the Tupamaros in Uruguay are not counted in that figure. Those are local struggles. But the actions of the IRA in London are included in the above total, as are the occasions when Tupamaros kidnapped foreign diplomats. There are two other deliberate omissions: acts of terrorism associated with the war in Indochina and the

23

numerous cross-border raids against kibbutzim or acts of terrorism in the Israeli-occupied territories, except for the major episodes, have not been included. These are still a part of local struggles and do not directly affect other nations. All truly international incidents of terrorism associated with the struggle in the Middle East are included, such as the killing of the Israeli athletes in Munich, the seizure of the Saudi Arabian embassies in Khartoum and Paris, and the killing of Palestinian leaders in Beirut and of suspected Arab terrorists in Europe by Israeli commando teams or agents. In all, since 1968, 520 people were killed, counting terrorists; 830 were wounded or injured.

Without minimising these casualties, and even allowing for some incidents that were overlooked or might justifiably have been included, the total amount of violence is not large. It is less than the homicide rate of any major American city: there are more than 18,000 criminal homicides a year in the United States. It is small compared with the casualties of any war; and it is perhaps significant that during periods when there are wars (such as the most recent one in the Middle East), incidents of terrorism elsewhere are not reported. Perhaps only in times of relative peace in the world can world attention be attracted by lesser episodes of violence. Had any of these terrorist groups somehow acquired the means of conventional war fought within the internationally accepted rules of warfare, would the toll have been any less?

The effect produced by the small amount of actual terrorist violence is much greater. Headlines have been captured and valuable television time has been devoted to the terrorists. Terrorists have created disruption and alarm and have compelled governments to divert more of their resources to protection against terrorist attacks. Some governments have been willing to release captured terrorists if holding them is likely to make the country a target of further terrorist attacks.

Paradoxically, while terrorists attack the basic rules of international order, they depend on international pressure to achieve their political goals. Through outrageous acts of violence directed against everyone, terrorists hope to persuade other nations to pressure their adversary into a settlement more favourable to the terrorists' cause than the terrorists themselves could achieve, not because other nations will always sympathise with their cause or their tactics, but because they simply want to end the violence.

The concept of using limited military means to generate international pressure was employed successfully during the anti-colonial struggles of the 1960s, when local insurgents attempted to attract international attention and embarass the government of the colonial power. The same tactic had also been used earlier by those fighting to bring about the withdrawal of British forces and create a Jewish homeland in Israel. International attention was a prerequisite to international pressure, which could achieve what the local insurgents could not achieve militarily — induce the colonial power to withdraw. The difference between the anti-colonial insurgents and today's terrorists is that during the colonial struggle the insurgents sought international attention by acts of violence in the colonies. Seldom was the metropole directly attacked. Now, terrorist violence may be exported anywhere in the world.

Recently, terrorism has been used most successfully on an international scale by Palestinian guerrillas. That there is now pressure for an Israeli withdrawal and the creation of a Palestinian homeland, that the Palestinian Liberation Organization may be accorded international recognition as the government of a stateless people, is owing, at least in part, to the success of Palestinian terrorists in bringing their cause violently and dramatically before the eyes of the world. Without endorsing terrorism, one must wonder what success they could have won had they operated within the established bounds of conventional warfare and polite diplomacy. At the same time, one must wonder what their success means for the future. Will it inspire groups with equal capacity for violence, but with far less claim to legitimacy, to try to extort concessions from the world merely in exchange for an end to their violence?

What has been demonstrated is that small groups with a limited capacity for violence can capture headlines, can cause alarm, and can compel governments to temporarily abandon their law enforcement function. To terrorists and to potential terrorists, that makes terrorism a success.

The Effect on the International Order

While terrorists have been able to attract attention to themselves and wring some concessions from vulnerable governments, terrorism has not yet had a major impact on the international order. Measured against other disruptive forces in the world, the activities of terrorists rank far below such things as the recent Arab oil embargo, soaring energy costs, worldwide inflation and food shortages, and conventional wars.

Campaigns of terrorism or specific incidents of terrorism directed against targets in the foreign diplomatic or business community have no doubt embarassed several governments, weakened some of them, and perhaps contributed to the downfall of a few. But where national governments did fall, were forced to step down, or grant greater authority to the military, as in Turkey, Argentina, and Uruguay, other factors were also present, such as grave economic problems, rampant inflation, widespread unemployment, or deep-rooted political struggles. No governments have fallen solely due to the activities of domestic or foreign terrorists.

25

Terrorism has exacerbated several local conflicts, expanding them beyond the locality involved. Terrorism has prolonged conflicts, making settlements more difficult to reach. This is particularly true of the conflicts in the Middle East and in Northern Ireland, but both of these are deep-rooted conflicts that would have been difficult to solve anyway.

Terrorism raises new questions about the feasible limits of protection a country may provide for its citizens once they are beyond its national borders. It also raises questions about the national responsibility. When terrorists from one nation train in another nation and board a plane in a third nation to carry out an act of terrorism in a fourth nation, who is responsible? What basic responsibilities does every nation have in deterring the acts of terrorism against citizens of another nation?

International terrorism also poses special problems for countries in which the 'battles' may occur. While most governments take the position that it is the responsibility of the host government to protect diplomats accredited to it, still unclear is how far its responsibilities extend in the case of citizens of another nation who may just be passing through one of its airports. Or how it should treat captured terrorists. Or whether or not it should endanger its own citizens in future attacks for the sake of a conflict that it does not view as its own. Or how it should treat foreign soldiers or agents sent to deal with terrorists in its territory?

Another problem area has to do with the legal status of the terrorists themselves. Do they deserve, as they claim, to be treated as prisoners of war if captured? If they violate local laws, are they common criminals, or, depending on their actions, war criminals? Are they international outlaws to be arrested wherever they are?

As it stands now, these questions tend to be decided *ad hoc* according to the realities of international politics as opposed to the merits of a case under international law. If international law is to have greater weight in this area of conflict, new laws must be created or old ones modified to deal with the unique problems of international terrorism.

In sum, terrorist violence has been greatly exaggerated, enabling the terrorists to gain publicity and some concessions. But, while raising some issues that still remain unresolved, terrorist violence cannot be said to have had as yet a major impact on the international order.

A Feeble Response

The international response to the threat posed by international terrorism, thus far, has been feeble. There has been only limited international cooperation against terrorists. Some nations directly or indirectly support with money, with weapons, and with training organisations that carry on terrorist activities. Nations continue to provide asylum to known perpetrators of terrorist acts, often giving them heroes' welcomes and even pensions. Many nations, while disapproving of terrorist tactics in principle, and who are unwilling to grant asylum themselves, are reluctant to condemn publicly acts of terrorism, or to condemn countries giving terrorists aid and asylum on the grounds that such condemnations might offend other nations with whom friendly relations are paramount. This is particularly true in the demonstrated reluctance of certain Western European nations to condemn Palestinian terrorists or their supporters. Arab countries may give weapons and asylum to terrorists, but they also possess the oil upon which Western Europe depends.

There are many reasons to explain the lack of international cooperation, some of which have already been discussed: few nations can agree on what international terrorism is, and since for reasons of ideology or politics, not all nations are threatened equally by the current wave of international terrorism, defining it, outlawing it, and carrying out counter-measures against terrorists tend to be matters of politics rather than issues of law. Furthermore, the overall effect of international terrorism, apart from the occasional publicity gained by terrorists, has been negligible. Most nations have more important problems to worry about than terrorists, especially someone else's terrorists. If lives can be saved and temporary tranquillity purchased by releasing a few prisoners, it does not seem unreasonable to do so, despite the offence thereby done to the law. Finally, it is difficult to enforce any sanctions against terrorist groups operating abroad and headquartered on foreign territory.

International law and the rules of warfare as they now exist are inadequate to cope with this new mode of conflict. The rules governing conflict were designed to deal with warfare between states. Conflict outside the 'system' poses a number of problems. First, the rules of war and consensual. The only means of enforcement are the moral force of international condemnation and the threat of retaliation in kind, a genuine constraint because the adversaries are normally roughly equal in vulnerability. Terrorist groups are not vulnerbale as nations are. They have no security responsibilities to any civilian population, and therefore they are less vulnerable to retaliation. On the other hand, when a government decides to take direct military action against a terrorist group abroad, it may be judged guilty of aggression, and it will bear the burden of any international condemnations or sanctions that result from the actions. The established system of diplomacy and the rules of war tend to be asymmetrical here. A state is at a disadvantage, not because it breaks the rules — so do the terrorists — but simply because it is a state.

Lacking international cooperation, nations have been compelled to deal with terrorism on their own. Some nations, such as the United States, have attempted to confront the challenge by increasing security against attacks by terrorists at home and abroad and by urging greater international cooperation against terrorism. The latter effort has achieved only limited success. Other nations, while bolstering their security measures, have attempted to establish a live-and-let-live relationship with foreign terrorists operating on their territory, acceding to terrorist demands when necessary and avoiding crackdowns that could provoke retaliation. A few nations, notably Israel, have chosen direct action against the terrorists, retaliating for terrorist attacks with direct military action or the assassination of key terrorist leaders. If terrorism continues to be a problem and the international response continues to be feeble, we may see more of this type of response.

New Targets and New Capabilities

Terrorism is not new, but a number of technical developments have made terrorism a more potent — and to groups that lack other means of applying power, an attractive — means of struggle. Progress has provided terrorists with new targets and new capabilities. Jet air travel furnishes unprecedented mobility and with it the ability to strike anywhere in the world. New weapons, including powerful explosives and sophisticated timing and detonating devices, are increasing terrorists' capacity for violence. The most ominous recent development is the discovery of Soviet hand-held, heat seeking, ground-to-air missiles in the hands of terrorists near the Rome airport.

Recent developments in news broadcasting — radio, television, communication satellites — are also a boon to publicity seeking terrorists. The willingness and capability of the news media to report and broadcast dramatic incidents of violence throughout the world enhances and may even encourage terrorism as an effective means of propaganda. Terrorists may now be assured that their actions will receive immediate worldwide coverage on radio, on television, and in the press. The world is now their stage. The whole world is probably watching.

This historical trend is important. The vulnerabilities inherent in a modern society increasingly dependent on its technology afford terrorists opportunities to create greater disruption than in the past. These increasing vulnerabilities in our society plus the increasing capacities for violence afforded by new developments in weaponry mean that smaller and smaller groups have a greater and greater capacity for disruption and destruction. Or, put another way, the small bands of extremists and irreconcilables that have always existed may become an increasingly potent force.

'Simultaneous Revolution' or Surrogate Warfare

What direction will terrorism take in the future? While it is incorrect to speak of terrorism in terms of an international conspiracy, as if all terrorists in the world were members of a single organisation, it is apparent that links are increasing between terrorists in various parts of the world. A number of terrorist groups share similar ideologies and are willing to cooperate. Alliances have been concluded between terrorist groups, such as that between the Popular Front for the Liberation of Palestine and the United Red Army of Japan. It was Japanese terrorists from the Red Army who were brought in by the Palestinians to machine-gun passangers at the Lod Airport in Israel two years ago. It has also been reported that the Irish Republican Army has developed close relations with members of the ETA, a Basque separatist group in Spain. And recently, four urban guerrilla groups in South America (the MRR of Chile, the ERP of Argentina, the ELN of Bolivia, and the Tupamaros of Uruguay), have created a 'junta for revolutionary co-ordination' in order to 'internationalise' their armed struggle. The better-trained, better-financed, and better-equipped guerrilla and terrorist groups are providing some military assistance and technical advice to less developed groups. Groups in one part of the world have shown themselves capable of recruiting confederates in other parts.

The growing links between terrorist groups are extremely important. They provide small terrorist organisations with the resources to under-take far more serious operations than they would be capable of other-wise. They make identification more difficult, since local citizens can be used to carry out attacks; and they could ultimately produce some kind of worldwide terrorist movement directed against some group of countries for vague ideological, political, or economic reasons, a con-cept that has been referred to by some terrorists as 'simultaneous revo-lution'.

A second possible trend is in the direction of more extravagant and destructive acts made possible by the creation of new vulnerabilities and new weapons, and made necessary as the public and governments become bored with what terrorists do now. There are many new vul-nerabilities. One that has received a great deal of public attention lately is nuclear power. The probable proliferation of nuclear power facilities in the next few decades, and the amount of traffic in fissionable material and radioactive waste that will accompany this, raises a number of new possibilities for political extortion and mass hostage situations on a scale that we have not yet seen.

At the same time, technological advances are creating a new range of small, portable, cheap, relatively easy to operate, highly accurate, and highly destructve weapons which, if produced on a large scale, will undoubtedly find their way into the hands of terrorists. Indeed, some of them already have — such as the Soviet manufactured SA-7. The SA-7 and its American counterpart, Redeye, are indeed already obsolete. Within the decade a new range of small, inexpensive weapons employing precision-guided munitions will be in mass production. The Federal Germans are deploying large numbers of a small anti-tank weapon with a semi-automatic guidance system that can be fired by one man, and have also designed another anti-tank weapon that has no back blast, making it possible to fire the weapon from inside a room, an ideal weapon for terrorists in urban areas. The Swedes have designed and are producing a weapon that fires a supersonic, surface-to-air missile kept on target by a laser beam guidance system. It is easily portable and can be operated by one man with minimum training. What will be the consequences of these weapons? What will happen when the 'Saturday Night Special' is not a revolver but perhaps a hand-held, laser-guided missile? Such weapons will provide terrorists with new capabilities and suggest new targets.

On the other hand, terrorist violence may be self-limiting in the sense that terrorists depend to a degree on the support of some constituency or the toleration of at least some governments. Too much violence could provoke harsh reactions and greater international cooperation against the terrorists.

A third possible trend is that national governments will recognise the achievements of terrorist groups and begin to employ them or their tactics as a means of surrogate warfare against other nations. Modern conventional warfare is becoming increasingly impractical. It is too destructive. It is too expensive. Few nations can afford it. The others must rely on external backers, but dependence on foreign support imposes constraints. There is always the danger, as we saw in the most recent war in the Middle East, that the superpower backers will themselves come close to the confrontation that could easily lead to a nuclear war. Before that happens, the superpowers are likely to tell their clients to cease hostilities and can always cut off supplies to ensure that they obey.

A nation planning to wage a modern conventional war must therefore plan to achieve its military objectives fast, before the cost of the war begins seriously to disrupt the economy, before world opinion can be mobilised to condemn its aggression or support a ceasefire, before the superpowers decide between themselves that the fighting should end, and, particularly in democracies, before the public at home watching the war on television turns off and domestic opposition to the fighting mounts. *Blitzkrieg*, always militarily attractive, has become a political necessity. Military occupation must now be a *fait accompli*, before political discussions begin. In recent years, we have witnessed several military offensives in which the advancing armies have raced the clock: the Israeli offensive in 1967, the Soviet invasion and occupation of Czechoslovakia in 1968, the Indian invasion of East Pakistan in 1971, the Egyptian offensive against Israel in 1973, the Israeli counter-offensive in which the last few hours of fighting were crucial, and the Turkish invasion of Cyprus in 1974.

But imposed ceasefires do not always resolve conflict the same way that surrender does. They temporarily stop the shooting, but they leave two hostile armies in the field, neither totally exhausted; even in retreat, the notion that a brief respite will suffice always exists. The fighting is likely to recur at a future date. This has resulted in recurring rounds of fighting between the same sets of contestants: India versus Pakistan in 1947, 1965, and 1971; the Arab nations versus Israel in 1948, 1956, 1967, and again in 1973.

The alternative to modern conventional war is low-level protracted war, debilitating military contests, in which staying power is more important than firepower, and military victory loses its traditional meaning as strategists debate whether not winning means losing or not losing means winning. These protracted wars seldom end, at least in any clear-cut fashion, though the level of fighting peaks and declines, often seasonally. War and post-war lose their traditional meanings. No nation or insurgent group can afford to mobilise all of its resources to fight for two generations. Protracted wars must compete with peacetime demands for resources. To fight long, one must fight cheaply; to fight cheaply, one must accept long periods of military stalemate. Local wars between lesser powers may be kept at low level through the collusion of external backers who refuse to allow the military contest to ascend to levels that will prove too costly, and too dangerous for them. The military contests in Laos and Cambodia are appropriate examples.

Terrorists, whatever their origin or cause, have demonstrated the possibilities of a third alternative — that of 'surrogate warfare'. Terrorism, though now rejected as a legitimate mode of warfare by most conventional military establishments, could become an accepted form of warfare in the future. Terrorists could be employed to provoke international incidents, create alarm in an adversary's country, compel it to divert valuable resources to protect itself, destroy its morale, and carry out specific acts of sabotage. Governments could employ existing terrorist groups to attack their opponents, or they could create their own terrorists. Terrorism only requires a small investment, certainly far less than what it costs to wage conventional war. It can be debilitating to the enemy. Prior to the 1973 Yom Kippur War, a senior Israeli officer estimated that the total cost in men and money to Israel for all defensive and offensive measures against at most a few thousand Arab terrorists was forty times that of the Six Day War in 1967. A secret backer of the terrorists can also deny sponsoring them. The concepts of

31

subversion sabotage, of lightning raids carried out by commandos, are not new, but the opportunities are.

How might terrorists be used in offensive surrogate warfare? Suppose a target nation has part of its strategic forces deployed overseas, including missile sites in another country. Perhaps there already has been some local opposition to the presence of these weapons. And perhaps also there are one or two extremist groups which have carried out relatively minor acts of violence. The groups have some international links but they lack the resources for any major undertaking. It is conceivable that through their links with foreign power local terrorists could be provided with the intelligence and some of the equipment necessary to launch an attack on one of the sites. Shortly before a bilateral treaty allowing the use of the sites is to be renewed, the terrorists attack, but, of course, fail. They penetrate the perimeter, but little damage is done to the missiles. Local newspapers, however, receive an anonymous tip that some lethal radioactive material has been released as a result of the attack. Indeed, checks with primitive geiger counters show some presence of radioactivity. The country whose missiles they are claims that no radioactive material escaped, and that probably the terrorists themselves deliberately spread a small quantity of radioactive waste material to alarm the population; there is said to be no danger; the denial is not convincing. Meanwhile, the terrorists warn of further attacks. Demonstrations against renewal of the arrangement by which the weapons are there in the first place begin and grow, aided perhaps by the fact that due to tightened security all locally hired employees of the country with the missiles have been temporarily laid off. The local government is shaken by the episode. There are further terrorist incidents. Relations between the two countries are strained. The owner of the missiles is finally asked to remove them.

Although the targets in this hypothetical example are military ones, the attack is a form of terrorism in that innocent civilians are endangered and the attack is carried out for its effect, not necessarily to destroy the target. With a little imagination, we could easily think of other examples. Suppose an atomic warhead is grabbed by what appears to be an international terrorist group, or suppose a relatively small and unimportant terrorist group finds itself the recipient of portable ground-to-air missiles whose original owner later claims were stolen.

We are reaching the point of industrialisation and population growth when the technical interdependencies of modern society — food on fertiliser on energy on fuel on transportation on communications — are so great and the margins of surplus so slim that a minor disruption in any single area can have tremendous cascading effects on nearly everything else. As a result, the vulnerabilities to disruption have increased. And as mentioned previously, so have the capacities for violence. Under such conditions, with a little help from their friends, any group of terrorists could ascend to the level of a genuine non-military threat to the national security of any advanced country.

Beyond Terrorism

International terrorism poses extraordinary problems for arms control. At present, the terrorist's capacity for destruction is limited, but the mass production and widespread distribution of increasingly sophisticated and increasingly powerful man-portable weapons will greatly add to the terrorist's arsenal. Weapons have become smaller, more potent, cheaper, and more widely available, all at the same time. Arms control efforts, which naturally have tended to focus on strategic weapons and on conventional war between nations, must now examine the consequences to be faced when weapons now being developed for tomorrow's infantrymen are passed second-hand or third-hand to tomorrow's terrorists.

At the same time, the world's increasing dependence on nuclear power may provide terrorists with weapons of mass destruction. Many fear that terrorists will steal a nuclear warhead, but the risks involved in taking such a device and the complicated tasks involved in actually detonating it may prove a deterrent to all but a handful of the larger and more sophisticated terrorist organisations. Recently, concern has shifted to the possibility that a group of terrorists might steal sufficient fissionable material to manufacture their own atomic bomb, but that, too, is a technically difficult and dangerous undertaking. Terrorists, however, need not steal a warhead or make an atomic bomb. A canister of radioactive waste material conceivably could pose a sufficient threat in any heavily populated area and provide terrorists with the means of radiological blackmail. The problems of security and control associated with nuclear weapons, and now with expanding peaceful nuclear programmes as well, are monumental.

But the consequences of international terrorism may go far beyond anything yet accomplished or contemplated by the terrorists themselves, militarily or politically. The developments that have made international terrorism feasible could in the future have a profound effect on the world. We are approaching an age in which national governments may no longer monopolise the instruments of major destruction. The instruments of warfare once possessed only by armies will be available to gangs. It will not be possible to satisfy the real or imagined grievances of all the little groups that will be capable of large-scale disruption and destruction or to defend everyone against them. The few examples of international terrorism that have occurred thus far are the harbingers of this new era. How will the world be affected by this development?

If the nature of warfare changes radically because of technical developments, then the concept of security, and of military power, and possibly of government itself may also change.

Warfare will have to be redefined. So will our ideas of what national defence means. Indeed the structure of government could change. Man's ability to invent new weapons is outpacing his ability to invent government institutions capable of controlling violence. Somebody no doubt said the same thing when the tommy-gun was invented — a machine-gun that could be concealed in a violin case — and no doubt, much the same was said when we first entered the age of nuclear weapons. And it is true that more people still die by knives or pistols in the hands of relatives and friends than are killed by tommy-guns, and that no one this side of Nagasaki has died in a nuclear war. But a sub-machine-gun can hardly be called a weapon of mass destruction, and nuclear weapons are still in the hands of a handful of governments who have a lot to lose if they use them. In the future, warfare — highly destructive warfare — may be waged, without the necessity for armies or governments, by people with little to lose.

Where does this take us? The primary purpose of government in whatever form is to provide security for its citizens. If governments cannot protect their citizens, as terrorists seem to be demonstrating, will governments as we know them become obsolete? The historical growth of national governments in the first place depended in part on national leadership, often a monarch, being able to monopolise the means of organised violence. If the military-power relationships are altered drastically in favour of small groups that obey no government, will we enter an era of international warlordism in which the people of the world and their governments are subjected to the extortion demands of many small groups? Or, in the face of growing terrorism and the threat of worldwide anarchy, will governments fall to the temptation of repression and use their still comparatively superior technical resources to become increasingly authoritarian? Or will governments put aside their political differences on this issue and delegate some of their jealously guarded sovereignty to an international force capable of dealing with international terrorists? Or will governments simply accept new concepts of warfare as redefined by terrorists, adopt their tactics to wage war against another nation, and take direct military action against enemy terrorists wherever they are?

Appendix: Chronology of Recent Incidents in International Terrorism

The following chronology lists incidents of international terrorism between January 1970 and July 1974. The list is representative and is not intended to be a complete catalogue of every incident. Acts of terrorism associated with the war in Indochina have been deliberately omitted. The numerous cross-border raids in the Middle East and acts of terrorism in the Israeli-occupied territories, except for the major episodes, have also been excluded. A complete chronology and a bibliography will be contained in a forthcoming research digest.[8] The author wishes to thank Janera Johnson for her assistance in compiling the chronology.

1 January 1970   A Brazilian revolutionary organisation hijacked an airliner en route between Montevideo and Rio. The plane was flown to Cuba. The hijackers stated that their purpose was 'to pay homage' to the dead guerrilla leader, Che Guevera.

20 January 1970   Unknown gunmen entered the British Consulate in Guatemala City where they shot and killed the consul's bodyguard.

10 February 1970   Three Arab terrorists killed one Israeli citizen and wounded 11 other passengers in a grenade attack on a bus at the airport in Munich. Two Palestinian organisations were responsible for the attack.

21 February 1970   A sabotaged Swissair plane en route to Tel Aviv crashed on takeoff killing all 47 passengers, including 15 Israelis. The Popular Front for the Liberation of Palestine was responsible.

21 February 1970   A bomb planted by the Popular Front for the Liberation of Palestine exploded in an Austrian plane that was carrying mail to Tel Aviv. There were no casualties.

1 March 1970   A bomb was found in the luggage aboard an Ethiopian airliner in Rome. The device was placed by members of the Eritrean Liberation Front.

6 March 1970   Members of the Rebel Armed Forces kidnapped the US Labor Attaché in Guatemala. In return for his release, the kidnappers demanded the release of four prisoners held by Guatemalan authorities. The Government agreed to meet the kidnappers' demands. He was released on 8 March.

11 March 1970   Japan's Consul General in São Paulo, Brazil, was seized by members of a leftist urban guerrilla group. The kidnappers' demands included the release of five prisoners and suspension of the massive search which had been launched by the Government. The Brazilian Government promptly suspended its search and announced that it would meet the kidnappers' demands. The hostage was released unharmed, after the plane with its prisoners arrived in Mexico.

24 March 1970   The US Air Attaché in the Dominican Republic was kidnapped by six members of a group calling itself the 'United Anti-Reelection Command', a leftist group which opposed the reelection of President Balaguer. The kidnappers demanded that twenty-one prisoners be set free. The Government agreed. The Attaché was released on 26 March.

24 March 1970   The Paraguayan Consul in the border town of Ituzaingo, Argentina, was kidnapped by members of the Liberation Armed Forces. They threatened to kill him and to begin killing the managers of the American

35

business firms if two of their members being held by the Argentine Government were not released from prison. The Government refused their demands. On 28 March, the kidnappers released the Consul, unharmed for humanitarian reasons, but vowed to execute police and government officials.

27 March 1970   A right-wing terrorist group threatened to kill the Soviet Ambassador in Argentina and his family in reprisal for the kidnapping of the Paraguayan Consul.

29 March 1970   Four members of a right-wing terrorist group attempted to kidnap the Soviet Assistant Commercial Attaché.

31 March 1970   Nine members of Japan's United Red Army hijacked a Japan Air Lines plane and ordered it to be flown to Pyongyang, North Korea.

31 March 1970   Members of the Rebel Armed Forces kidnapped the West German Ambassador to Guatemala. The kidnappers threatened to execute the Ambassador unless the government released seventeen — later twenty-five — prisoners. The Guatemalan Government refused to meet the demands. A last-minute attempt at negotiations failed and on 5 April the authorities received an anonymous phone call telling them where to find the Ambassador's body.

5 April 1970   The US Consul General eluded a kidnapping attempt in Porto Allegre, Brazil.

26 April 1970   A Brazilian VASP airliner was hijacked and ordered to be flown to Cuba by a left-wing urban guerrilla leader.

4 May 1970   Two Palestinian Arabs burst into the Israeli Embassy in Asunción, Paraguay, and shot and killed the wife of the First Secretary and seriously wounded an Embassy employee. The assailants were reported to be members of Al Fatah.

13 May 1970   Eight armed nationals of the Domincan Republic took over a Dutch Antilles Airways plane and ordered it to be flown to Cuba.

22 May 1970   Eight children were killed and twenty-two wounded when a school bus in Israel was hit by three bazooka rockets fired by *fedayeen* who had crossed the border from Lebanon.

5 June 1970   A Polish airliner was hijacked to Denmark by persons seeking asylum.

7 June 1970   The US Political Secretary in Jordan was kidnapped by Palestinian guerrillas. The guerrillas demanded the release of forty prisoners held in Jordan. He was released unharmed on 8 June.

9 June 1970   Sixty foreigners were held hostage in two Amman hotels by members of the Popular Front for the Liberation of Palestine. The guerrillas threatened to blow up the two hotels if their camps in Jordan were smashed by Jordanian army units. The hostages were released unharmed on 12 June.

10 June 1970   The US Assistant Military Attaché in Jordan was shot to death by guerrillas.

11 June 1970   The Federal German Ambassador to Brazil was kidnapped in Rio de Janeiro by members of two leftist urban guerrilla organisations. In return for his safe return, the kidnappers demanded the release of forty prisoners and the publication of a revolutionary manifesto. The Brazilian Government agreed and the forty prisoners were flown to Algeria. The

Ambassador was released unharmed on 16 June.

21 June 1970   An Iranian Boeing 727 was hijacked by three armed Iranians and flown to Baghdad. The hijackers requested political asylum in Iraq.

21 July 1970   Members of the National Liberation Army kidnapped two Federal German technicians in Bolivia. They burned the offices of an American-owned goldmining firm, stole $5,000, and fled into the jungle with their captives whom they threatened to execute unless the Bolivian Government released ten prisoners within 48 hours. The government yielded on 22 July and the two technicians were released unharmed.

22 July 1970   Six Arab guerrillas hijacked an Olympic Airways 727 over Rhodes, Greece, after it had taken off from Beirut, and ordered it to be flown to Cairo. They demanded the release of seven other Arab guerrillas being held by the Greek Government. The Greek Government promised to release the prisoners within one month, and the fifty-five passengers and crew of the aircraft were released. The Popular Struggle Front claimed credit for the operation.

31 July 1970   An American public safety adviser in Uruguay was kidnapped by the Tupamaros. The kidnappers demanded that 150 Tupamaros being held in jail be freed in return for the hostage held by the Tupamaros. When the President of Uruguay refused to negotiate with the kidnappers, the Tupamaros killed the adviser.

31 July 1970   The Brazilian Consul was kidnapped by Tupamaros. He was finally released on 21 February 1971.

31 July 1970   Tupamaros attempted to kidnap the Second Secretary to the US Embassy in Montevideo, and also the Cultural Attaché.

7 August 1970   An American agricultural adviser in Uruguay was kidnapped by the Tupamaros. During his extended captivity, the man suffered a heart attack. He was driven to a hospital and released on 2 March 1971.

6 September 1970   Members of the Popular Front for the Liberation of Palestine hijacked three airliners bound for Europe and diverted them to the Middle East. Two aircraft were flown to a landing strip in the Jordanian desert. A fourth hijacking of an El Al plane from Amsterdam was foiled when a security guard aboard the plane killed one of the hijackers and wounded another. The hijackings were announced to be in retaliation for American support of Israel and the American peace initiatives in the Middle East. The hijackers demanded the release of imprisoned Arab guerrillas in Switzerland, Great Britain and Federal Germany. On 9 September the same group hijacked a BOAC VC-10 and also had it flown to the airstrip, bringing the total number of hostages held in the desert to over 300. Negotiations were complicated by the outbreak of fighting between Jordanian troops and Palestinian guerrillas. On 12 September the remaining passengers (women and children had been removed earlier) were evacuated, and the three airliners were blown up. Most passengers were soon released, but the hijackers continued to hold fifty-eight hostages to exert pressure on the European governments. The remaining hostages were released in September in exchange for seven Arab guerrillas.

12 September 1970   Members of the Jewish Defence League in London announced that they had kidnapped three employees of the Egyptian Embassy and would hold them hostage until the airline passengers held in Jordan were released.

5 October 1970   The British Trade Commissioner in Quebec, Canada, was kidnapped by members of the Quebec Liberation Front. The ransom demands included the release of thirteen prisoners, the publication of a manifesto, and the payment of $500,000 in gold. On 10 October other Front members kidnapped the Minister of Labor in the Quebec Government. The kidnappers warned that they would kill him if the demands made by the kidnappers of the British diplomat were not met. The Government again rejected the demands, but offered the kidnappers a safe conduct out of the country if the two hostages were released unharmed. On 18 October the body of the Minister was found in the trunk of a car. On 3 December the kidnappers released the British diplomat unharmed and were flown to Cuba in accordance with an agreement that had been worked out earlier.

9 October 1970   An Iranian airliner was hijacked to Baghdad by Iranian terrorists seeking the release of twenty-one prisoners held in Iran.

1 November 1970   The Polish Deputy Foreign Minister was assassinated in Karachi, Pakistan, by a Pakistani truck driver who drove a truck into an airport reception line for the Polish officials.

1 December 1970   The honorary Federal German Consul in San Sebastian, Spain, was kidnapped by members of a Basque nationalist party dedicated to achieving independence for the Basque provinces in northern Spain. The kidnappers warned that his fate would depend on the sentence given to fifteen Basques accused of murdering a head of the provincial police. On 24 December the Consul was released unharmed.

7 December 1970   The Swiss Ambassador to Brazil was kidnapped in Rio de Janeiro by leftist guerrillas. The kidnappers demanded the release of seventy prisoners, the broadcast of a revolutionary manifesto, and the immediate publication by the press of any other rebel communiques. After lengthy negotiations, the Brazilian Government agreed, on 14 January 1971, to release the prisoners. The Ambassador was released unharmed on 16 January.

8 January 1971   The British Ambassador in Uruguay was kidnapped by Tupamaros. In return for his release, the kidnappers demanded the release of 150 prisoners. The Government refused to negotiate with the kidnappers. The Ambassador was released on 9 September, just three days after 106 of the prisoners on the kidnappers' list escaped from jail.

8 January 1971   A bomb placed by members of the Jewish Defense League exploded in the Soviet cultural offices in Washington, D.C.

2 February 1971   Two armed Kashmiri nationalists hijacked an Indian Airlines plane to Pakistan. They demanded the release of thirty-six prisoners held in Kashmir by the Indian Government. When the Government rejected their demands, they blew up the airliner.

10 February 1971   Two Croatian emigrés seized control of the Yugoslav Consulate in Göteborg, Sweden, in an unsuccessful attempt to ransom its occupants for convicted terrorists held in Yugoslav jails.

4 March 1971   Four American servicemen stationed near Ankara were kidnapped by four members of the Turkish People's Liberation Army. The kidnappers demanded the publication of a manifesto attacking American imperialism in Turkey, and the payment of 400,000 Turkish lira. The Turkish Government captured one of the kidnappers who divulged the names of his accomplices. The kidnappers released the four airmen unharmed on 8 March.

30 March 1971   Six members of a Philippine leftist student organisation hijacked a Philippine Airlines domestic flight to Peking, China.

7 April 1971   The Yugoslav Ambassador to Sweden was assassinated and two Yugoslav diplomats were wounded by Croatian terrorists in Stockholm.

17 May 1971   The Israeli Consul General in Istanbul was kidnapped by members of the Turkish People's Liberation Army. The kidnappers demanded the release of all guerrillas being detained by the Turkish Government. The Government rejected the demand and launched a house-to-house search. The Consul's body was found, shot to death, in an apartment on 23 May.

23 May 1971   The honorary British Consul in Rosario, Argentina, was kidnapped by members of the People's Revolutionary Army.

29 May 1971   Basque Nationalists attempted to kidnap the French Consul in San Sebastian, Spain. He resisted and escaped.

24 August 1971   A bomb placed by Al Fatah damaged a Jordanian airliner in Madrid, Spain.

28 November 1971   The Jordanian Prime Minister was assassinated in Egypt by members of Black September. This was the first public mention of the group. A statement by the group said that the killing was in revenge for the slaying of Palestinian guerrillas in the Jordan civil war in September 1970.

15 December 1971   Black September members attempted, unsuccessfully, to assassinate the Jordanian Ambassador in London.

16 January 1971   An American nurse was killed and several persons wounded in a terrorist attack in Israeli-occupied Gaza.

26 January 1972   Croatian emigrés claimed responsibility for bombing of a Stockholm-to-Belgrade airliner which crashed, killing twenty-six.

26 January 1972   The New York offices of Sol Hurok, who manages tours by Soviet performers, were firebombed by members of the Jewish Defense League.

22 February 1972   A bomb planted by the Irish Republican Army exploded at Aldershot army base in England, killing seven and wounding five.

22 February 1972   A Lufthansa jet airliner en route from New Delhi to Athens was hijacked by five Palestinian guerrillas who described themselves as members of the 'Organisation for Victims of Zionist Occupation'. They released the passengers and crew on 23 February. Later, the Federal German Government disclosed that it had paid $5 million in ransom for the release of the hostages and airliner.

21 March 1972   The managing director of Fiat in Argentina was kidnapped by members of the People's Revolutionary Army. On 10 April police discovered the kidnappers' hideout. The kidnappers executed the victim just before they were captured.

27 March 1972   Three NATO radar technicians were kidnapped by members of the Turkish People's Liberation Army. When their hideout was surrounded, the three hostages were executed.

3 May 1972   Four Turkish students claiming to be members of the Turkish People's Liberation Army hijacked a Turkish airliner to Bulgaria.

8 May 1972   A Belgian Sabena Airlines plane en route from Vienna to Tel Aviv was hijacked by four members of Black September who ordered the plane flown to Israel's Lod Airport. Upon their arrival they demanded the release of 317 Palestinian guerrillas held in Israel. Israel paratroopers disguised as mechanics burst through the emergency doors and killed two of the hijackers and wounded a third. Five passengers were wounded in the gunfight.

31 May 1972   Three Japanese gunmen attacked passengers at Israel's Lod Airport with machine-guns and hand grenades, killing twenty-five and wounding seventy-six. The gunmen, who were members of the United Red Army of Japan, were recruited by the Popular Front for the Liberation of Palestine for the assault.

3 June 1972   A lone hijacker claiming to be a member of the Black Panther Party seized a Western Airlines jet in the United States and ordered it to be flown to Algiers after collecting $500,000 ransom.

20 June 1972   Nineteen Croatian guerrillas infiltrated into Yugoslavia. Near the town of Bugojnok, they attacked and killed thirteen local security officers before they were defeated.

30 June 1972   The president of the Buenos Aires branch of the Banco di Napoli, a leading Italian bank, was kidnapped by four armed men.

17 July 1972   The First Secretary of the Swedish Embassy in Bogotá, Colombia was shot to death by unidentified gunmen.

31 July 1972   Hijackers claiming to be sympathisers of the Black Panthers took over a Delta Air Lines jet over Florida, directing the plane to Algeria after collecting $1 million in ransom.

5 August 1972   An oil storage facility in Trieste, Italy, was set on fire by Black September terrorists. The fire caused an estimated $7 million damage.

16 August 1972   An El Al airliner was damaged by a bomb in its luggage compartment shortly after take off from Rome. A new guerrilla group calling itself 'Nationalist Youth Group for the Liberation of Palestine' claimed credit for the attack.

22 August 1972   A Southern Yemen DC-6 airplane en route from Beirut to Cairo was hijacked by three armed men who said they were members of a group called the 'Eagles of National Unity'. The plane was flown to Benghazi, Libya, where the hijackers requested asylum.

5 September 1972   Eight Palestinian guerrillas broke into the Israeli quarters at the Olympic Games in Munich, killing two Israeli athletes and taking nine others hostage. The guerrillas demanded the release of 200 Palestinians imprisoned in Israel and safe passage for themselves and their hostages to another country. In a subsequent gunfight five of the terrorists and all nine of the hostages were killed. Black September claimed responsibility for the attack. (On 21 February 1973, Israel, in retaliation for Munich, raided refugee camps in Lebanon killing thirty-one. They also shot down a Libyan airliner that strayed over Sinai, killing 107 aboard.)

5 September 1972   A Dutch citizen, who headed the Philips Argentina electronic firm, was kidnapped by a Peronist urban guerrilla group.

15 September 1972   Croatian emigrés hijacked an SAS airliner and ransomed its passengers for Croatian terrorists held in Swedish jails.

19 September 1972   A letter-bomb mailed by Arab guerrillas exploded and killed a diplomat in the Israeli Embassy in London. In the next few days, nearly fifty letter-bombs addressed to officials in Israel and Israeli Embassies were intercepted throughout the world. Eight more letter-bombs were found in the first half of October. Black September claimed responsibility.

6 October 1972   Palestinian students entered the Federal German consulate in Algiers and held hostages for about an hour, demanding release of three Arab terrorists held in Munich.

22 October 1972   Four men hijacked a Turkish airliner to Bulgaria, and threatened to blow it up along with sixty-nine passengers if Turkey did not release twelve terrorist prisoners, restore the right of workers to strike, and reorganise the universities.

29 October 1972   A Lufthansa Boeing 727 en route to Ankara was taken over by two hijackers claiming to be members of Black September and was ordered to be flown to Munich. The hijackers threatened to blow up the plane unless the Federal German Government released the three Black September terrorists captured in the Munich attack.

2 November 1972   Three youths bombed the French Consulate in Zaragoza, Spain, fatally injuring the French honorary Consul and slightly injuring two others.

6 November 1972   A letter-bomb exploded in a post office in Bombay, India, wounding a post office worker.

7 November 1972   An Italian industrialist was kidnapped in Buenos Aires.

8 November 1972   Four members of the 'Armed Communist League', a small guerrilla group in Mexico, hijacked a Mexican airliner. They demanded arms, the release of five imprisoned guerrillas, a Government promise to drop charges against two fugitives who joined them, and $330,000 in ransom.

10 November 1972   A letter-bomb exploded when it was being opened by the managing director of a diamond brokers' firm in London. In the next few days, fifty-two more letter-bombs addressed to Jewish firms in Europe were intercepted in Bombay and New Delhi, and twenty more were intercepted by British authorities. Swiss authorities intercepted an additional five.

6 December 1972   A Spanish industrialist in Argentina was kidnapped by unknown persons.

8 December 1972   The chief representative of Al Fatah in Paris was killed by an explosion which destroyed his Paris apartment.

10 December 1972   The managing director of the British Vestey industrial group in Argentina was kidnapped by members of the People's Revolutionary Army.

20 December 1972   The US Embassy in Beirut, Lebanon, was hit by two rockets. Black September was suspected of the attack.

27 December 1972   An executive for the Argentine subsidiary of International Telephone and Telegraph was kidnapped.

28 December 1972   Four members of Black September took over the Israeli Embassy in Bangkok, Thailand, and held six hostages for nineteen hours. They demanded the release of thirty-six Arab guerrillas imprisoned in Israel. Thai officials and the Egyptian Ambassador in Bangkok persuaded the guerrillas to release their hostages in return for safe conduct to Egypt.

41

8 January 1973   A bomb exploded destroying the offices of the Jewish Agency in Paris which arranges for the emigration of Jews to Israel. Black September claimed credit.

23 January 1973   Two Italian businessmen residing in Ethiopia were kidnapped by members of the Eritrean Liberation Front.

23 January 1973   Two armed gunmen and one woman kidnapped the US Ambassador to Haiti, and held him hostage along with the US Consul General. In return for the two hostages, the kidnappers demanded the release of thirty prisoners and a ransom of $1 million. In subsequent negotiations, they agreed to accept the release of twelve prisoners and $70,000. The kidnappers released their hostages after eighteen hours and flew with the released prisoners to Mexico.

25 January 1973   A representative of Al Fatah was killed in a hotel in Nicosia, Cyprus, by a time-bomb. Palestinians claimed that Israeli agents were responsible.

26 January 1973   Black September claimed responsibility for the assassination of an Israeli tourist in Madrid, Spain, who they claimed was an Israeli intelligence officer.

27 January 1973   The Turkish Consul General and Vice-Consul in Los Angeles, California, were murdered by a man of Armenian origin in revenge for Turkish attacks on Armenians in 1915.

20 February 1973   Three Pakistani youths attacked the Indian High Commission in London and held staff members hostage, injuring some of them. British police shot two of the gunmen and arrested the third, who said they belonged to a group called 'Black December'. They had intended to take hostages in order to obtain an audience with Prime Minister Indira Ghandi and to demand the release of Pakistani prisoners-of-war.

1 March 1973   Eight members of Black September took over the Saudi Arabian Embassy in Khartoum and seized several hostages, including the US Ambassador, the US Deputy Chief of Mission, and the Belgian Chargé. The Jordanian Chargé d'Affaires and Saudi Arabian Ambassador were also held. Many other diplomats escaped. The terrorists demanded the release of sixty Palestinian guerrillas being held in Jordan, all Arab women detained in Israel, Sirhan Sirhan (the killer of Senator Robert Kennedy), and imprisoned members of the Baader-Meinhof gang in Federal Germany. When negotiations failed, the terrorists executed the two US diplomats and the Belgian Chargé on the night of 2 March. The terrorists then tried to bargain for safe passage to another country, but this was rejected. They surrendered on 3 March.

4 March 1973   The Greek charter ship 'Sanya' − carrying 250 American tourists bound for Haifa, Israel − sank in Beirut harbour following an explosion on board. There were no casualties.

8 March 1973   Two bombs exploded in London, killing one and injuring two hundred. The Irish Republican Army was believed to be responsible.

12 March 1973   An Israeli businessman subsequently branded by Cairo's *fedayeen* radio as a 'Zionist intelligence officer' was shot and killed on the steps of the Nicosia Palace Hotel in Cyprus. Black September claimed responsibility.

28 March 1973   The manager of the Rosario, Argentina, branch of the First National Bank of Boston was kidnapped by Argentine guerrillas.

2 April 1973 A naturalised US citizen, serving as a technical operations manager for Eastman Kodak Company in Argentina, was kidnapped on his way to work by guerrillas. He was the first American businessman kidnapped in Argentina.

8 April 1973 The president of Nobleza Tobacco Company, an Argentine subsidiary of British and American Tobacco Company, was kidnapped outside his home in Buenos Aires.

9 April 1973 A group of Arab guerrillas blew out the entrance to a Nicosia apartment building where the Israeli Ambassador resided, and escaped in an automobile. Shortly after the bomb exploded, two cars crashed through the gates of the Nicosia airport. There the guerrillas engaged in a gunfight with Cypriot police and an Israeli security guard. Three Arabs were wounded in the fight; one later died. Some reports credit Black September with the operation.

10 April 1973 Israeli commandos, in a raid on Beirut, killed seventeen, including three high-ranking Palestinian guerrilla leaders, and wounded several others.

27 April 1973 An Italian employee of El Al Airlines was shot and killed outside a department store in Rome. Police arrested a Lebanese citizen who said that he was a member of Black September and had been ordered to kill the Italian because he was an Israeli spy responsible for the killing of an Al Fatah official in Rome in October 1972.

2 May 1973 Rockets were fired at the US Ambassador's residence in Beirut.

4 May 1973 Two Soviet doctors working in Burma were kidnapped by rebel Shan tribesmen.

4 May 1973 The US Consul General in Guadalajara was kidnapped by members of the 'People's Revolutionary Armed Forces'. They demanded the release of thirty prisoners held in Mexico. Later, they asked for a ransom of $80,000. The Mexican Government acceded to all of the demands and the Consul's wife arranged for payment of the ransom. He was freed unharmed on 6 May.

18 May 1973 Four members of the 'People's Revolutionary Army (Zero Point)', a leftist guerrilla organisation, hijacked a Venezuelan airlines plane and ordered it to be flown to Mexico City. The hijackers demanded the release of seventy-nine prisoners held in Venezuela, a demand which the Venezuelan Government rejected. Mexican officials persuaded the hijackers not to destroy the plane but rather to fly to Cuba. The hijackers accepted the offer and flew to Havana.

21 May 1973 Gunmen belonging to the People's Revolutionary Army wounded an executive and another employee of Ford Motor Company, Argentina, one of whom later died. The organisation issued a communiqué on 23 May stating that the victim had been shot resisting a kidnapping attempt and warning that the kidnapping of Ford executives would continue unless the company paid $1 million ransom.

30 May 1973 A Colombian airliner was hijacked by two armed men who demanded the release of forty-seven imprisoned guerrillas and $200,000 ransom. The Colombian Government refused both demands. The hijackers accepted $50,000 instead and escaped. All passengers and crew were released and unharmed.

31 May 1973   The People's Revolutionary Army threatened to attack and kidnap top executives of Otis Elevator Company and their families unless the company made $500,000 in charitable contributions similar to those made by Ford and doubled the wages of 1,300 Otis employees in Argentina.

2 June 1973   An American military adviser in Iran was shot and killed by gunmen believed to be members of a leftist guerrilla group.

6 June 1973   A British executive of an Argentine affiliate of Britain's Acrow Steel was kidnapped by six gunmen believed to be members of the People's Revolutionary Army; but in a press conference, the group denied responsibility for the kidnapping and for the threats against Ford and Otis. The kidnappers may have been members of a splinter group. In the negotiations the kidnappers asked for $7.5 million ransom.

9 June 1973   An arms plant in West Berlin was partially destroyed by a Black September unit. The group issued a communiqué stating that it was because the company deals with Israel.

10 June 1973   A Royal Nepal Airlines plane was hijacked while on a domestic flight by three armed men, one of whom was identified as a leader of a Nepalese student organisation connected with the Nepalese Communist Party. The plane was carrying a bank shipment of approximately $400,000 which the hijackers seized. They ordered the plane to be flown to India and escaped.

18 June 1973   A Federal German clothing manufacturer in Argentina was kidnapped by guerrillas and held for $100,000 ransom.

18 June 1973   The President of Firestone Tyre and Rubber Company's subsidiary in Argentina was kidnapped by members of the People's Revolutionary Army who demanded $3 million ransom.

25 June 1973   The Italian Vice-President of the Bank of Italy and Rio de la Plata was kidnapped by gunmen believed to be members of the People's Revolutionary Army. The kidnappers demanded $2 million in ransom.

28 June 1973   An Algerian supporter of *fedayeen* terrorist operations was killed in Paris by a bomb in his car.

1 July 1973   The Israeli Military Attaché in Washington, D.C., was shot to death outside his home. Arab terrorists were believed to be responsible.

2 July 1973   The assistant manager of First National City Bank of New York in Córdoba, Argentina, was kidnapped.

19 July 1973   A lone Palestinian guerrilla armed with a machine-gun and hand-grenades attempted to attack the El Al offices in Athens. He was prevented from entering the office by the closed bullet-proof inner glass doors. The terrorist then fled to a nearby hotel where he cornered seventeen hostages. Negotiations, undertaken by the Ambassadors of Egypt, Libya, and Iraq, continued for several hours. It was finally agreed to allow the terrorist to be flown to Kuwait where he vanished. The hostages were released unharmed. The man claimed to be a member of the 'Organisation of Victims of Occupied Territories'.

20 July 1973   A Japan Air Lines Boeing 747 was seized by one Japanese and three Arab hijackers shortly after it took off from Amsterdam. A fifth hijacker, a woman reported to be a Latin American, was killed shortly after the plane was taken over when a hand-grenade she was holding accidentally exploded. The three Arabs identified themselves either as members of the

'Organisation of Sons of Occupied Territories' or the 'Mount Carmel Martyrs'. The Japanese hijacker was identified as a member of the 'Japanese Red Army acting for the people of Palestine'. The hijackers ordered the plane to Lebanon where they were refused permission to land. They finally landed in Dubai. Officials at Japan Air Lines arrived there to negotiate, but the hijackers rejected negotiations and flew on to Benghazi, Libya, where the passengers were released and the aircraft destroyed with grenades and a bomb by the hijackers.

21 July 1973   A Moroccan waiter resident in Oslo, Norway, was murdered by several persons believed to be members of the 'Wrath of God', a militant wing of the Jewish Defense League or Israeli counter-terrorist agents.

5 August 1973   Two Arabs armed with machine-guns and hand-grenades opened fire on passengers at the Athens airport. Three passengers were killed and fifty-five wounded. The terrorists then seized thirty-five hostages but later surrendered to Greek police. Later, a new group calling itself the 'Seventh Suicide Squad' claimed responsibility for the attack which it named the 'Bahr al-Bakr' operation after a Cairo suburb where Israeli planes bombed a school in 1970.

18 August 1973   Members of the Irish Republican Army of sympathisers launched a fire- and letter-bomb campaign in London, Birmingham, and Manchester. By September 28 more than forty bombs had exploded. Many others were discovered and defused. At least twenty-nine people were injured. Letter-bombs were discovered at British Embassies in Paris on 28 August, and in Lisbon on 17 September. A letter-bomb sent to the British Embassy in Zaire wounded a British official on 17 September. British officials in Gibraltar and Brussels also received letter-bombs.

22 August 1973   A US citizen and member of the military anti-Castro Cuban Revolutionary Directorate was killed in a bomb explosion in his hotel room in Avrainville, France.

27 August 1973   A British citizen and manager of Leigib's Meat Company in Paraguay was kidnapped.

5 September 1973   Five Palestinian commandos broke into the Saudi Arabian Embassy in Paris and seized thirteen hostages. They demanded the release of an Al Fatah leader imprisoned in Jordan. After twenty-eight hours of negotiations in which a number of Arab ambassadors participated as inter-mediaries, the commandos dropped this demand and asked for safe passage out of the country. They agreed to release all but four of the hostages and were allowed to board a Syrian aircraft which flew them to Kuwait. On 7 September the commandos and their hostages transferred to a Kuwaiti plane and flew over Riyadh, Saudi Arabia. The commandos threatened to throw the hostages out of the aircraft unless the Saudi Arabian Government helped them obtain the release of the Al Fatah leader. When Saudi Arabian officials refused, the aircraft was ordered to return to Kuwait. On 8 September the hostages were released and the commandos surrendered. The five claimed to be members of a group called 'Punishment'.

5 September 1973   Italian military police arrested five terrorists when they said they were planning to shoot down an El Al airliner at the Rome airport. One of the terrorists possessed two Soviet portable heat seeking ground-to-air missiles.

8 September 1973   Two men and a woman were injured seriously when terrorists exploded two bombs in King's Cross and Euston railway stations in London. At least ten other persons suffered lesser injuries in the explosions. It was believed that the Irish Republican Army's Provisional urban guerrillas or some of their ultra-militants were behind the bombings.

23 September 1973   A British executive of the Nobleza Tobacco Company in Argentina was kidnapped and held for ransom in Buenos Aires.

28 September 1973   Three Jewish emigrés en route from the Soviet Union to Israel and an Austrian customs official were seized by two armed Arabs who claimed to be members of the 'Eagles of the Palestinian Revolution'. The terrorists seized their hostages aboard a train, later commandeered a car, and drove to the Vienna airport. They demanded that the Austrian Government close Schönau Castle, a transit camp for Jewish emigrés operated by the Jewish Agency. The Austrian Government agreed and the terrorists released their hostages and were flown to Libya.

4 October 1973   Two American employees of the Frontino Goldmines in Colombia were kidnapped. The kidnappers, believed to have been members of the National Liberation Army, sent a letter on 5 October to the International Mining Company which owns the mines, demanding $168,990 ransom.

10 October 1973   The honorary British Consul in Guadalajara, Mexico, was kidnapped by terrorists who demanded the release of fifty-one political prisoners and $200,000 ransom. The Mexican Government refused to release any prisoners. The Consul was released unharmed on 14 October.

20 October 1973   A Boeing 737 carrying forty-three passengers and a crew of six was seized on a flight from Buenos Aires. Four hijackers, including two women, forced the plane to fly to Tucuman, then to Bolivia. The guerrillas identified themselves as Tupamaros. An offer of safe conduct out of Bolivia, presumably to Cuba, was accepted by the terrorists in exchange for the release of the hostages they had threatened to kill.

22 October 1973   A Swissair executive in Argentina was kidnapped by the People's Revolutionary Army. A $10 million ransom was demanded.

25 October 1973   The American head of an Argentine subsidiary of Amoco International Oil Company of Chicago was kidnapped in Buenos Aires.

22 November 1973   An American executive of Ford Motor Company, Argentina, and three bodyguards were killed in Córdoba, Argentina. A terrorist group called the Peronist Armed Forces announced that it was responsible.

25 November 1973   Four Palestinian guerrillas, belonging to the Arab Nationalist Youth for the Liberation of Palestine, hijacked a Royal Dutch KLM jumbo jet. The aircraft was forced to fly first to Damascus and then on to Nicosia, Tripoli, and Malta. The hijackers demanded that KLM cease transporting arms to Israel and that the Netherlands Government change its 'pro-Israel stance' drastically and no longer render aid to the emigration of Soviet Jews to Israel. All 247 passengers were released unharmed on 27 November; the hijackers surrendered after getting a safe passage guarantee from Dubai.

6 December 1973   An American executive with the Exxon Company in Argentina was kidnapped by the People's Revolutionary Army. The guerrilla group demanded that $10 million in food and medicine be distributed to the poor.

12 December 1973   An American engineer was kidnapped in La Plata, Argentina. $500,000 ransom was asked for his release.

17 December 1973   Thirty-two persons died and eighteen were wounded when five Arab guerrillas attacked the Middle-East-bound Pan American World Airways jet airliner in Rome, spraying it with bombs and machine-gun fire, hurling hand-grenades into it, and setting it on fire. The guerrillas then commandeered a West German Lufthansa airliner to Athens with a number of hostages. From Athens, the hijackers flew to Kuwait, where they released their twelve remaining hostages in exchange for 'free passage' to an unknown destination. The terrorists surrendered to the Kuwait Government.

18 December 1973   Two bombs in cars and a parcel-bomb exploded in London in what is believed to have been reprisal attacks for the jailing of Irish Republican terrorists.

27 December 1973   A Federal German industrialist who is also his country's honorary Consul was kidnapped from his home in Ireland.

29 December 1973   The Director of Safrar-Peugeot, a subsidiary of Peugeot of France, was kidnapped by seven armed men in Buenos Aires, Argentina. The kidnapping has been attributed to the Revolutionary Armed Forces, but the guerrilla group denied responsibility.

31 December 1973   One of Britain's leading Zionists was shot in his London mansion. The victim was an honorary vice-president of the Zionist Federation of Britain and president of Joint Palestinian Appeal, which collects funds for welfare in Israel. The Popular Front for the Liberation of Palestine claimed responsibility.

31 January 1974   Two Japanese belonging to the radical Japanese Red Army and two Arabs of the Popular Front for the Liberation of Palestine tried to blow up a Shell refinery in Singapore, then seized eight hostages aboard a ferryboat and threatened to kill themselves and the hostages unless they were given safe passage to an Arab country. On 6 February, five members took over the Japanese Embassy in Kuwait, holding about twelve hostages including the Japanese Ambassador. They demanded that the Japanese Government supply an airliner to bring their comrades from Singapore to Kuwait. The airliner carrying the four guerrillas from Singapore landed in Kuwait and, after picking up the other five who had released their hostages, went on to Yemen-Aden, where it arrived on 8 February.

2 February 1974   Three members of a group called Moslem International Guerrillas seized a Greek freighter in the port of Karachi, Pakistan, and said they would blow up the ship and kill two hostages unless the Greek Government freed two Arab terrorists who had received the death sentence.

3 February 1974   A 50-pound bomb, apparently concealed in a suitcase, smashed a bus as it was travelling through Yorkshire, Great Britain, carrying soldiers and their families back from leave to their camp. Eleven were killed, fourteen were injured. Officials in London attributed the attack to the Provisional Irish Republican Army.

12 February 1974   A 50-pound bomb exploded in the records section of the Latimer National Defence College in England, injuring ten persons. Authorities blamed terrorists of the Irish Republican Army.

3 March 1974   A British Airways VC-10 on its way from Bombay to London was hijacked by two Arabs after a brief stop at Beirut Airport. The guerrillas planted explosives and ordered the pilot to land at Amsterdam's Schiphol Airport. After freeing the ninety-two passengers and ten crew members, they blew the plane up before being taken prisoner by Dutch security

forces. They had told passengers that they belonged to the Arab Nationalist Youth for the Liberation of Palestine.

25 March 1974   The US Vice-Consul stationed in Hermosillo, Mexico, was kidnapped. A note demanding a reported $500,000 was found on the consulate floor.

26 March 1974   The Eritrean Liberation Front kidnapped five employees of Tenneco, an American-based oil company in Ethiopia. The company broke off talks after one person who was sent to retrieve the company's five employees was kidnapped and another was killed. An American nurse was then kidnapped by the same group on 27 May. The rebels planned to try three of the five Americans on charges of exploiting the national resources of Eritrea, a province in northern Ethiopia.

12 April 1974   The head of the US Information Service branch in Córdoba, Argentina, was wounded and kidnapped by the People's Revolutionary Army. The guerrillas released him the same day apparently because of the seriousness of his wounds.

12 April 1974   Eighteen people were killed and sixteen were wounded in Kiryat Shemona, Israel, by three Arab guerrillas who stormed a residential building. The guerrillas, who said they belonged to the Popular Front for the Liberation of Palestine, General Command, died in an explosion at the end of a gun and grenade battle with Israeli troops. Israeli forces carried out retaliatory raids across the Lebanese border after the victims of the Arab terrorist raid were buried.

15 May 1974   Three Arab guerrillas belonging to the Popular Democratic Front for the Liberation of Palestine crossed the border from Lebanon into Israel where they attacked a van bringing Arab women home from work. Two were killed, one was wounded. The three then entered the Israeli town of Maalot where they killed three more before seizing about ninety teenagers in a school building. The guerrillas demanded the release of twenty-three jailed terrorists. Israel agreed but negotiations subsequently broke down and minutes before the deadline, Israeli security forces rushed the school. The three Arabs were killed along with one Israeli soldier and twenty children. Seventy were injured. On 16, 17, and 21 May, Israeli planes struck targets in southern Lebanon in retaliation for the Maalot killings.

19 May 1974   A bomb placed in a car exploded at London's Heathrow Airport injuring three persons and damaging fifty cars.

13 June 1974   Four Arab terrorists shot their way into an Israeli settlement killing three women before they themselves were killed. They carried leaflets from the Popular Front for the Liberation of Palestine demanding the release of 100 prisoners, including the captured survivor of the attack at Lod Airport in May 1972.

15 June 1974   An unknown individual scratched the letters 'IRA' on the face of one of the world's most valuable masterpieces, a Rubens painting in Cambridge, Great Britain.

16 June 1974   A bomb believed to be planted by the IRA Provisionals exploded in Westminster Hall in London, injuring eleven people.

17 June 1974   A foreign executive of Mercedes Benz was kidnapped by leftist guerrillas in Argentina.

48

24 June 1974   Three Arab terrorists entered Israel and seized hostages in an apartment building in Nahariyya. They killed four persons and wounded eight before they were killed in a gun battle.

15 July 1974   A lone Japanese hijacked a Japan Air Lines jetliner. He demanded the release of an imprisoned Red Army member and an aircraft to fly both men to North Korea. The hijacker was captured by Japanese police.

16 July 1974   Two persons in Manchester, Great Britain, were injured by a bomb planted by the IRA.

17 July 1974   A bomb believed to have been planted by the IRA exploded in the Tower of London killing one person and injuring forty-one.

Notes

1. This study was originally written under the auspices of the California Arms Control and Foreign Policy Seminar. Portions of the study were contained in an earlier written statement submitted to the Subcommittee on the Near East and South Asia, Committee on Foreign Affairs, House of Representatives, Congress of the United States, 24 June 1974. I wish to express my gratitude to Dr Ciro Zoppo, Director of the California Arms Control and Foreign Policy Seminar, for his encouragement and support in the completion of the paper, and to Professor Carlo Schaerf, Director of ISODARCO, for his invitation to offer the present version at Urbino, Italy. I would also like to thank the distinguished international group of scholars and students who attended the meeting at Urbino for their many helpful comments. Finally, I am indebted to Dr David Ronfeldt and Dr Ralph Strauch of the Rand Corporation for their thorough and penetrating reviews of the paper. With their permission, I have incorporated several of their points into the text.
2. Inter-American Juridical Committee, *Statement of Reasons for the Draft Convention on Terrorism and Kidnapping*, Document CP/doc.54/70, Organisation of the American States, 5 October 1970, rev. 1 of 4 November 1970; quoting Eduardo Jiminez Arechaga in a study published in *Anuario Uruguayo de Derecho Internacional, 1962*. The Committee's statement provides an excellent account of attempts to define terrorism in legal terms.
3. Carl Leiden and Karl M. Schmitt, *The Politics of Violence: Revolution in the Modern World* (Englewood Cliffs, New Jersey, 1968), pp. 30-1.
4. United Nations, General Assembly, *Report of the Ad Hoc Committee on International Terrorism*, General Assembly Official Records: 28th Session, Supplement No. 28 (A/9028), 1973, p. 22. Italics supplied.
5. *Ibid.*, p. 21.
6. *Ibid.*
7. A brief chronology of international terrorism is appended to this paper. For a complete chronology of incidents of international terrorism, see Brian Jenkins and Janera Johnson, *International Terrorism: A Chronology 1968-1974* (a forthcoming work to be published by the Rand Corporation, Santa Monica, California).
8. *Ibid.*

2. DEFINITIONS OF TERRORISM

Gaston Bouthoul

Introduction

All manifestations of conflict, inflexible demands, and ideological
hatreds between rival groups, have a tendency to culminate in forms of
collective violence. In general, such violence, which is intermittent, is
produced by two basic motives. The first arises from the love of power,
shown in what Machiavelli called 'wars of domination'. Each hostile
group, brought into conflict with the other, tries by force to impose its
will on the other, or to subject it to its own physical supremacy. The
second basic set of motives for violent action falls under the general
category of genocide, which may be either the physical destruction of
the adversary or that annihiliation of his social identity which
has become known as 'ethnocide'.

As far as collective psychology is concerned, the result of such
conflicts is to make fear predominate over every other one of the
weaker adversary's other sentiments: he will then resign himself to sub-
mitting to the will of his conqueror from fear of still greater evils.

Terror, culminating in the threat of death, is the *ultima ratio* of
every socio-political and hierarchical organisation. Terror sanctions that
authority whose ultimate expression is: 'obey or you will die'. The conception of territory, so vital amongst animals as among the most
primitive of tribes, is founded upon the same underlying threat. By
definition, a frontier is a line which must not be crossed, unless author-
ised, without danger to life. Actual examples are the Berlin Wall and
other contemporary frontiers marked by minefields, barbed wire, and
defended by armed guards.

The first feeling of the newly born is one of fear which is the basis
of every hierarchy and manifestation of force, the function of this
hierarchy being ambivalent. On the one hand, it has a protective function against threats from without and from within: this is its role of
reassurance. On the other hand, the authority it wields is founded on
penalties and punishments. These two aspects of hierarchy are contradictory and complementary; both act on the instinct of self-preserva-
tion which they reassure and disturb at the same time.

Terror underlies every armed conflict and every manifestation of violence. Invariably the aim is to subdue or paralyse the enemy by fear.

It is not, however, in man's nature to confuse terrorism and war. The battles of Cannae and Zama, of Austerlitz and Waterloo, were not acts of terrorism, nor were the battles of Lepanto or Trafalgar acts of piracy. Terrorism differs equally from the brief, violent actions which are intended to seize power by surprise, such as conspiracies, palace revolutions, *coups d'etat* and *putsches*.[1] These seek to surprise, but not to terrorise systematically.

Neither is guerrilla warfare necessarily terrorist action, but rather a way of conducting hostilities in certain circumstances. It is, in the last analysis, a particular form of military tactic characterised by the dispersal of forces, mobility, sudden strikes and what we today call commando action. Guerrilla tactics consist of refusing to be committed to large-scale engagements. Often it is delaying strategy, awaiting propitious political and military circumstances. These were the methods of the famous Fabius Cunctator in the Second Punic War.

All these forms of violence have one common trait, namely that they are confrontations, on a small or large scale, and seen as such by both sides. Each side recognises the other as its enemy and declares this openly. In this formal, almost gentlemanly, warfare, violence is practised between uniformed and recognisable combatants but does not involve enemy civilians. The last war to conform to these conventions was that of 1914. Since then, the new techniques of war, aerial bombardment of towns and later, the permanent targeting of nuclear weapons on great centres of population, seems superficially to resemble terrorism. Nonetheless, a distinction from some forms of terrorism remains in that targets are invariably the cities of the enemy.

Characteristics of Terrorism

Certain specific qualities of terrorism thus begin to appear. They are:

1. Its clandestine nature: terrorist actions are the work of small and very secret groups. Even whilst collaborating, they are often ignorant of each other's identity for fear of treason and betrayal.

2. Terrorist action is not a battle: terrorists do not restrict themselves to attacks upon an overt enemy, but also strike at the innocent in order to create fear and insecurity. Today the availability of explosives permits murder and destruction at all times and in all places: booby-trapped vehicles, time-bombs, letter-bombs, plastic-bombs, and so on.

3. Terrorism attempts to act in secrecy: the anonymous, unidentifiable threat creates huge anxiety, and the terrorist tries to spread fear by contagion, to immobilise and subjugate those living under

this threat. At the same time, secrecy and anonymity strengthen the terrorist's pride in his impunity, producing a paranoic emotion of infinite power. He feels himself the possessor of supreme authority, the right to give life or death, the symbol of absolute power. There are, however, ambivalent tendencies in the psychology of the terrorist. Although at one and the same time, he feels himself to be judge and martyr, added to this is a sporting factor: it seems at times as though he is involved in an exciting and dangerous game. In the chase, he feels himself to be not only the hunted but also the powerful hunter. Included also in this game with death — the death of others as well as his own — is a kind of necrophilia, which is akin to that of the sect of Thugs, the worshippers of the goddess Kali. The deaths of nearly a million victims during the nineteenth century have been attributed to this cult.

4. Extreme terrorism exhibits two other traits: the first is psychological; it is a tendency towards obsession, single-minded fanaticism, the logic of paranoia taken to its ultimate. The greatest atrocities are ennobled in the eyes of their perpetrators by an ideological justification which overrides the suffering of the victims and the mourning of the bereaved. Such acts are for the perpetrator an emotional release and, at the same time, a thrilling expression of his personality. The second trait may often be the manifestation of an Adlerian compensation complex, created by deeply resented frustrations and humiliations.

5. Terrorism is much influenced by intellectual and doctrinal fashions. In examining its motivations, one discovers the changing ranks of ideological values. One after another, ideological trends unleash a series of terrorist outrages whose justification is based, according to current thinking, on patriotism, nationalism, racism, cultural intolerance, religious fanaticism and political dogma. At the same time, it often presents itself as a form of propaganda action, aiming to promote a certain doctrine or set of demands, using the modern techniques of publicity. Thus Basque terrorists, Irish extremists and other contemporary movements justify outrages in order to draw attention to their cause.

6. There is also noticeable in terrorism an element of imitation in the techniques employed. For example, there were the many assassination attempts on heads of state during the nineteenth century, outrages by single terrorists at point blank range. Then came the fashion for bombs flung at processions. Today, after aircraft hijacking, there is a tendency to turn to massacres of crowds, such as that of Fiumicino (with forty-six dead), or at the Tower of London, or the murder of hostages at Maalot. A spectacular action, especially if the perpetrators escape with impunity, will in general inspire a series

of imitators.

7. Among terrorists there is the power of suggestion: there are, for example, solitary men who are controlled by an *idée fixe*. This is often the case with regicides such as Ravaillac and Damien, or assassins such as those of King Umberto or President Kennedy.

When terrorism involves groups, romanticism predominates, its variety reflecting the character of the struggle, hatred or fervour, a territorial demand or love of a cause. Such romanticism and the *idée fixe* are sustained by constant repetition, propaganda and auto-suggestion. There are famous examples which show these characteristics. That of the Grand Master of the Sect of Assassins (also known as 'the Old Man of the Mountain') is one. In the eleventh century, he succeeded in creating a body of trained men, the 'faithful', ready to carry out, even at the risk of their own lives, the crimes he commanded them to commit. Some of them, cultured and distinguished, were successful in gaining entry to princely courts, living there for years, until the day when they would murder their host or one of his ministers to serve the policy of their Grand Master. It is related that when caught and tortured, before dying, they would denounce as their accomplices the leading men of the court who were opponents of the Sect. By means of these tactics, 'the Old Man of the Mountain' was able to dominate by terror the sovereigns of all the Near East and to impose his policies upon them. This enormous power has been attributed to the fact that he not only indoctrinated the 'faithful', but added to this the use of hashish, which has given rise to the word assassin, to give them a glimpse to paradise.

Certain recent crimes committed by those under the influence of drugs have shown how they favour the forms of suggestion mentioned above. The 'family' directed by Charles Manson is a notable case: the addicts, under the influence of the 'Master' murdered a film star and six of her guests in California.

A power of suggestion just as effective is found among some of the most notable figures to have used terrorism, such as Hitler and other dictators of the twentieth century. Having flourished in Europe, this type of leader is now to be found in other continents, reviving the ancient traditions of despotism.

Forms of Terrorism

1. *Terrorism in Power*

In its usually most terrifying form, terrorism is the instrument of a source of power which uses it against its fellow citizens or subjects. Thus one may say that the Inquisition terrorised Spain for centuries.

The September Massacres of 1792 and the Reign of Terror of Revolutionary France, executions and deportations by the Gestapo and the Stalinist Purges, are other examples. This form of official terrorism is often accompanied by a technique of suggestion in order to obtain self-incrimination from the victims. By a combination of persecution, solitary confinement and torture, it was found to be possible to obtain astonishing confessions. The victims become their own accusers, and themselves demand punishment.[2]

A government sometimes also uses the most violent terrorist methods when waging war. Examples are submarine warfare practised by the Germans in both world wars, or the Japanese kami-kaze pilots, who, when first used, imperilled the American fleet by their suicidal attacks. And militarily, throughout the ages, it has been the practice of states to create regiments of shock troops (elite regiments of infantry for assault, janissaries, imperial guards, parachutists and commandos) who are surrounded by a reputation for fearlessness and sometimes for ferocity. This is virtually terrorism, often playing a deterrent role.

2. *The Balance of Terror*

Today in suppressing our anxieties, we are becoming gradually more accustomed to what is probably the most fearsome situation in history. It has been called the 'Balance of Terror'. The inhabitants of all the great cities of the world serve as atomic hostages, living under the permanent aim of intercontinental missiles, capable of annihilating them within a few seconds.

Humanity has again learnt to live dangerously. Ancient history was characterised by a strategy aimed at cities; its most spectacular events are the destruction of great capitals after centuries of splendour – Nineveh, Babylon, Persepolis, Carthage, Rome, Alexandria, Baghdad, Cordoba and others. Then came centuries in which Christian civilisation learned to spare cities, even during its most violent wars. Today we have rediscovered the ancient threat of cities razed to the ground and of annihilated populations.

3. *The Export of Terrorism*

There have been many occasions in the past when governments have organised or aided terrorism in other countries. They install training camps for paramilitary terrorist groups, deserters or exiles, arming them and providing for them; then they await a favourable moment. In this way Louis XIV financed and armed the Catalonian insurgents. During the French wars of Religion, England helped the Protestants while Spain went to the aid of the Catholic League. Similarly, France gave official aid to the American insurgents before herself entering the War of Independence. During the wars of decolonisation, the neighbour of former colonies have served as an inviolable retreat for the forces of insurgents.

Another common form of terrorism is that used by defeated states who no longer have the necessary troops and resources to engage in open war and fight set battles. They therefore attempt to make the situation of the enemy untenable by the use of small groups practising terrorist techniques. This has been found in anti-colonial wars and in the European Resistance Movements against occupation during the Second World War.

One of the most hideous forms of terrorism is found when two populations of the same country, living side by side for centuries, come into conflict with each other over religious or ideological differences. In such cases an escalation of atrocities often results, as in the unhappy province of Northern Ireland. In addition, it may lead to the export of terrorism. Innocent foreigners find themselves attacked in their own countries under the pretext of the terrorist's need to interest other countries in his cause.

Terrorism and International Institutions

The problem of terrorism has become such a matter of moment that it enjoyed the honour of a special debate at the United Nations. From the beginning, however, the complexity of the problems which it raised became evident. As a result, the delegations of different nations took up contradictory positions. Finally, it became impossible to discuss the question seriously and the examination of proposals on terrorism was postponed *sine die*.

Certainly the nature of terrorist action — assassination, kidnapping, bomb outrages and hijacking — is easy to establish; it is an incontrovertible fact. However, the United Nations has inherited the shortcomings of its predecessor, the League of Nations. Public debates have often poisoned relations further, exciting in some countries nationalistic and religious passions, chauvinism and intransigence. Thus, in a famous precedent, the World Disarmament Conference which opened in 1932 never succeeded in defining the soldier. When the question is posed, whether it concerns soldier or terrorist, each delegation questions the ulterior motives of the others and asks itself which particular definitions and which measures would be favourable to its own policies and embarassing to those of others.

New Techniques of International Terrorism

Although international terrorism has always existed, it has become in recent years a subject of worldwide preoccupation. The reason for this

55

lies, above all, in the new techniques that have been developed, notably the hijacking of aircraft. The heroic times of bandits, highwaymen and pirates have been revived in this new form. The 'Pax Britannica' of the nineteenth century put an end to piracy by means of stern laws and summary justice: those caught in the act of piracy were at once hung from the yard arm. But these laws dated from the beginning of the last century and their authors obviously could not have foreseen air piracy. For the development of aviation and techniques derived from it, notably the use of the parachute, has increased the efficacy of violence, even that of attacks on the ground. The aeroplane makes possible the organisation of an operation from afar, and enables the fully prepared executants to be transported with lightning rapidity. The proliferation of airlines also facilitates the covering of tracks in escape, as well as easy arrival.

To this is added the perfection of the terrorist's armoury: guns and carbines of increased range, telescopic sights for snipers, miniature grenades and bombs, and the whole gamut of booby traps, explosive letters, time-bombs and remote-control bombs.

The spectacular nature of hijacking is caused by the varied age, sex and nationality of the passengers, and as a result, of all acts of international terrorism, it has made the most striking impression upon the public mind. Added to this is the fact that the public anxiously asks whether certain air disasters, whose causes are officially unknown, may not in reality be the disastrous results of failed hijacking. One nervous passenger or terrorist may unleash catastrophe. One can understand that governments and airlines, in cases of this sort, may prefer to keep silent in order to avoid panic.

Our society has become increasingly vulnerable. The concentration of populations in vast, inadequately policed cities, the multiplication of dams and viaducts, of industrial concentrations, harbours, power stations, oil wells and petroleum refineries, have created numerous targets which are not only extremely important but also highly vulnerable. For example, in November 1972, two American 'air pirates' circled several times over the nuclear power station at Oakridge in an aeroplane they had seized, threatening to crash into it.

International Legislation and Terrorism

In discussing organised violence, the distinction, posed by St Thomas Aquinas in his theory of the just war, is always present, expressing as it does a general tendency of human nature. Where terrorism is concerned, as with all other homicidal violence, our first instinct is to distinguish between just and unjust terrorism, one unjustifiable, the other excusable.

This Manichean tendency has been shown once more in the recent debates on terrorism at the United Nations. The greatest, the most modern supranational world institution found itself divided: a number of states wanted the motion to introduce a distinction between international acts of terrorism, according to the motives invoked by the terrorists and the political ends to which they appealed. This suggestion aroused the indignation of some delegates: that of Austria declared 'the philosophy which has just been expressed here is based upon the principle that the end justifies the means . . .' Thus where terrorism is concerned, especially if it is involved in international conflicts, there is a collision between the various jealous sovereignties of states and the moral and legal theories which derive from them.

Almost three centuries after St Thomas Aquinas expressed his theory of the just war founded upon 'the best intention', several notable Spanish theologians developed it further. They claimed that when belligerents are sincerely convinced of the legitimacy of their cause, both sides at the same time are fighting a just war.

In the modern world, the question of collective terrorism was tragically posed during the First World War. German submarines torpedoed without warning merchant shipping, which provoked the entry of the United States into the war. The second time that these legal problems were posed was when the Tribunal of Nuremberg judged crimes committed by the Nazis.

Classification and Statistics of Terrorist Acts

It is extremely difficult to classify terrorist acts on the basis of the declared intentions of those who commit them, even when one accepts them as sincere. The task is further complicated by the controversial and often illogical justification offered. Where sociology deals with violence, it finds no solid base but the factual description of the actions and statistical enumeration: all motives remain subjective.

For five years, the French Institute of Polemology has attempted to take a census of manifestations of collective violence and aggression throughout the world. Early on, it ran up against several principal difficulties:

1. The difficulty caused by the various versions given by commentators, the perpetual divergence of the investigators, which caused the Institute to give up the attempt to classify these manifestations according to the accounts given by those involved.

2. These statistics are limited to a certain number of countries. Neither those of Eastern Europe nor most Asian or African countries, publish statistics of criminal acts. Incidents of political terrorism, whether the work of the state or directed against it, are state secrets.

57

3. It is often difficult to distinguish between acts of political terrorism and armed crime carried out by groups involved in robbery, gang warfare, protection rackets and kidnapping.

4. Setting aside terrorism committed by the state — and we know it can produce the most appalling massacres where there is a fanatical ideology — it seems that the number of victims of 'pure' terrorism — terrorism, that is to say, which is not the instrument of crime or brigandage — is very small. The statistics of the Institute of Polemology indicate at least two actions of collective violence for every one of terrorism.[3] In 1973, taking all countries in the world which publish figures, 'the number of victims', one commentator has said, 'has not been more than the deaths in car accidents in France during a fine weekend in summer'.

The Effects of Terrorism

Terrorist actions are essentially meant to strike the imagination, arouse strong feelings of fear, of indignation, sometimes of sympathy — but these sentiments are blunted by repetition. In some areas, Ulster for example, the population becomes resigned and learns to live with terrorism. Weariness allows, and indignation provokes, the enactment of special anti-terrorist measures, as with the exceptional laws provoked by the anarchist outrages of the late nineteenth century. In democratic countries, repetition of terrorist acts agitates public opinion, which demands increased protection and this always results in such laws. In general, they are effective enough, both against political terrorism (on condition that the state be determined to prevent the creation of private militias such as were maintained by fascist groups) and against criminal terrorism by private groups. An example of the latter is the famous case of the 'Bonnot Gang', and acts of banditry so often disguised as idealistic terrorism in troubled times. American legislation against gangsterism, given the extent of the problem in the United States, is more controversial as to its effect. It appears, however, that on the whole the worst excesses of violence are to a great extent contained.

Notes

1. For example, the type of action described in the works of Cardinal de Retz or in *Technique du Coup d'Etat* by C. Malaparte. It is the same with insurrections, riots and rebellions. These are examples of overt violence.
2. These techniques are described in works inspired by the Inquisition, such as

the *Manual of Inquisitors* composed at Avignon by the Dominican Nicolas Eymerich in 1370, and the *Hammer of Witches* by Henry Institoris and Jacques Sprenger (1487). On the same subject, see Arthur Koestler, *Darkness at Noon* (London, 1940).

3. These statistics are published regularly in *Etudes Polémologiques*.

3. MEASURES AGAINST INTERNATIONAL TERRORISM

Steven J. Rosen and Robert Frank

Introduction

What is shocking about international terrorism as a method of warfare is not the amount of bloodshed, which by any account is minimal compared to more conventional methods of armed struggle, but the character of the victims. The law and custom of conventional war permits almost unrestricted violence against the active armed forces of a hostile target state, but at the same time extends the maximum possible protection and exemption to innocent non-combatants, civilians, and neutrals of third states. In the terrorist mode of action, on the other hand, it is exactly these exempted and innocent parties who are the main target of action. The immediate victim may have no organic connection to the political policy of the target state, and may indeed not even be a citizen of that state nor have any influence over its policy, but if his victimisation might by some process of reasoning contribute to the weakening of that state or to the strengthening of the revolutionary movement, the action is considered legitimate. According to critics, this lack of proximity between the victim and the policy under attack thus puts terrorism on a different moral plane as a method of violent political behaviour.

States not parties to a dispute may be expected to object to the all-encompassing scope of the terrorists' field of battle, and at the minimum they will feel a responsibility for protecting the lives of their nationals at home and abroad. In principle, they may insist on a differentiation between creditable ends and unacceptable means — a distinction that is already well-established in the law of warfare, for example in the prohibition of germ warfare. The question, then, is what can the international community do to protect innocent civilians from random victimisation if international terrorists continue to claim an unrestricted global arena as a legitimate theatre of combat?

Whose Ox is being Gored?

The question, as posed, assumes the existence of an 'international community' prepared to take action against a common threat. This vision of a community of shared values, inspired by the universal doctrines of the three great monotheist creeds, is the moral foundation of the United Nations Charter and underlies the body of international law. With regard to international terrorism, however, the assumption of a community of nations is a rhetorical invention. The lines of fissure that have formed in debates of terrorism at the United Nations and at the International Civil Aviation Organisation reveal instead the existence of at least three distinct 'communities': (1) a loose Western coalition of liberal democratic states orientated to security and international order; (2) the multifarious and shifting Afro-Asian coalition of 'non-aligned' states, many of whose governments trace their history to a violent birth in the war against colonial rule; and (3) a no longer monolithic Communist bloc torn between Marxist imperatives of world revolutionary struggle and the reality of a fragile *status quo* to defend in Eastern Europe. On one side of the question in the United Nations General Assembly are the American and Federal German delegations, to whom it is obvious that the international community cannot tolerate the slaughter of innocent athletes at an international sporting competition or condone 'senseless acts of violence' against airline passengers in far-flung places in the name of remote political struggles unrelated to the victims. On the other side of the question there is the Kenyan delegate, who remembers the profound contribution of Mau Mau violence to the liberation of his country from the British, or the Algerian delegate, who may himself have participated in unconventional and spectacular acts of terror in the resistance to France. Even seemingly random violent acts cannot be openly opposed by the 'non-aligned' group if the claim is made by their perpetrators that they will disrupt the sensitive economic and political processes of a target state recognised as a legitimate enemy. Thus the cleavage.

The Soviet delegate, bound in Marxist-Leninist unity with all revolutionary movements against Western imperialism, still is constrained by other realities. Could not the bombing of El Al offices and aircraft today be duplicated in Ukranian or Estonian or Jewish actions against Aeroflot tomorrow? What if Czech liberals or emigré Hungarians or East German nationalists in West Berlin discover that *their* target states also have sensitive economic and political processes that may be disrupted in one country or another? The Soviet Union, as the world's 'other' great imperial power, cannot be unrestrained in its enthusiasm for the ability of small Davids to inconvenience big Goliaths.

The Yugoslav delegate typifies the dilemma in another way. He too is impelled by socialist ideals to embrace the terrorist as brother. And like the Kenyan and the Algerian, he remembers the noble role of violent action by Tito's partisans (even against civilian targets) in the liberation of his country from Hitler. And he is well aware of the efforts of his government since it sponsored the Belgrade conference of non-aligned countries in 1955 to project itself into the Third World camp as a second sphere of action to counterbalance participation in the Communist bloc. Indeed, on these and other grounds, the Yugoslav delegates have been among the most active opponents of international measures against terrorism. But in 1974 the trial took place in Zadar of sixteen 'terrorists' of the Croatian separatist movement known as Ustashi. And (portents of a post-Tito future?) the alarming accusation was made that exile groups of Croatians in West Germany, France, and Canada are supporting a campaign for airline hijackings, bombings, and assassinations against Serbian targets and the Yugoslav state. If these expectations materialise, may we expect a shift in the priorities of Belgrade's policy on terrorism?

Some potential for revolutionary states to support actions against terrorism if their interests are affected is suggested by the example of Cuba. For several years prior to 1973, hijackers of American aircraft seeking asylum and a haven against American prosecution regularly forced captured planes to land in Havana. It appeared a safe assumption, given the hostility between Castro and Washington, that Cuba would not extradite hijackers nor prosecute those able to make a claim of 'political' motivation. At the same time, anti-Castro Cubans developed a lively traffic in the other direction of Cuban boats and aircraft carrying illegal emigrants to the United States. Here again, it appeared a safe assumption that the United States would provide sanctuary to the 'legitimate resistance to Castro's dictatorship'. But over time, the two states found that a mutual interest developed to put a halt to the illegal seizure of vessels on both sides. Negotiating through intermediaries, and putting aside their enmity in favour of a higher interest. Washington and Havana signed an anti-hijacking agreement on 15 February 1973. On Cuba's side, this represented an obligation by a militant socialist state to extradite and subject to prosecution opponents of the world's leading imperialist state.

Could, then, the incentives that induced Cuba to support certain actions against piracy be reproduced for other anti-imperialist states? This would appear to depend on the realisation of a number of threats that are now only hypothetical possibilities: Estonian emigré attacks on Aeroflot, Ibo actions against Nigerian offices abroad, Tibetans against China, Sikhs against India, Pathans against Pakistan, Kurds or Shi'ites against Iraq, Ewes against Ghana, Eritreans against Ethiopia, Bugandans against Unganda, and so on *ad infinitum*. So far this potential risk of victimisation has not induced many governments to accept the political cost of supporting actions that are opposed by influential revolutionary movements (notably the Palestinian Liberation Organisation [PLO]).

Instead of general measures against terrorism they have preferred to rely, in case of international terrorist violence directed against themselves, on the *ad hoc* use of political influence to secure the cooperation of other states to deal with individual cases. This was the case, for example, in the punishment of the renegade PLO faction that hijacked a jet to Tunis to embarass Arafat immediately after his appearance in the General Assembly.

Even if some of the enumerated threats materialised, international terrorism would remain in its essential character more a problem for the liberal democratic states of the West than the authoritarian regimes of the Communist states and most of the Third World. The leverage achieved by small groups of terrorists against powerful opponents depends on focusing wide publicity on small events to create the largest psychological impact. The killings of Israeli athletes ay Munich or Puerto Rican passengers in the Lod airport have no political value in themselves but are 'media events' which derive their power from the transmission of the news to large numbers of people by electronic or printed means. While liberal states characteristically enjoy a free press, the authoritarian government can sever the link between the terrorist and his media audience in the target country. Moreover, within its own borders the authoritarian government is in a superior position to restrict freedom of movement, access to materials, freedom of organisation, means of communication, and other necessities of terrorist groups. This does not exempt authoritarian states from terrorist actions abroad nor from those at home that do not depend on publicity for their impact, but it does reduce the scope of the threat. And even when revolutionary states are forced to take a stand against terrorism, they may, in the words of Salah Khalaf (PLO Chief of Operations), distinguish between 'criminal terrorist acts staged by adventurers' and 'legitimate actions carried out as part of the strategy of armed struggle'. There is much less incentive to support unqualified international actions against terrorism.

Even some Western states have been restrained in giving general support to actions against terrorism in the Legal Committee of the General Assembly and elsewhere. Some have failed to prosecute or refused to extradite persons accused of participation in terrorist acts against other states. In several notorious cases, European governments have peremptorily and even eagerly surrendered prisoners to appease the demands of terrorists holding hostages. The reluctance of these governments to support firm anti-terrorist action may be based in the fear of reprisals by terrorist organisations, or they may be constrained by commercial interests in the Arab world. Whatever the reason, even the West has failed to achieve a general consensus on measures to respond to the threat.

Thus the unhappy cast of characters for the moribund international debate on measures against terrorism: a faltering West, crippled by moral and economic decay, pitted against a coalition of Afro-Asian states committed to the PLO and supported by the Communist bloc. The conflict of ideologies is reflected even in the official title of the debate item in the General Assembly agenda:

> Measures to prevent international terrorism which endangers or takes innocent human lives or jeopardizes fundamental freedoms, and study of the underlying causes of those forms of terrorism and acts of violence which lie in misery, frustration, grievance and despair and which cause some people to sacrifice human lives, including their own, in an attempt to effect radical changes.

And with regard to organisational capacity to deal with this kind of problem, one may note a steady decline in efficacy from Metternich's Concert of Europe to the failed design for Great Power government in the League and the UN Security Council, to the present period of populism and Third World hegemony in the ideologised General Assembly.

Areas of Issue

Do the above limitations on concerted international action against terrorism necessarily lead to the conclusion that united action is impossible? The recent history of negotiations on anti-terror measures suggests that the limitations apply with varying degrees of severity depending on the area of issue and forum in which international policy is proposed. Critical dimensions of difference can be seen in a comparison of three areas of issue: protection of diplomats and consular personnel; prevention and punishment of air piracy; and deterring the export of terrorism. International cooperation has been most successful in the first area and least successful in the third.

The mutual interest of states in the immunity of their diplomatic agents abroad from harassment and attack is an ancient and established principle of international affairs, stretching back as far as the tradition of innocent passage of messengers between warring tribes. But in the past five years a total of more than twenty-seven diplomats from eleven countries have been kidnapped and at least four have been killed. A dozen of the incidents involved kidnappings and violence against American personnel in six Latin American republics. The perpetrators of these unconventional acts are not hostile governments, but guerrilla movements who find foreign diplomatic agents a vulnerable target for insurgent action against their own regimes.

The first Convention on this problem was drafted by the Organization of American States (OAS) at a special assembly in 1971. The OAS

Convention provides that kidnapping, murder, and other assaults against the life or personal integrity of those persons to whom the state had the duty under international law to give special protection, as well as extortion in connection with those crimes, shall be considered common crimes of international significance, regardless of motive. If the fugitive is not surrendered for extradition because of some legal impediment, the state in which the offender is found is obligated to prosecute as if the act had been committed in its territory. To make this procedure effective, it has been necessary to establish first, a firm obligation to prosecute where extradition is withheld, and secondly, a clear basis for jurisdiction based on the character of the offence, regardless of the place in which the crime is committed. No significant opposition to the OAS Convention emerged, and it moved easily to the status of 'hemispheric policy'. The issue then passed to the International Law Commission and subsequently to the United Nations General Assembly, which on 14 December 1973 unanimously adopted a Convention on the Prevention and Punishment of Crimes against Internationally Protected Persons, including Diplomatic Agents, patterned after the OAS Convention. These actions draw upon a reservoir of prior agreements on the necessity to protect ambassadors and diplomats, including Article 29 of the Vienna Convention on Diplomatic Relations, and they have been taken without even token dissent.

The issue of hijacking and sabotage of civil aircraft would appear to be another problem of universal concern, but here the commitment to action has been less than unanimous. Three measures have been taken by the International Civil Aviation Organisation.

1. The Tokyo Convention (1963) deals with ordinary criminal offences aboard aircraft, establishing standards of jurisdiction and an obligation to return supervened aircraft to their owners. It commits contracting states to establish punishments for the commission of illegal acts on aircraft, but carefully avoids laying any positive obligation to punish or extradite offenders.

2. The Hague Convention (1970) responds specifically to the more recent wave of hijackings and establishes an obligation of each state to make hijacking punishable by severe penalties and without exception to punish or extradite any hijackers on its territory regardless of where the hijacking took place.

3. The Montreal Convention (1971) extends the terms of the Hague Convention to cover persons who commit acts of sabotage or otherwise endanger or destroy aircraft, harm passengers, or perpetrate bomb hoaxes.

The Tokyo Convention has been ratified by more than sixty-one nations, but the Hague and Montreal Conventions, with their no-loophole requirements to prosecute, have not been widely ratified. Specifically, they have not been ratified by several Arab states which continue to provide safe havens for hijackers who land in their territory to escape prosecution. The motive of this non-compliance is generally understood to be support for the Palestinian movement and especially for the goal of disrupting Israel's fragile transportation network.

The United States and Canada have proposed a fourth convention which would bring pressure to bear on non-compliant governments by authorising the suspension of all air service to states which allow hijackers to use their territories as sanctuaries. However, this proposal was stillborn at the International Conference on Air Law in Rome in September 1973. Several states objected to the infringement of national sovereignty that is implied in forcing a government to observe a treaty that it has not signed or ratified. Moreover, since the Yom Kippur War which erupted two weeks after the Rome conference, the climate has worsened considerably for unified actions which might be interpreted as hostile to the PLO and which appear to be opposed by the wealthy Arab states. Also, the issue may lessen in intensity following Arafat's appearances before the General Assembly in November 1974. The PLO is reported to have offered to several delegations a reduction in terrorist activities outside Israel as a *quid pro quo* for the support and recognition given by the international community to the Palestinian cause. (To the extent that governments were persuaded by this incentive to improve their attitude to the PLO, the efficacy of terror as a political weapon is once again demonstrated.) In summary, the position taken by various states on the issue of hijacking may be described as a function of relative threat perception at a given moment in time and of ideological distance from the hijackers political goals.

The third area of issue, broadly known as the 'export of terrorism', was raised by a general convention proposed by the United States in September 1972. The killings at the Munich Olympics and the flood of letter-bombs mailed from Amsterdam, New Delhi, Belgrade, Singapore, Bombay, and Malaysia to addresses in Canada, Austria, Argentina, Great Britain, Australia, Egypt, Brazil, Cambodia, Italy, Federal Germany, and Jordan raised the spectre of traumatic disruption of societies on a global scale as a means of calling attention to disputes in particular countries. The draft Convention for the Punishment of Certain Acts of International Terrorism was designed to focus on 'the common interest of all nations in preventing the spread of violence from countries involved in civil or international conflict to countries not a party to such conflict'. This approach is based on the principle that, 'the containment of violence within the narrowest feasible territorial limits has been a traditional function of international law in cases where it has been difficult to eliminate violence completely'.

Essentially, this draft convention extends the provisions of the Hague and Montreal Conventions and obliges states to prosecute or extradite offenders in a wider category of crimes. These include acts involving unlawful killing, serious bodily harm, or kidnapping where these are aimed at civilians outside the target state. Violent acts against nationals of state A while travelling in state B in the name of a political campaign against state C would be prohibited. Violent acts within the target state or committed by nationals of the state within which the acts occur would not be covered by the draft convention, on the grounds that these are subject to the ordinary jurisdiction of each state. The draft convention is aimed at the limitless spread of terrorism and seeks to answer the claim of some terrorist groups, notably the Palestinian Liberation Organisation, to a global theatre of conflict. Implicitly, the draft convention establishes the principle that terrorist acts must be confined to the narrow geographical scope of a recognised insurgency.

These were described as fairly modest demands by the American representatives, but they were received with considerable opposition from the Afro-Asian coalition. The Libyan delegate called the American initiative 'a ploy . . . against the legitimate struggle of the peoples under the yoke of colonialism and alien domination'. The General Assembly took no action on the American draft but created a 35-member Ad Hoc Committee on Terrorism to study the issue and make recommendations for action. Within the Ad Hoc Committee, a counter-proposal was offered to the American draft by a 'Non-Aligned Group' of fourteen states: Algeria, Congo, Southern Yemen, Guinea, India, Mauritania, Nigeria, Syria, Tunisia, Tanzania, Yemen, Yugoslavia, Zaire, and Zambia, comprising almost half the committee. Terrorism is defined in Paragraph one of this counter-proposal as 'Acts of violence and other repressive acts by colonial, racist, and alien regimes against peoples struggling for their liberation . . .', while in Paragraph three we are reminded of the legitimacy of the struggle of national liberation movements. In another section, fourteen 'measures against international terrorism' are recommended, of which the first three are: '(a) The definitive elimination of situations of colonial domination; (b) intensification of the campaign against racial discrimination and apartheid; (c) the settlement of situations of foreign occupation and restoration of their territory to populations who have been expelled from them'. The thirteenth article reasserts that 'when people engage in violent action against colonialist, racist, and alien regimes . . . the international community, when it has recognized the validity of these objectives, cannot take repressive measures against any action which it ought, on the contrary, to encourage, support, and defend'. Cynics have suggested the possibility of a General Assembly resolution directly endorsing the slaughter of the Israeli athletes in Munich as a 'measure against

67

terrorism'.

After two months of debate, the Ad Hoc Committee reported to the General Assembly that it was unable to agree on concrete recommendations for dealing with the problem. The Assembly's only direct response to the American intiative was the adoption by a roll-call vote of 46 to 35 of Resolution 3034 (XXVII) on 18 December 1972, which the United States strongly opposed as an attempt to bury the issue. Resolution 3034 focused its primary attention on 'finding just and peaceful solutions to the underlying causes which give rise to such acts of violence' and reaffirms and 'upholds the legitimacy of the struggle of all peoples under the colonial and racist regimes and other forms of alien domination'.

Self-Defence

It is manifest that states threatened by international terrorism cannot, in the present period, give much credence to the idea of positive action by 'the international community'. Threatened states and groups of states will rely on the 'inherent right of individual and collective self-defence' that is affirmed in Article 51 of the United Nations Charter. Without concerted international action it will be impossible to deny funds to the terrorist organisations (the PLO will get $50 million in 1975) and to cut off their supply of arms (the Soviet Union will supply to the PLO the Strella SAM-7 and the Sagger anti-tank missiles). It will be impossible to realise more ambitious plans for institutional response to the problem of terrorism, such as the creation of an effective international criminal court.

But states will have some instruments against terrorism directly at their disposal, including:

Coordinated intelligence and contingency planning.
Improved technology of electronic surveillance to detect metals and explosives.
More stringent customs procedures.
Stepped-up security at embassies and airports.
Development of screening profiles to identify terrorists.
Improved aircraft construction to partition passengers from pilots.
Bilateral and multilateral extradition agreements.
Direct pressure on states which harbour terrorists.
Development of clandestine counter-terrorist organisations to combat guerrilla groups or to create incentives for other states to support actions against terrorism.

4. LEGAL ASPECTS OF TERRORISM

George Sliwowski

The social life of an individual may cause many conflicts. Not every conflict, however, has the same significance. Some may be regulated and thus provoke no serious social damage. But others may be transformed dramatically into such a dangerous form that acute damage occurs. In such cases we may speak of the perpetration of offences.

The nature of these offences varies. The most important are major crimes, the slightest are contraventions of minor police regulations. They differ also according to the intensity of social danger involved. But − and this fact is essential and most important − each offence implies human responsibility. This responsibility is always linked to the commitment of an offence and may be treated as a violation of divine authority or as disobedience of a sovereign or as a violation of public order. Recognition of this responsibility is often reflected by the award of damages to the victim but is primarily seen in the imposition of a punishment for the offence. In the background of every punishment is the idea of retaliation. Today of course students of penal policies also underline the necessity for the re-eduction and the socialisation of the offender. Accent is often laid on prevention, by creating conditions that will make the perpetration of crimes, felonies and misdemeanours less likely, but nevertheless the modern states may not and have not dispensed with penalties, for the infliction of penalties is understood to be a symbol of the strength and stability of the public authorities. Punishment thus remains as a powerful measure in the hands of the state even if the results in the fight against crime are often either overvalued or seen to be disappointing.

We like to distinguish between domestic and international offences, but such a classification is not satisfactory. Domestic offences are traditionally those committed within a state by its citizens. International offences are traditionally those perpetrated on the territory of other countries and which produce consequences of an international character and involve the application, directly or indirectly, of international law. But the notion of international offence has recently attained a broader applications. Among such offences are those infringing the social order imposed by international law. For example, one may cite trade in women and children, forgery, and wire tapping. But above all, there is the use of violent means liable to endanger general security, that is international terrorism.

It is theoretically possible to imagine terrorist acts perpetrated by a single person. But the term 'international terrorism' almost always implies the collaboration of a larger number of persons. The term should not, however, be taken to refer to the actions of sovereign states. Of course some authors write of terrorism on the part of states when, for example, a state uses terrorist methods to strangle the activity of a minority or to impose harsh conditions on its own citizens or on other states which are dependent on it. But in such a case, however, we are dealing with a quite different phenomenon, bearing no relation to the 'classic' picture of international terrorism.

International terrorism is a phenomenon which has been much in evidence in modern times. Its features, its essence and its origins are complicated. Later we will try to analyse these aspects in more detail. Here it is appropriate to mention only that acts of terrorism are often linked by their authors with wars or movements of liberation. This creates problems for international lawyers. In every case we must distinguish two strategies of terrorism: that involving acts directed against specific enemies and that involving acts directed against persons extraneous to the conflict. On the face of it, the latter have every right in international law to be left in peace and thus in such circumstances no terrorist would seem to be entitled to claim immunity from punishment on the grounds that he is engaged in a just liberation struggle. But only an International Criminal Court is likely to be able to resolve the complicated problems involved.

The problem of terrorism has concerned criminal and international lawyers for more than one hundred years. The first important sign of such interest was the well-known 'Brussels Clause' of 1856. Its origin lay in a series of attempts on the lives of heads of states and their families. This clause was narrowly concerned with the problem of extradition. It still retains validity and remains of great importance.

In the field of criminality there remain of course several offences, whose existence we acknowledge but for which it is very difficult to provide a precise legal definition. This problem has arisen, for example, in countries which have sought to combat 'hooliganism'. And this same difficulty evidently applies to terrorism. For all the attempts to establish a legal definition of this phenomenon have more or less failed; and it is indeed quite possible that we may never establish such a definition with any real legal precision. Different reasons for this may be cited. But optimists would stress the relatively novel character of the offence and hence argue that the scientific analysis of the problem of international terrorism is in itself a form of progress, if so far without great practical results.

It is obvious that terrorism involves the spreading of fear by threats to a large part of the population as a means of realising their goals. Terrorism may be carried out in various ways and each way has its own peculiar significance. Such operations may include the elimination of certain persons; or the kidnapping of certain persons; or the seizure of valuable objects. The aim is to compel individuals and ultimately states to adopt a certain manner of conduct.

In spite of their different characteristics terrorist activities have some common features. In almost all cases the terrorists are seeking their goals by spreading fear and by undermining confidence in accepted human values. Often among the specific goals are: a change in the head of state; or a change in the direction of current policy; or a change in the political regime; or the liberation of arrested persons; or the payment of a ransom. But all these specific acts are designed exclusively to further a general strategic goal, the 'social goal', which the terrorists acknowledge as the principal aim of their activity. This 'social goal' distinguishes terrorist acts from similar or identical acts by ordinary criminals.

The character of terrorist methods has been subject, however, to some evolution. In particular, in recent times the main accent has been placed on jeopardising general security, while the destruction of particular targets seems to be in decline. This of course does not imply that the elimination of individuals is no longer even considered by terrorists. It signifies only that a general threat is in the majority of cases quite sufficient to achieve at least the tactical goals of terrorists — a proposition which has been totally vindicated in practice. Individual persons, organisations, public authorities and even states have often surrendered in the face of terrorist threats, thereby rendering other measures such as homicide and destruction of property unnecessary. Human fear and insecurity have then been demonstrated to be more successful and useful in promoting the aims of terrorists than the acts of destruction. Obviously this phenomenon has been linked to the great advances in means of communication and the growth of mass media.

The attempt to give a precise definition of terrorism involves us in a tautology, for the notion of terrorism is a kind of abbreviation, instead of a regular juridical notion reflecting all the legal descriptions of an offence such as apply to theft, larceny and homicide. Terrorism as a juridical denomination has its roots in the terroristic behaviour of its authors. This kind of behaviour, this peculiar mechanism of action has given the name to the offence. Tautology is thus in this sense obvious.

Nevertheless some attempt to define terrorism is essential. First, it may be contended that the notion of.terrorism is directly linked to the creation of a general atmosphere of threat and fear. This has particular importance for the understanding of international terrorism, especially when the means used by the terrorists receive wide publicity. Those who disseminate terror seek to destroy both psychological resistance and belief in the usefulness of self-defence on the part of the potential victims. When a terrorist inflicts bodily harm or damages property he is threatening potentially identical or similar action against persons who in the future may offer him resistance. Thus we may formulate a broader conclusion: terrorists seek the violation or elimination of certain laws which may form an impediment on the way to the realisation of their ultimate goal. Terrorists seek to invoke the fear of a future implementation of their threats in circumstances where a future victim might be expected to resist. On the other hand, terrorists also hope that the current victim will comply with their demands.

An increasingly important aspect of the subject is *international* terrorism. This, as the term indicates, signifies cooperation of several people of different nationalities to accomplish acts to damage the territory of different states or the citizens of other states. International terrorism, then, differs from internal terrorism not by the means used but by the range of activity of the terrorists.

Attempts at the construction of a worthwhile definition of terrorism have been numerous. But, as has been mentioned, previous international efforts to this end have had no practical result. It is nevertheless worth underlining the pioneering endeavours of the conferences of the Bureau for the Unification of Criminal Law. This was an international organisation which no longer exists. Before the Second World War the Bureau held its meetings at first every year and afterwards from time to time. The first conference (Warsaw, 1927) established the criterion of an international offence − *delictum iuris gentium* − in the case of intentionally making use of a means which may endanger the general security. Such a statement has direct importance for the problem of defining terrorism although it is perhaps possible that such activity could be performed also by non-terrorists.

But only the third conference (Brussels, 1930), the fourth (Paris), the fifth (Madrid) and the sixth (Copenhagan, 1935) were concerned directly with the problem of terrorism. This period saw the clear emergence of the term, 'terrorism'.

It is impossible to mention here all relevant resolutions carried at these conferences. But it is important to indicate the general trend of the evolution of the idea of terrorism and of terroristic offences. In all the resolutions the use of measures able to jeopardise general security finds a prominent place. They refer especially to the causing of fire and flood; the spread of suffocating matters; the destruction of buildings; the disruption of normal communications; the pollution of waters and articles of consumption; and the causing of disease among men, animals and plants. The perpetration of such offences is stricly linked to terroristic activities in the sense that these activities are considered as a way of causing general danger. This was made very distinct and precise in Articles One and Two of the Resolution of the Brussels Conference. The same resolution also refers to the creation of organisations designed to damage personal property as constituting a danger to general security.

The Paris Conference devoted the first five Articles of its Resolution to the problem of terrorist activities. We may observe here also the link between terrorist activity and the causing of general danger. Although the resolution does not employ precise legal terms, there is a clear inclination to see the essence of terrorism as the terrorising of the general population. The tendency to enlarge the framework of terrorism is also evident in the Paris Resolution not only by the inclusion of the view that the creation of an organisation having terrorist goals is an act of terrorism in itself, but now in addition, the encouragement of this activity and its approbation were also so regarded. The same arguments were confirmed in the Resolution of the Madrid Conference. The last conference before the Second World War, at Copenhagan in 1935, returned to the idea of linking terrorist activity with the endangering of general security. In the introduction to the relevant resolution reference was made to the necessity of introducing special penalties for offences endangering general security or causing a state of terror such as those designed to impede the functioning of public authorities or to poison international relations and thus to jeopardise the maintenance of peace. The resolution underlined, in other words, the existence of mutual ties between general danger and terrorist activities. The common denominator is obviously the factor of threat. In particular, Article Two is of great interest in establishing this link. For it recognised as symptoms endangering general security and at the same time as features of terrorism deeds which are generally considered as belonging to the first category, namely such acts as causing a railway crash, a disaster at sea, or explosions; the spreading of inflammable of suffocating materials; the destruction of means of communication or of warning signs; and the perpetration of other deeds which may threaten human life and cause in this way a general danger.

In addition, one must not overlook the Convention of the League of Nations concluded at Geneva on 16 November 1927 even though it was not ratified and has never come into use. This Convention, adopting the same approach as at the Copenhagan Conference, considered as a symptom of terrorist activity attempts to force changes in government, the disruption of the activity of public services or enterprises, the poisoning of international relations and assassination attempts against heads of state and other government representatives. In addition, however, the League Convention extended this catalogue of symptoms of terrorism to include the destruction and the damaging of public buildings, public utilities, means of communication and every intentional act jeopardising human life by means of causing general danger such as interrupting means of communication by the use of inflammable matters and explosive material, the provocation of epidemics, and the pollution of water and food. The production, storage, import, export, transportation, selling and distribution of the means of causing these results and indeed every other means of support were also considered as symptoms of terrorist activity. This Convention of the Legaue of Nations thus clearly reveals the influence of ideas spread during the conferences of the Bureau for the Unification of Criminal Law.

The tendency to seek to give precision to the normative definition of terrorism continued after the Second World War. In the first place we must mention the draft of the Code concerning Crimes against Peace and the Security of Mankind elaborated by the International Law Commission during the Sixth Session of the United Nations in 1954. According to this draft, terrorism is regarded as an international offence. The evolving tendency in the description of the essence of terrorism was also here confirmed. According to this draft, this terms covers all persons who undertake, support or tolerate terrorist activity on the territory of another state, comprising attacks on persons exercising public duties or on public property or attempts to cause general danger liable to jeopardise human life.

We find another attempt at a formulation in the draft of a Convention elaborated by the General Assembly of American States, which took place at Washington in January-February 1971. The text of Article Four of this draft has general importance. It calls the attention of the legislators of individual states to the need to give precision to the legal notion of terrorism, but in the absence of such precision it formulates its own definition: acts of terror should be considered acts procuring general threat or panic among the population or among its parts and causing a general danger as a result of the use of means, which cause or may cause by their substance great damage or a serious disruption of the public order or elemental disasters. Terrorism also consists, according to the draft, of the destruction of or the unlawful appropriation by the use of force of ships, aircrafts or other means of public communication. This attempt at definition is characteristic not only because it is influenced by the idea of the offence of endangering, but also because it attempts to link this in a harmonious way to precise examples. In this way the idea of jeopardy ceases to be a mere abstract criterion.

We should not forget also several Conventions concluded to secure the safety of air traffic. We may mention here: the Convention on Offences and Certain Other Acts commited on Aircraft, signed at

Tokyo on 14 September 1963; the Convention regarding the unlawful Seizure of Aircraft, signed at The Hague on 14 December 1970; and finally the Convention for the Suppression of Unlawful Acts against the Safety of Civil Aviation, signed at Montreal on 23 September 1971. All these conventions have a peculiar character in that they limit their application to aviation and to aircraft. They all relate of course to terrorist activities, although this is not made precise.

The Convention to prevent and punish the Acts of Terrorism taking the Form of Crimes against Persons and related Extortion that are of International Significance, signed at Washington on 2 February 1971, involves a totally different point of view. In the title of this Convention emerges at first sight the notion of terroristic activity as the item against which the edge of repression should be directed, but the Convention itself does not offer a precise definition of terrorism, as might have been expected from the title. According to Article One of the Convention, terrorist acts should be considered to be: rape, homicide of persons whose life is to be specially protected by international law, and extortion connected with these offences. These acts are considered as common (non-political) offences having repercussions of international character and they involve the extradition of the offender according to the conventions concluded by the states concerned, or, if such conventions have not been concluded, according to the laws of the state. The Convention thus affirms the principle: *aut dedere aut iudicare (punire)*, that is to extradite or to judge the offender. The authors of this convention, however, declined to give a precise definition of terrorism, enumerating only the offences, which constitute its features. It seems, then, that here a certain contrast exists between the title and the text. For the acts declared as having a terrorist character may be committed by non-terrorists. We thus cannot conceal the disappointing fact that the text does not fulfil the promise made in the title.

Terrorism is unanimously considered to be an international offence. In fact terrorism has long been such an offence. But the frequency of such acts during recent years has given to it a quite peculiar importance. The incidence of hijacking of aircraft and of kidnapping during recent years have contributed to the great interest in this problem shown by those involved in international criminal law. Two recent events should be mentioned in this connection: the Symposium of the International Institute of Higher Studies in Criminal Sciences (held at Syracuse in 1974) and the Eleventh Congress of the International Association of Criminal Law (held at Budapest in September 1974) on the hijacking of aircraft. The final statement of the Symposium read as follows:

Hardly a day passes without some violent event labelled terrorism taking place somewhere in the world. Acts of terrorism which are often done under the claim that they are intended to uphold human rights in fact also violate human rights.

But the construction of a valuable definition of terrorism is indeed difficult. Yet the attempt to find a very precise definition of terrorism is justified by the weight of the problem and by the frequency of terrorist offences which is necessitating a stern struggle against this phenomenon. But a larger problem arises at once: is it possible to construct such a definition? In fact it seems fairly doubtful. The most essential criterion of terrorist activity remains the intention of the offender. This criterion forms the difference between a murder arising out of a robbery and one arising out of terrorism. The fact is that a different social evaluation applies to each case, whatever the legal position. The terrorist has no egoistic goals in the traditional sense of this term. But these goals are very difficult to make precise in legal terms, since they may be evaluated in different ways and divergences of opinions militate to a high degree against the construction of such a precise differentiating criterion. Hence it has been necessary to use the doubtful methods of legal technique in the construction of the definition of terrorism. There are two faults to notice: the tautology method in the description of terrorism and the quoting of offences as if they were in themselves acts of terrorism.

Acts of international terrorism are perpetrated by persons with differing citizenship; they are also perpetrated on the territory of different states. It also often happens that the authors of terrorism seek refuge in the territory of other states. In this case the problem arises in the terms of the known principle: *aut dedere aut iudicare (punire)*, that is that the relevant state has only two choices: to try the offenders itself or to extradite them to the state which has the right to try them. This principle upholds the Rule of Law in the sense that no offence can remain unpunished. Adherence to this principle could also be strengthened by the idea of universal jurisdiction: the tribunals should have the right to judge terrorist offences committed anywhere. The principle *aut dedere aut iudicare (punire)* evokes immediately the problem of extradition: the transfer of the arrested offender by one state, which has no right to or will not judge him, to another state which has the right and the will to do so.

This principle as such seems to present no difficulties but problems do arise concerning the exceptions to the principle. The most important exception concerns political crimes. The authors of such crimes are not subject to extradition and this principle is deeply rooted in international criminal law. The other side of this principle is supported by the idea that political offenders may request the granting of asylum. The great majority of terrorists evoke the political character of their deeds and claim the application of the principle of asylum. They seek also to go to countries where their ideas are approved and where they are sure not to be extradited.

It is impossible to mention all the legal problems which arise in the field of asylum and extradition. But it must be underlined that in recent times many concerned with the science of international criminal law have been showing a tendency to seek to limit the right of terrorists to evoke the political character of their activity. This tendency is very easy to understand. The numerous acts of hijacking of aircrafts and kidnapping have endangered people absolutely remote from the conflict, in whose framework the terrorists have sought to engage them. It is thus absolutely necessary to eliminate the occurrence of such events and to reduce the principle of the non-extradition of the authors of political offences to its real and just range, so as to assure the necessary defence of people who cannot be held responsible for the grievances alleged by terrorists. For such people have human rights to remain in peace and not to be disturbed.

The thesis that terrorism is an international offence involves serious consequences. First, there is the necessity to vest the legislation of all states with universal jurisdiction, that is with the right to try all terrorist offences wherever they may be committed. That is a first step already achieved in several pieces of national legislation. But this principle seems to be insufficient. The rivalry between the individual states and their often controversial interests may enable the delinquents in several cases to avoid taking responsibility for their crimes. In such circumstances the answer would seem to be an International Criminal Court of Justice, which would be competent to try *inter alia* terroristic offences carried out in different countries.

The creation of such a court has been for many years a dream of students of international criminal law. The idea has not so far been realised in the form of a permanent institution. An International Criminal Court was of course established after the Second World War to try the principal criminals of war, being a tribunal *ad hoc*. But nothing comparable for terrorism exists. In 1937 a draft convention was proposed to this end but was never ratified. Then, in 1950, the International Law Commission elaborated a draft statute for such a court. Its jurisdiction could protect world public order. The Court would be competent to recognise terrorist offences. But, again, this has not yet become a reality.

The creation of an International Criminal Court would represent a most important and valuable achievement for international law. Its compulsory character would overcome the current difficulty which some states have created by granting asylum to terrorists who have no right to claim the exception of political offence.

5. REVOLUTIONARY ORGANISATIONS: SPECIAL CASES AND IMPERFECT MODELS

J. Bowyer Bell

Introduction

The temptation in the academic analysis of revolutionary organisations for many at least is to construct elegant cross-national models, generalisations for all seasons and most campaigns. In a sense, this tendency is little different from that of guerrilla analysis where the rebels assume that the rules of revolution and the laws of all national liberation struggles are universally applicable; what worked for Mao in China or Castro in Cuba should so work in Quebec or South Africa. The academician need only fear learned dissent with the prospect of fashioning a new and more elegant model, while the guerrilla, on the other hand, may have to pay a higher price for his conviction about the universality of revolutionary forms. In any case, a certain circumspection might be wise in proposing generalisations of all-inclusive schemata, and stages of development. In point of fact, there appear to be a whole spectrum of revolutionary organisations, employing various strategies and tactical mixes selected for varying reasons. These movements are limited or emboldened by varying traditions, differing cultural heritages, and special historical conditions.

Certainly these revolutionary organisations, like any set of organisations — parliaments, formal armies, trade unions — share certain common characteristics. After all, the overriding purpose in every revolutionary case is to seize power by violent means. Nevertheless, each has been shaped by very special conditions. Few are classical models even when the leadership strives to copy an ideal and admired model — for example, Guevara constructing his *foco* à la Castro in the Bolivian bush. It might thus be a worthwhile exercise to examine in some detail three revolutionary movements — there are, of course, no terrorist organisations which is the nomenclature of threatened authority. Each is a very special case. All, however, do share common characteristics.

The Provisional Irish Republican Army

The struggle for an Irish Ireland, free and Gaelic, at times to observers eems to have continued for centuries; arisen at some distant point in he Celtic twilight. Certainly, the present guerrilla campaign in Northern reland traces its origin to the Republican ideals of Wolfe Tone and the Rising of 1798. In one form or another since that time, Irish Republicans have been engaged in fashioning strategies of physical force to break the connection with England that Tone called the never-failing source of all Ireland's ills, and again as Tone advocated, unite Catholic, Protestant, and Dissenter in the common name of Irishman. And with one notable exception they have largely been frustrated by the power of Britain, by their own incompetence, by bad luck or perhaps at times by Celtic malice.

Despite French aid, the Rising of 1798 failed and began the long litany of Irish debacles. In 1803 a hapless plot aborted, in 1848 the Young Irishmen did no better. Later in the century, the Irish Republican Brotherhood and the Fenian assassins proved no more effective. Officials were assassinated, bombs detonated but the Republic came no closer. By the end of the century, the Irish rebels had tried most revolutionary means, even an invasions of Canada from American soil, a most elegant example of transnational revolution. Simultaneous with the plots and plans of the men of physical force, others, at times in isolation, at times in a conscious mix, had been applying other strategies: parliamentary agitation; boycotts; intimidation and extortion; monster meetings; and civil disobedience. And by the end of the century, much had been won — the land question largely solved, the Catholic Church recognised, the habits of parliamentary democracy instilled and the opportunities offered by the British Empire available to all. There seemed no place in the new Ireland for the old, pure Republicans, the assassins and bombers of the past, who still clung to the dream of an ideal Republic.

In 1916 a small band of hard-core Republicans, directed by the Irish Republican Brotherhood, hopeful of German aid, and supported by the tiny Irish Citizen's Army — a militia created by the Labour leader James Connolly — rose in revolt. This Easter Rising of 1916, limited almost entirely to Dublin as a result of bad luck, the collapse of the German connection, and poor planning, was regarded by most Irishmen of the time as a mad act of mad men, a futile gesture, that razed the centre of the city for no good purpose. On their way to prison, the Irish Volunteers — the Irish Republican Army (IRA) — were hooted by the crowds. Yet the swift British repression — the immediate execution of the leaders of the Rising — transformed Irish opinion and created a base of popular support that would permit a less spectacular but more effective revolt within two years. Between 1918 and 1921, the reorganised IRA waged what was to become the archetypal national liberation struggle. There were assassins in the cities, guerrilla columns in the hills, ambushes, sabotage, arms raids, arson and murder from a ditch. Simultaneously an effort was made to establish parallel, revolutionary Irish institutions — a Parliament, Republican judges and tax collectors. The British were largely able to limit this shadow structure to a symbolic role but could not impose order on the country except by recourse to means — counter-terror — that the British public found unpalatable. In 1921 a political solution to the impasse was found in the Treaty which created an Irish Free State in twenty-six largely Catholic counties; which established a small six-county Province of Northern Ireland, two-thirds Protestants, still under the Crown; and which guaranteed Britain certain economic and strategic concessions. For some Irishmen, the Treaty after an 800-year struggle gave Ireland the Freedom to be Free. To the purists in the IRA, the Treaty was a betrayal and so they turned on the 'Free Staters' in a bloody civil war. The pure Republicans lost first the war and then many of the faithful when a few years later Eamon De Valera took his new 'slightly constitutional' party into the Irish parliament and conventional politics. The purists and militarists persisted, went underground, and organised the IRA for the next round.

By the late 1920s, the IRA had assumed its present form, defined the essential task, and thus evolved into a covert underground revolutionary army that regularly, in all but predictable cycles, has since troubled the Anglo-Irish political scene. In 1938, at last giving up hopes of a second round in the South where De Valera had assumed power democratically and gradually dismantled the more odious parts of the hated Treaty, the IRA decided on a bombing campaign in Britain. This futile exercise in erratic and uncoordinated explosions eventually, as civilian casualties resulted, alienated even much of Irish Republican opinion. The bombs coupled with gun battles between IRA volunteers and the Irish police in Dublin destroyed the movement. The activists were dead or in jail and support in the country limited to the faithful few. At the end of the Second World War, when most of the internees and prisoners were released, the knowledgeable assumed that the IRA was dead and a romantic thread to the past at last broken. The patriot game was at last over.

This did not prove to be the case, for the faithful few began at once to re-create the IRA. This time the IRA Army Council decided on a guerrilla campaign in Northern Ireland, no action in the South, and the co-option of the tiny Republican Sinn Fein Party for use as a political base. Beginning with a spectacular raid on a British military barracks at Armagh in 1954, the campaign formally opened in December 1956. Briefly, the IRA gathered momentum and then gradually settled into a long, futile guerrilla war of such low intensity that the security forces of Northern Ireland could cope without strain. In 1962, at last, the IRA called off what had become known as the Border Campaign. Even the perpetual optimists of the Army Council assumed that in the foreseeable future the gun could play no serious part in Irish politics. The IRA moved to the Left, the volunteers became involved in social and economic issues and so alientated the old purists. The men of physical force suspected *their* army was going 'Communist' and neglecting the proper, military role.

The new Army Council engrossed in the rising tempo of Northern events, where a civil disobedience campaign led by young radicals threatened the old Protestant regime at Stormont, ignored the conservative quibbles. Then in 1969, as the astute had long predicted, the challenged Protestants who saw 'civil rights' as a plot to create a united Ireland ran amok first in Derry and then in Belfast. The police could not, many felt would not, keep the mobs in control and London had to send in the British army. Within the Irish Republican community, there was a feeling that the IRA had failed to protect the Northern Nationalists because the Army Council had been too busy playing radical politics. The Northern militants, particularly in Belfast and later Derry, began reorganising and when it became clear to them that the 'new' IRA was even willing to give up abstention and, like De Valera, go into parliamentary politics, a split was all but certain. At the beginning of 1970, a Provisional Army Council commanded one IRA in opposition to the 'political' Official IRA. The Provos had been born.

The Provos arrived on the Irish scene as a small group of zealots who knew the reason for all Irish ills — the British connection — knew the means to correct the situation — physical force — and who had the skills to undertake such an exercise. Provo strategy was relatively simple and ultimately highly effective. By gradually escalating the level of violence, they provoked a British army possessed of a doctrine of anti-guerrilla tactics. The use of such tactics all but guaranteed the alienation of the Nationalist community. The British army, reacting by the book to Provo violence, first rocks, then petrol bombs, and eventually sniping, did in fact alienate the Nationalists who were gassed, arrested, man-handled, intimidated and who became involved in what the British army chose to see as an anti-insurgency campaign. The British army became the enemy. The Provo campaign grew more intense. The Protestants' administration at Stormont felt grave concern as they saw order dribbling away. To redress the balance, they persuaded the Cabinet in London to intern suspects without trial. All those suspected of treason, namely known dissident Catholics, would be swept up. Internment unleashed a tide of Nationalist resentment at this obvious sectarian manoeuvre. The province collapsed into open war with a level of violence so high that the British Home Secretary admitted in December 1971 that he could only hope that at some

81

future date a tolerable level might be reached. Ultimately, in March 1972, the Northern Ireland Stormont Government – a Protestant State for a Protestant People – was closed down by London. In July the Provos actually bombed their way to the bargaining table where the British Minister in charge of Irish affairs managed to negotiate a brief truce. After that the Provo bombing collapsed and sniping returned. The Protestants turned to random assassination of Catholics, all by definition traitors. The British security forces soldiered on with increasing success. The Government in London fashioned first a new power-sharing executive that collapsed under the weight of Protestant resentment and then proposed a constitutional convention.

Through the more than four years of their campaign, the Provos have remained faithful to the power of the gun, persisted despite arrests, and internment, despite the losses in the field, and despite the opposition of practically everyone from the Official IRA to the Dublin Government. For the Provos *the* source of Irish ills remained the British connection maintained by *the* enemy, the British Army. Their Provisional Sinn Fein political organisation, however, was delighted to discuss various federal formulas, present programmes for a new Ireland, shape overtures to the Protestants in the North. The Provos were not in fact the simple-minded bombers so often depicted in a hostile press. On the other hand, they insisted on seeing complex and intractable problems in terms of the simple Republican formulas of the past. The main task was to expel the British, for after that Irishmen – Catholic, Protestant, and Dissenter – unhindered could cope with their own Irish problems. No matter that many Irishmen feared a British withdrawal would usher in an era of sectarian strife, civil war and general chaos. No matter that it had become increasingly obvious that no one but the small Irish Republican minority wanted a united Ireland – certainly not the politicians in Dublin nor the Roman Catholic Church, nor of course the Northern Protestants.

The Provos knew better and when the campaign began to falter in Northern Ireland, the decision was made in 1973 to begin a campaign of symbolic bombing in Britain under the assumption, not altogether mistaken, that disgusted with the revolting Irish, with the endless and often mindless violence and, most of all, with the 'ungrateful' Protestants, the British public would demand an end to the Irish connection. In this new strategem, the Provos were helped, so to speak, by the independent efforts of small schismatic groups who had unlike the IRA no compunctions about setting off bombs without prior warning, thereby guaranteeing innocent civilian casualties and, it was to be assumed, subsequent British horror and disgust.

In any case, with Irish bombs detonating in London and the Midlands, the IRA had entered the ranks of transnational revolutionaries by opting for tactics very much in an Irish tradition that the guardians of order, not altogether unjustly, could label as terrorism. Actually from the very beginning – and also traditionally – the IRA had acted within a transnational medium, for the funds to maintain the dependents of prisoners, to pay the active service men and to acquire arms had largely come from abroad, mainly but not entirely from the United States. IRA arms purchasers were active throughout Europe and even eventually made a Libyan connection as a result of Colonel Gaddafi's militant anti-imperialism, Britain apparently still being an Empire in Libyan eyes. In fact, the distinction between a parochial insurgency and an 'international' revolutionary movement is largely artificial. The IRA is simply acting within a long tradition, allying with England's enemies, using familiar resources, striking into Britain as did their revolutionary ancestors. After hundreds of years, there is little unfamiliar to the Irish rebel except for the smell of success and the Provos still are quite convinced – as were their revolutionary ancestors – that *this* time the connection will be broken, the gun in politics justified, and the long road to Irish freedom travelled at last to the end.

EOKA-B in Cyprus

While the Cypriot revolutionary movement, EOKA, cannot match the long Irish revolutionary tradition, the aspiration of the Greek Cypriot community for *Enosis*, union with the Motherland, has a venerable history. For the most part after the arrival of the British in 1878, this aspiration found form as petitions and patriotic oratory, for the Greek community was relatively content. After all, the Greek island was no longer ruled by Turks who had long been a minority of less than 20 per cent. Still, there had been agitation, one serious riot, but all with no visible result since the British did not take the Greeks seriously. After the end of the Second World War, events led some Cypriots to anticipate change and movement toward self-determination. This could mean *Enosis* on the instalment plan or it might even mean that Great Britain would agree to what for most Greeks was the logical and just solution to the future. Great Britain paid no attention either to the rising movement on the island for *Enosis* led by the radical new Archbishop Makarios or to the initiatives of the government in Athens. As much to attract British attention as any other reason, Makarios agreed to the plans of a retired Greek colonel, George Grivas, to establish an underground army, EOKA, recruited from devout anti-Communist young men. When Makarios too lost patience, Grivas and EOKA began a classical insurgency campaign: guerrilla columns in the hills, assassins along Murder Mile in Nicosia, all the old familiar violence the British could recognise from Ireland, Palestine and Malaya. The EOKA campaign led not to *Enosis* but in 1960 to a tripartite solution between Turkey, Greece and Britain that created an independent Cyprus, protected the Turkish minority, and guaranteed the British military bases. The unrepentant advocates of *Enosis*, including Grivas, were despondent but could not be more Hellenic than the Athenian regime. EOKA was dissolved, Grivas went into retirement as a hero, and the optimists waited to see what President Makarios could make of Cyprus.

It gradually became clear that there was no real trust between the Greeks and Turks on the island and that while Makarios was a shrewd politician and could manage the Greeks by balancing off the devout advocates of *Enosis* with the dubious members of AKEL, the large Cypriot Communist Party, he could not dissolve Turkish suspicions and create a Cypriot nationality. There was rising tension and in 1964 intercommunal violence which precipitated a serious crisis. A Turkish invasion fleet was already at sea when an accommodation was reached through American auspices. There was no Greco-Turkish war and NATO was saved. But Cypriot politics became more complex, poisoned now by the massacres and murders. In 1966 the entire cycle was replayed almost exactly and once more the island struggled out of the far side of violence bitterly divided, Greek flags on one side, Turkish on the other and a few lonely white Cypriot national flags in the front of government buildings. Intercommunal talks led nowhere. The only 'positive' development had come in April 1966 with the military takeover in Athens that meant *Enosis* seemed much less attractive, certainly to AKEL and to many liberals as well. Perhaps Makarios would have a breathing space to create a Greek Cypriot consensus, to mould a real and viable Cyprus.

This did not prove to be the case for the Athenian colonels took an increasingly intimate interest in a Greek island with a democratic government, a huge Communist party and an Archbishop as President who seemed to seek a Third World role rather than follow the dictates of the Motherland. Parochial, unsophisticated, narrow in education and dominated by crude ideas, the Athenian colonels easily perceived Makarios as an enemy of Greece, an affront to their dignity, and at best an unwitting tool of the International Communist conspiracy that loomed so large in their minds. Although Athens already had considerable leverage in Cyprus because almost all of the officers of the Cypriot National Guard were mainland Greeks, the colonels encouraged General Grivas to return to the island and organise another EOKA — EOKA-Beta. Grivas, who was no one's tool, saw a congruence of interests and left for Cyprus. His arrival hardly delighted Makarios but he felt it more polite to suffer the machinations of the 'poor, sick man' than to treat his EOKA-B seriously. In fact, Makarios soon found he had to suffer more than Grivas, for in 1971 there was a spectacular assassination attempt that forced his helicopter to crash land in the ground of the Archbishopric Palace. Despite efforts to hide their trail, the evidence led to the unspoken conclusion that the attempt had been by Greek officers on orders from Athens to rid them of the Red Archbishop. It was not the last attempt, but Makarios scrambled along, apparently more popular than ever, was re-elected President by a vast majority, untroubled by assassins, Grivas, and EOKA-B. Certainly, as the years had passed George Papadopoulos and some of the colonels grew more sophisticated, recognised some of the risks Grivas's presence entailed, and hedged their bets.

Then in December 1973, a new lot of colonels overthrew Papadopoulus. Dominated by Brigadier Dimitrios Ioannidis, the new lot had all the vices of the old regime compounded by a lack of experience and even cruder ideas about reality. Grivas undoubtedly could have taken care of himself despite the new regime but in January 1974 he died. As had been the case with EOKA, Grivas had organised his new movement as his personal tool: an army with one Field Marshal, a few lieutenants and the rest soldiers. Every string came to Grivas; at every level he exerted personal control. Without Grivas, EOKA-B would collapse, for it would take months at best, perhaps even years, for a new leadership to evolve. At this point the Greek Central Intelligence Agency, KIP, moved into the vacuum. The Greek liaison officers assigned to Grivas's district commanders came into effective control of their areas, more mainland talent and advice appeared, and the Greek officers of the National Guard proved most helpful in the matter of arms and training. Instead of collapsing EOKA-B within months was flourishing, but as an agency of KIP. The Colonels had a new lever. EOKA-B undertook operations, first arms thefts, then assassinations. The odds had shifted against Makarios.

Makarios's attempts to reduce Greek leverage were either not very successful or engendered further tension. His purchase of Czech arms to strengthen his new Tactical Police Reserve had caused a serious and quite public row with Athens. His effort to reduce the length of service in the Greek National Guard had evoked little enthusiasm even among his own supporters. His recommendations that certain candidates not be appointed to the officers' training school had been ignored by the Greek officers. As the EOKA-B struggle evolved into a classic insurrection, fuelled by the Greek officers and directed by KIP, Makarios apparently gave up hope in subtle ploys and intricate plots. EOKA-B was outlawed. During 1974 there was a rising number of arrests. EOKA-B advocates who were teachers, held positions in the civil service or police were threatened with dismissal. The pro-EOKA-B editor of *Ethniki* was twice tried and convicted of insulting the President. There were further arrests, rumours of torture and leaked plans for further purges. Finally, in a most unsubtle manoeuvre Makarios decided to send Greek President, Phaedon Gyzikis, an ill-disguised ultimatum to remove the Greek officers, accusing the Athenian regime of directing EOKA-B, of attempting to subvert them and the Cypriot State and of complicity in the various assassination plots. Not only was the letter immediately released to the public but the text contained a series of most undiplomatic slurs on the Athenian regime. Logically Greece had three choices: first, back down, remove the officers and close down EOKA-B; secondly, to do nothing and continue as before, since Makarios could not force an evacuation; or thirdly, to get rid of Makarios.

The final option contained special risks but offered real advantages. After a long and active career Makarios had a wealth of enemies; had become frozen into positions; had lost the confidence of the Turks and had polarised Cypriot Greek opinion. Certainly there were many on the island who felt that there would be an easing of tension if the Archbishop had a sudden seizure or stepped in front of an omnibus. If the Athenian regime was serious, and there were hints that they were because of the sense of outrage caused by Makarios's public insults, the major risk was that an attempt to depose Makarios might spark off a civil war on an island filled with covert, private political armies, in addition to EOKA-B, the Tactical Police Reserve, and the National Guard. And this is very nearly what KIP, the Greek officers, and EOKA-B managed. For instead of an assassin being despatched, tanks were rolled up before the Presidential Palace, giving Makarios time to flee out of the back, to reach his home district at Phapos and to rally support. Two days of bitter fighting followed before it became clear that sufficient support for Makarios did not exist. He then went into exile, making triumphant appearances in London and before the United Nations. The Greeks had not removed an old enemy but had precipitated a most serious crisis, in particular because they appointed as the new 'President' of Cyprus, Nicos Sampson, a hopelessly provocative selection. An old EOKA gunman with an unsavoury reputation, Sampson had claimed responsibility for 'operations' during the intercommunal fighting which the Turks saw as massacres. His appointment almost guaranteed Turkish intervention, By the time that the Turks did in fact invade the island, the nature of the EOKA-B organisation had changed. Essentially the 'revolutionary' organisation became an adjunct of the National Guard, participating in the defence of the island.

There had in fact been two EOKA-Bs: that of Grivas, fashioned with the hope of toppling Makarios and/or moving toward *Enosis*; and that of KIP, actually an agency of the Greek regime to be used as an armed pressure group against Makarios. If the first — a right-wing, covert guerrilla army dedicated not to national liberation but to the end of the Cypriot 'nation' — resembled a relatively common type of revolutionary organisation in structure and tactics, the second EOKA-B of KIP was most unusual. Friendly regimes have aided sympathetic revolutionary organisations in the past for ideological or pragmatic reasons. There have often been volunteers in revolutionary armies from Layfette to Guevara. There have even been stage-managed coups from abroad. Yet EOKA-B became a willing instrument of KIP to be used by Athens in a policy that led from one disaster to another until the discredited colonels fled from the stage leaving the old democratic leaders with the ruins.

Ethiopian Separatism: The Eritrean Liberation Front

The Ethiopian Empire, descended through endless genealogies from the Queen of Sheba, has for centuries faced the problems of maintaining centralised control and absorbing diverse and unruly peoples. The Amharic elite, Christian Copts, have traditionally felt besieged, surrounded in their highlands by circling tribes and alien religions. And the very nature of those highlands cut by steep valleys has made many regions all but impenetrable to the agencies of the government in Addis Ababa. The old institutions – the Coptic Church, the Emperor, the feudal landlords – have given a coherence to Ethiopia while the new Western-educated elite has offered the prospect of modernisation. Yet in this century, as in the last, a crucial question has remained that of national survival and as much because of divisions within the Empire as the threats from the outside.

In 1935 Ethiopia did in fact succumb to alien enemies at last when the Italians, still humiliated by their defeat at Adowa in 1896, drove out Emperor Haile Selassie and incorporated the country with their colonies in Şomaliland and Eritrea into an Italian East African Empire. The Emperor eventually returned with the British armies and in turn laid claim to both Eritrea and Somalia as traditional parts of his Empire, a historically dubious posture but one that resulted in a United Nations decision to permit the federation of Eritrea with Ethiopia, while British British and Italian Somaliland would merge and become independent. The enlarged Empire was thus immediately faced with two new but traditional problems: alien claims from the outside and dissidence within. The new Somali Republic to the east immediately laid claims to most of the huge Ethiopian province of Ogaden largely inhabited by nomadic Somali tribes. In Ethiopian eyes, this was the old Islamic threat in different terms. And to the north in Eritrea there was articulate opposition to incorporation in a 'medieval' empire, opposition by Moslems to the anticipated Christian domination, and grave doubts in general whether federalism would be to Eritrean advantage. Such opposition, however, took no effective form until Addis Ababa, disquieted by the dangers of separatism, began to chip away at Eritrean 'rights', a process that ultimately led in 1960 to annexation.

This time Eritrean opposition was more anguished but equally in-effectual. The United Nations seemed uninterested. Few had ever heard of Eritrea and the Emperor's prestige because of his opposition to Italian imperialism remained high. Most of the opponents of annexation had to resign themselves but a few did not. These formed the core of the Eritrean Liberation Front, established in Egyptian exile, who, using obsolete weapons purchased in South Arabia, opened an armed struggle in September 1961. One tremendous local advantage was that the militant nomadic tribesmen had a long heritage of armed disobedience. Banditry and brigandage were endemic and the bleak and inhospitable country was ideal for the guerrilla. The leadership of the new ELF thus found willing, enthusiastic, and skilled volunteers who were in effect being paid to do what came naturally. Secondly, although for obvious reasons there was more Islamic than Christian sympathy, the ELF was non-sectarian representing a liberal political position keyed on the national issue rather than a dissident tribe or religion. The ELF could claim, although few listened, to be the only serious liberation move-ment in Ethiopia fighting for all and not simply for narrow Eritrean interests. The ELF struggled along as a low-level rural guerrilla campaign with the odd operation in the towns largely ignored even by the central government in Addis Ababa. Some support dribbled in from progressive Arab states approached for ideological reasons, while devout Moslems gave for Islamic purposes. Still, the campaign remained one of Africa's forgotten wars; in fact, the creation of the Organisation of African Unity in Addis Ababa in 1963 under the auspices of the Emperor made the separatist ELF's task more difficult — no new African state, Somalia excepted, could afford to condone separatism or seek border changes and few wanted to alienate the Emperor now the symbol of African unity. Unable to organise the countryside effectively, where the Provincial Governor-General Raz Asrate Kassa's policy of benign neglect seemed to work, preventing an over-reaction from Addis Ababa and the warping of Ethiopian priorities; unable to escalate the campaign in the cities or extend the struggle beyond the province; and most of all unable to attract the international attention so necessary, the ELF as had others before them opted for a new and violent tactic: attacks on Ethiopian airliners. Attack squads machine-gunned airliners on the ground in India and Germany, others hijacked internal flights and found refuge in Aden and Tripoli. Further attempts were made in Europe and ELF agents also sought to bomb Ethiopian embassies in Rome and Dijibuti. The Ethiopian response was dual. In Eritrea the ELF was de-fined as a bandit problem. The passing journalists were informed that it was a low level agitation funded from abroad by radicals and militant agents of Islam. And it was quite true that much of the ELF leadership appeared to be perpetually in exile and increasingly dedicated to an 'Arab Eritrea' — this in a province that probably did not have a Moslem majority and certainly was only marginally Arab. As for the transnational hijackings, the Ethiopian security forces adopted a hard attitude, refused to bargain, flooded their flights with agents ordered to shoot on the spot no matter what the risks. An attempt above Madrid resulted in a gun-battle and the summary execution of the surviving ELF cadres — they were dragged into the first class cabin, had blankets put behind their heads, and their throats were cut. Such a policy failed to deter the ELF and still another attempt over Addis Ababa led to another gun-battle and the death of all the ELF hijackers.

In the meantime, conditions changed on the ground. After the Arab states recovered from the June 1967 War, new aid, particularly from Ghaddafy in Libya, flooded down the Red Sea. A new collection of ELF leaders used the policy of benign neglect to infiltrate the isolated villages. Finally, on 21 November 1970, outside Asmara, the ELF assassinated Major-General Teshome Ergheto, military commander of the Second Imperial Division. At last aware of the potential threat of the ELF, the Emperor took the wraps off the army. There were great sweeps, air strikes on dissident villages, a new military governor, and the ELF over six months was beaten back into the bush. The fear was that in the process large segments of the population had been alienated by the violence of the 'pacification'. So the long slow process of winning the loyalties of the people while keeping up the pressure on the ELF continued with no clear end in sight.

Ethiopia seemed in Eritrea to be cursed with an endemic insurgency, for the ELF had enough assets to continue despite the splits, despite the flawed Arabic cause, despite the exiled leadership, but not enough to triumph in the field. And it seemed most unlikely that *any* government in Addis Ababa could afford to concede in Eritrea and thus almost surely begin a train of defections. Certainly during 1974, when the army intervened in politics in a series of radical initiatives, policy concerning Eritrea remained ambiguous. A Governor-General in Eritrea and a Chief of Staff in Addis Ababa were appointed who advocated a 'political' solution but no one knew what this meant and in August 1974 the new Prime Minister, Michael Imru, indicated that any accommodation would be within an Ethiopian context. During the chaos in Addis Ababa, the ELF soldiered on, taking the opportunity to open operations in the towns, shooting down a helicopter and kidnapping various foreigners. After a decade, a solution seemed no closer, Ethiopian strategy no more or less effective, and the ELF, flaws and all, still determined to pursue their national liberation struggle.

The Imperfect Models

All of these particular case studies are very special indeed, chosen in part to underline the scope of revolutionary activity by groups far from the classical models of Mao or Guevara. Still, they offer certain insights into the nature of 'International Terrorism' even if they form an unstable foundation for an elegant theoretical castle or provide more exceptions than examples to the model maker.

First, in nearly every case, the distinction between domestic, international, and transnational 'terror' is artificial. Revolutionaries, no matter how parochial their armed struggle or how deeply isolated within the wilds, have an impact beyond the bounds of the avowed target. At the moment the struggle is initiated, they are almost guaranteed external friends and enemies. Even the isolated Irish found a friend in Gaddafi, thereby greatly complicating British and Western relations with the radical Arab states. More to the point, even without a friendly Libya, the activities of Irish-American sympathisers had become a serious criminal and then political problem in the United States. Even without extra-territorial operations, IRA agents seeking to purchase arms illegally, Irish representatives drumming up support before student conferences, foreign television correspondents rushing into Northern Ireland to interview the men on the run had permitted the conflict to bleed out into the international medium. In the case of the KIP-controlled EOKA-B, the international impact of the proxy coup was great and yet – technically – the EOKA 'rebels' operated solely within Cyprus and before the flawed attack on the Presidential Palace had been responsible for less than a handful of serious incidents. In the case of the ELF, organised in Egyptian exile, there could not even be a beginning until arms had been illegally purchased in South Arabia, nor could the insurrection continue withour external aid. Thus those deeds that seemed to make the IRA or the ELF international – a bomb in the White Tower in London or the machine-gunning of an Ethiopian airliner on the ground at Frankfurt – were simply spectacular military tactics based on an economic-diplomatic-logistic foundation with extensive international contacts. Such contacts may well exacerbate or engender international tensions far more serious than the result of one bomb detonating.

Secondly, when revolutionaries have recourse to acts that are relatively easy to define as terrible – the slaughter of innocents for example – there has been an academic tendency to place all such terrorists into a special category – a universal set with describable characteristics, motivations, and means. Yet the three present examples fit only uneasily into the various schemata offered. In a single area, that of the purpose behind the introduction of a 'terrorist' operation, they varied greatly. The IRA bombs in Britain were not meant to 'terrorise' individuals or the population at large; in any case, there is no rigorous scientific, political or psychological definition of 'fear' or 'terror' — terror like love appears easy to recognise but difficult to define. The IRA had two immediate aims: first to drive the news of the British-sponsored plebiscite on the existence of the border off the front pages and second to create an atmosphere of British horror and disgust that might accelerate British withdrawal from such a revolting and ungrateful country. Less overt but still present was the recognition that the campaigning in Northern Ireland was not going as well as had been hoped and such a new stage would improve internal IRA morale, stretch British resources, and attract wide attention. In the case of the ELF hijacking, the overwhelming motive was not to instil fear but rather to make propaganda by the deed — the target was not even the Ethiopian government, except incidentally, but rather that mysterious creature 'international public opinion'. That the Ethiopian state airline and tourist industry might be damaged was simply a spin-off benefit. In the case of EOKA-B, the assassination attempts on Makarios, including the final clumsy tank attack, were abortive efforts to remove a single actor from the Cypriot stage so that Athens could direct the drama along lines more congenial. As an aside, there had been no evidence that the first attempt intimidated Makarios into shifting his political posture or greatly altering his way of life. There was no climate of fear within the Presidential Palace — in fact, rather the reverse, an atmosphere in public at least of serene forbearance. In sum it is difficult to recognise a universal strategy of terror but easy to see similar acts performed for quite special local and traditional motives by revolutionaries acting within narrow limits. Certainly the techniques of terrorism are freely borrowed but only within cultural restraints; for example, IRA leaders have expressed horror at the massacres in Rome and Lod while EOKA people see no point in mindless bombing. All revolutionaries operate within certain restraints, if often pliable ones, and cannot be profitably viewed as absolute opportunists.

In fact, as noted, it is difficult even to discuss all terrorists, as Gaston Bouthoul does in his paper in this collection on the psychology of terrorism, except on a level so ethereal, if elegant, that the real men responsible for real acts become literary figures. Since real revolutionaries perform similar acts that require similar preparation, organisation and talents, it is hardly surprising that real similarities exist; but they are much less interesting than those suggested by Bouthoul. Most active service rebels are idealistic males, unmarried, physically fit, between the ages of sixteen and twenty-eight, — and a variant, educated below capacity or beyond effective use. With the exception of the latter — university students — the profile is exactly the same as one would expect in any elite military organisation, the British commandos, American Special Forces, French paratroops. The inclusion of the university graduate indicates the political component of a revolutionary army. Just as Prussians make different kinds of soldiers than Italians, so too do the Irish, Greek, and Eritrean rebels differ. This is even more so when the leadership is involved — contemplate the vast psychological differences in a 50-year-old former Belfast bookmaker, a talented and arrogant Greek colonel, and a failed Eritrean politician converted in a decade of exile to the most militant ideas of Arab nationalism. They do, of course, share a commitment to the efficacy of force, tend to have tunnel vision in excluding compromising options, and are convinced of ultimate and complete victory of their just case — but *this* profile fits most generals and many politicians.

A final summary would suggest that while the construction of models, however, imperfect, is essential in the understanding of the phenomenon classified as terrorism, at present the state of analysis leaves much to be desired. There are either too many special cases or else the effective generalisations are neither particularly profound nor ready of application. But there should by no means be a total academic investment in the special cases simply because broad generalisations present very severe problems. Rather on all levels there should be a search for rigour, a commitment to disinterested analysis of this all too fashionable form of political violence.

6. THE ROLE OF INTERNATIONAL TERRORISM IN THE MIDDLE EAST CONFLICT AND ITS IMPLICATION FOR CONFLICT RESOLUTION

Daniel Heradstveit

The term terrorism is highly ambiguous and several meanings can be attached to it. Here, I shall not try to define terrorism because I believe that discussions on definitions do not take us further with the problem with which we are dealing. It must be pointed out, however, that the word itself tends to be used to propagate certain opinions about a conflict, often implying a moral judgement designed to put more blame on one party to the conflict compared with another.

In this analysis of international terrorism in the Middle East conflict attention will be confined to the activities of certain Palestinian guerrilla organisations like those of the Popular Front for the Liberation of Palestine, the Democratic Front for the Liberation of Palestine, the Popular Front for the Liberation of Palestine General Command, Black September, and so on. But it is important to underline the fact that the activities of the Palestinian guerrillas is not the only form of terrorism that we have in the Arab-Israeli conflict. Terrorism has occurred in many forms in the Middle East. It has been used by both sides and has always been a part of the conflict ever since Jewish immigration into Palestine started on a serious level. But the form of terrorism that causes most concern today, at least among Europeans, is that which directly threatens the security of outsiders, namely hijacking, killing of diplomats and so on. Today these tactics are mostly employed by so-called 'extreme' guerrilla organisations on the Arab side.

It was after the terrible defeat of the conventional Arab armies in the Six Dar War of June 1967 that a psychological vacuum was created that favoured the growth of the Palestinian guerrilla movement. In the years 1968, 1969 and 1970, the guerrilla movement had spectacular success and enjoyed considerable influence in the Middle East. The guerrillas moved into a psychological vacuum, and in this vacuum they managed to create an image of themselves that in turn became a source of power. The favourable image generated more support and in turn created the foundation for an even more favourable image built on more substance. So the initial success of the guerrillas had a spiralling effect. We do not act in the world as it really is, but in what we think it is. The October War is a striking example of this and of how so-called 'area experts' do not know what the objective conditions are. Some observers have been surprised to see how even a minor military success by the guerrillas had a tremendous effect and looked like a major military victory to the Arabs. But analysed within the psychological context of how the Arabs see the Arab-Israeli conflict this is not so astonishing. It matters little that the Israelis were saying that the guerrillas were bluffing and their military power meant nothing. The gap between beliefs and 'reality' was striking, but what really mattered was what the Arabs believed that the guerrillas were. The source of their power was the image of the guerrilla in the Arab world, not their military capacity.

When the guerrillas were confronted, however, with the military challenge of King Hussein's army, there was not much left of the guerrillas. The most important aspect of that defeat was that the image of the guerrillas was destroyed. The spiralling effect went the other way. This might mean that the guerrillas, in striving for power from now on, must rely more on the 'objective conditions' rather than image-building in order to gain credibility in the Arab world. There will be no such sudden way to success as after the June War of 1967.

The Palestinian guerrilla movement has two basic goals: a national goal and a revolutionary goal.

The national goal aims at regaining the territory of Palestine and creating a Palestinian democratic state including the territory that is now covered by the State of Israel. This goal would of course imply the end of Zionism and the removal of at least some Jews, even though it can be disputed and argued to what extent the guerrillas really mean that all Jews should leave the country. It is emphasised by the guerrillas that the Oriental Jew should be allowed to stay on.

The other goal is the social goal of creating revolution in the Middle East. By revolution is meant socialist regimes of a shade that would be so much to the 'left' that only South Yemen today would pass as a true socialist regime. It is obvious that this goal is not shared by the Arab governments, as it is a direct threat to their legitimacy, but furthermore this goal is not even shared by all the guerrillas. The Arab governments, especially at the time when the guerrilla movement was at its peak of power, paid lip service to the national goal, that of liberating Palestine, while entertaining great fear of the revolutionaries, although this did not come out into the open too clearly until after the defeat of the guerrillas in Jordan when Egypt said very clearly that some guerrilla organisations had to be fought.

Not only did the guerrillas pose a threat to the traditional Arab regimes, but they also challenged traditional Arab doctrines in the struggle with Israel. In this way also the guerrilla movement was not very popular with established state interests.

94

The guerrillas also employed different strategies derived from their different goals. They agreed on keeping the issue hot by making the maximum of disturbance: the existence of the State of Israel should be constantly questioned. But there was serious disagreement on what would lead to the road of liberation. One key issue was whether there should be cooperation with the conventional armies and the conventional regimes, or whether there should be a policy of confrontation. Yassir Arafat was the foremost exponent of cooperation with conventional armies and conventional regimes, while George Habbash with his revolutionary ideas was the foremost exponent of confrontation with the conventional regimes and the conventional armies. The net result of these disagreements was that the proponents of confrontation facilitated and legitimised King Hussein's slaughter of the Palestinian guerrillas.

This happened on the local scene, but the struggle is also a global one. Internationally George Habbash engaged in hijacking of aeroplanes and other extreme methods. Yassir Arafat, on the other hand, said that this was damaging to the liberation struggle. Yassir Arafat was building up cells of students and others, particularly in Western countries, actively working to gain sympathy for the Palestinians. For Yassir Arafat it was not only a question of mobilising Arab masses, it was also important to engage in building up a sympathetic image of the guerrillas' fight in the Western World and in this way undermine the sympathy for Israel and thereby also its support from the Western World. Yassir Arafat had learned a lesson from the wars in Algeria and Vietnam where influence on Western public opinion proved to have a decisive significance. Again, image-building was an important part of the strategy.

No doubt there was a definite shift in sympathy after the Six Day War. We may say that the 'objective conditions' for exposing to Western public opinion the 'evils' of Zionism had never been so good because of the occupation of Arab land. The guerrilla fight and the activities of El Fatah probably accelerated this process. But the activities of George Habbash and the Popular Front for the Liberation of Palestine probably proved to be detrimental. In the internal debate between Habbash and Arafat on this issue, Habbash had his arguments ready, saying that the fight between the Jews and Arabs must be evaluated in a global context where the fight is between revolutionaries and reactionary forces. Israel and the United States were two sides of the same coin and hence in order to fight Israel, one also had to fight the United States. There was no point in trying to gain the sympathy of the public opinion in the United States because that country would always stand beside Israel. If, however, the United States could be involved directly in the fighting in the Middle East, this would be excellent, because it would increase the chances of exhausting the American resources, thus improving the possibilities of defeating Israel.

These different goals and different tactics seemed to be based on a certain logic or rationale. But the situation was not quite like that of course in real life. My own talks with Palestinian guerrillas, including people like George Habbash, indicate that their ideology tends to be rather diffuse, as are their ideas of ends-means relationships. We very often attribute to their goals and their strategy a clarity and a logic that the guerrillas themselves lack. The differences in strategies, the extreme methods and the various confrontations may also be explained by a plurality of causes, for the differences just described should not in themselves lead to numerous groups or organisations. Such differences can in fact also be partly explained in a cultural context where the Palestinians have always been quite divided. They may also be partly attributed to the political milieu which is characterised by such an intense rivalry that instead of fighting the enemy the guerrillas sometimes end up fighting each other. Nevertheless, the analysis of the different goals and strategies that have been outlined tells us something essential about the guerrillas even if it is a simplification.

One general observation can be made that should be of interest to students of terrorism generally. The adoption of extreme methods seems definitely to be related to the question of size. Small groups have a tendency to adopt more extreme methods than larger groups. Looking at the Palestine guerrillas, methods of extreme violence have always been used by the smaller groups. After the slaughter in Jordan, Black September, probably closely linked to El Fatah, adopted extreme tactics. But at this stage El Fatah could be considered to be in a weak position. El Fatah, at the peak of its power, adopted what we generally associate with a more 'responsible' way of advancing its interests.

The correlation of weakness and extreme violence does not only apply to guerrilla groups, of course, for even governments can use extreme violence under pressure of frustration and weakness. Indeed, the possibility that governments should act in this fashion in the Middle East should in no way be ruled out. Imagine, for example, what would happen if Israel should be defeated by the Arab armies. It is generally assumed that Israel would retaliate with all means available. It is a striking asymmetry in the conflict that Arabs have received one military defeat after another while Israel could hardly be expected to swallow this. According to Israeli strategic doctrines, to accept a military defeat would be the beginning of the end. Of course, the very fact that this is believed to be their position can be exploited by Israel as a means of putting pressure on Western governments.

It seems fair to conclude that the use of extreme violence has not served its purpose for the guerrillas in the Middle East notwithstanding the increased international recognition of the PLO, and, moreover, that the use of extreme violence seems to be closely related to the problem of the subjective feeling of being strong or weak.

The possibilities for extreme violence and how useful it is must also be related to a discussion of technological developments. Briefly, it seems justified to assert that technological developments, generally speaking, favour the employment of extreme violence. Take, for example. the October War in the Middle East. The efficiency of such light weapons as the anti-tank and anti-aircraft weapons used by the Egyptians was clearly demonstrated. These weapons are easy to produce and easy to handle. Therefore, it is reasonable to conclude that the use of these weapons offers a clear military advantage to the Arab side in the conflict. It also opens up the possibilities that smaller groups like the guerrilla organisations may use these weapons efficiently. Imagine, for example, the alarm which would be caused in the Western World if there were indications that Palestinian guerrillas were in possession of anti-aircraft weapons in Europe. Thus both psychological aspects and the objective conditions where technological developments constitute an important part must be taken into account when assessing the possibilities for extreme violence.

At this point it is appropriate to attempt to assess the implications of extreme violence for those seeking conflict resolution in the Middle East. But the question arises how conflict resolution should be defined. Obviously a solution of the conflict in the Middle East can be many things. But for the purpose of analysis it is necessary to limit the focus of the problem. Hence we will limit our discussion of conflict resolution to a 'solution' along the lines of the UN Resolution 242, whose essential elements are Israeli withdrawal from the territories occupied in June 1969 in return for Arab recognition of Israel and better arrangements for the Palestinians. But an implementation of this 'solution' would not mean that the conflict would be solved in the sense that conflict would be alienated. On the contrary, it is very likely that a considerable amount of conflict would continue.

It is also a common phenomenon in international conflicts that resolution on one level of conflict can lead to the intensification of the conflict on another. This is clearly demonstrated in the Middle East conflict: for example, whenever Egypt approaches a bargain with Israel, this leads to more intense and militant tactics on the part of some of the guerrilla organisations. Issues can also change over time and original issues can be replaced by new issues. Resolution of one issue can lead to intensification of other issues in a conflict.

A sharp distinction is often made between what is called conflict management and conflict resolution. Many writers are concerned with the management of conflict while others focus on conflict resolution. But at the same time it is clear that once there is conflict management some elements of conflict resolution are also achieved. And it is difficult to imagine a process towards conflict resolution that does not at some stage start with management of conflict — some sort of agreed accommodation of differences. We will choose to regard conflict resolution as a process where one does not find a static situation in the international system, but where the interaction of states will move along a scale from open extreme violence (in our study called conflict rancorous) to conflict resolution (see Figure 1).

Figure 1

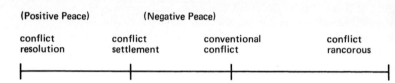

We will only consider different degrees of progress towards conflict resolution. While conflicts can be solved partly, we can hardly imagine a situation where conflict is non-existent. We also make a basic assumption that the implementation of the UN Resolution is a step forward towards conflict resolution, but of course this can be disputed.

We have come up with three basically different goals pursued in the conflict area. The actors in the area will be classified according to their attitude towards these three goals. Empirically, of course, the situation is far more complex. The pluralism and the complexity of a conflict of this character is enormous. For analytical purposes, however, we have to move towards simplification. In spite of pluralism in goals pursued we find that these three different goals cover the most interesting tendencies in the conflict for the purposes of evaluating the possibilities for conflict resolution. Those seeking these goals are:

1. Adherents of reaching a settlement through negotiations along the lines of the UN Resolution of 1967.
2. Adherents of a Palestinian democratic state having as its preconditions a military solution.
3. Adherents of the *status quo*. This means being in favour of the present situation in the absence of other options, but envisaging a settlement at some unspecified time in the future.

Goals 1 and 2 are mainly shared by people in the Arab world while goals 1 and 3 are mainly shared by people in Israel. It follows from this that it is only goal 1 that is shared by both conflict parties and thus the only goal about which there is scope for compatibility.

In Figure 2 we have classified the actors in four groups. This is based on our previous classification. The only difference is that we are now defining their attitude along the dimension of positive-negative towards the UN Resolution. When positive the actor is characterised by moderate, when negative he is called extreme.

Thus:

Arabs	Extreme	(Ae)
Arabs	Moderate	(Am)
Israelies	Extreme	(Ie)
Israelis	Moderate	(Im)

As previously we define conflict resolution as a solution along the lines of the UN Resolution. The adherents of a Palestinian democratic state will in our analysis be defined as extreme, because they favour a solution which is far removed from what we have defined as conflict

Figure 2: Compatibility-Incompatibility

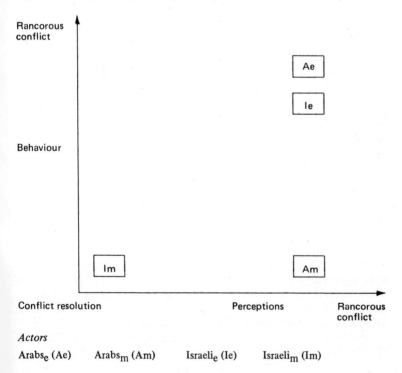

Actors

Arabs$_e$ (Ae)   Arabs$_m$ (Am)   Israeli$_e$ (Ie)   Israeli$_m$ (Im)

resolution. Correspondingly we have defined the adherents of the boundaries after the June War of 1967 as extreme on the Israeli side. This classification may, of course, be criticised for characterising these groups as extreme. For example, it can be argued that the Palestinian guerrillas are standing for the only humane and just solution of the conflict and that those opposing this solution are the extreme ones. Thus the descriptions, 'moderate' and 'extreme' must be understood in relation to to our definition of conflict resolutions. Research is not something neutral. Our subjectivity is expressed quite clearly in our definition of conflict resolution and classifications of actors. But instead of the words 'moderate' and 'extreme', we could have used 'negative' and 'positive', which perhaps are less subjective terms.

A basic assumption for our model is that sometimes there is congruence between images on the one hand and action on the other. In other instances we will find incongruity. It is this observed lack of congruence that makes it interesting to separate perception and behaviour for analytical purposes.

Looking at the value of Arab unity, for example, and the actual behaviour of the Arabs, there seems to be an incongruence between image and behaviour. But any intelligent analysis of Arab behaviour must take this value into account and estimate the chances of this value being realised, since it constitutes an integral part of the image of the Arab states. Today it is political ritual, tomorrow it may or may not be part of a political reality.

As a general rule we may say that the lack of congruence between image and action is a result of the constraints that actors are faced with. When the Arabs, for example, cling to the idea of a Palestinian democratic state the obstacles on the practical level are such that many Arab actors will not pursue the goal in day-to-day politics. This might lead to frustration because they do not achieve what they think is right — but the frustration may not lead them to give up the image.

We have reached the conclusion that incompatible perceptions might potentially be just as detrimental to conflict resolution, not only because the other party might fear that goals on the perceptual level might emerge on the behavioural level, but also because 'objective conditions' can make this less or more likely. Constraints in the operational environment may also change.

In Figure 2 we have pleaced the actors along the dimensions perceptions and behaviour. Here we see that Im comes close to conflict resolution because Im comes close both on the behavioural and perceptual levels to a fulfillment of the UN Resolution. Am is close to the UN Resolution on the behavioural level, but moves far away from the UN Resolution on the perceptual level. Ae and Ie are far removed from the UN Resolution both on the perceptual and behavioural levels.

Another basic assumption in our model is that this relationship changes over time. We have observed that sometimes values that at some periods are transferred into behaviour at other times just survive as part of the image. Events may happen that reinforce the image which in turn have consequences for the behaviour of the actors. Events may also take place that almost eliminate the image, but changes in the image will only be accepted with great reluctance. If we take a given image that is strongly instituted, the general trend will be that events will either re-inforce the image or leave it unchanged. For example, the defeat of the Palestinian guerrillas in Jordan had serious consequences for the behaviour of the Arab states in respect to the efforts towards establishing a Palestinian democratic state, but this does not necessarily mean that the value itself — a Palestinian democratic state — is weakened even though for the time being it has been severely weakened as a feature of Arab behaviour and that there is a wider gap between image and behaviour. Our conclusion is, therefore, that when a conflict party gives up pursuing a goal for the time being, this does not mean that the goal is un-interesting for the study of conflict resolutions if this goal still remains a part of the actors' image.

The support that each goal is able to mobilise changes over time. Thus the time dimension also here becomes important. In the course of time the amount of support for the different goals has varied substan-tially. Thus the dynamics of the relationship between these goals has to be explored in order to make an evaluation of the possibilities for conflict resolution. Figure 2 does not tell us anything of the strength behind each goal, but the essential thing is to realise that this is not static.

In an earlier analysis we became aware of the competition between different goals and also competitive strategies dividing each separate conflict party. A very simple empirical example will serve to illustrate the point.

We first concluded that there seems to be a very even power relation-ship between the adherents of a military solution and the adherents of a political solution in the Arab world. We then concluded that if the adherents of a military solution in the Arab world, of which the guer-rilla was the primary exponent, should be defeated, it would be far easier to reach a negotiated settlement along the lines of the UN Resolu-tion. But we are guilty of the fallacy of leaving out the interaction process with the adversary in the conflict. The defeat of the guerrillas in Jordan did not increase the possibilities of a political solution. For the day-to-day troubles with the *status quo* went down sharply in Israel which had the effect of strengthening the position of groups in Israel wanting more expansion and not a settlement along the lines of the UN Resolution.

The competing relationship between different goals is of course in no way unique to the conflict in the Middle East. This is probably true of all conflicts and political relationships. It is, therefore, not sufficient to study the doctrine currently enjoying the most support. The chances of other doctrines taking its place must be estimated.

Generally speaking, of course, the growth of the guerrilla movement has no doubt led to a polarisation of the conflict and has seriously obstructed efforts towards a negotiated settlement. To assess the influence of the guerrillas, however, it is not enough to look at the actions that they have been able to carry through. Their influence on Arab governments, on the superpowers and on Israel, must also be taken into consideration.

In evaluating the influence on Israel, we must look at how Israel forms her image of her enemy and how this in turn affects her actions. It is characteristic of conflict of this type that, in the portrayal of the adversary, extremist groups or signals with very low credibility but with content of an extreme character are taken as indicators of the intentions of the adversary as a whole. In this way the extreme groups on both sides will gain a strong position in the sort of polarised conflict situation with which we are dealing. It might be that Israel has not been very much frightened by the fighting capabilities of the guerrillas, but it seems safe to assume that the guerrillas have greatly strengthened the Israeli image of the Arabs wanting to liquidate them. Thus the guerrillas have played an important role psychologically in strengthening the hawkish elements in Israel (*Ie*).

Moreover, the guerrillas have managed to obstruct peace initiatives from the Arab side. Therefore, the guerrillas have served to reinforce extremism on both sides. But, on the other hand, the guerrillas by their military activities have made it more necessary for Israel to negotiate. In addition, the guerrilla movement has served to focus attention on the 'Palestine Problem'. It is also clear that the Palestinians would not have obtained the same share of the cake in Geneva. Thus the guerrillas have served both to strengthen extreme actors which has weakened the possibilities for a negotiated settlement and at the same time strengthened the hand of the guerrillas if negotiations should come about. The influence of the guerrillas has worked both ways — both increasing and decreasing the chances of a negotiated settlement.

Looking at the situation in a longer-term perspective, the situation is not so easy to assess. Some people will say that the approach of Henry Kissinger is useless because it does not solve the conflict. The underlying sources of conflict would remain the same. What Kissinger has tried to do is to isolate the parties so that they cannot fight — but basic hostility remains. Critics would further contend that Kissinger's approach to peace contains strong elements of force and hence, sooner or later, such a 'peace' will result in new wars. This is not the place to explore these arguments in detail. For our purpose it is sufficient to say that a 'Kissinger peace' *may* lead to more stability, but that the possibility of new wars would still be there. At this point it is again worth looking at the problems of perceptions versus behaviour in our model of the conflict. Presently the Arabs might compromise with the State of Israel in the form of a 'Kissinger peace', but will they give up the idea of a Palestinian democratic state? This is surely a key issue when evaluating the possibilities for conflict resolution. General theory on perceptions tells us that these change very slowly. Repeated military defeats of the Arabs, for example, have not led them to give up the idea that some day they will be strong enough to defeat Israel. On the other hand, if an event occurs that is in line with an already established image, it might have a spiralling effect on the image. For example, the idea of Arab unity faced failure after failure, but suddenly with the October War and the oil boycott a relatively high degree of unity was achieved. Probably this will have a spiralling effect on the Arab image of unity and, in turn, on the image of Arab fighting capacity.

Transferring this to the guerrillas, defeats may not lead to the renunciation of the goal — new guerrilla movements may be organised and the idea of a Palestinian democratic state may be taken up by others. Moreover, we have seen the linkage of the guerrillas to revolutionary values. So the question arises to what extent the revolutionary movements in the Middle East will adopt in the future the doctrines of George Habbash. Again, will revolution and the fight against Israel be viewed within the same framework; or will a compromise be possible, whereby Israel is not attached to this revolutionary framework? History provides many examples of values being abandoned mostly because of the constraints in the system: the costs are too much. But history also offers examples of the contrary. A basic dilemma in the Arab-Israeli conflict is to assess which attitude is more likely to prevail in the present case.

PART II

THE ARMS RACE

7. AN OUTLINE HISTORY OF NUCLEAR PROLIFERATION

Herbert F. York

In December 1938 a discovery was made in Germany of a new nuclear process called fission and the scientific community of the Western World was prepared for it — not that it was not a surprise — in the sense that it was very widely and quickly recognised that this new discovery made possible the chain reaction and made it possible to release the energy of the atomic nucleus. It had been know for up to forty years that the energy locked up in the atomic nucleus was of the order of one million times as great on a unit weight basis as the energy available from chemical processes. But during the first forty years that this fact was recognised there was no way known whereby this energy might be released in a way and at a time chosen by man. The discovery of fission in 1938 meant that within months the Western World recognised that here was the key to the release of nuclear energy. The result was that in 1939 five countries — Germany, France, Great Britain, the United States and the Soviet Union — began programmes for the development of this new process, first for the work designed to understand it and later to exploit it.

In all of these countries the people who did the work immediately recognised the possibilities and began fundamental work designed to explore them. In the main this work was unsupported by governments or armies. The persons who did it were already employed in university laboratories or in research institutes. These university laboratories and institutes had already on hand the equipment and facilities necessary for the conduct of this work. It is difficult to estimate the total effort in this early period, 1939-40, on a world basis, but trying to judge from the number of papers published in the journals there must have been the better part of a thousand persons involved; and the amount of money being spent on atomic energy must have been, in modern terms, allowing for changes in value, perhaps tens of millions of dollars. All this was essentially at the initiative of the scientists themselves without any substantial involvement of governments or military organisations.

Of these five states Germany's efforts were the least impressive. A major reason was that German science was in a chaotic state through the expulsion and emigration of Jewish scientists. Moreover, the political situation was such that those who remained were unable to create

105

a unified programme. A number of small programmes designed to study atomic energy were initiated, but there was no national programme. The belief, apparently, was that the war would be short and that atomic energy was a long-term prospect. At any rate, there was in Germany no national conclusion that there should be a major programme and so no national programme was instituted although work continued for the next few years.

Let us now turn to the second country, France. Here research centred around Frederic Joliot-Curie and his collaborators, including Lew Kowarski and Hans Halban. Their work proceeded during 1939 and into 1940 and they were able to do some of the best of the early research in determining the nature of the fission process and what were the possibilities for producing nuclear power, and they were well on the way to a thorough understanding of the question when the German invasion of France took place in 1940 and the work was suddenly cut short. The French group split up. Some chose to stay in France. For example, Joliot-Curie took this course although he continued to do fundamental work during the war and participated in the French Resistance. Others left and went to Great Britain and took with them the knowledge which they had acquired and what was most of the world's supply of heavy water at that time. It was a somewhat adventurous escape, those concerned being prepared to take extreme measures to prevent this heavy water from falling into German hands. They arrived safely in Great Britain where they then resumed their work as best they could, in conjunction with British colleagues. To complete the preliminary part of the French story one must record that in 1942 when the British work was transferred to North America, the French work was also transferred there but specifically to Canada. We shall return later to the subsequent history of the French programme.

The third case was that of Great Britain. There the same thing happened as in France and Germany. Physicists were able to use facilities and equipment already available to them to find out how to use the process for the production of nuclear weapons and of nuclear power. The programme in Great Britain was augmented beyond what it otherwise would have been by the influx of refugees from the Continent. The prospects for atomic energy were brought to the attention of the British Government fairly early on. The notion of instituting a major programme designed to exploit these new possibilities was approved by Churchill and it was he who gave the code name to the project which persisted for many years, both in Great Britain and in the United States, namely 'Tube Alloys' — a code name which was in some later circumstances to give some unexpected difficulties. The British during the next several years developed a fund of basic data. They began to develop the information necessary to make the first reasonable estimate of what a critical mass might be; what the size of an explosion might be; what it might take actually to build a nuclear reactor, and so forth. It became evident during the course of this work that, on the one hand, it was feasible but, on the other hand, that the industrial base required and the total size of the effort required was going to be much larger than had seemed likely in 1939. This requirement for a very large industrial base and the growing intensity of the war in Europe, and particularly the growing severity of the aerial attacks on Great Britain, led to the British programme being transferred to North America, largely to the United States, in the period 1942-3. We shall return in due course to the subsequent history of the British effort.

The same thing that had happened in the three countries mentioned so far also took place in the fourth, namely the United States. Probably a larger total number of persons were involved but again in 1939-40 physicists in laboratories in a number of major cities and a number of major institutions studied the basic process and began to speculate what it would take to build bombs and reactors, and to speculate what it would mean in terms of the political situation of the time, the dominant feature of which was of course the war in Europe. There were some early approaches by some of these physicists, in particular refugee physicists, to the US Government and to military authorities. But although they were sometimes received politely they were never given the backing which they felt was merited by the project. The main argument they used, incidentally, in pointing out the situation to the politicians was that fission had been discovered in Germany and it was clear that in the political situation of the time the Germans would be eager to exploit such a new device and it was absolutely essential for the survival of civilisation that it not be the Germans who succeeded first in developing atomic weapons. They had of course no direct information about what was going on in Germany but they had their general views about the capabilities of German science and the likelihood of the Germans moving in this direction, and they were convinced that a race was going to develop and that it was necessary for the United States and its future allies to win it. The United States was not yet in the war but was becoming more and more directly concerned with the allied cause, and the emotional if not the direct military involvement was growing. In 1941, as the war fever heightened in the United States, special institutions of all kinds were established to manage the war programme. Among these were the National Defense Research Council (NDRC) and later the Office of Scientific Research and Development. This meant that institutions were established in the US Government whose purpose was to arrange for the maximum possible exploitation of science and technology to the benefit of the war. This brought about some novel situations. There had been for many years contacts between science and the military in the United States, as in all countries, but generally speaking it had been between the middle echelons of the military and the scientists who could be best described as technological experts in the design of one kind of gadget or another. This new creation, the NDRC, brought top-level scientists with national and world reputations for the first time into contact with top-level military and political leaders and into contact with the President himself.

The creation of this general apparatus for the exploitation of science and technology in the interests of winning the war meant that there was now a direct and natural channel for nuclear scientists as well as all other scientists to the top decision-making levels, and it was through this channel rather than through the individual importuning of individual scientists that the programme was able finally to get under way. The National Academy of Sciences conducted a study of the prospects of nuclear weapons in 1941 and submitted a report concluding that they were feasible, that the time-scale was consistent with the war programme and that the industrial base needed could be found. At the same time that this question was being studied at home in the United States by the scientific groups, a liaison had been established with the British across the board in military science and technology and had been growing more effective as time went on and as the war intensified. It dealt with a very wide range of subjects, such as radar, anti-mine warfare, and eventually with operations research and many other things. It included simply as a natural part exchange of information with respect to nuclear energy and with respect to the prospects for the application of this new discovery of fission. Again, in the autumn of 1941, at the same time as the National Academy of Sciences was producing its report to the effect that the new weapon was feasible, the British had arrived at a similar conclusion. Americans who were at that time in Great Britain, exploring various scientific topics, came back and reported to the NDRC the British conclusions with regard to the feasibility and prospects for making a nuclear weapon. Putting these two things together, on 6 December 1941, the day before Pearl Harbour, Vannevar Bush, who was the Director of the NDRC, drew up a report recommending to President Franklin Roosevelt the institution of a high priority programme in the United States to develop a new weapon. During the spring of 1942 the committee apparatus — the NDRC consisted actually of a collection of committees — tried to run the programme directly as best it could but it soon became evident that the size and complexity was far beyond anything that could be run in that way, and so the military in the United States were brought in for the first time, not because of their expertise in weaponry, but because of their expertise in organising large industrial projects. The Government in fact did not turn to the Ordinance Corps or any of the other military organisations expert in the building and operating of weapons. Instead it turned to the Corps of Engineers who were expert in building dams and handling similar civil projects. In the autumn of 1942 the project, which the world knows as the Manhattan Project, then got under way and involved the personnel from Great Britain. I will not describe the programme itself – it took just under three years from when it got into high gear until the first bomb was tested in the summer of 1945, followed by the use of the two bombs in August 1945 at Hiroshima and Nagasaki. There has frequently been speculation since then that the timing of these explosions had been carefully adjusted so as to relate to various problems not only in the Second World War but in connection with the then incipient Cold War. I believe that the facts do not support that approach. The dates at which the first bombs were used, the date at which the first test was made, the date at which the first military applications were conducted, were determined by the technological events involved. The tests took place on the first date that it was possible for them to take place, and the uses in the war in Japan took place at the first date at which the bombs were available for that purpose. To a limited extent some of the political features that appear on the scene in 1945 – the timing of some of these events – may have been juggled to fit the nuclear programme but not vice-versa. For instance, the date on which the Potsdam Conference was actually held was delayed somewhat so that President Harry S. Truman could go there knowing for sure whether the atomic bomb actually worked or not. The purpose of using the two bombs in Japan was to terrorise the Japanese Government into surrender. By that time the rate of bombardment of Japan had reached something in the neighbourhood of a thousands tons, a kiloton, a day. It was scheduled to go up to something like 10 kilotons a day in 1946, something which, of course, never happened. The use of the bombs and the use of two of them in relatively quick succession thus had as its purpose the tipping of the balance in Japan in favour of unconditional surrender, which was what the Allied demands had become. But even before this event, before the bombs were tested and before they were used, it became known that the Germans had no programme and the question was then naturally raised why should the American programme continue. It was raised by particular individuals, especially those who in the first place had argued that the United States must initiate a programme because there was a chance the Germans would do it first. When it was discovered through the collapse of Germany that there was no German programme, it was natural that some people at least should raise the question, 'As there is no race for the atomic bomb what does that imply?'. So the question was raised and at the highest levels, the names of Leo Szilard and James Franck being associated with this development. But the proposals to stop the programme had no chance whatsoever. By that time the reason for the programme had passed from the rather particular goal of beating the Germans to the more general one of contributing to ending the war at the earliest possible date. The scientists and people in the project, like everyone else, were determined to do their best to achieve that goal, one which was then generally perceived as proper and noble.

It was out of these first discussions before the first atomic bombs were used that what we can call the arms control and disarmament movement, which still persists today, grew. After the bombs were used and the war ended, the three Western allies, the United States, Canada, and Great Britain raised the question with their Soviet ally as to how two almost contradictory goals might be achieved. On the one hand, they wanted to prevent a nuclear weapons arms race, and on the other hand they wanted to promote the application of atomic energy to the general benefit of mankind. They were able, during the autumn of 1945 and spring of 1946, to generate a set of proposals which sounded good, but when they finally tried to put them into concrete terms they were unable to arrive at an East-West agreement. The basic American proposal, which could also be thought of as the Western plan, is known to history as the 'Baruch Plan'. It was in fact largely authored by J. Robert Oppenheimer and David E. Lilienthal; it acquired its name mainly because Bernard Baruch was the man who was chosen to present it to the world. It had as its purposes the same ones previously mentioned: the promotion of atomic energy under circumstances which would somehow prevent the spread of nuclear weapons. It is interesting to recall that Oppenheimer and the others recognised then that a scheme of inspection of facilities would not be adequate. It would not be possible to conduct independent nuclear programmes and invent a scheme of control involving inspection which could assure that no nuclear resources were being diverted to improper purposes. For that reason they invented what was for that time and even today an extremely radical proposal, one in which essentially all work in atomic energy would be internationalised. All atomic energy facilities including mines, laboratories and so forth would be controlled by an international agency under the United Nations. The notion was strongly counter to all current ideas about private enterprise and equally counter to the prevailing notion of national sovereignty, and so it was rejected at that time.

Let us now turn to the fifth nuclear programme, namely that of the Soviet Union. The Soviet programme started in 1939, the same time as the programmes in the four other countries. It had the same general characteristics as the others. A group of physicists and other scientists working with laboratories already available to them, employed by the research institutions and universities they were already working in, simply turned aside from their usual research programmes to research into this particular field without the necessity of any particular special permission or endorsement from higher governmental authorities. During 1939 and the early part of 1940 the work proceeded, as it did in the Western countries. The Soviets, like the other scientists, devoted their machines and their talents to elucidating the basic features of the phenomenon and to making estimates about what would be required to build devices of both military and peaceful application. Then, in 1941, the Germans turned eastwards and invaded the Soviet Union and the programme was effectively terminated by that operation. The persons in leadership positions ended up by taking on other more immediate tasks. The man who eventually was to lead the programme when it was later re-instituted, Igor Kurchatov, went off to the Crimea where he worked on problems of 'degaussing' ships to make them safe from attack by mines. Thus the Soviet programme started off like the others and in 1941 was effectively stopped. During the next several years, some people kept track of what was going on and studied the available literature, for there was still quite a bit published on the subject even after 1941, and they thus became convinced that there was a Western programme. There may well have been other good ways through which the Soviets were aware of the Western programme and at least in their own literature on the subject they say that they reached a conclusion that there was a major programme in the United States because of a steady decrease in the amount of literature published on the subject. A curious example is sometimes cited. This concerned a cable sent by Flerov and Petrzhak, two of Kurchatov's co-workers, to *The Physical Review* (an American journal) announcing the discovery of a phenomenon known as 'spontaneous fission' in uranium. The cable was duly published, but it evoked no response from any American scientist. Some Soviet scientists reportedly saw this failure to respond as further proof of the existence of a 'secret' American A-bomb programme. However, in trying to understand what happened in the Soviet Union it seems clear that the most important single event was the purely technological event, the proof by the American test and the American use in Japan that the bomb was feasible. Prior to these events, there apparently had been, as is perfectly plausible to suppose, arguments within the Soviet establishment with regard to the appropriateness of devoting resources to the somewhat long-range and questionable end. Hence the major effect of the American test was to settle this argument in favour of those who insisted it was practical. That more than any other political or strategic consideration is what inaugurated the major Soviet programme in 1945.

The Soviet programme from that point follows a remarkably parallel path to the American programme as far as time intervals are concerned.

The period from the 1945 decision to when the Soviets had a working reactor is within a few weeks of the corresponding period between when Bush recommended to Roosevelt all-out support of the American programme and when the Americans had a working reactor. Similarly, the period from when the Soviets first had a working reactor to the first test is within a few weeks of the period which separared the same two weeks in the United States. These rather elementary facts, plus additional though sparse information, indicate that the two programmes followed a similar course. In this connection we must note that in September 1945, immediately after the American explosion, there was published in the United States a report, called the Smyth Report (written by an American physicist who was involved in the programme and who later became one of the Atomic Energy Commissioners) which described, within fairly restrictive limits of secrecy, all the major elements of the programme. This was published in an edition of 40,000 copies in the Soviet Union very shortly after its release in the United States and no doubt proved helpful. But in addition to the most important scientific fact — namely that it worked — and in addition to the information available in the Smyth Report — namely that not only did the bomb work but there are several different ways to make it and several different ways to prepare the explosive material — the Soviets also had available to them at that time some very good intelligence information. Klaus Fuchs, a refugee who had made his way first to Great Britain to become part of the British programme and had then gone with the British team to the United States, had become part of the American team at Los Alamos, where the bomb was designed. Throughout this period he was reporting what he know back to the Soviet Union. Incidentally, just to complete the story, as far as he is concerned, there was a conference held at Los Alamos in the spring of 1946 called the *Conference on the Super*. It was a post-war conference whose purpose was to discuss the prospects for making a still bigger bomb, a super bomb, a bomb that we now know as the hydrogen bomb, a bomb which would have an explosive power about a thousand times as big as the atomic bomb. This conference was conducted before the British returned home and Klaus Fuchs was one of the members of the group which worked in it, one of the forty people whose names are listed on the front of the report of the conference. He was also co-author of at least one patent relating to the development of the hydrogen bomb. Thus he was not only involved in the atomic bomb but in the early work on the hydrogen bomb as well.

The Soviet programme started in the autumn of 1945. Nine months later came the Baruch proposal which, if accepted, would have called for a halt in that programme, including problems intrinsic to the Baruch Plan itself, but also simply because the Soviets had a programme and

112

were not about to stop it. They gave all sorts of political reasons at the time but in later years when Nikita Khrushchev was willing to gossip about it to various visitors, he said that as far as the Soviets were concerned they were determined to be of co-equal status with the United States and there were only two ways of achieving that: either get the United States to give up the bomb or to get it themselves, and the prospects of getting the United States to give it up did not really look realistic. And, in fact, while the Baruch Plan did eventually call for the Americans giving up the bomb, that feature was the vaguest and most remote element in the plan.

So to summarise the cases of the first two authors of proliferation — the United States and the Soviet Union — the Americans did it inspired by the fury of the Second World War in general and by the notion of a race with Germany in particular; while the Soviets did it for the simple reason that they found the American monopoly intolerable.

We must now turn to the case of Great Britain. During the war many arrangements were made for sharing nuclear technology between the Americans and the British but, partly because of the unusual level of secrecy from the initiation of a high priority programme which has always surrounded the field, Churchill and Roosevelt made the agreements on sharing nuclear energy private and in some important cases they did not even bring their immediate staff in on it. They simply had some documents drawn up; they initialled them; then had them filed away to bring them out after the war. Roosevelt died and with his death knowledge of some of these key documents died too.

I mentioned earlier the question of 'Tube Alloys', a code name for uranium invented by Churchill. Some of these documents were in the US Navy files under 'T' for 'Tube Alloys' and so when the British brought up the question of these arrangements, which they recalled having made during the war, no American copies of these documents could be found nor were found until ten or fifteen years later when somebody happened to come across these agreements filed under 'T' for 'Tube Alloys'. In any event, partly for that particular set of reasons and partly for more general reasons, the cooperation which had grown up between the Americans and British during the war began to come apart after the war: the Americans began to distrust foreigners when it came to atomic secrets, strict laws were passed with regard to controlling information and Anglo-American cooperation was replaced by a series of barriers blocking the transfer of information.

The British team which had been at Los Alamos and at other American installations, returned home after the war. Some of them left atomic energy and went to rejoin whatever programmes they had previously been involved with. But others continued their interest in atomic energy and formed the nucleus in Great Britain of what amounted to a technological nuclear lobby. As the cooperation with the Americans continued to decrease and the prospects for reopening it continued to deteriorate, these people began to propose that the British should simply continue the programme that they had initiated and should go on and develop a bomb of their own. Apparently the basic notion of the time was not a question of whether or not a programme should be started but whether or not a programme already started should be continued. The notion that what was involved was a question of continuation rather than a question of initiation made it quite a different question from a political point of view and Clement Attlee apparently took the final decision to initiate a nuclear programme in 1948 without checking with Parliament or even with the full Cabinet. At least in part this was possible because it could be seen as a small detail about how to continue rather than as a major decision about how to start. In 1952 something like four years after that decision was made, the British conducted their first nuclear test. So Great Britain, the third nuclear power, derived its nuclear bombs from a programme started in 1939 which simply came to fruition in 1952 without any further major decisions being made.

There was a new attempt to control the spread of atomic weapons, a new attempt to control the arms race, in 1958. At that time the Soviets, the Americans and the British, then the only nuclear powers, were able to agree on a nuclear test moratorium. The moratorium was meant to be temporary and it was instituted with the purpose of providing an appropriate political climate in which to achieve a nuclear test ban treaty. They were able to institute the moratorium successfully but it was not in fact adequate in creating the necessary climate. And so after more than a year had gone by (one year had been the time period allocated) the moratorium was denounced, first by President Eisenhower who said the United States was no longer bound but would not begin testing without giving notice and then three days later by Khrushchev who told an Argentine newspaper man the Soviet Union was not bound either but would not start testing unless the West did so first. And that is where the fourth case of nuclear proliferation comes in. Just a few months later the French began testing nuclear weapons and Khrushchev seized on it as an alibi. He claimed that 'the West' was testing new weapons and that they must stop it.

Now the French programme, like the British programme, also actually began in 1939. The French, as described earlier, started their own programme. They then moved first to Great Britain, then to Canada, and finally, at the end of the war, back to France. Because they had been in Canada they had not been privy to as wide a spectrum of information as the British. The information to which they had direct access related mainly to the construction of reactors, to reactor theory and technology and to the technology of plutonium. When the French asked permission to take this information home with them, they were not allowed to take the basic documents themselves, but they were allowed to extract whatever could be fitted into three small notebooks with no limit to how small the writing should be. Lew Kowarski has reported elsewhere on his efforts to make the smallest and finest possible notes to get the maximum possible information back to France. This information, which followed the same continuous line beginning in 1939 and came from a programme whose origins were in 1939, returned to France and became the basis for the French programme again. In the minds of the people conducting it, it was a continuation of the programme continuous from 1939. However, it was nowhere near as advanced as the British programme and did not have the same priorities as the Soviet programme and so took very much longer. They began by building up a base for peaceful uses of power reactors and other kinds of research at first, but this automatically led to the accumulation of facilities and knowledge that led in the direction of a bomb, and apparently in the mid-1950s, Pierre Mendes-France took the decision to accumulate fissile material for the possible use in a bomb. Then when Charles de Gaulle came to power in 1958, if not before, the decision actually to build the bomb was made. But the technological base was already there and had been accumulating since the discovery of fission in 1939. Hence, as in the British case, at no point was a radical decision necessary — that is, a decision between doing nothing and doing something. The technological base accumulated in a slow and natural way that was determined by the technological needs of other programmes.

So much for the four cases whose origins date back to 1939. The fifth case is that of China. The Peoples' Republic came to power in early 1949. Chinese intervention in the Korean War followed hardly a year later and dominated relations between China and the West and was also an extremely important feature in their relations with the Soviet Union. The Soviets in fact began to assist the Chinese in a variety of ways and according to their own lights. In particular, the Soviets have always placed a high importance on the training of technocrats and the use of technology as a means for economic and social advancement and hence they helped the Chinese to establish the same kind of base. Included in the early Soviet assistance to China was assistance in nuclear energy: the Soviets helped them with the provision of material and equipment, the provision of information, and the training of cadres of persons to establish a reactor programme and a research programme. They even went so far as to assist them in the setting up of a plant for the separation of nuclear isotopes. While this was going on there was a period of confusion. Joseph Stalin died, was replaced temporarily by George Malenkov and then by Khrushchev. Later came the split between the Peoples' Republic and the Soviet Union. It is clear that arguments over just how far this help in atomic energy should proceed were a major element in what finally became the Sino-Soviet split. Khrushchev, again in some of his various instances of gossiping, has talked about his difficulties with Mao, especially with regard to Mao's ideas about nuclear energy. It is clear that Khrushchev was, appropriately, frightened by the prospect of nuclear war and he was disturbed by the fact that Mao was not. The famous statement, attributed to Mao — he may or may not have made it — that if half the Chinese were killed China would still be the biggest country in the world, came to us via Khrushchev. Khrushchev told that story a number of times, and it is obvious that he was deeply impressed by it and by what he took to be Mao's attitude. At any rate, the Soviets, as a result of the split, stopped practically all of their technological support, including support in the nuclear field. But before the split occurred, the Chinese had acquired from the Soviets a very substantial base including isotope separation facilities, reactors and so on. In any event what finally happened is that China tested her first atomic bomb in 1964 and her first hydrogen bomb in 1966. If one discusses, or rather gossips about this with a Chinese, even the proverbial taxi driver, the latter will tell you that the Chinese were kicked around by the West for two hundred years (and by the West he means the Russians as well as everyone else) and that Chinese acquisition (this is said by Chinese with no connection with the Peoples' Republic) of an atomic bomb puts an end to this particular period of history.

Moving to the sixth case, that of India, we find it is distinct from all of the other five in that it has more recent roots. The Indians, unlike any of the previous five, are signatories to the Partial Nuclear Test Ban Treaty, though as is well known they refused to sign the Non-Proliferation Treaty (NPT). Moreover, they have certain bilateral agreements particularly with the Canadians that inhibit their use of things which the Canadians have actually given to them and there are other arrangements that the Indians have made in regard to international atomic energy which distinguishes this sixth case from the previous five. In all the previous five cases there were no prior agreements of any kind, either with respect to going slowly, or going secretly, or going openly, or exchanging information other than in certain specific information cases. All of the other five started at an early date and without any inhibitions, without ever having promised or indicated to anybody that they would not. The Indians are the first case where a nation had indicated that they might not and had gone a certain number of steps down the road of agreeing not to, although they had not taken the final step. The events which influenced the Indians very strongly are the failure of other powers to live up to the obligations in Clauses Four, Five and Six of the NPT. The Indians very frequently in arms control circles claim that the NPT is very unfair, and that the provisions with regard to peaceful uses of nuclear explosives are not adequate. Thus, they charged that the overall situation for these and other reasons was essentially unfair, and they were finding it increasingly intolerable. Other events entirely aside from these which are usually cited as being important to the Indians are, first, the Chinese Himalayan expeditions of 1962 which were a shock to everybody, especially to the Indians; secondly the first Chinese test of 1964; and thirdly the Chinese satellite of 1970. The last of these matters may not be too important because the timing may be wrong; the Indian nuclear programme was apparently initiated in 1969, although it is hard to be quite sure of this.

8. PLOWSHARE, PROLIFERATION, AND THE N+1 COUNTRY

Thomas Blau

Proliferation – A Political Problem

The problem of nuclear weapons proliferation has, for years, been conceived to be that of limiting weapons to nations already possessing them and preventing their spread to the would-be next member of the nuclear weapons club, the so-called N+1 country. Unfortunately, the Non-Proliferation Treaty of 1969 (NPT) is in a disappointing tradition: the attempt to reduce the likelihood of war by restricting formally, through written international agreement, various kinds of military hardware.

Narrowly construed, such a conception ignores the non-nuclear weapons, and even non-strategic, incentives for proliferation in the particular circumstances of each N+1 candidate. It is extraordinarily difficult to deal, for instance, with internal factors, for responses may range from aesthetically unattractive covert involvement in the domestic affairs of others, to the ineffable prospects of 'improving social and economic conditions'. In any case, the first is likely to backfire and the second, if it reaches, astonishingly, the stages of effective operationalisation and implementation, has no demonstrated relationship with non-proliferation or even peacefulness.

There are, however, logically intermediate problems which fuel proliferatory pressures which have not received important attention from most analysts or policy-makers. Specifically, major incentives to proliferate include the attenuation of close relations between certain states, the weaker of which often perceive the attenuation as an increasing external threat. Given the rapidly decreasing costs of nuclear weapons and delivery systems, national nuclear systems can be viewed as a substitute of sorts for fair-weather great power friends. Additionally, given economic stringency, rising costs for conventional forces, and an almost worldwide antipathy toward military service, nuclear weapons can be seen as a cheap alternative to further investment in conventional forces.

It is easy for an American to show how his country's failure to assure its allies may stimulate national nuclear forces. The United

States is, after all, the home of the unfortunate Multilateral Force idea, which attempted to deal with this problem in the NATO context. In the Middle East Israel's only 'friend' simultaneously attempts the role of referee between it and those who challenge its very existence, an ambiguity which must surely stimulate proliferatory pressures in Israel. The stimulus can only be sharpened when the Unites States-as-referee attempts to bribe the region into stability with, of all things, reactors. The primary issue remains that of American reliability. Reliability is not an issue in terms of diplomatic guarantees, and is unlikely to be much help should the Arabs seek to exploit militarily the territorial and strategic gains they will win in exchange for vague and indirect murmurs of non-belligerency.

Stability in the Middle East may, then, be threatened more by Israel perceiving itself as increasingly inferior in conventional weaponry than by its possession of a 'bomb in the basement' capability.[1] At the same time, constraints on the United States include the 'oil weapon', which gains its edge from the danger of Soviet military involvement. If the Soviets are perceived as being in some ways more powerful and more reckless — and there is much evidence for both views — then the United States will not be perceived as a reliable ally.

In the case of India, the Nixon-Kissinger 'tilt' toward Pakistan, shocking in terms of strategy, history, and morality, raised doubts about the value of American friendship in more countries than just India. Ironically, it is not unequivocally fortunate for the West that astute observers in India, for instance, may understand the constraints on alternative patrons. The Director of the Indian Institute of Defence Studies and Analyses writes of the Indo-Chinese border war of 1962:

> In the scale of values calculated by Soviet leaders — naturally enough — the security of the Soviet Union was placed higher than rendering assistance to India. Such a three-way situation could always occur again . . . Soviet deterrence, even if successfully invoked under Article IX of the Indo-Soviet Treaty, has serious limitations and ought not to be relied upon under all circumstances.[2]

As in the Israeli case, moving toward a national capability is not an outlandish response to the political and strategic environment, particularly the dubiousness of any great power guarantees. American guarantees are especially dubious because of the coming primacy of Soviet strategic power (ratified by the various SALT agreements), Soviet conventional power, especially in the naval sphere, and a greater Soviet capability for if not reckless action, then dire threat. The United States has done much to create this environment, and it is proliferatory. In such a situation, to focus attention on the achievement of signatures to pledges of hardware limitations may be 'legalism' in the worst sense.

119

If the United States is weaker, then it cannot be relied upon. Self-help is one alternative to Soviet patronage or lonely weakness.

Casual Proliferation by Joint Product

The United States has been the greatest propagandist of non-proliferation as well as the major proliferatory influence in the world. Beginning almost immediately after the end of the Second World War the US Atomic Energy Commission, in its previous incarnation as the Manhattan Project, has been a zealous promoter and exporter of the peaceful uses of nuclear energy. 'Peaceful uses' include reactor technology and civilian-applications explosives for underground excavation and natural resources retrieval. India exploded such a shot in 1974; the Soviet Union has an extensive programme under way for varied applications; and the American programme, called Plowshare, has been kept alive by the demands for cheap retrieval of energy resources such as natural gas.

Plowshare is threatened regularly with budgetary extinction on economic and ecological grounds, as well as simple fear raised by the prospect of 'routine' nuclear explosions. An even more important problem is the proliferatory momentum that Plowshare and its Soviet counterpart engenders. The programme's enthusiasm encourages others to consider such applications. Naturally enough, Plowshare economics are presented in 'positive' ways: for instance, current prices for natural gas, set artificially by the Federal Power Commission, are viewed as given, constant, and reflective of true costs. The programme's costs and benefits are not compared to the alternative of deregulation, which would induce a great deal of private retrieval of new gas by conventional technologies.[3]

Such calculation has particular political effectiveness in a time of energy crisis, where the anxiety created by the problem compounds the difficulty of complex analysis demanded. Its casual and even enthusiastic discussion by great powers; its positive implication in a treaty on *non-proliferation*; its possible salience for an internationally shared 'crisis'; all contribute to the legitimisation of the idea of peaceful bombs. There is strong temptation to forego investment in other technologies when this one may have a joint product 'for free': a weapons capability.

While the original nuclear powers sought explicitly a weapons capability, the N+1 candidates present relatively little clear connection between their political goals and their technological developments. The result is unpredictability and the confounding of the ability to interact and plan intelligently, not least for the candidates themselves. As Van Cleave has written: 'For the first three nuclear weapons powers, civil nuclear programs grew out of the weapons programs. The point has now been reached where weapons programs can grow out of civil nuclear development'.[4] This may be a rare case of the popular fear of post-Trinity man, in which events follow technology. The original case of France is instructive. As Van Cleave quotes Lawrence Sheinman:

> The action of responsible political leadership was the last in a long chain of events . . . The question is not so much what induced France to take the nuclear plunge as it is a question of whether the eventual outcome could have been otherwise.[5]

Non-Proliferation by Carrot and Stick

Within its hardware focus, the American approach has been dichotomous and this dichotomy is embodied in the NPT. The damage done is accepted rather than confronted. A carrot-and-stick strategy ensues. A distinction between peaceful and military atoms, rarely believed to have much validity, is nonetheless made solemnly. American policy-makers are resigned to the inevitability of proliferation of nuclear capabilities of some sort, and subsequently choose not opposition but selective encouragement. The hope seems to be that the United States might gain some sort of control over the nature and rate of proliferation by being in the van of its proponents. The United States has narrowed explicitly its opposition to only military applications, but such a nice distinction is technically dubious.

The American position was presented frankly by Adrian Fisher, Deputy Director of the Arms Control and Disarmament Agency, before the Eighteen Nation Disarmament Conference. He acknowledged that, 'the development of nuclear explosives for any purpose by a state which does not now possess nuclear explosives would inevitably involve the acquisition by the state of a nuclear weapons capability'. Yet the American position was that,

> if and when peaceful applications of nuclear explosives that are permissible under test-ban treaty limitations prove technically and economically feasible, nuclear weapons states should make available to other states nuclear explosive services for peaceful applications. Such a service would consist of performing the desired nuclear detonation under appropriate international observation, with the nuclear device remaining under the custody and control of the state which performs the service.[6]

The proliferatory implications of this position came to fruition in the NPT because attractive applications appeared to exist on territories of some non-nuclear weapons states. Such applications raised problems of formal and informal arms control hardly discussed with the same intensity as have the possible projects. While the Treaty made no attempt to deal with problems of control, Article V pledged, vaguely, the projects.

Many experts are sceptical that much of weapons usefulness could be learned by the host country from such events. This may indeed be true, for example, for India, since what the hosts of a nascent programme can learn depends on where they are on the learning curve toward achieving the technology. A very knowledgeable Australian, for instance, has suggested privately that there is 'no way' his country could allow the United States to so completely control the firing of a project such as the proposed West Australian harbour excavation without learning something useful about weapons applications. In any case, should such applications be successful in any respect, enormous pressures will be created within host countries for increasing local control over future shots, in the name of 'sovereignty'. They will be difficult to deny, since the superpowers have labelled the technology 'peaceful'.

If there is a difference between military and civilian bombs, it may be that the military type are developed usually with particular delivery systems in mind. (Perhaps delivery systems are blissfully absent from the minds of peaceful bomb developers.) Yet such questions were largely foregone in the negotiation of the NPT as the American aims became quite limited, leading to a similar condition in the analysis offered; the world has been seen as made up of nuclear and non-nuclear nations, the latter amenable to being bought off by the former. William Bader offered a different view: 'Better the United States deal with the highly particular circumstances which motivate a country to want nuclear weapons rather than vainly try to deny them the technology'.[7]

While the United States has not dealt with 'particular circumstances', it has, in a sense, abandoned with alacrity the policy of 'vainly trying to deny them the technology', by offering to give it away, as in President Nixon's Middle East tour. The great powers have attempted to assuage the feelings in non-nuclear states that non-proliferation is an attempt to gain nuclear monopoly. The great powers are responding to a 'historical inevitability' that is not clear except as self-fulfilling prophecy.[8]

The NPT encourages underdeveloped nations to allocate their limited resources to what has been, to date, the premature expectation of the benefits of nuclear technology. The NPT uses nuclear development aid as its carrot in approaching the non-nuclears. Those who sign will receive aid in developing their peaceful nuclear capabilities and those who do not, will not. Article IV, Section 2, reads

All the Parties to the Treaty undertake to facilitate, and have the right to participate in, the fullest possible exchange of equipment, materials and scientific and technological information for the peaceful uses of nuclear energy. Parties to the Treaty in a position to do so shall also cooperate in contributing to the further development of the application of nuclear energy for peaceful purposes, especially in the territories of non-nuclear-weapon States Party to the Treaty, with due consideration for the needs of the developing areas of the world.

These 'developing areas' bear resemblance to the then non-existent 'power-starved' areas to which President Eisenhower referred in creating 'Atoms for Peace' over two decades ago. Even in today's energy crisis, there is little compelling in the vision of nuclear development in the poorer areas of the world. Much of the underdeveloped world's petroleum shortage is for agricultural and chemical applications rather than energy. As for the remaining energy shortfall, it is not clear that nuclear sources are much of a substitute, especially if all economic and military costs are calculated against the expected benefits. Before deciding to encourage and export nuclear capabilities, the economics should be carefully analysed and found to be positive.

The carrot-and-stick approach to proliferation, begun in the 1953 Eisenhower speech and reaching culmination in the NPT, assumes that small nations will be, by engaging in nuclear activities, caught up in 'solving' their economic problems with the new technology. Scepticism is called for not only by the sorry historical records but because of the nature of the technology itself, particularly the case of explosives. The goals of a civilian applications programme are those that create modernity, economy, and physical and tactical mobility in a weapons programme: improving the yield-to-weight ratio, miniaturisation, 'ruggedising', radiation 'cleanliness', and the development of data about bomb effects phenomenology.

Finally, the very logic of the NPT is proliferatory. The distinction between the nuclear weapons 'haves' and 'have-nots' is well known. The NPT suggests a newer, vaguer, but not visibly less compelling distinction to prestige hungry leaders: between those engaged in nuclear activities and those not. The gamble of the NPT is that engaging in non-nuclear weapons activities will satisfy appetites for weapons; the danger is that they will be whetted. Gains to big-power intelligence gathering will be scant consolation as certain activities, involving the use of explosives, blur the line between the peaceful and the military.

The Control of Testing

When President Eisenhower proposed the test-ban talks in 1958, he suggested that any agreement should deal separately with weapons tests and peaceful-purposes detonations. Detection and control of detonations were very difficult problems, both technologically and politically for the negotiators. The Eisenhower proposal complicated the problems for 'how could the purpose of an explosion be determined and how would it be possible to be certain that a device allegedly designed to produce a huge natural cavity would not also have military applications?'.[9]

Jacobson and Stein noted as early as 1966 that the military applicability of Plowshare-like activities was an explicit problem:

> ... there has always been a significant link between the Plowshare experiments and the attempt to achieve 'clean' bombs or neutron weapons, for using nuclear detonations as a means of excavation would be practical only if one could minimize the radioactivity resulting from the detonation ... the Plowshare experiments could have been in the very forefront of nuclear weapons research since they involved minimizing the amount of fission products in nuclear explosions.[10]

A possible next step in arms control agreement, then, the cessation of all weapons testing, implies also the cessation of civilian explosive applications. Myers and others have attempted to revive the possibility of a comprehensive test-ban.[11] Most of the debate that preceded the original Test Ban,[12] similar to that now revived, revolved around re-assurance against clandestine testing by the other side. Impetus was provided in the original case by the desire to halt atmospheric fallout but this is no longer significant. Underground testing was exempt from the original ban because the threat of fallout was not a factor and because of the detection dilemma. Low-yield underground tests are progressively difficult to detect and distinguish from natural seismicity.[13]

Some authorities favouring a comprehensive ban argue that the passage of over a decade has lessened the military gains to be had from further testing in what is now a 'mature' technology. Those of Weisner's and York's persuasion may suggest, for instance, that the remaining potential for weight reduction through device design, holding yield constant, is approaching a limit. Any possible marginal gain should be less significant for entire systems into which these warheads fit. The benefits of device weight reduction for an entire missile may have reached a point where further reduction is not an important contribution to the entire system's performance. Indeed, calculated against the cost of system re-design, the contribution may be negative.

The difficulty with this argument is that if it is valid an international agreement to ban the useless should not be necessary. It would be worse than ironic if, in serving the cause of peace and arms control, international agreements channelled military research in more destructive directions. Such events are not, however, unknown in this century.

124

But it is in fact not at all clear that testing is no longer important militarily. Diminished weight-to-yield ratios, for instance, allow much greater flexibility in the development of the entire weapons system, including a range of delivery systems. Weight reduction is important in achieving greater missile accuracy, which will not stop with the astonishing CEPs of today. The importance of effects testing will not diminish, especially as newer systems evolve. Testing is important for considerations of safety. Since warheads are made in lots, with demand for command and control effectiveness of 100 per cent, proof testing by random detonation of lot samples is necessary, particularly when a system is complex and tooling variation in one component may produce disaster particularly for persons in the vicinity.[14]

What we can say, in sum, is not very satisfactory. Leaving aside questions of military significance, if one is committed to the cessation of testing, then the elimination of Plowshare, whatever its possible benefits or importance for NPT, is likely to be perceived as a small price to pay. As Brooks and Myers have suggested, perhaps ruefully:

> Statements made by persons associated with the U.S. Atomic Energy Commission, its contractors, and industries involved in nonmilitary applications of nuclear explosives (and their equivalents in other nations) tend to be sanguine about the prospects. Persons whose dominant interest is arms control and the nonproliferation of nuclear weapons tend to give more emphasis to the factors indicating that the economic utility will not be substantial. Those who are concerned with the preservation of the environment weigh heavily the possible costs associated with various polluting effects.[15]

Hopefully, this discussion has suggested the possibility of an alternative and more differentiated approach to these problems. But the nature of Plowshare-like activities compounds the difficulty of evaluation because military bombs and civilian bombs are not, to put it mildly, clearly different. Although certain differences of interest may exist, for example, in the relationship between yield, weight, and radioactivity, these are only differences of emphasis. In any case, information about the 'wrong' end of the spectrum of effects may not be without use to a military programme. For instance, particular problems such as the minimisation of radioactivity and weight in the low yields may be of major interest to tactical weapons programmes.[16] One is led, then, to question current attempts at arms control which emphasise the limitations of particular technologies. In any case, they are not that particular.

India: the N+½

The Moscow accord of July 1974 not to test underground above 150 kt. after 1976, appears to have thrilled Richard Nixon and Henry Kissinger, but it bans almost nothing. Rather, it points the direction of future weapons development. Neither the NPT nor this accord deals with issues of 'vertical proliferation', a frequent concern of non-nuclear weapons states. Not only does a 150 kt. limit allow the superpowers to work on their interests; it would also pose no difficulty, if it were extended, for states such as India, which tested a shot of one-tenth that yield.

The Gandhian tradition made it inevitable that the Indian bomb would appear under an aegis of 'peaceful application'. Thus India has, in some degree, succeeded in blurring the issue of the 'N+1 Country'; perhaps it is the 'N+½'. While an Indian scholar, Chandrasekharo Rao, has acknowledged that 'the recent explosion of a nuclear device is a major event in the history of Indian strategic evolution', he also suggests that 'there is no warrant to conclude either that what was tested in Rajasthan was a bomb, or that the next Indian test would necessarily be with a bomb'. While the writer regretfully acknowledges 'the tendency for other powers not to distinguish between an explosion for peaceful purposes and one designed to lead to the acquisition of the bomb', he himself does not provide such a distinction, except to refer to his country's bomb as a 'device'.[17] A lesson well learned from the United States!

The Indian situation is an example of the prophecy of inevitability becoming self-fulfilling. Neither the United States nor Canada are pleased, yet their aid was critical in the past. As to the future, Rao is blunt:

> [Bleak] . . . is the prospect for the continued supply of nuclear material . . . these developments might means a continued dependence of Moscow . . . It is more than probable, however, that in order to prevent India from moving towards Moscow, Western countries might still soften their policies.[18]

The implications of current events are grave and unclear, but it is difficult to believe that India will stop merely with a 'device'. As George Quester wrote a few years ago: 'One can easily imagine India half entering the nuclear club with a simple plutonium bomb, and then, feeling desperately obliged to tidy up its membership, its "retaliatory second strike", with missiles and hydrogen bombs'.[19]

Such a 'tidying up' would not be a casual decision. This internal effort made for the bomb programme may well seem 'wasted' to many Indians without a delivery programme to make the capability a serious factor for adversaries. This will not be cheap, especially for a nation in India's present straits. Hence, even if based on incorrect estimates of weapons costs, further uncertainty about the Indian economy and polity may have international consequences fully as serious as those conjured up by visions of arms races and new balances of power in Asia. It must, however, be admitted that the question of the costs of a *serious* deterrent is no longer one that can be dealt with by the expression of a few reasonable generalities. Because the costs of weapons and delivery systems are now far less than generally believed, the particular situations of N+1 candidates must be subjected to empirical analysis. This water is further muddied by accomplishing much of the weapons development under civilian-applications programmes, which increase, of course, the attraction of such 'peaceful' development.

Incredibility Breeds Proliferation

The errors of the powerful tend sometimes to become 'correct' because they are put into effect. Notions about the inevitability of proliferation have formed the behaviour of the powerful and, consequently, proliferation becomes increasingly 'inevitable'. There may, however, still be alternatives in helping the monster to grow up, in the wistful hope of being able to control its maturity by right of parentage.

The alternatives to continuing 'arms control by filial piety' involve the hard work of Bader's admonition to deal with the circumstances that motivate a country to go nuclear.[20] These circumstances, however, are 'particular'. Every potential N+1 country has security concerns that are serious, particularly to that country. In the case of the NPT, Rao complains, with good reason, that it does not 'expressly provide . . . for protection to a non-nuclear weapons state against a threat from a nuclear weapons state'.[21]

Westerners can muster excellent arguments against, for example, India's attempting nuclearly to deter China, including the asymmetries of development, resources, and geography. In addition, attempting to deter a Chinese attack may provoke it. Surprisingly, this relatively reasonable ground for attack has yet to occur. It should be unnecessary to point out that this happy state is not inevitable. It is a political environment which includes insecurity about China which spurs the Indian programme. However, a spurred programme, relatively limited at the outset can induce a worsening of relations, especially when doubts are held about the effectiveness of command and control and force protection. The logic remains that, as such a programme *approaches but does not reach* strategic effectiveness, it will tend to induce a harsh political and military response. This did not happen to the Soviet and Chinese infant programme notably because they were 'preserved' by factors external to the immediate strategic environments. It is important to ask whether such factors will be salient in the case, for example, of the Indian programme. I have not seen evidence that this question has been seriously considered.

The extraordinary systems nature of such weapons is often ignored. The bomb demands integration into delivery systems, which demand integration into systems for command and control, force protection, and accident avoidance. All this must be integrated within a weapons posture, which must be part of the general political goals of the nation. Although the technology may be disseminated and the costs have come down, there can be little doubt that the cardinal issues in national nuclear forces policy retain much of their historic difficulty.[22]

Yet to Indians and Japanese, concerned about nuclear coercion by China, the independent deterrent is an option that must be considered seriously because Soviet and/or American guarantees will lose all credibility in the 1980s, with the evolution of Chinese delivery systems. Speculations about being willing to defend Tokyo even at cost to San Francisco cannot be and do not deserve to be taken seriously.

It may be argued that a major proliferatory event was the accord limiting the wrong kinds of systems in SALT, namely, missile defence. Not only did the superpowers choose to limit weapons that kill other weapons and thus reduce the dangers of cataclysm rather than limit weapons that kill people in Premier Kosygin's terms of a decade ago. SALT also channelled arms competition toward the most destructive of weapons, with no measurable increases in anyone's security. Thus recent Soviet-American accords confirm and exacerbate the dire predictions of ABM defenders a half-dozen years ago. The failure to go to defence also gave comfort to the dubious French programme, for not only could the United States not defend New York in order to defend Paris, but to the East, perhaps the French *could* tear off an arm of the Russian bear, and thus deter him. If such calculations are valid for traditional American allies such as the French, they are more so for Indians and Japanese.

It should be needless to say that indefatigable diplomacy is called for in order to alleviate the political, social, and economic sources of tensions between nations. This is, however, a piety that calls for a long, complex, and rarely emotionally satisfying series of processes. It will not be accomplished by shuttle. A re-evaluation on the part of all the great powers of missile defence, as an *alternative* to offensive weapons, may be due.[23]

Notes

1. Avigdor Haselkorn, 'Israel: From an Option to a Bomb in the Basement?' in Robert M. Lawrence and Joel Larus (eds.), *Nuclear Proliferation: Phase II* (Lawrence, Kansas, 1974), pp. 149-82.
2. K. Subrahmanyam, 'India, Keeping the Option Open' in *ibid.*, p. 125.
3. See, for example, Robert B. Helms, *Natural Gas Regulation* (Washington, D.C., 1974).
4. William Van Cleave, 'Nuclear Technology and Weapons' in Lawrence and Larus, *op. cit.*, p. 58.
5. *Ibid.*, p. 59; Lawrence Sheinman, *Atomic Energy Policy in France under the Fourth Republic* (Princeton, New Jersey, 1965), p. 215.
6. 280th ENDC Plenary Meeting, 9 August 1966.
7. William Bader, *The United States and the Spread of Nuclear Weapons* (New York, 1968), p. 127.
8. The text of the NPT indicates clearly that American is not to present blanket opposition but to encourage selectively, and thus gain influence over the growth of nuclear capabilities. American enthusiasm for NPT was implied by President Lyndon Johnson's hailing it as a move that 'will truly deserve to be recorded as the most important towards peace since the founding of the United Nations'. He promised to 'share our nuclear research fully – and . . . without reservation'. Address to the UN General Assembly, 12 June 1968.
9. Harold Karan Jacobson and Eric Stein, *Diplomats, Scientists and Politicians* (Ann Arbor, Michigan, 1966), p. 91.
10. *Ibid.*, pp. 35-6.
11. Henry K. Myers, 'Extending the Nuclear Test Ban', *Scientific American*, CCVI (1972), pp. 13-23; and 'Comprehensive Test Ban Treaty: Grounds for Objection Diminish', *Science*, CLXXV (1972), pp. 283-6; Robert Neild and J. P. Ruina, 'A Comprehensive Ban on Nuclear Testing', *Science*, CLXXV (1972), pp. 140-6; Gerald Wick, 'Nuclear Explosion Seismology: Improvements in Detection', *Science*, CLXXV (1972), pp. 1095-7. See also Howard C. Rodean, *Nuclear Explosion Seismology* (US Atomic Energy Commission, Division of Technical Information, Washington, D.C., 1971); and US Congress, Joint Committee on Atomic Energy, Subcommittee on Research, Development and Radiation, *Status of Current Technology to Identify Seismic Events as National or Man-Made*, 92nd Congress, 1st Session, 1971.
12. See, for example, Robert Gilpin, *American Scientists and Nuclear Weapons Policy* (Princeton, New Jersey, 1962); Henry A. Kissinger, 'Nuclear Testing and the Problems of Peace', *Foreign Affairs*, XXXVII (1958), pp. 1-18; James H. McBride, *The Test Ban Treaty* (Chicago, 1967); Jacobson and Stein, *op. cit.*, Edward Teller and Albert Latter, *Our Nuclear Future* (New York, 1958); Jerome Weisner and Herbert York, 'National Security and the Nuclear Test-Ban', *Scientific American*, CCXI (1964), pp. 27-35; US Congress, Senate Committee on Foreign Relations, Subcommittee on Disarmament, *Hearings: Control and Reduction of Armanents*, 85th Congress, 2nd Session, 1958.
13. Myers, for example, argues that advances in the state of the seismologist's art now permit the distinction between natural and artificial phenomena. Myers, 'Extending the Nuclear Test Ban', *loc. cit.*, and Myers, 'Comprehensive Test Ban Treaty', *loc. cit.*
14. A practitioner's discussion is found in R. W. Henderson, 'Making Nuclear Weapons', *Ordinance*, XLV (1961), pp. 623-5.

15. David R. Brooks and Henry Myers, 'Plowshare Evaluation' in Bennett Boskey and Mason Willrich (eds.), *Nuclear Proliferation: Prospects for Control* (New York, 1970), p. 100.
16. See, for example, 'Over the Threshold', *Army*, July 1972, pp. 17-21, which notes renewed discussion of tactical nuclear weapons for European defence.
17. R. V. R. Chandrasekharo Rao, 'Proliferation and the Indian Test: A View from India', *Survival*, XVI (1974), p. 210.
18. *Ibid.*, pp. 212-13.
19. George Quester, 'India contemplates the Bomb', *Bulletin of the Atomic Scientists*, XXVI (1970), p. 14.
20. Bader, *op. cit.*, p. 127.
21. Rao, *op. cit.*, p. 212.
22. See Albert Wohlstetter, 'Nuclear Sharing: NATO and the N+1 Country' in Richard N. Rosecrance (ed.), *The Dispersion of Nuclear Weapons* (New York, 1964), pp. 186-221.
23. The author is indebted to Bob Lawrence for comments on the text.

9. NUCLEAR ENERGY – FACT VERSUS MYTH

Bernard T. Feld

Some Facts about Nuclear Reactors

We adopt, as the standard reactor, the power level of 1,000 megawatts thermal = 1 GWt. As a conversion factor to produced electric power, we use 1 watt (We) $\cong$ 2.5 Wt.

1. Stored Radioactivity: In the steady state of operation, 1 Wt of fission power implies a level of stored fission product radioactivity of 1 curie (3.7×10^{10} disintegrations/sec). Thus, 1 GWt $\to$ 1,000 megacuries (or 1,000 tonnes of radium equivalent). Very roughly, this is equivalent to the total radioactivity (prompt plus fission products) produced by the exposion of one Hiroshima or Nagasaki type atomic bomb (10-20 kilotons of TNT equivalent). If distributed over a fair-sized city, this could result in some 10,000 to 100,000 deaths. It should, of course, be noted that the radioactivity would, in this case, all be delayed, that is not containing the prompt component associated with a nuclear weapon explosion, so that large-scale evacuation of the population – if rapid enough – could reduce the lethal effects. Nevertheless, the level of radiation would probably be high enough so that, even under ideal arrangements for the evacuation of the exposed populations, the number of individuals suffering radiation sickness, not to speak of genetic damage, would still fall within the above-mentioned range.

2. Plutonium Production: Let R be the breeding ratio (number of plutonium nuclei produced per nucleus undergoing fission). Depending on factors such as the reactor type and design, $0 < R < 1.5$. For some reactor designs now in use or planned,

> LWR (light water reactor), $R \cong 0.4$
> HTGR (high temperature gas-cooled reactor), $R \overset{\sim}{>} 0.5$
> LMFBR (liquid metal-cooled fast breeder reactor), $R \cong 1\text{-}1.2$
> HWR (heavy water reactor), $0.5 \geqslant R \geqslant \text{'O'}$.

Among the above-listed reactor types, only the HWR uses natural (unenriched) uranium as its fuel element. The value R = 'O' corresponds to the assumption that the spent fuel elements are discarded (buried) without any attempt to recover the produced plutonium; nor need it be separated from the fission products. Such an apparently 'wasteful' use

131

of uranium adds very little to the cost of electricity to the consumer; nor is it precluded by any scarcity of available uranium ores.

In terms of R, then, our standard reactor (1 GWt) produced 400 R kilograms of plutonium per year, or 1 GWe → R tonnes Pu/yr. Note that, at 5-10 kg. per bomb, this is sufficient for 1-200 × R atomic bombs per year. The present rate of plutonium production, confined to the main technologically developed nations, amounts to perhaps a few tonnes per year. However, this is expected to grow rapidly, as indicated in Table 1.

Table 1:   IAEA Nuclear Power Projections and Approximate Equivalent Potential Bomb Production Rates

	1980		2000	
	GWe	bombs/yr (R ~ ½)	GWe	bombs/yr (R ~ ½)
Less Developed Countries	25	1,000	750	30,000
Developed Countries	290	10,000	4,550	200,000

3. Fuel Costs – the Breeder Myth: At the current raw materials cost of $10-15 per pound of uranium oxide, only around 5 per cent of the cost of the electricity to the consumer comes from the cost of the fuel. Hence raising the fuel cost to around $100/lb. (which would increase the economically usable uranium supplies by a factor of around 100) would only raise the cost of electricity by 50 per cent. The cost of extraction of uranium from sea water probably falls within these limits. Considering that the uranium present in sea water amounts to around seven parts per million, the available supply of uranium from this source is sufficient to supply projected demands – even on the most 'optimistic' of current estimates – for centuries to come.

Some Facts about Energy Consumption

1. Current Figures: For the purposes of our discussion, we divide the current (1972) world population of around 3.6 billion into the less developed countries (LDCs), which contain two-thirds of the total or 2.4 billions, and the developed countries (DCs) with one-third or 1.2 billion. Actually, affluence, as measured by any one of a number of possible indicators, such as *per capita* energy consumption, GNP and rate of population increase, does not vary in a continuous fashion from country to country, but shows an appreciable and unfortunately growing gap between the rich third and poor two-thirds of the world, so that the division of the world's peoples between the DCs of the affluent

'North' and the LDCs of the underdeveloped 'South' is an operationally meaningful one. The current average rates of power consumption (energy used for *all* purposes) are given in Table 2.

Table 2:   Current (1972) World Energy Consumption

	Average (KWt per person)	Population (10^9)		total (1,000 GWt = 10^{13} KWh/yr)	
LDCs	0.2	2.4	(67%)	0.5	(9.5%)
DCs	4	1.2	(33%)	4.8	(91%)
worldwide	1.5	3.6		5.3	
Indonesia	0.1	0.1	(2.8%)	0.01	(0.2%)
United States	12	0.2	(5.5%)	2.4	(45%)

To provide an idea of the spread in energy consumption rates within the two larger categories, we also give the figures for Indonesia and the United States. The numbers speak for themselves.

2. Distribution among Sources and Projections into the Future: The above-mentioned IAEA projections also break down energy use into its fuel sources. The numbers for 1980 (which may be considered as reasonably realistically representative of the immediate future, since most plants planned for 1980 are already being designed) and for the year 2000 (much more speculative) are shown in Table 3.

Table 3:   IAEA Energy Use Projection

Fuel	1980 (1000 GWt)	2000 (1000 GWt)	Factor of Increase
solid (coal)	2.4	4.1	1.7
liquid (oil)	4.1	5.2	1.3
natural gas	2.0	3.3	1.7
hydro	0.6	1.6	2.7
nuclear	0.6	9.4	16.0
	9.7	23.6	2.4

We shall return in the next sections to the question of the realism and/ or reasonableness, or lack thereof, in these projections.

Alternative Models for the Year 2000

Based on the current rate of worldwide population growth — approximately 2.3 per cent or a 30-year doubling time — the world population in the year 2000 will be around 7 billion. This figure is not very dependent on our assumptions as to the success or failure of population control measures in the next few decades, since demographic factors, associated with the changing patterns of age distribution in the population would assure continued population growth, even if the LDCs were today to achieve the desideratum of 'zero population growth' (each couple just reproducing itself). For the sake of simplified computation, and in the spirit of and within the accuracy of our projections, we assume a total world population of 8 billion in the year 2000, of which 2 billion are in the DCs and 6 billion in the LDCs (reflecting the considerably greater rate of population increase in the LDCs).

We now consider three models for the growth in energy production (and consumption) up to the year 2000. These are chosen to emphasise the most important aspects of the problems of reconciling actual possibilities with real needs, and also to highlight the necessity of distinguishing between the hopes and aspirations (demands) and the undeniable requirements (needs) of mankind in respect to energy.

1. Uniform Growth (*status quo*) Model: We assume a continuation of the pattern of the past century, with a 5 per cent yearly increase in energy consumption (14-year doubling time), uniformly applied world-wide (i.e., no distinction between the growth rates of the LDCs and the DCs). In the 28 years between 1972 and 2000, we have two doubling times, or a four-fold increase over the rates of total energy consumption shown in Table 2, resulting in:

Table 4a: Energy Consumption in Year 2000

Model a

	Total (1,000 GWt)	Average (KWt per capita)
LDCs	1.9	0.32
DCs	19.0	9.6
Worldwide	21.0	2.6

Two comments are in order. First, comparing the worldwide energy consumption figure of 21,000 GWt with the total (23.6) in the IAEA projection of Table 3, we note that that projection is probably based on a similar model. Our suspicion is that this is, in fact, the case, and that the distribution as between the different energy sources has been determined in a somewhat arbitrary fashion, with the main input being the IAEA projection of nuclear energy output which, on their estimate, should amount to around 40 per cent of the total energy production in the year 2000. Even accepting the projected total, there is considerable leeway in the possible means for its achievement; some other possibilities will be noted in the next section. Secondly, since this model assumes a uniform pattern of growth in total energy consumption, the fractions projected for the LDCs and the DCs remain as given in Table 3. However, owing to the greater rate of population growth of the LDCs, the *per capita* energy consumption gap increases on this model, growing from a factor of 20 in 1972 to a factor of 30 projected in the year 2000. This is a dramatic illustration of the problem faced by the LDCs: even running like mad, they continue to fall behind.

2. Pangloss Model (best of all possible worlds): We assume that necessary measures are taken to equalise the worldwide average energy consumption, aiming at a uniform figure of 4 KWt *per capita*. This assumes the immediate adoption of a policy of zero energy growth on the part of the DCs, with the entire effort going into raising the level of the LDCs. The relevant figures are given in Table 4b.

Table 4b: Energy Consumption in the Year 2000

	Model b	
	Total (1,000 GWt)	Factor over 1972
LDCs	24.0	50.0
DCs	8.0	1.7
Worldwide	32.0	6.0

   (i)   The relatively small, 70 per cent increase in energy consumption for the DCs arising only as a result of the same population increase, is far less than is now envisioned by any of the governments concerned. This would clearly require very considerable and unaccustomed restraint on the part of the affluent peoples. The total increase in energy capacity of the DCs is easily within the range of available resources; the entire projected need (8,000 GWt) is even less than the total nuclear energy capacity envisioned for the year 2000 by the IAEA (Table 3).

   (ii)   On the other hand, the required increase in energy available to the LDCs is immense. It would consume the *entire* available energy projected by the IAEA (Table 3). More significant, it would require 5½ doublings in 28 years, or a 5-year doubling time (14 per cent annual increase) of energy capacity in the LDCs. This is clearly an unrealistic goal in the contemporary world.

3. Optimistic but possible Model (where there is life, there is hope): Between the two models described above, there must be some middle ground, in which it may be envisaged that the gap between the DCs and the LDCs will be narrowed even if not completely overcome. The model

expounded below is one of many possible ones, leaning admittedly toward the optimistic end of the spectrum. Even if it may not be easily attainable, it is useful to present is as a not completely unrealistic goal towards which it is worth aiming.

We assume zero energy growth for the DCs, as in Model b. For the LDCs, we aim at an average *per capita* energy consumption of 1 KWt which, coupled with the adoption of a life-style appropriate to a labour-intensive form of agriculture and industrialisation, should provide the Third World with the possibilities for attaining a life standard commensurate with the potentialities arising from the humane application of modern science and technology. The model is summarised in Table 4c.

Table 4c: Energy Consumption in Year 2000

	Model c	
	Total (1,000 GWt)	Factor over 1972
LDCs	6.0	12.5
DCs	8.0	1.7
Worldwide	14.0	2.7

(i)   For the DCs, the model is the same as (b) above.

(ii)   For the LDCs, the required rate of increase is 9 per cent per year (8-year doubling time — 3½ doublings in 28 years) which is large, but not completely outside of what has previously been attained by countries like Japan and China. We note that the total energy need, anticipated in this model for the year 2000, is considerably less than that projected by the IAEA for the year 2000 (Table 2). In fact, it could *all* be achieved without the need for any nuclear fission energy.

(iii)   However, we must also consider the capital investment cost that would be required to accomplish the contemplated raising of power consumption in the LDCs. We may adopt as a rough, but reasonably realistic estimate of the average capital cost of installation of power producing capacity the figure of $1 per watt (Wt). This figure varies little with the type of fuel consumption under consideration. On this basis, the increase by 5,500 GWt in power consumption in the LDCs between the present (500 GWt) Table 2 and that projected in this model (Table 4c), would require a capital investment of $5,500 billion over 28 years, or $200 billion per year. It is significant as a measure of the problems involved in attaining this goal, that the current world expenditure for armaments is roughly this same figure of $200 billion. On the other hand, the increased income of the oil-producing countries, resulting from the recent increases in oil prices, is also within a factor of 3 or 4 of this figure. The reader may draw his own conclusions as to the prospects for making available the capital investment resources required for the achievement of the levels envisaged in this model.

Some Other Aspects of the Energy Dilemma

We set forth, in the following, a number of corollary questions associated, especially, with the role of nuclear energy in the coming decades. While we suggest some provisional answers, our aim is more to raise the issues than to make any attempt at their settlement.

Fission Energy – Who Wants It?

From the above analysis, primarily the DCs want it, but only if they propose to continue to increase their rate of energy consumption into the indefinite future. Any of the reasonable needs of the LDCs, at least until the year 2000, can be met with conventional, readily available sources, not to speak of such prospects as solar, geothermal and fusion energy in the longer term. Note, however, that if fission energy is really demanded, its production via the HWR route (R = 'o') avoids the Pu proliferation problem.

How About the LMFBR? Who Needs It?

As noted in the preceding, the need for breeder reactors is based on the assumption of a scarcity of economically recoverable uranium – an assumption which does not appear to be borne out by the facts. At the very least, there should be serious reconsideration of the present commitment of the technologically advanced nations to an energy economy based on plutonium breeding. Such reconsideration should take place *now*, before we become irrevocably committed to the breeder route.

Aside from Political and Economic Considerations, are there any Physical Limits on Energy Uses in the Future?

(i)   Oil supplies are severely limited, and should therefore be conserved for special future needs such as protein production and the extraction of petroleum-based chemicals – certainly not for transportation or heating. The same goes for natural gas.

(ii)   Coal supplies are much more abundant; but we must learn to use them in a non-polluting fashion. Programmes of research and development for coal gassification and liquefaction processes should be pursued as a matter of the highest priority.

(iii)   Nuclear fusion is potentially an unlimited energy source – the amount of heavy water in the oceans is enough for all envisageable

137

energy needs for many centuries — but its technical feasibility is yet to be established. There is also an associated radioactive problem (more amenable to technical solution than that associated with fission power), and the problem of 'thermal pollution'. However, fusion also has, in the long run, the possibility of direct conversion into electric power, thereby greatly diminishing the thermal pollution problem (increased efficiency).

(iv)   There are thermodynamic limits to the total amount of energy consumption that can be tolerated by the atmosphere, before the onset of drastic climatological changes such as the melting of the polar ice caps. We are already within a factor of less than 100 of such limits. Another problem, relating to the burning of fossil fuels (coal and oil) relates to the release of carbon dioxide into the atmosphere, leading to the 'greenhouse effect' — heating up of the earth due to the absorption of infra-red radiation from the earth, thereby upsetting the earth's energy balance between radiation received from the sun and radiated back into space.

(v)   The Malthusian nightmare. All possible solutions are predicated on the ability to limit the rate of population growth, so that any increase in world resources, especially as applied in the developing world, are not overtaken by the necessity to feed more mouths. Note that population, food and energy are intimately connected, since modern agricultural methods of food production are all very energy-intensive: the 'Green Revolution' needs large quantities of fertiliser and water, the provision of both of which require large inputs of energy.

Hopeful Aspects

Most of the foregoing sections have been relatively pessimistic as to future prospects. Do I have anything good to say? There are in fact a number of very hopeful prospects for meeting our energy needs for the rest of this century, short of widespread use of nuclear fission energy (which is both feasible and available, if used sensibly and if it were adopted as a temporary expedient, to be phased out as soon as more reasonable sources become available).

1. Coal — as noted, supplies are abundant. The problem is atmospheric pollution, which can be averted by the development of the technology of gassification and liquefaction, especially *in situ*.

2. Geothermal energy — utilisation of the earth's thermal gradient (increase in temperatures in going towards the earth's centre) is being vigorously pursued in many laboratories. This is an interesting and hopeful source.

3. Solar energy — a finite but very important source, especially of small units for limited use. As a rough gross figure, we note that the

absorption of the solar energy falling on 1 per cent of the earth's surface, utilised with an efficiency of 3 per cent (not unreasonable with currently available technology), will yield a total of approximately 10,000 GW (only about twice the current world energy consumption rates, see Table 2). On the other hand, limited as it is in quantity, solar energy is mainly available where it is most needed — in the underdeveloped 'south'. And it is far less polluting than other available energy sources.

4. The problems of the transportation of energy over large distances and the use of energy for transport can both be solved by the development of methods for the conversion of thermal energy into free hydrogen or into hydrogen-active compounds. Work is in progress in this area, but it should be pursued with greater vigour.

5. Wild blue yonder solutions — research on the availability of space technology, for solar energy absorption, for dispersal of waste energy without affecting the earth's thermal balance and so on, is only in its infancy. Although these applications are obviously not relevant to any discussion of energy problems of the twentieth century, they may be very relevant for considerations that go much beyond the year 2000.

Conclusion

If we are smart enough not to blow ourselves up en route, we should be able to make it into the twenty-first century.

10. FUELLING THE WESTERN WORLD'S REACTORS: PROBLEMS AND ISSUES

Victor Gilinsky

Introduction[1]

The purpose of this paper is to identify, and to provide background for discussion of broad security issues related to provision of nuclear fuel — in practice, enriched uranium — for the West's nuclear power programmes, in particular for those of Europe.

Advanced countries are planning to sharply increase their reliance on nuclear power to generate electricity over the next two decades, a period during which electricity production is expected to absorb an increasing fraction of primary energy. This trend to nuclear energy, already strongly under way, has been accentuated by the recent oil crisis: Western Europe, Japan, and the United States look to an accelerated installation of nuclear power plants to reduce dependence on imported oil.

Assuring supplies of uranium is an essential part of this strategy. In this regard, a wide spectrum of circumstances applies to the advanced countries. Large reserves are found in the United States, Canada, Australia, South Africa, and presumably in the Soviet Union; modest reserves are found in France and in some African countries economically associated with France; other Western European countries and Japan have essentially no domestic sources of uranium.

Although there is some uncertainty about the extent of the world's supply of cheap uranium, more important for the short term is that the number of major uranium ore producing states — and known potential major producers — is relatively small, probably smaller than the number of major oil producing states. The shift to nuclear power, therefore, implies for Western Europe and Japan not a reduced dependence on foreign sources of fuel, but a shift in fuel dependence.

Secure access to uranium enrichment services is also criticial. Almost all the nuclear power reactors to be installed in the remainder of the century will likely use enriched uranium fuel. The United States at present has the bulk of the world's uranium enrichment capacity; Western Europe has developed its own enrichment technology and plans to supply a substantial share of its enrichment needs after about

1980. Japan is just starting to develop the requisite technology.

The United States Atomic Energy Commission (USAEC) gaseous diffusion facilities currently supply almost the entire Western world's requirements for enriched uranium. A few years ago it seemed to many in the United States that this near monopoly could continue indefinitely. Since then the situation has changed considerably. USAEC enrichment capacity, even after presently planned expansion, will be inadequate to meet world needs soon after 1980. Since existing capacity is now largely committed and no firm plans have been made for further increases in American enrichment capacity, the USAEC has stopped taking orders for uranium enrichment services. Although the action was not unexpected, it nevertheless heightened concern throughout the Western countries over the future provision of uranium enrichment.

The question of how future world uranium enrichment requirements will be met is still open. Europeans and others are moving to secure an assured supply of enriched uranium in the 1980s from a variety of sources: the United States, Western Europe, and the Soviet Union.

There are now two major competing European organisations developing new enrichment capacity: the French-led Eurodif enterprise and the tripartite-sponsored (Britain-Federal Germany-Netherlands) Urenco enterprise.

The Soviet Union has also emerged as an actor on the uranium enrichment scene. With presumably substantial uranium enrichment capacity as a consequence of its military nuclear programme, but only a relatively small civilian nuclear power programme of its own, the Soviet Union has indicated a willingness to supply enrichment services to others on attractive terms.

Given the importance of energy, the political overtones of some of the new enrichment enterprises, and their potential military significance, the strategic importance of the competition among uranium enrichment enterprises is considerable. And, just as in the case of oil, the need for uranium to fuel reactors in the leading industrial countries will affect relationships between producing and consuming countries and may become a source of conflict.

Key nuclear fuel-related questions and issues facing Europeans are the following:

(a)   Are Europe's nuclear power plans consistent with Europe's nuclear fuel supply?

(b)   How can Europe assure itself of an adequate supply of the world's cheap uranium?

(c)   Are there possibilities for sharp price increases through collusion of suppliers, as in the case of oil?

(d)   How will Europe's need for uranium affect its relations with uranium producing countries?

(e) How can Europe assure itself of adequate access to uranium enrichment services? What will be the terms of sale?

(f) Who will supply the necessary capital for expansion of West European uranium enrichment capacity?

(g) To what extent can Europe rely on the United States or other non-European sources for future access to enrichment services?

(h) To what extent can Western Europe afford to rely on the Soviet Union as a major supplier of enriched uranium? What would be the political consequences?

Subsequent sections will outline the projected Western requirements for nuclear fuel and the assumptions on which these projections are based, and will briefly discuss future supply prospects.

Nuclear Electric Generating Capacity

Estimates for future uranium requirements and requirements for uranium enrichment services depend on a host of factors. Although our subsequent discussion will not be sensitive to the detailed forecasts, it is useful to exhibit some of the underlying assumptions.

Uranium demand forecasts depend most directly on forecasts for nuclear electric generating capacity and its expected average utilisation. These in turn depend on forecasts for total energy consumption and the associated total electric generating capacity.

For many years electric generating capacities in industrial countries have been doubling approximately every ten years. In the wake of the recent energy crisis, the earlier awakening to the environmental implications of continued growth in energy use, and reduced population estimates, it now appears that growth in total energy consumption and in electric generating capacity in advanced countries will be below earlier estimates. Nevertheless, there is a continued increasing trend toward use of energy in the form of electricity; even recent projections of electric generating capacity in advanced countries forecast a considerable degree of growth over the coming years.

An example of projected growth in total energy is provided by a February 1974 USAEC forecast for total American energy consumption and the portion to be consumed in the form of electricity, reproduced in Table 1. The relevant USAEC document presents four series of forecasts.[2] Table 1 displays an intermediate forecast, falling between the extremes of minimum and maximum growth, that assumes a general reduction in the growth rate of electricity use. Corresponding 1974 aggregate forecasts of nuclear electric generating capacity in the United States and in the rest of the world are given in Table 2. These indicate rapid growth for the rest of the century. It should be noted that many

142

Table 1: A 1974 Forecast of US Energy Consumption and Electric Generating Capacity*

	1960	1970	1980	1990	2000
Energy consumed *per capita* (million BTU *per capita* per year)	247	329	399	494	624
Fraction for electric generation	0.18	0.24	0.32	0.41	0.50
Electric generating capacity *per capita* (kilowatts *per capita*)	0.97	1.67	2.99	4.62	7.45
Electric generating capacity (thousands of megawatts)	168	341	680	1160	2020
Apparent capacity factor†	.49	.52	.49	.51	.52

* *Nuclear Power 1973-2000*, USAEC, WASH-1139 (74), February 1974.
† The average utilisation of capacity.

Table 2: A 1974 Forecast of US and World Nuclear Electric Generating Capacity* (thousands of megawatts)

	1970	1975	1980	1985	1990	1995	2000
US	6	47	102	250	475	760	1090
Non-US		45	140	387	780	1367	2130
World	6	92	242	637	1255	2127	3220

* *Nuclear Power 1973-2000*, USAEC, WASH-1139 (74), February 1974.

of the factors that depress total and electric energy growth — high fossil fuel costs, uncertain fossil fuel supplies, and increasing environmental constraints — in the long run favour increased dependence on nuclear power. In sum, advanced countries are turning to nuclear power to diversify fuel sources and to lower electrcity generation costs. For example, at $10 per barrel the fuel costs associated with an oil burning power plant are approximately 17 mills/kwh, and utilities have recently paid a good deal more than $10 per barrel. Of course, long-term oil prices could well be below that figure (or above it) since the price is determined by market controls rather than by any intrinsic production costs. The break-even cost for oil to compete with nuclear plants is about $4 per barrel.

Table 3a: A 1972 Forecast of Total Electric and Nuclear Capacity in Selected Countries* (thousands of megawatts: Nuclear portion in parentheses)

	1960	1970	1980	1990	2000
France	20.2 (0.03)	36.9 (1.65)	64.0 (10.0)	105.0 (40.0)	150.0 (90.0)
West Germany	25.9 (0.0)	49.0 (0.74)	101.0 (18.6)	166.0 (69.0)	227.0 (130.0)
Italy	16.3 (0.0)	30.0 (0.6)	59.0 (4.7)	102.0 (22.5)	150.0 (55.0)
Spain	6.38 (0.0)	17.24 (0.15)	32.0 (8.0)	57.5 (30.0)	101.4 (64.0)
United Kingdom	34.8 (0.30)	66.1 (4.16)	101.6 (18.9)	163.7 (64.2)	264.2 (130.0)
Other Western Europe	27.4 (0.0)	43.7 (0.4)	87.7 (19.3)	136.3 (54.6)	191.6 (99.4)
Total Western Europe	131.0 (0.3)	243.0 (7.7)	445.0 (79.5)	730.0 (280.0)	1094.0 (568.0)

* Taken from USAEC December 1972 forecasts. (The number of significant figures is clearly excessive for 1980 and beyond.)

Table 3b: A 1972 Forecast of Total Electric and Nuclear Capacity in Selected Countries (thousands of megawatts; Nuclear portion in parentheses)

	1960	1970	1980	1990	2000
Western Europe	131.0 (0.3)	243.0 (7.7)	445.0 (79.5)	730.0 (280.0)	1094.0 (568.0)
Soviet Union and Eastern Europe	104.0 (0.0)	273.5 (1.68)	690.0 (19.5)	1460.0 (146.0)	2300.0 (600.0)
Japan	- (0.0)	- (0.9)	- (31.9)	- (97.2)	- (195.0)
United States	174.7 (0.02)	349.2 (5.9)	631.9 (131.6)	1153.8 (508.0)	2012.1 (1202.0)
Canada	23.2 (0.0)	43.4 (0.2)	77.0 (11.5)	135.0 (33.0)	228.0 (87.0)
Other	26.0 (0.0)	59.0 (0.4)	141.0 (6.7)	351.0 (85.0)	830.0 (296.0)
Total world	542.0 (0.3)	1148.0 (16.8)	2138.0 (292.0)	3983.0 (1233.0)	7418.0 (3261.0)

144

Table 3 displays an earlier (1972) forecast of total electric generating capacity and of the nuclear portion for selected countries. While the detailed estimates are now changed, broad trends observed in the breakdown are still valid. As indicated in Table 3, the United States is expected to install a substantial fraction of world nuclear electric generating capacity. By comparison, the Soviet Union is expected to lag the United States by about ten years in installing nuclear reactors.

It should be emphasised that the range of forecasts has been suppressed in our tables; official forecasts indicate a fairly broad range of uncertainty after about 1980, growing to about a factor of two by the year 2000.

But a further word of caution is appropriate about relatively short-term forecasts. A comparison of current and earlier USAEC forecasts provides some perspective and suggests that on the whole little weight can be attached to forecasts more than ten years in advance. Perhaps most surprising is that the February 1974 'most favoured' forecast for 1980 (102,000 Mwe) is not only far below the forecast made about a year earlier (132,000 Mwe, reported in December 1972) but is well outside the earlier range of estimates (127,000-144,000 Mwe). Moreover, the 1974 range of estimates (85-112,000 Mwe) does not even overlap the range of December 1972 estimates. Predicting the future is clearly a risky occupation.

Reactor Strategies

To move from the electric generating capacities (such as those given in Table 2) to nuclear fuel requirements involves a series of further assumptions. Perhaps the most important additional assumptions relate to the type of nuclear reactors to be installed.[3] For our purposes — considering, say, the rest of the century — these include mainly US-type light water reactors (LWR)[4] which utilise low-enrichment uranium (about 3 per cent uranium-235); and to a lesser degree US- and European-type high temperature graphite-moderated reactors (HTGRs), which use medium- to high-enrichment uranium, up to 93 per cent uranium-235.

Other types of reactors have received attention, and it is useful to indicate why they are less significant for our purposes. The principal categories are:

(a) Heavy water reactors (HWR).
(b) British and French gas-cooled reactors (GCR and AGR).
(c) British steam generating heavy water reactors (SGHWR) which use ordinary (light) water for cooling and heavy water for moderation.
(d) Fast-breeder reactors (FBR).

Heavy water reactors have not had much success in advanced countries with the exception of Canada. Their principal appeal stems from their use of natural uranium and the independence they consequently offer from ties to uranium enrichment facilities. In the past, in view of the USAEC's effective world monopoly of uranium enrichment, this has meant independence from control by the United States. As a result, HWRs appealed to a number of independent-minded, less industrialised countries such as India, Argentina, and others. These reactors, although few in number, are disproportionately significant for their military potential: they can be refuelled during operation of the reactor and therefore for technical reasons lend themselves more easily to the production of plutonium for military purposes. (The plutonium for India's first nuclear explosion is reported to have come from a heavy water research reactor supplied by Canada.)

The British and French gas-cooled natural uranium reactors have proved too expensive. This reactor design, marginal at best, was adopted for political reasons: to avoid dependence on American uranium enrichment facilities. Both the British and French nuclear programmes have suffered from these decisions. Over the past few years the French have decided to switch to US-type light water reactors, and simultaneously to expand France's uranium enrichment facilities using French gaseous diffusion technology developed to supply highly enriched uranium for French nuclear warheads. The pressure for the switch came from the French state electric utility, which finally overcame the resistance of the government nuclear agency that developed the French line of natural uranium reactors.

The British case is more involved. When the difficulties with the earlier Magnox line of reactors became evident, the British shifted to the so-called advanced gas-cooled reactor (AGR) which uses enriched uranium, hoping still to capitalise on the long British development of gas-cooled reactor technology. At the same time, Great Britain expanded efforts to develop its own enrichment technology, especially gas-centrifuge technology. But problems developed with the AGR, and Britain has been forced to abandon the AGR in favour of a new reactor system.

In summer 1974 the British Government announced a tentative decision to turn to the British-developed hybrid SGHWR, which also utilised enriched uranium, for future installations of nuclear power plants.[5] There are some advantages to this design, but it seems doubtful whether they can compensate for the enormous amount of engineering that has already gone into light water reactors. Like the French EDF, the Central Electricity Generating Board, which has responsibility for providing electric power, preferred the LWR, but the British Government decided for the third time to stick with an as yet commercially unproven British reactor technology.[6] It may again prove to be a costly mistake. From the point of view of uranium and enrichment demand, it matters little which type of reactor is installed: the SGHWR uses enriched uranium in approximately the same amounts as the LWR.

All nuclear power programmes plan to move eventually to dependence on fast-breeder reactors (FBR).[7] When this will occur, however, is unclear. Fast-breeder R & D programmes are under way in all the leading industrial countries — the United States, the Soviet Union, Great Britain, Federal Germany, France and Japan — all of which are pursuing the sodium-cooled design, the so-called liquid metal fast-breeder reactor (LMFBR). But fast-breeder development programmes have been delayed, at least in the United States.[8] It seems doubtful whether significant numbers of commercial FBRs will go into operation before about 1990, although some installations may take place in Europe earlier. On the whole, it appears that the slow-down and eventual reduction in uranium requirements and in uranium enrichment requirements, implied by the expected shift to fast-breeders, will not be significant before the turn of the century. As a consequence we can safely ignore the fast-breeder in our analysis.

HTGRs have been included because of all the alternatives to the LWR they seem closest to commercial acceptance. The HTGR offers better thermal efficiency (about 40 per cent as opposed to about 30 per cent for LWRs), better utilisation of uranium, and possibly some safety advantages. It is being promoted by energy companies with considerable financial resources, and a number of large HTGRs have been purchased by American utilities: approximately six large plants are under construction or on order.[9]

To sum up, most of the reactors to be installed around the world for the remainder of this century — mainly LWRs with some additional number of HTGRs — will burn enriched uranium.

Enriched Uranium Requirements and Current Supply

Detailed analyses show that, based on the broad conclusions of the previous section, the requirement for enriched uranium for the next two decades depends most strongly on the projected use of nuclear energy for the generation of electricity;[10] it depends to a lesser extent on the mix and rate of installation of reactor types and their characteristics, and the extent to which plutonium, a by-product formed during the operation of most reactors, is subsequently recycled as a fuel to reduce uranium-235 requirements.

The precise demands for *natural uranium* and for *separate work* (SW), or enrichment effort, depend on the aggregate enrichment levels of the fuel and on the mode of operation of the enrichment facilities:

a given amount of enriched uranium can be produced from a range of combinations of natural uranium feed and separative work.[11] The operating parameters of enrichment facilities are chosen so as to minimise overall costs.[12]

1. *Separative Work*

Table 4 lists a series of recent USAEC and OECD/IAEA estimates of future separative work requirements: the USAEC estimates are consistent with the forecasts of nuclear electric generating capacity presented in Table 2. The totals can be compared with present American enrichment capacity of about 17,000 tons SW per year (actual 1974 production is expected to be about 13,000 tons SW). The American enrichment plants are undergoing two capacity expansion programmes,[13] which will raise the total capacity of the three gaseous diffusion plants to about 27,000 tons SW per year in 1983.

Table 4:   Some Recent Forecasts of Annual Separative Work
Requirements
(Thousands of tons SW per year)

		1980	1985	1990	2000
USAEC (1974) Intermediate Case*	US	14.2	24.6	42.7	75.3
	Non-US	14.1	33.9	60.7	121.0
	World Total	28.3	58.5	103.4	196.3†
OECD/IAEA (1973)**	World Total:				
	Extreme range	26-33	45-68	62-124	
	Medium range	30-31	57-58	91-97	

* *Nuclear Power 1974-2000*, USAEC, WASH-1139 (74), February 1974, Table 2, p. 2. Based on intermediate growth of nuclear power — Case D for USA, Case Y for non-US; assumes enrichment plant tails assay of 0.3 per cent U-235, some recycling of plutonium; includes the so-called centrally planned economies (Soviet Union and Eastern Europe).
** *Uranium: Resources, Production and Demand*, Joint Report by the OECD Nuclear Energy Agency and the IAEA, August 1973. Assumes 0.275 per cent tails assay, some plutonium recycle; excludes Soviet Union and Eastern Europe. Inclusion of these countries would raise the estimate slightly. On the other hand, using a 0.3 per cent tails assay would lower the enrichment demand by about 5 per cent.
† The cumulative requirement to the year 2000 comes to about 2.4 million tons SW. At a nominal $40 per kg. SW, this comes to about $100 billion. Note that with 0.2 per cent tails assay the cumulative separative work requirement would rise to about 3 million tons SW.

148

West European enrichment capacity in 1974 is accounted for by the UKAEA plant at Capenhurst (about 400 tons SW per year), the French gaseous diffusion plant at Pierrelatte (about 200 tons SW per year), and the Urenco gas centrifuge plants (about 50 tons SW per year). Soviet enrichment capacity is unknown — but on the basis of their military programme is presumably large, perhaps a significant fraction of American capacity.

On the whole, the estimates of future uranium enrichment demand overlap fairly closely. For example, the results of a recently published joint OECD-NEA/IAEA study on world uranium supply production and demand for early years are slightly higher than those of the more recent USAEC intermediate cases despite the fact that they exclude countries (Soviet Union, Eastern Europe) included in the USAEC estimates, but they also assume slightly different operating parameters designed to reduce uranium consumption.

A somewhat higher French estimate presented in an article by Michel Pecqueur, a director of the CEA, is shown in Table 5. Estimates presented at a colloquium of the Swiss Association for Atomic Energy in September 1973 by the Eurodif organisation are given in Table 6. On the whole, these estimates are reasonably consistent. Note that given the rapid expansion in civilian nuclear power, the various projections take the form of steeply rising curves, and hence estimates for any particular year are very sensitive to assumptions concerning delays in various nuclear programmes.

A number of observations emerge from these forecasts. American enrichment capacity even after the planned expansion will be inadequate to meet Western world needs by around 1980. In fact, because of some preproduction in American facilities and some existing capacity in

Table 5:   CEA Estimates of World Enrichment Requirements*
            (Thousands of tons SW per year)

	1975	1980	1985	1990
United States	7.0	17.0	30.0	40.0
Europe	4.5	11.0	24.0	37.0
Japan	2.0	4.0	9.0	14.0
Other Third World Countries	0.5	2.0	6.0	13.0
World Total	14.0	34.0	69.0	104.0

* Michel Pecqueur, 'l'Europe va-t-elle manquer d'uranium enrichi?', *Revue Francais de l'Energie*, April 1973, pp. 272-8. Assumes 0.275 per cent tails assay and some recycling of plutonium; excludes Soviet Union, Eastern Europe.

Table 6:   EURODIF 1973 Estimates for Uranium Enrichment
            Requirements*
            (Thousands of tons SW per year)

	1980	1985	1990
Europe	10-11	18-20	35-38
Western world	34-40	67-75	over 90

*   Reported in *Nuclear Engineering International*, November 1973. Estimates
    assume 0.275 per cent tails assay, 25 per cent plutonium recycling.

Europe, major new capacity additions will not be needed until the
early 1980s. But after that point, say from 1985 on, rapid increases in
capacity will probably be required. All the estimates agree that by
about 1990 the world will need something over five times present
American enrichment capacity. Clearly, civilian needs will dwarf what
were once thought to be enormous military requirements.

2. *Natural Uranium*

On the basis of the assumptions used to calculate separative work
requirements, one obtains requirements for natural uranium feed.
Recent (1974) USAEC forecasts are presented in Table 7. Compared
with earlier forecasts, they indicate a reduction in projected requirements. Roughly comparable recent OECD/IAEA projections are presented in Table 8.

Recent estimates of world uranium resources are given in Table 9.
The available estimates are probably conservative; the American figures
quoted in Table 9 represent an increase of about 25 per cent over a
similar compilation published in January 1970.[14] The estimates presented both in the latter compilation and in a joint report of the OECD
Nuclear Energy Agency and the IAEA of August 1973,[15] suggest that
uranium reserves in the higher $10-15 per lb range are comparable with
those in the less than $10 per lb category. On the whole, the estimates
for more expensive uranium are highly uncertain, presumably because
not much prospecting has been done for uranium in this category.

One arrives at the result that known world uranium supplies currently described as extractable at less than about $10 per lb are adequate
to supply world needs until a little after 1990.[16] This ignores, however,
the need of the mining industry for a forward reserve covering about
eight years' use to cover the time it takes to develop an ore discovery
to the start of production. In effect, the critical point would be reached
in 1979[17] when presently known reserves would just correspond to an
eight year reserve. The Joint Report of the OECD Nuclear Energy

Table 7: An Intermediate USAEC 1974 Forecast for Enrichment
Plant Uranium Feed Requirements*
(Thousands of metric tons per year)

	1980	1985	1990	2000
USA	26.7	42.4	71.5	120.0
Non-US	28.6	66.1	115.0	216.0
Total	55.3	108.5	186.5	336.0
Cumulative Requirements (from 1973)				
USA	110.0	253.0	579.0	1600.0
Non-US	138.0	352.0	872.0	2652.0
Total	248.1	605.0	1451.0	4252.0**

* *Nuclear Power 1974-2000*, USAEC, WASH-1139 (74), February 1974.
Assumes 0.3 per cent tails assay, and intermediate growth of nuclear power;
Case D for USA and Case Y for non-US.
** Note that the cost of 4 million tons of uranium at a nominal $25 per kg.
comes to $100 billion.

Table 8: OECD/IAEA Forecast for World Uranium Requirements*
(Thousands of tons per year)

	1975	1980	1985	1990
Extreme range	23-26	51-66	79-127	100-224
Medium range	25	60-61	103-108	156-173
Cumulative requirements				
Extreme range	58-64	241-297	581-799	1045-1713
Medium range	62	272-273	695-712	1367-1441

* *Uranium: Resources, Production and Demand*, Joint Report by the OECD
Nuclear Energy Agency and the IAEA, August 1973.

Agency and the IAEA of August 1973 stressed that if considerable
uranium discoveries are not made before 1979 it will be impossible for
known reserves to support the required uranium production rates. The
present rate of discovery is considered inadequate for this purpose.

The present low rate of discovery is said to be related to the generally depressed state of the uranium market, characterised by excess
capacity and large stockpiles and inventories. The projections for
sharply increased demand do not seem to have impressed the uranium

151

mining industry.

Of course, more expensive ores can be used without markedly affecting the cost of nuclear generation of electricity. At $10 per lb natural uranium contributes only about one-half mill per kilowatt-hour, or about 3 per cent of the total cost of power.[18] However, the price of uranium may increase sharply.

Table 9:   World Resources of U_3O_8 at $10/lb*
            (Thousands of tons U_3O_8)

	Reserves**	Estimated Additional†	Total
Australia	140	48	188
Canada	241	247	488
France	47	31	78
Niger	52	26	78
Gabon	26	6	32
S. and S.W. Africa	263	10	273
Others, Non-Communist	68	69	137
Total Non-US	837	437	1274
USA	340	700	1040
Total (rounded)	1180	1140	2300

* Statement on Uranium Resources by Mr Frank P. Baranowski, Director, Division of Production and Materials Management, US Atomic Energy Commission, FY 1973 Authorization Hearings Before the Joint Committee on Atomic Energy, 5 March 1974. See also *Uranium: Resources, Production and Demand*, Joint Report by the OECD Nuclear Energy Agency and the IAEA, August 1973.

** 'Reserves' refers to uranium which occurs in known ore deposits of such grade, quantity and configuration that it can be profitably recovered with currently proven mining and processing technology.

† 'Estimated Additional' refers to uranium survival to occur in unexplored extentions of known deposits or in undiscovered deposits in known uranium districts, and which is expected to be discoverable and economically exploitable in the given price range.

Future Enriched Uranium Supply

The countries with major uranium resources are the United States, Canada, South Africa, Australia, and presumably the Soviet Union.

The United States is unlikely to export significant quantities of uranium. It may itself be in short supply since it will have a major share of the world's reactors and is expected to become an importer of uranium.

Canada has indicated it may tie uranium sales to sales of Canadian heavy water reactors.[19] If this were to happen, it would pose an awkward choice for European countries, which would not normally purchase HWRs.

South Africa has extensive reserves but uranium production is tied to other mining operations and uranium production may not be expanded sufficiently rapidly to cover European needs.

Australia has indicated interest in exporting enriched uranium. There have been government statements to the effect that until Australia has an enrichment facility — which is not likely for a long time — exports of uranium will be restricted.[20] This could set a pattern for uranium producers.

Altogether it seems that efforts to find and develop uranium resources will have to be expanded rapidly if Europe is not to find itself short of uranium.

As indicated above the USAEC facilities supply almost the entire Western world's commercial requirements for uranium enrichment services. The sale of enrichment services has now been put on a more business-like basis than heretofore, and customers are required to place orders eight years in advance and to advance a substantial deposit. More recently the USAEC announced that it would no longer accept new orders for enrichment services because existing contracts will fully commit American capacity even after currently planned increase in capacity.

Additional world enrichment capacity, beyond the planned programme which will raise USAEC capacity to about 27,000 tons SW per year, can come from various sources. Several possiblities exist for the 1980s:

(a)   The USAEC could build additional capacity using either gaseous diffusion or gas centrifuge technology. On the whole, this has been the preferred solution of the USAEC bureaucracy and of the Joint Committee (whereas the Administration has been determined not to build any more government-owned enrichment plants).

(b)   The USAEC could license private firms — American or foreign or both — to use either its gaseous diffusion or gas centrifuge technology in a new enrichment plant.[21] Several industrial groupings announced their intention to enter the enrichment business.

(c)   The Soviet Union could become a major supplier of enriched uranium to the non-Communist nations. Soviet capacity is presumably second only to that of the United States. The Soviets have signed agreements with a half dozen Western States; have contracted to supply enrichment services to French and German utilities; and have discussed possible arrangements with a number of other

Western organisations. They are apparently offering not only prices slightly below American prices but also much more flexible terms. That the Soviet Union would sell enriched uranium to Federal Germany even before it has ratified the Non-Proliferation Treaty, may be an indication of the Soviet Union's eagerness for a major share of Europe's market for enriched uranium.

(d)   The small gas centrifuge enrichment plants being built by Urenco under a tripartite British-Dutch-German sponsorship will be followed by larger enrichment facilities. Urenco has announced plans to expand its enrichment plant capacity to about 2,000 tons SW per year in 1980 and then about 10,000 tons SW per year in 1985.[22] They have accepted orders for enrichment services at $48 per kg. SW. The expansion of capacity is limited principally by the state of the technology. That is, it will take some time to prove the technology in a commercial sense.

(e)   A gaseous diffusion plant will be built by the French-sponsored Eurodif, a group initiated by the French CEA. Eurodif originally included participants from a large number of countries including some involved in the Urenco enterprise. Most of these have dropped out and direct participation is limited to France, Spain, Italy, and Belgium. Japan has purchased a share of Eurodif's capacity. Eurodif originally planned to expand to 5,000 tons SW per year in 1980 and to 9,000 tons SW per year in 1985. It has now announced an accelerated schedule. Orders for separative work are being taken at about $57 per kg. SW.

(f)   Japan has indicated interest in building an enrichment plant and is making efforts to acquire the necessary technology.

(g)   South Africa apparently has an enrichment plant under construction, but the details, including the type of technology being used, have been kept highly secret.

Europeans must decide how to invest in competing enrichment technologies and enterprises. Each country must decide what value it places on secure domestic, or at least European, sources of enrichment services. Investment decisions in this area have been complicated by an interweaving of national and international technical, economic, and political factors.

The relative advantages of the two major competitive enrichment technologies, gaseous diffusion and gas centrifuge, depend on the individual circumstances of a planned enrichment enterprise. The cost of a 'standard' enrichment plant of either type with a capacity of about 9,000 tons SW per year is estimated at roughly $1.5 billion. A gaseous diffusion plant of this size requires an additional investment of perhaps $1 billion to provide roughly 2,400 MWe of electric power. The gas

154

centrifuge process has the advantage that its power requirement is less than one-tenth of the gaseous diffusion process. It also appears that gas centrifuge enrichment plants can be built on a considerably smaller scale without significant economic penalty. But commercial performance of gas centrifuge technology is still comparatively uncertain, whereas gaseous diffusion technology is well proven on a commercial scale, and capital and operating costs — apart from power — are predictable with accuracy.

Decisions in uranium enrichment are further complicated by military considerations. No aspect of the nuclear fuel cycle is so close to the military side of nuclear affairs because, in effect, the same facilities that produce enriched uranium for civilian reactor fuel could produce highly enriched uranium for nuclear weapons. Present government-owned enrichment facilities in the United States, Great Britain, France, and the Soviet Union owe their existence to military requirements, and the technology of uranium enrichment has been kept secret at the government level. In the United States uranium enrichment technology is essentially the only aspect of the nuclear fuel cycle that has not shifted to the private sector, and the technology has been closely held on grounds of national security.

It was earlier remarked that, as in the case of oil, the need for nuclear fuel in advanced countries may become a source of conflict. The problem of supplying nuclear fuel for Western power plants differs, however, significantly from that of supplying oil. Both the principal sources of uranium and the main present and projected enrichment facilities are in the so-called Western world. Therefore, the problem of supplying nuclear fuel can in principle be resolved within the Western alliance; it does not significantly involve the Third World; and it need not involve the Communist countries. Whether it will be resolved on a more orderly basis than the oil problem remains to be seen.

Notes

1. This study was originally written under the auspices of the California Arms Control and Foreign Policy Seminar.
2. *Nuclear Power 1974-2000*, United States Atomic Energy Commission (USAEC), WASH-1139 (74), February 1974.
3. The price of nuclear fuel does not feed back significantly to the estimate for nuclear electric generating capacity because nuclear fuel costs are such a small proportion of total electric generating costs, so far at any rate. Fuel costs may, however, affect the choice of nuclear power plant design.
4. So called because they use ordinary (or 'light' as opposed to 'heavy') water for slowing down neutrons and for heat transfer. LWRs are divided into two types: pressurised water reactors (PWRs) and boiling water reactors (BWRs), but for our purposes the distinction is not significant.

5. *Business Week*, 20 July 1974; and *Weekly Energy Report*, 15 July 1974.
6. A 100-MWe prototype SGHWR has operated for several years.
7. These reactors in effect burn uranium-238, the isotope which makes up over 99 per cent of natural uranium and which is burned hardly at all in ordinary reactors. As a result, FBRs extract about 30-40 times as much energy from a given amount of uranium. They do this by first converting the uranium-238 into plutonium (breeding) and then burning the plutonium, and also burning some of the uranium-238 directly. In fact, the cost of natural uranium becomes such a negligible fraction of FBR fuel costs that for practical purposes the availability of nuclear fuel ceases to be a problem for the indefinite future.
8. The French programme is on schedule — a prototype 250 MWe Phénix FBR recently joined the French electrical grid. A 1200 MWe Super-Phénix is scheduled to start up around 1980, (*Nucleonics Week*, 11 July 1974). French fast-breeder technology seems to have moved into the lead and the possibility of a GE licence has been reported, (*ibid.*, 18 July 1974).
9. US-type HTGRs utilise over 90 per cent highly enriched uranium (uranium-235). Extensive installation of such reactors implies considerable requirements for enrichment. The use of these reactors also entails special problems of material and facility security: each large HTGR will contain over a thousand kilograms of highly enriched uranium. Extensive installation of HTGRs therefore also implies very large flows of highly enriched uranium in commercial channels.
10. Tom Roberts, 'Uranium Enrichment: Supply, Demand and Costs', *IAEA Bulletin*, February/April 1974, p. 14; see also *Uranium: Resources, Production and Demand*, Joint Report by European Energy Agency and the IAEA, OECD, September 1970.
11. For example, 6.6 kg. of natural uranium (0.7 per cent uranium-235) can be used to produce 1 kg. of enriched uranium at 3 per cent uranium-235 using 3.4 kg. SW. The rejected material would consist of 5.6 kg. of uranium with 0.3 per cent uranium-235. Alternatively, 1 kg. of 3 per cent enriched uranium could be produced from only 5.5 kg. of natural uranium with a greater enrichment effort — 4.3 kg. SW — with a 'tails assay' of 0.2 per cent.
    It is a little confusing that separative work is measured in units of mass: kg. and tons. This comes about because the enrichment effect is proportional to the material throughout (times a dimensionless factor which depends on the enrichment levels of the incoming and outgoing material). Sometimes kg. SW is given as SWU or separative work units.
12. The adjustable variable is the so-called 'tails assay', the enrichment level of the enrichment plant waste stream. The tails assay is fixed in such a way as to minimise overall costs. For the recent prices of uranium (about $7 per lb — prices for future delivery are now much higher) and separative work (about $40 per kg. SW), the appropriate tails assay is about 0.3 per cent. The total cost varies little for small changes in the tails assay.
13. Cascade improvement (CIP) — to raise capacity by 5,800 tons SW per year at the same power level; Cascade uprating programme (CUP) — to increase capacity by an additional 4,700 tons SW per year while increasing the plant power level.
14. *Uranium: Resources, Production and Demand*, Joint Report by European Nuclear Energy Agency and the IAEA, OECD, September 1970.
15. *Uranium: Resources, Production and Demand*, Joint Report by the OECD Nuclear Energy Agency and the IAEA, August 1973.
16. The market price for uranium has been about $7 per lb, but the price for future delivery is apparently much higher.

17. *Uranium: Resources, Production and Demand*, Joint Report by the OECD Nuclear Energy Angency and the IAEA, August 1973.

18. Estimated generating cost for a 1000 MWe LWR plant, including escalation to 1981, is about 15 mills/kwh (11.7 mills/kwh for capital, 2.5 mills/kwh for fuel, a mill/kwh for operation) based on fairly standard assumptions. Major fuel cost components are mining and milling, enrichment and fabrication. *The Nuclear Industry 1973*, USAEC, WASH-1174-73, 1974.

19. *Weekly Energy Report*, 1 July 1974.

20. *Nucleonics Week*, 16 May 1974.

21. Described in *ibid.*, 2 May 1974.

22. As of July 1974 Urenco already had contracts for 1,800 out of the 2,000 ton SW per year capacity expected in 1980. *Weekly Energy Report*, 22 July 1974.

11. NATIONAL SECURITY AND THE ARMS RACE

L. J. Dumas

Introduction

Because of the enormous political, social, military and technical complexities of the arms race, analysts have often focused on particularly important sub-issues. But the sum of all the analyses of all of the sub-issues does not provide the same insight as an analysis of the situation as a whole. It is precisely this kind of overview which is required to understand the present status of world security, and to set effective future policy. It is the purpose of this paper briefly to sketch some of the major implications for military security of the continuation of the arms race.

To sharpen the discussion, I will define 'military security' as the prevention of property damage, injury and loss of life caused by military means as well as the limitation of such damage, casualty and death in the event of war. 'National' security focuses only on the destruction imposed on the people and property of a given nation. Further, the analysis will be focused on weapons of mass destruction, including nuclear, biological and chemical weaponry. Conventional weapons will not be included. Additionally, all questions of direct expense, social cost, politics and morality will be set aside — only the effectiveness of the expansion of military force in maintaining or increasing the military security of the participants in that expansion will be considered.

The central thesis of this paper is that, in fact, as the sum of world armaments increases due to the progression of the arms race, the military security of every nation decreases. Furthermore, it is held that this deterioration of national security accelerates as the level of world armaments rises.

There are four essential reasons why national security declines as the amount of world armaments grows. These are: (1) the possibility of accidents; (2) the possibility of accidental war; (3) limitations on the ability to control inventories; and (4) the widening gap between offensive and defensive military technology. Each will be discussed briefly in turn. It should be noted that although these categories are somewhat interrelated, they do constitute largely separate effects.

Accidents

The term 'accidents' refers in this context to the unintended detonation of a nuclear device or the unintended spreading of toxic chemical, radiological or biological military materials. The US Department of Defense has officially acknowledged the occurrence of twelve major accidents involving nuclear weapons over the period 1958-66.[1] However, in 1969, the Stockholm International Peace Research Institute (SIPRI) published a somewhat more comprehensive list, including thirty-three major US nuclear weapons accidents between 1950 and 1968.[2] Although none of these involved the actual nuclear explosion of a nuclear device, a number were extremely serious accidents coming very close to disaster. A summary description of just two of those will suffice to convey the seriousness of the problem:

On January 23, 1961, a B52 bomber from Seymour-Johnson Air Force Base crashed into the area of Goldsboro, North Carolina. The plane was carrying two unarmed 24 megaton bombs, one of which was recovered from the wreckage. The second bomb was jettisoned by parachute, falling into a field without exploding. According to Dr Ralph Lapp, former head of the nuclear physics branch of the Office of Naval Research, the bomb was fitted with six interlocking safety mechanisms all of which had to be activated in sequence to detonate the weapon. Lapp contends that five of the six mechanisms were triggered by the fall, leaving only one switch preventing the explosion.[3] A twenty-four megaton weapon detonated at say 11,000 feet, has a fireball radius of about 2 miles, would destroy all standard housing within a radius of about 12.5 miles and ignite all flammable materials within a radius of about 34.5 miles. In 1969, the Department of Defense indicated that not one, but two switches remained untriggered and that the bomb was unarmed.[4]

On January 17, 1966, at 10:16 a.m., a B52 bomber collided with a refueling tanker and crashed near Palomares, on the Medterranean coast of Spain. Four hydrogen bombs of 20-25 megaton class fell out of the plane. One landed undamaged on a dry river bed. The conventional explosives in two others exploded scattered plutonium over a wide area of fields (2/10,000 of an ounce of plutonium is lethal when inhaled or ingested — a minimum critical mass for a kiloton class Hiroshima type bomb is about 11 pounds). Removal of 1,750 tons of radioactive soil and vegetation was required for decontamination. It took nearly three months to recover the fourth bomb from the Mediterranean. It was intact. The extent of ecological damage which would have resulted had that weapon ruptured is nearly inestimable.[5]

It should be noted that there is virtually no information available concerning the number, extent or seriousness of damage resulting from nuclear weapons accidents of the Soviet Union — or for that matter of the other nuclear powers. If a nation as generally safety conscious as the United States has had at least thirty-three accidents, the world total is likely to be considerably higher.

Accidental War

A major study undertaken at Ohio State University's Mershon Institute resulted in a 1960 report stating ' . . . there is a significant chance that a major accidental war may occur at some time in the 1960s'.[6] By accidental war is meant an exchange of weapons of mass destruction, most likely nuclear, which though not triggered with purposeful calculation of the governmental decision makers in authority, nevertheless follows a pattern indistinguishable from intentional war after the initial incident.

Accidental war could be precipitated in a variety of ways. For example, an accident, similar in type to those discussed above, but perhaps resulting in a nuclear explosion, could be misinterpreted during a time of peak international tension as an intentional attack, calling for retaliation. There is often some degree of confusion as to the exact circumstances surrounding an accident for a significant period after its occurrence, which heightens this possibility. Examples of such periods of peak international tension are the Cuban Missile Crisis of 1962 and the American nuclear alert surrounding the October War in the Middle East in 1973.

A false defence communications signal could also be the trigger, especially at a time of international crisis. A number of such signals are known to have occurred. For example:

1. On 5 October 1960 in the main defence room at North American Air Defense Command (NORAD) headquarters near Colorado Springs, Colorado, an emergency light began flashing indicating, in the words of one observer, ' . . . it was highly probable that objects in their air were moving toward America. An attack was likely'.[7] The Canadian Air Marshall in charge ' . . . refused to be panicked by radar information which made it appear that long range missiles had been launched against North America'.[8] It took about 15-20 minutes for the signal to be verified as false. The early warning radars in Thule, Greenland, had not picked up a missile attack — they had echoed off the moon.[9]

2. On at least four occasions since 1971, SECT (Submarine Emergency Communications Transmitter) buoys have been released from

Polaris nuclear missile submarines because of mechanical failure, according to Representative Les Aspin (Wisconsin). Each time the buoys escaped they began broadcasting distress signals. On at least two of these occasions, the message was that the submarine had been sunk by enemy action. In each case, the submarines were forced to surface to countermand the distress signal.[10]

It does not require much imagination to see how false signals of this seriousness could trigger accidental war during a period of high international tension.

Inventory Control Limitations

There is always some part of any inventory whose precise position and status is unknown at any given point in time. It is simply not possible to keep absolute 100 per cent control of any inventory for any extended period. This is as true of nuclear weapons and nuclear explosives as it is of nuts and bolts or candy bars. As an example of the official recognition of the impossibility of perfect inventory control even where maximal control is vital, consider the control of inventories of nuclear fuels.

The US Atomic Energy Commission has an explicit category in their nuclear materials accounts called 'material unaccounted for' (MUF), defined as:

The algebraic difference between a *physical* inventory and its concomitant *book* inventory after determining that all known removals (such as *accidental losses, normal operational losses* and authorized *write-offs*) have been reflected in the book inventory.[11]

According to the Director of the Office of Safeguards and Material Management of the US Atomic Energy Commission,

examination of historical performance of nuclear fuel cycle operation . . . shows that, in general, the long term MUF is not zero but of the order of 0.5% throughout. The common conclusion is that such apparent shortages are due to unmeasured losses or measurement bias. However, from a safeguards standpoint continuation of the same MUF could also indicate or mask a consistent diversion – a matter of . . . serious concern from a national security . . . standpoint.[12]

Furthermore, in a detailed evaluation of the *capabilities* of a material balance accounting system, the system which is used to keep track of nuclear fuels inventories, it was estimated that under conditions of *best performance* such a system would only have a 50-50 chance of even detecting the diversion of up to 0.5 per cent of the plutonium input to a chemical processing plant.[13]

To be sure, there are significant differences between inventory control in processing plants and control of weapons inventories. But the basic fact of the inability to obtain better than 99.5 per cent control, even where the materials involved are highly expensive and dangerous, implying strong pressures for precise control, indicates a pressing against theoretical control limits. Yet, even if control were to be bettered by another factor of five, increasing accounting capability to 99.9 per cent for nuclear weapons inventories, that would still leave an average of seven American nuclear warheads in Europe alone in the uncontrolled fringe of 0.1 per cent of the inventory. Theft or diversion by terrorists, for example, or even by extremist national governments are frightening possibilities.

Two Exacerbating Factors

There are two general problems which severely aggravate the three causes of insecurity discussed above. First are the human factors, namely limits on human sensory/motor capabilities and, even more important, the psychological and emotional limits of human beings. These limits make the likelihood of accidents, accidental war and theft or loss from inventories much greater. Space restrictions prevent the presentation of the volumes of evidence on human limitations here but I think the following short item will convey the point:

> A total of 3,647 persons with nuclear weapons access were removed from their jobs within a single year because of drug abuse, mental illness, alcoholism or discipline problems. . . . each year at least 3% of the approximately 120,000 . . . who work with the American nuclear arsenal are discovered to be security risks. Twenty percent of the disqualifications are because of drugs.[14]

Second, the larger, the more geographically dispersed and the more complex weapons and warning systems are, the greater the problems of accidental war, accidents and inventory control become. More people, more installations and more components have to function properly for the system to operate as desired. It is a basic principle of engineering design of machine and human-machine systems that there should always be a strong bias in favour of simplicity. Even very substantial increases in the reliability of every individual component are easily overwhelmed, leading to decreased overall system reliability, by an increasing complexity which multiples the number of components. This is precisely what has happened to our military systems with the progress of the arms race.

Offensive-Defensive Gap in Military Technology

There has been a widening gap favouring military offence versus defence since the Second World War. The most extraordinary sophisticated developments in defensive technology have been readily overwhelmed by minor offensive advances or even by mere alterations in offensive strategy. Beyond this, there have been major advances in offensive technology that have vastly widened the gap. The following two sets of estimates will provide a quick picture of the end results of three decades of military technological advance.

In 1964, the former science advisors to Presidents Eisenhower and Kennedy, Herbert York and Jerome Wiesner, estimated that a full-scale attack by the Soviet Union on the United States countered by the American defensive systems would have resulted in millions of American casualties; by the late 1950s, the casualties would have numbered in the tens of millions; by the mid-1960s the figure 'could very well be on the order of one hundred million'.[15] Developments such as MIRV in the last decade have made matters substantially worse.

In a second estimate, York points out that whereas the ability to destroy 10 per cent of the incoming bomber fleet was sufficient for defensive 'success' in a Second World War-type conventional war, a 99 per cent destruction of the American SAC bomber fleet would still allow the penetrating 1 per cent of that fleet to deliver 10,000 times as much explosive power as was directed against Hiroshima.[16] In other words, in the nuclear age, the penetration required for offensive 'success' is less than 1/90 what was required for conventional military aerial offensive 'success'.

Conclusion

If the purpose of the massive research, development, production, and deployment of weapons of mass destruction which has dominated the international scene for the past three decades has been either to increase or even maintain the military national security of the participants then that effort has been counter-productive. The arms race has produced an inexorable and accelerating deterioration in the security of all the world's nations. Each of the four problems discussed in this paper has been and will be severely aggravated by its continuation.

We have lost the ability to defend against full-scale external military attack. We are in real danger of destroying from tens of thousands to even millions of human lives by mere accident. The shadow of accidental war, with its potential for dragging us into a nuclear holocaust in which hundreds of millions will die, falls ever more strongly upon us with every expansion of military mass destruction systems. The growth of stockpiles of nuclear, biological and chemical weapons vastly increases the possibility for terrorist murder on a scale which will make the most terrible terrorist acts committed to date seem trivial by comparison.

What is to be done? Neither arms limitations nor even a complete halt to the arms race is enough, though both are clearly preferable to the species of arms control that has, in fact, become guided armament. Freezing of weapons at the current levels merely maintains the probability of accident, accidental war, and theft or loss from inventories (with its possible terrorist implications) at a constant level. Given enough time, disaster will still occur. Massive reduction at least of weapons of mass destruction, is seemingly the only military strategy available which can actually successfully increase military national security.

Notes

1. *New York Times*, 23 January 1968.
2. 'Accidents of Nuclear Weapons and Nuclear Weapons Delivery Systems' in *SIPRI Yearbook of World Armaments and Disarmament 1968/69* (Stockholm, New York and London, 1969), pp. 259-70.
3. Joel Larus, *Nuclear Weapons Safety and the Common Defense* (Ohio, 1967), pp. 93-9.
4. *SIPRI Yearbook 1968/69*, pp. 261-2.
5. Larus, *op. cit.*, pp. 93-9.
6. J. B. Phelps *et al.*, 'Accidental War: Some Dangers in the 1960s', Mershon National Security Program Research Paper RP-6 (Columbus, Ohio, 1960), p. 18.
7. *Boston Traveler*, 12 December 1960.
8. *New York Times*, 23 December 1960.
9. *Ibid.*
10. L. Aspin (Democratic Congressman from Wisconsin), Press Release, 16 January 1974.
11. US Atomic Energy Commission, Office of Safeguard and Materials Management, *Safeguards Dictionary* (July 1971), p. 31.
12. D. L. Crowson, 'Safeguards and Nuclear Materials Management in the U.S.A.' in *Safeguards Papers from ANS/AIF Winter Meeting, November, 1968* (Office of Safeguards and Materials Management, US Atomic Energy Commission, Washington, D.C., 1970), p. 18.
13. R. Schneider and D. Granquist, 'Capability of a Typical Material Balance Accounting System for a Chemical Processing Plant', *Safeguards Systems Analysis of Nuclear Fuel Cycles* (Office of Safeguards and Materials Management, US Atomic Energy Commission, Washington, D.C., 1969).
14. *Newsday*, 28 January 1974, report of Congressional testimony of Dr Carl Walske, former Assistant Defense Secretary for Atomic Energy Matters.
15. J. B. Wiesner and H. F. York, 'National Security and the Nuclear Test-Ban', *Scientific American*, CCXI (1964), p. 35.
16. Herbert F. York, *Race to Oblivion* (New York, 1970), pp. 190-1.

12. UNILATERAL DISARMAMENT RE-EXAMINED

Tom Stonier

Whatever comes out of any disarmament conference is determined by the instructions to the delegates emanating from their home governments. Those instructions reflect the perceptions of the world which those governments possess. And the vast majority of these are not ready for total and complete disarmament. Will Pakistan, for example, be ready to disarm unless her neightbour to the East disarms? And is India willing to disarm if it is likely to result in the revolt and secession of ethnic minorities from Bengal in the East to Kashmir in the West? Will the Soviet Union disarm in view of the restiveness of the Soviet Bloc in Eastern Europe? I do not think so. The time is not ripe, and any real hope that total and complete disarmament will come out of such a conference is a delusion, and in a sense a cruel hoax.

Having said that, I would like to introduce two or three concepts which I hope will be helpful in formulating the kind of agenda which might yield positive results. The attainment of total and complete universal disarmament, would mean that an ancient social institution, namely war, would have been abolished. And if we intend to do that maybe we should use as a model another ancient social institution which did become abolished, and that is slavery. Let us look at the history of the abolition of slavery as a model and see what relevance this history may have for the abolition of war.

The institution of slavery was abolished because as an institution it had become disfunctional. Slavery disappeared as a consequence of the changing requirements for labour accompanying the spread of industrialisation.

Let us examine this proposition in somewhat greater detail. No ancient civilisation could have arisen without both the institution of war and the institution of slavery. War had to come first because of the need for military power to coerce a large labour force into doing the work which would relieve the ruling classes, the artisan classes, the priesthood, and the military. Until the Industrial Revolution displaced it, slavery was all-pervasive. It is important to realise that slavery was not abolished because of the abolitionists. The abolitionists expedited the demise of slavery. They certainly hurried history along, but they did not alter its course. Slavery was not considered a problem until the middle of the eighteenth century. Not even so enlightened a group as the

Quakers began to be preoccupied seriously with its evils before then. At that point, of course, the Industrial Revolution was already well on its way, and the pattern of labour utilisation had begun to shift dramatically. The primary motivation for slavery was the need to maintain the economic infrastructure which supported society. Slaves worked in the mines, on the roads, and on the irrigation systems, as well as in the fields and houses. In short, they did most of the dirty work which maintained pre-industrial society.

With the Industrial Revolution the labour patterns changed. Capital was better invested in machines than men and, with minor exceptions, it became cheaper to hire and fire labour. Thus began the demise of slavery around the world beginning with the Somerset Decision in Britain in 1772, and with the formal outlawing of slavery by Denmark about twenty years later. This was followed by other countries, one at a time – a process which continued for about two centuries, Southern Yemen outlawing slavery in 1968. Slavery still exists in parts of the world untouched by the Industrial Revolution. It also exists in some parts of the world which are highly industrialised, but such practices are now kept out of sight. It is fair to say, therefore, that although slavery still exists in a number of hidden spots on the planet, basically, the institution has been eliminated.

How does the abolition of slavery relate to the abolition of war? To answer this question, we must first analyse human society in terms of various degrees of complexity. (This analysis rests heavily on the writings of the Harvard sociologist Daniel Bell, and those of Johan Galtung, Director of the Norwegian Peace Research Institute.) If one looks at the world, there are at least four levels of social organisation discernable. It is important to understand these four levels if we are to understand the role war plays on each. There is *primal* society, *traditional* society, *industrial* society, and *electronic* society. In *primal* society, social organisation is dependent on face-to-face communication. The level of organisation extends from hunting/gathering bands to villages. That is to say, we are dealing with a social organisation involving from perhaps a dozen to a few thousand individuals. A hundred per cent of what economy exists, is devoted to the primary sector of the economy: to produce food and obtain water, although there may also exist a little part-time mining activity, fashioning tools and weapons and so on. *Traditional* society involves much larger units. It involves 'supra-village' organisation, which may become as extensive as did the old empires. Here we are dealing with tribal groups of the order of several thousand to about a million individuals. Ninety per cent, perhaps 95 per cent of the labour force is occupied with the primary sector of the economy, namely with the production of food and raw materials. Traditional society is held together by a system more elaborate than face-to-face communication, such as a network of foot, or mounted, messengers. The introduction of the horse-drawn coach and the establishment of regular postal services coupled with the advent of newspapers began to herald the next level of social organisation: the *industrial* society. There are different levels of industrial society, but at the middle industrial level, the railway dominates social organisation. The railway is not only a highly efficient form of transportation, but it is also the mainstay of the communications technology of the industrial society. The railways fostered the evolution of a highly developed postal service, which, coupled with newspapers, represents the chief mode of communication capable of holding together units which contain anywhere from about a million to a hundred million individuals. In the middle level industrial society perhaps no more than 50 per cent of the labour force is devoted to the primary sector of the economy.

Lastly (thus far), there is the *electronic* society. The United States was the first country to develop into an electronic society in the mid-1950s. Electronic society is characterised by several things, two of which are highly significant. The first is that television becomes the mass medium, supplementing the other three primary forms of electronic communcation: films, radio, and the telephone. Secondly, something happens to the economy which classical economists said could not happen, namely that a larger sector of the gross national product went to services than it did to production. This reflected, of course, the increasing automation of the production processes. By the time American society had reached the electronic era, the portion of the labour force engaged in the agricultural sector of the economy, for example, was approaching the 10 per cent mark. At least as much, if not more of the labour force was already way off in the quarternary sector, that is to say, people who made their living by handling abstract symbols, whether it involved typing or writing, or teaching, or accounting, or working with computers. They had begun to live and work in a very abstract world.

The reason why it is important to use this analysis of world society is because at each of these levels of social organisation, the institution of war plays a very different function, just as did the institution of slavery. Primal society really does not engage in war *per se*. It may, where a society is on the edge of becoming a traditional society. But even then, it would be more appropriate to consider violent encounters as skirmishes. It is probable that prior to the advent of settlement life there were, in fact, skirmishes. However the primary though not sole function of those skirmishes was to insure the proper spacing out of the clans or villages. Primal war fulfilled the functions of its biological roots: the maintenance of territories. Territoriality acts to limit population densities so as not to stress the environment to a point

167

where it collapses.

It was not until the rise of settlement life and civilisation when war became sufficiently profitable that we find groups engaging in its systematically. And from the time that civilisation arose until now, human history has been one sordid quarrel after another as it became apparent to each group that the only way to extend its own resources was to take away somebody else's.

That is the primary motivation for war: the extension (or defence) of resources. By the time traditional societies arose, the globe was covered with people. In most instances, no group could acquire new resources without taking them away from somebody else. It will not do to condemn war in moral terms. An outcry against war does not account for its popularity.

With the coming of the industrial age both the function of war and its practice changed. Initially, during the early phases of industrialisation, war became extremely profitable as a means for attaining colonies. Areas of the world still organised at the 'traditional' level were unable to muster large armies with the same efficiency as an industrial power. Industrial powers arose as they developed their railways in the middle of the nineteenth century. The German nation arose with the development of a rail network — with the adroit use of these railways it defeated Denmark, Austria and France in quick succession. Von Moltke advised his generals 'Build railways, not fortifications'. Thus could one muster large numbers of well-equipped soldiers in a short time. The British became supreme with steam-driven, steel ships. It was possible for a British regiment, properly armed and trained, to conquer areas that involved hundreds of thousands, and even millions of people. When it was possible for native forces to muster large numbers against the British, as Kipling tells us, 'they broke our British square'. The British were not invincible. They were, however, industrialised. And industrial powers could colonise with impunity. Only other industrial powers might stand in the way.

There is irony in history: as the Industrial Revolution moved into the twentieth century, colonies became more of a liability than an asset. The abolition of colonialism following the Second World War was helped by resistance abroad and a moral outcry at home. But the moral outcry did not cause de-colonisation. Nor did violence and rebellion: they merely acted as the midwife for a society pregnant with change. The economic realities had shifted. The price for maintaining political control over most colonies substantially exceeded the benefit derived from them. As the industrial societies were beginning to move into the electronic era an entirely new phenomenon had arisen — an increase in the standard of living was achieved much more effectively by technical ingenuity than by taking away somebody else's resources. Ideological conflict still persisted. After all, people are resources – the ideological wars which are supposedly aimed at men's hearts and loyalties are really aimed at their productive capacity and their military potential. Nevertheless, just as slavery became an anachronism in industrial society war has become an anachronism in electronic society.

If we look at the world today where are the areas of unrest? Where are the wars taking place? It is not in Western Europe, it is not even in Eastern Europe, it is not in the United States and it is not in Canada and New Zealand, and it is not in Japan. It is from Bangladesh to Nigeria. War and violence are most prevalent in those countries which are moving into the nation-state system, those areas which are industrialising. And those countries are not ready for disarmament.

Let us return to slavery. The first country formally to abolish it was Denmark, the most recent was Southern Yemen. The abolition of slavery was done, not by a universal convention 'let us abolish slavery', but bit by bit, each nation finding the institution unpalatable, then abolishing it. And that, I think, must be our clue. Unilateral national initiative!

Is there any indication that this is happening in our world today? The answer appears to be positive. An increasing number of countries are moving away from national military forces into transnational security schemes. This is true in spite of the fact that in other parts of the world, where countries are moving from traditional to industrial society, we witness an increase in national military forces. We must look to countries like Costa Rica to understand the future. Costa Rica abolished its army in 1948. In 1949 it was invaded by General Samoza of neighbouring Nicaragua. Samoza hoped to re-establish the dictatorship in Costa Rica which was overthrown by the revolution of 1948. Samoza was forced to withdraw by pressure from the Organisation of American States. Thus there exists at least one clear-cut instance of a country disarming, being invaded, and successfully repelling that invasion by non-military means.

Nobody doubts that Japan is a major power. Its armed forces, however, are smaller than those of South Korea. This is true in spite of a traditional enmity between Japan and Korea, an enmity which in earlier times would have led to an arms race. One can also look to Franco-German relations as another example. There were no two countries which bore each other greater enmity than France and Germany. The hatred dates back well into the sixteenth century when Emperor Maximillian referred to a 'hereditary enmity'. Nobody seriously expects France and Germany to go to war. Both are now part of a transnational economic system, the EEC, and they are each other's largest trading partners. We must recognise this fact as being of paramount significance.

It should become apparent that a number of nations, beginning with

Costa Rica and finally including even Japan, are ready to rely on transnational security systems and to dismantle their own national military establishments. One can envisage countries like Holland or Denmark simply saying, 'Look, who in the world is our army going to defend us against? We will maintain some forces available for United Nations duties, and we will maintain some for NATO for the time being, but we will not have any strictly national forces of our own'.

We are dealing with a world in which the global society is fragmented into subgroups which are at different levels of development. Those societies which are well into the electronic age have become part of transnational economic systems, and for many of those countries, the armed forces have basically become non-functional. Our strategy should therefore be to encourage those countries to take unilateral initiative in disarming. Rather than clamouring for total universal disarmament now, we should use the abolition of slavery as a model and press for unilateral national initiative. This would not interfere with potential agreements on universal arms *reduction* and a significant amelioration of the arms race, which does stand some chance of becoming a reality.

A strategy aimed at universal disarmament should recognise clearly the following principles:

1. Only countries moving into electronic society develop transnational economic interests sufficiently strong to force such countries into transnational political systems. Of these countries it is the smaller countries for whom security is much more effectively attained by being part of a transnational system. Therefore countries such as Costa Rica (utilising the Organization of American States), or countries such as Holland and Denmark (using the security of NATO) are the ones which will be the first to abolish their armies. The situation is parallel to that encountered towards the end of the eighteenth century among the industrialised Western European countries which began to abolish slavery. Just as slavery became an anachronism for countries as they entered the industrial era, so are armed forces becoming such an anachronism today. We must encourage unilateral national initiative among these countries.

2. If we wish *most* countries to reduce their national forces, we must fulfill certain prerequisites first. For example, we must held the Third World to industrialise, and then help it to move rapidly through the industrial, into the electronic era.

3. Global society is not yet sufficiently far advanced to allow the major powers to disarm, even though they are well into the electronic era. This does not mean that there is no movement away from the institution of war. It is significant that in spite of repeated opportuni-

ties for conflict — the Berlin Wall, the Middle East, the Far East and Cuba — there has been no actual military confrontation between the superpowers except by proxy. The reason for this is, of course, the awareness that there can be no victory following nuclear war. This pressure to avoid a nuclear disaster continues to operate. Yet in the long run, this motive will be overshadowed by the increasing economic interactions between the major powers. Hence the superpowers as well as the transnational security blocks which exist now (or are developing) will continue to evolve into global systems. It must become a primary aim to accelerate that process.

4. To that end it becomes imperative to foster serious and systematic investigation of the technological bases which will underlie the creation of a global community. All governments should be urged to fund research in academic and other institutions and to establish new institutions which devote their energies to understanding contemporary social evolution and how best to make it serve the needs of humanity.

PART III

EUROPEAN AND MIDDLE EAST SECURITY

13. THE POLITICAL ASPECTS OF EUROPEAN SECURITY

Pierre Hassner

The Changing Dimensions of Security

This paper was originally presented in a country, Italy, where the headlines of newspapers and the attention of citizens have been divided between three forms of insecurity: the *individual* and *domestic* insecurity brought into the open by terrorist bombings; the potential *military* insecurity connected with the war in another Mediterranean country, Cyprus, and by the changes of regime in several countries of Mediterranean Europe; and the *economic* insecurity brought about by the energy and balance of payments deficits and by worsening job prospects for individuals.

Yet when we speak of European security, we are mainly concerned with the state of three negotiations whose present stage either of stalemate or of recess permit the drawing up of a provisional balance-sheet: the negotiations on strategic arms limitation (SALT II), the Conference on Security and Cooperation in Europe (CSCE) and the Conference on Mutually Balanced Force Reductions (MBFR – or MFR, since the 'B' for 'balanced', has been dropped at Soviet request).

The contrast between the two perspectives – that of current events and that of the negotiations – calls for an explanation which may shed some light on our problem itself. There are three paradoxes associated with these three conferences.

First, the one whose title includes the word 'security' is also the one which has least to do with security in the strict and narrow sense. Economic cooperation, the legitimisation of the political *status quo*, peaceful change through increased communications between societies have been its main themes, with military so-called 'confidence-building' measures relegated to a marginal role and practically abandoned. The military security of Europe is much more the concern directly of MBFR and indirectly, although just as importantly, of SALT II.

Secondly, even in these cases, the negotiations are not meant to put a stop to any open conflict or to redress any situation which inspires a feeling of dramatic insecurity. On the contrary, they are made possible precisely by the feeling of security which obtains between the two superpowers and between their respective European alliances — a feeling which was given concrete form by the SALT I agreements and by the Federal German treaties with the Warsaw Pact countries. One may, then, wonder whether security in Europe is indeed a subject for negotiations or whether these do not consist essentially of registering an already existing security. But of course this recognition or this confirmation through negotiation are not neutral; they have an effect on other aspects of European security. This effect can be positive if the same security can be maintained but at a lower cost, or if some of the same security which obtains between superpower blocs or alliances can be brought within alliances or to neutral and non-aligned powers. They can also lead or contribute to a negative evolution which could culminate in a calling into question or jeopardising of the security of Europe by creating a military or psychological imbalance or a feeling of social and ideological vulnerability.

Thirdly, public opinion seems particularly indifferent to these negotiations. It seems to share neither the hopes which Eastern propaganda wanted attributed to it or to inspire about the Security Conference, nor the fears, which many experts, in the West, have voiced about the effect of that conference and of the two other negotiations. Citizens think of security in the terms we have illustrated through the Italian example: in terms of individual, psychological or economic security.

The key to these paradoxes seem to lie in the ambiguity and the evolution of the notion of security itself.

As far as the three negotiations are concerned, it is clear that their meaning has much more to do with politics than with security. They are the expression of a new type of relationship of the Soviet world with Western Europe (based on the acceptance, by the latter, of the *status quo* in Eastern Europe) and with the United States (based on the acceptance, by the latter, of nuclear parity). In both cases the new type of relationship is supposed to lead to a new type of cooperation and also to a new type of competition, both between and within alliances. Both the new cooperation and the new competition raise new problems concerning the relationship between the strategic balance, inter-state relations, and the links between societies — hence between the international system and social evolution.

We have, then, to distinguish between at least four forms of security: (1) *military security*, focused on the avoidance of war — through deterrence or arms control; (2) *political security*, based, in its inter-state dimension, on the compatibility between the objectives of the various governments, and, in its domestic dimensions, on the compatibility between the objectives of governments and those of their respective populations; (3) *economic security*, or the avoidance of crises of supply or of production; (4) *socio-psychological security*, or the

174

confidence of the citizens in the legitimacy and viability of their regimes.

No attempt will be made, of course, to consider each of these dimensions in its own right. But it is important, when considering the military and political inter-state dimension to see them in the light of the others. This is particularly so at the present time when considerations of military power and balance have not lost their importance but have, to some extent, lost their immediacy and their simplicity. They have to be seen as part of a global political process in which economic and psychological, domestic and transnational factors play an equally important and mutually influencing role. Security can no longer be seen in essentially military terms — as the deterrence by one alliance of a military attack by the other: we all know that this attack is extremely implausible. But it cannot be conceived, either, in purely cooperative terms, as a common effort against the costs and dangers of the arms race similar to the fight against cancer: despite a general acceptance of the suicidal character of war, the political struggle for influence continues, and it continues to be influenced, often in a direct and unconscious way, by considerations having to do with the military balance or with the resolve of great powers in the use of force against smaller ones. Only a conception of security which includes both the elements of cooperation and of conflict, of interdependence and of inequality, can do justice to a situation where neither the Cold War model of the two blocs ranged against each other in hostile confrontation nor the idealistic model of collective security apply — but rather a complex interplay of divergent and common interests between the superpowers, between them and their allies, between the various governments and the various domestic and transnational social forces.

European security can only be seen against the background of the fundamental changes which have occurred on the European scene in the last ten or twelve years. By and large, these changes have gone in the direction of complexity:

1. from bipolarity (based on the nuclear superiority of the United States and the conventional superiority of the Soviet Union) to a mixture of bipolarity (with a certain trend towards Soviet superiority), of multipolairty and of anarchy;

2. from hostility between the two camps, accompanied by unity within, to a mixture of that situation and of cooperation between the two camps and quarrels (although to a very different degree) within them;

3. from the Cold War, defined as the primacy of an external, frozen conflict, to Hot Peace, defined as the primacy of multiple, fluctuating domestic conflicts;

175

4. from the danger of war to the reality of disorder.

We are, them in a new period of transition comparable, to some extent, to the years 1947-8. Europe was already divided, much on today's lines, but there was no certainty about the permanence of the United States' presence, about the character of Soviet rule in Eastern Europe, about the fate of Greece and of Yugoslavia, about the role of Communist parties in France and in Italy, about the evolution of each part of Germany. Today, the situation is of course more stable, especially in the two Germanys, but the strict correspondence between a country's geographical situation, its diplomatic and military alignment and its domestic regime, is being called into question, at least in the Western half of the Continent; and this differentiation and uncertainty is being held in check, in the East, only by the Soviet Union's willingness to use force within its camp — which itself has consequences for the relations of the camp with the West, in an era of increasing and possibly destabilising contacts.

The Cold War could be characterised by the primacy of the defensive, each camp being united and protected from the other by their mutual hostility. Today we have more a state of mutual vulnerability — to each other's indirect influence through contagion or demonstration effects, to domestic turmoil or to the world economic crisis. The strange character of the negotiations on European security is that they are based on contrasting bets over long-range trends. Everybody accepts the *status quo* but everbody hopes that long-range change will influence it, in particular by the domestic transformation of the other side, in a direction more favourable to its own interests: liberalisation of the East or 'Finlandisation' of the West.

What makes the impact of the negotiations so difficult to assess is that the structure and the evolution of the different dimensions of international reality are fundamentally diverse. The strategic and regional balances have, until recently, remained fairly stable, but may be affected by their 'decoupling'. Diplomatic alignments have shifted, in the case of Romania, of France, perhaps of Greece and Portugal, but not in a central or decisive way. Perhaps the most important dimension is the third one, that of change in the perceptions and aspirations of social groups and forces within societies — but the question of the degree to which they will be held in check by the other two dimensions or will suddenly or progressively modify them remains entirely open. And this is the evolution which the various governments hope to encourage or to block, to channel or to control.

Common and Conflicting Objectives

For the Soviet Union, the primary objective is to prevent any of these changes from endangering either its own regime or its control of Eastern Europe. European society means above all the security of the Moscow leadership — which would be challenged by Western influence on East European or Soviet societies, or by an alliance of the United States or of Western Europe with China. On the other hand, the same goal of maintaining their authority also drives the Soviet leaders to seek the economic cooperation of the West, which is necessary given the demands of their societies and the unwillingness to run the political risks of satisfying them through decentralising reform. The first objective leads to the exclusion of alien influence, the second to contacts and the acceptance of interdependence. Both are conservative or defensive in intent, but both, leaving aside ideological or power political ambitions, lead to a third, more dynamic goal. Since interaction and interdependence with the West are seen as both dangerous and necessary, leverage or influence upon Western developments are sought at the very least in order to prevent these developments from going into directions which might have undesirable consequences — if only in terms of example or indirect influence — on Soviet and East European societies. In this game of comparative influences the Soviet Union seeks above all to prevent the emergence of a strong political and military Western Europe. It tries to decrease American influences but to prevent its replacement by a West European power. It tries to increase differences between Berlin and West Germany, West Germany and Western Europe, Western Europe and the United States but not to the point where Western structures would crash down, thereby creating problems for the Soviet bloc itself.

Beyond that, it is not clear whether the Soviet Union has any long-range view, whether it is looking seriously towards a stage of military *détente* which would bring the dismantling of existing military organisations and would leave it the sole dominant power in the European continent, or replace the existing structure by a Soviet-American condominium weighted, in Europe, on the Soviet side.

It may even be the case that the economic crisis of the West and the developments in Southern Europe could be starting a revision of the relatively conservative Soviet stance towards a more direct exploitation of political expectations of political opportunities in Western Europe coupled with lesser expectations of benefits from its prosperity.

The position of the United States is less ambiguous. Basically, on European security, the United States is a *status quo* power. What it wants is mostly to preserve the alliance system which, in its view, has kept the peace on the European continent. First, it wants to slow down the global arms race, with its dangers and its costs; hence its interest

177

in SALT which has inevitable consequences for European security. Secondly, domestic considerations (above all Congressional pressures for troop reductions of which the Mansfield amendment is the most spectacular expression) have made the American administration desire a positive course for the MBFR talks. Thirdly, tensions with Western Europe on non-military issues (such as trade and energy) have made the American Government try increasingly to extract some leverage out of its crucial position in European security, thereby both affirming its role as a protector of Western Europe and putting it into question.

The American interest in European security negotiations is, then, an essentially indirect and primarily damage-limiting one. It has led the United States to be in favour of the SALT negotiations, unfavourable to the CSCE in which it has seen first an anti-American enterprise (which it was before 1968), then a way for the Europeans to address impossible demands to the Soviet Union and hence to create problems for the stability of the Soviet-American *détente*. Finally on MBFR it has led from a tactically favourable but actually reserved position to a genuinely favourable one.

Among the other powers, the two most crucial ones for European security are the two Germanys. The German Democratic Republic was primarily interested in the CSCE, in which it saw an indirect way to get international recognition of its sovereignty. Now that she has obtained this, her interest has declined. Federal Germany has the symmetrical and opposite interest of seeing in European society a way to multilateralise the *Ostpolitik*, namely to push for a 'change through rapprochement' with Eastern Europe, that is, essentially, with the German Democratic Republic.

The other East European countries see in European security negotiations a way of encouraging *détente* which they all favour, and, at least in the case of Romania, a way of breaking their *tête-à-tête* with the Soviet Union through a multilateral dialogue which would constitute both a protection and a chance for self-assertion.

Clearly, while the Soviet Union shares the objective of *détente*, the Romanian objective of greater freedom of action for small powers clashes with the Soviet one of consolidating the unity of the Socialist Camp, just as the West German one of increasing communication with, and liberalisation in, East Germany clashes with that of *Abgrenzung*, or of formalising the division of Germany and of Europe.

The other European states, whether or not they belong to Western organisations, are closer in their objectives to Romania or to Federal Germany than they are to the Soviet Union. They do want *détente* for its own sake: this is a feeling particularly strong among the smaller, in particular Nordic, countries. But they also want it to be an occasion for the various States of the Continent to increase their autonomous activities and for their societies to communicate. France, which claims to have shown the way to East-West *détente* and wants to keep an original role in it, yet sees SALT and MBFR as superpower or bloc-led operations, has, contrary to the view of the United States, indicated a clear preference for CSCE as being both less dangerous to the military balance, more accessible to the role of individual states and more relevant to the evolution of societies and to the fate of individuals. The neutral countries have shown considerable activity, especially in CSCE, as well as solidarity with small countries cutting across the borders of alliances. The nine countries of the Common Market have also taken negotiations on European security as an opportunity for affirming their distinctive identity and their ability of working together, although again, this has emerged in the context of CSCE and its preparation more than in MBFR. Even there specific West European and neutral concerns are being expressed, albeit negatively, and appear as an essential political aspect of European security.

The Political Consequences of the Three Negotiations: a Provisional Balance

A first aspect which has already been mentioned is that the political issue, very often, has less to do with *what* is being negotiated about than who is doing the negotiating. In this respect there is a clear difference between the three negotiations: SALT is bilateral not only in the discussions but in the institutionalised commission they have set up; the MBFR talks are essentially run between the two alliances, despite the presence of several other concerned countries; finally the CSCE is the only one which includes all European States on a basis of formal equality. It is not surprising, then, that the order of preference of the United States and, perhaps increasingly the Soviet Union — SALT, MBFR, CSCE — is the opposite of that of the small and medium European states who identify essentially with the CSCE. Unfortunately, it is probably not by chance that the conference which the Europeans have the greatest role in is also that which has the least bearing on the problems of European security in a strict sense. Moreover, it may well be that the great role played by West European, neutral and small states in it has been proportional to their lack of relevance even in terms of the conference itself. For while they have dominated the parliamentary proceedings and the endless committee discussions, there are signs that the conclusion of the conference, both in terms of timing and of the level of the meeting, is being planned under a Soviet-American agreement which is a sort of bargain involving the two other negotiations. In a deeper more general and partly symbolic way the CSCE and the unexpected realignments it has witnessed are nevertheless at least as relevant as the other two conferences to the evolution of European security. The three negotiations may be said to converge towards the latter: the CSCE means the multilateralisation and, to some degree, the institutionalisation of European *détente*, which means grappling with the fundamental problems concerning its nature and the structure of the political relationships involving the continent of Europe. SALT II, on the other hand, means the Europeanisation of the superpower strategic dialogue: while SALT I had dealt essentially with their global relationship, SALT II is inevitably raising problems directly relevant to Europe, such as the status of the Forward Based Systems (i.e. the American planes stationed on the European continent or in the Mediterranean and capable of striking the Soviet Union with nuclear weapons). Both sets of issues converge in MBFR, where the fate of nuclear weapons in Europe, the nature of the relations between the superpowers and their European allies, and the role of defence establishments and budgets in their relation to the evolution of European societies are centrally raised by the apparently abstruse discussions on numbers of men and weapons.

The political consequences of the SALT negotiations, as seen through the reactions of European public opinion, fall into three categories.

From the point of view of global strategy, the Moscow Agreement of May 1972 (or SALT I) means a codification of the notion of parity, and, through the renunciation (for all practical purposes) of anti-ballistic missile defence, the confirmation of the doctrine of mutually assured destruction. In both cases, the agreement only confirms an existing situation. This situation certainly raises problems about the credibility of the American deterrent as the basis of European security. However, while these problems are felt by European experts and while some expressions of doubt or fear about American protection have appeared here and there, on the whole the SALT agreement has produced no panic and has been received rather favourably. For one thing, the Europeans have been taking parity for granted long before it was there; for another, this situation, rightly, or perhaps wrongly, does not worry them too much, for they assume that, even in the situation of parity, as long as the American presence and involvement on the European continent are given concrete form by American troops and tactical nuclear weapons, the Soviet Union, which is not considered likely to plan any massive military undertaking against Western Europe anyway, will be deterred by the impossibility of being sure of avoiding escalation into a strategic war with the United States. Hence, the nature and the degree of the American involvement in the regional European balance are felt more acutely as affecting European security than the variations in the strategic balance.

This is why the second aspect, involving the links between the regional and the global balance, which seems likely to be at the centre of the SALT II negotiations, is much more sensitive and provokes many more doubts and, potentially, much more criticism on the West European side than the global aspect which was at the centre of SALT I. The issue raised by the Soviet Union, of the American Forward Based Systems (i.e., the nuclear-capable vehicles based in Europe and able to reach the territory of the Soviet Union) and the associated problem of the definition of strategic and tactical weapons touches directly upon the nature of the American presence in, and guarantee to, Western Europe. The apparent trend towards accepting the Soviet definition of 'strategic' (i.e., weapons capable of reaching the territories of the super-powers themselves) and towards reducing the role of tactical nuclear weapons, seems to lead towards a growing separation between the re-gional (or theatre) balance and the global one, towards a growing 'sanc-tuarisation' of the two superpowers themselves, towards a growing unwillingness to risk escalation in the case of a conflict in continental Europe and hence towards a growing 'decoupling' between its fate, or at least its system of deterrence and defence, and that of the United States. This feeling, which as yet is limited to specialists is likely to grow if and when negotiations in SALT II bring these issues to the fore-front of public discussion.

In fact, even this second set of concerns is not of an essentially strategic nature. What feeds it, and what has provoked the most worries and protests in Western Europe is the basic question of the political priority, for the United States, between its relationship with the Soviet Union and its relationship with its Western European allies. This in-volves much more than the SALT I agreement and the SALT II talks themselves. It is the Declaration of Principles of May 1972, the institu-tion of a bilateral Soviet-American standing commission and the Agree-ment for the Prevention of Nuclear War of June 1973 which have stirred the accusations of 'a new Yalta', of a 'Soviet-American con-dominium', and of the superimposition, over the old structure of European security, based on the opposition and balance of the two alliances, of a new structure, based on the collaboration of the two superpowers in protecting a passive Europe and in controlling its politi-cal evolution sufficiently to nip any conflict in the bud before it becomes open and creates risks of escalation.

This same fear of the creation of a passive, more or less denuclearised and more or less neutralised Europe is central to most of European concerns about the MBFR. Before the negotiations themselves really began, two Western concessions, both made at the instigation of the United States, concerning the dropping of the notion of *balanced* force reductions (the 'B' in MBFR) and the exclusion of Hungary from the proposed zone of reductions in Central Europe, have given substance to European fears that what started as a Western bid to prevent a European security conference as proposed by the Soviet Union and the unilateral withdrawal of American troops as proposed by Senator Mansfield may end in a Soviet-American understanding which would lead to a partial American disengagement without satisfying Senator Mansfield while consolidating Soviet superiority in Europe and advancing the Soviet conception of 'military *détente*', that is, of a continent where a reduced American presence, combined with Soviet-American collaboration, would act as a permanent inhibition to the emergence of a West European political and military power.

The issues in MBFR can be summarised under the headings Who? What? Where? and How Much? applied to the notion of force reductions and deployment. The only universal common ground is that everyone would like to reduce costs, and hence troops, although some European countries, like Federal Germany, who were at first for this reason eager to participate in the first stage of reductions, have revised their position because of the political implication of the answer to the question: who? But even the quantitative question implies a basic political difference reflected in the quarrel around the 'B'. The West wanted asymmetrical reductions leading to a common ceiling, that is, changing the present situation of Soviet superiority in Europe into one of stabilisation through true parity. The Soviet Union, not illogically, argued that this would give the West a unilateral advantage and, less reassuringly, declared the aim of the negotiations to be the stabilisation or the freezing of the present relation of forces, considered as being part of the *status quo*. This means that whether for defensive or offensive, regional or global reasons, the Soviet conception of European security implies Soviet military superiority in Europe.

On the other questions, too, the Soviet position after some wavering, is, today, simpler and more logical than the Western one but is also, obviously designed politically to influence the evolution of intra-West European and intra-Atlantic relations in a direction unfavourable to the strengthening of Western unity or of West European autonomy.

The questions 'who?' and 'what?' raise primarily two dilemmas — national, foreign, or non-European troops, or all of them?; nuclear or conventional weapons, or both? In both cases the Western position, while unclear or contradictory at first, has crystallised on the more restrictive answer: in the first case, by suggesting a reduction limited to American and Soviet troops in the first stage, so as not to jeopardise chances of West European troops making up for American ones; in the second case, by restricting the negotiations to conventional weapons, so as not to put into question the American nuclear presence. Conversely, the Soviet position after some hesitations on the first point, has crystallised on the more inclusive formula, asking for the dismantling of national troops and the withdrawal of nuclear weapons, as well as for withdrawals of stationed troops and conventional weapons. Again, logic seems on the Soviet side, so much so that it is doubtful that the Western position is tenable for long. But the details of the Warsaw Pact proposals as well as the public Soviet comments show very clearly that the first priority of the Eastern position is to prevent the emergence of a Western European defence capability and, in particular, to place constraints on the West German Bundeswehr. National troops belonging to the controlled zone are to be dismantled while stationed troops are to be redeployed; the latter are, after reduction, submitted to a freeze and to controls which not only would prevent their strengthening and their uniting but would put them in a special situation of surveillance by the parties to the treaty, including the Soviet Union.

Hence, the relevance of the question: 'where?'. Since these controls do not apply to all the countries concerned, they would tend to put a special zone, of which Germany would be the most significant part, in a special situation. Hence the question of the implication of these measures for the political future of Central Europe and, especially, for Federal Germany's relations with Western Europe.

Paradoxically, the limitation to Central Europe raises no less delicate questions for the regions which are not included – the so-called Northern and Southern flanks. These countries are particularly concerned with the question: 'how?', with putting constraints on the movement and the redeployment of forces rather than on their quantity. Without these constraints, the reductions on the politically relatively stable Central Front might make the already unstable flanks, especially Southern Europe, even more insecure.

However, while, in case of reductions in Central Europe, an agreement not to redeploy the same troops elsewhere is likely, the chances of any more far-ranging measures limiting the threat and the use of force, which were the whole point of the MBFR talks for the smaller nations and, at the beginning at least, for Federal Germany, seem to be very remote indeed. Such proposals come up against the clear opposition of the Soviet Union and the almost as clear lack of enthusiasm of the United States.

While the MBFR talks seem blocked at the time of writing, a first agreement is by no means impossible. But the chances are that it would reflect the political interests of the Soviet Union and the United States rather than those of the Europeans except in the most limited and indirect way. It would be a symbolic reduction, designed to 'keep the détente going' in spite of the obstacles which are blocking the more serious SALT negotiations. Beyond that, and beyond tactical considerations linked to the US Congress and to the CSCE negotiations, the question remains whether both sides want to retain the present military structure of European security, but at a lower level of troops and of costs, or whether they want to prepare the ground for a new structure. In particular, are Soviet statements about the 1980s being the years of 'military *détente*' built upon the successes of political and economic *détente* and leading to the dismantling of the two military organisations to be taken seriously? How is one to reconcile or to balance the Soviet desire for the *status quo*, their insistence on the continuing confrontation of the two systems, on the one hand, and their stated objective of getting rid of 'military blocs' in favour of a new European structure based on 'collective security'? This, at bottom, is also the basic problem of the Conference on Security and Cooperation in Europe.

Ambiguity belongs to the essence of CSCE, even more than of MBFR. In a sense it has been, from the beginning, a comedy of errors. The Soviet Union had been pressing for it since 1965, and so had small countries like its rebellious ally Romania and non-aligned Yugoslavia. But they obviously did so for exactly opposite reasons: the Soviet Union in order to solidify the Eastern bloc and the division of Europe, the smaller countries in order to introduce more flexibility into the system and more freedom of action for themselves. Someone was bound to lose his bet. Similarly, the Soviet Union wanted to consolidate the regimes of Eastern Europe, and to have its own predominance over them recognised and legitimised by the West; but, by the same token, it was renouncing, to some extent at least, the propaganda benefits of playing up the imperialist, and particularly the West German revanchist, danger; and it was, again to some extent at least, opening Eastern Europe to some Western penetration which is inseparable from trade and *détente*. As regards attitudes to the West, the campaign for the CSCE started with a pronounced anti-American character: it was meant to isolate both Federal Germany and the United States and to promote the idea of a pan-Europe in which the Soviet Union but not the United States would be included. After 1969 the American and Canadian presence were welcomed more and more and, today, the Soviet Union is appealing to the United States to moderate the demands of the West Europeans and a certain communiy of interests and attitudes between the two superpowers is making itself felt increasingly just as, conversely, a certain community of interests and attitudes is emerging between the small and middle states of Europe irrespective of their alliance positions.

Finally, the CSCE and the whole pan-European theme was feared by many West European circles as highly dangerous to West European integration: the Nine would be drawn into divergent or conflicting attitudes, the Community would be submerged in a wider, pan-European framework. In fact, the preparation of the CSCE and the negotiations themselves have turned out to be, so far, the most — one might almost say the only — successful exercise in political cooperation among the Nine. Consultation, representation of the Community, the hammering out of a common position, have functioned remarkably well. Contrary to most expectations and to some earlier experiences with Gaullism and *Ostpolitik*, the dialogue with the East has seemed — at the CSCE at least — a more unifying than divisive theme for the European Community.

Of course, one might argue that this has proved so precisely because, at the CSCE, the Nine were dealing more with procedural and symbolic issues rather than with substantive ones involving sovereignty, security or bread and butter matters like money or energy. The same could be said about the exhilerating activity of the small and neutral countries from Switzerland to Romania. The whole conference may be seen as a psychodrama, a game in which the less powerful can 'do their thing' with the two superpowers adopting a more passive or withdrawn attitude until they decide that the fun has lasted long enough and that it is time to go home — to the real world.

This, indeed, is the present issue, with the Soviet Union pressing, with American concurrence, for an early conclusion at the summit, while the Nine and the neutrals would like to continue the conference until they obtain more concessions on freedom of movement, and the Romanians wanting an institutionalisation which would make the conference into a forum. While it is too early to predict the time and form of the conclusion, the essential elements of the balance are not likely to change nor to lose their basic ambiguity.

The balance-sheet can be presented in the jargon of the conference — in terms of the weights attached to the results in so-called 'Basket I' versus the results in so-called 'Basket III'. After many discussions in the preliminary talks at Helsinki, it had been decided to divide the issues into four 'baskets' handled by four Commissions. The first dealt with the principles of European security, above all with that of the inviolability of borders; the second with economic cooperation; the third with human contacts and information, with what the West calls the free movement of people and ideas; the fourth with the follow-up to the conference.

It emerged fairly quickly that the two essential 'baskets' were the first and third. The second, economic, could only be filled with declarations of interest; one political point emerged, however, namely the decisive role of the representatives of the Common Market Commission in discussions on economic relations, and the tacit acceptance of this role by the Eastern side. The fourth basket was — for all practical purposes — set aside, as the Western delegations did not want to be committed on the follow-up of the conference before evaluating the results of the conference itself, and were rather hostile to institutionalisation anyway, while the Soviet enthusiasm in its favour seems to have considerably diminished in view of the opportunities offered by multilateral institutions to small states. The Soviet interest was concentrated on 'Basket I', that is, on the legitimisation of the territorial and political *status quo*, including the division of Germany and, implicitly at least, the political regimes in Eastern Europe. The interest of the West Europeans is concentrated on 'Basket III', namely on contacts between individuals and societies going beyond the traditional, state-controlled, cultural relations.

On 'Basket I', despite protracted battles on 'inviolability' versus 'immutability' of borders, and despite having to accept principles like self-determination and religious freedom, the Soviets essentially achieved their objective, which was at the same time their main (or at least their main minimum) objective for the Conference itself. But they did not achieve it in the expected manner: through one solemn proclamation — but though painstaking discussions in which they had to bargain and were often put on the defensive by lesser powers. This is why they are anxious, having made their essential point, to put an end to the exercise.

On 'Basket III', the situation is in some respects the same and in others the opposite. The very admission of 'Basket III' as a separate subject, of 'human contacts' as a legitimate issue for negotiations represents a hard-fought-for and a worthwhile victory for the Western point of view. On the other hand, contrary to the Soviet victory on 'Basket I', where the symbolic and the substantive coincide, on 'Basket III' a symbolic victory (itself heavily qualified, upon Soviet insistence, by declarations reaffirming state sovereignty) remains empty if it does not lead to concrete measures facilitating the circulation of people or of information: and here the basket remains desperately empty and the Soviet position, so far rigidly intransigent. This is why the Nine and the neutrals are trying to continue the discussions and to deny the Soviets the final satisfaction of a festive celebration at the summit to conclude the conference, until some more substantive progress has been achieved on 'Basket III'.

What Next?

As between the two baskets and the two positions, two different conceptions of *détente* are at play. One, the Soviet one with which the United States agrees in important respects thereby turning it into a great power one, is based on the primacy of security, and hence of the *status quo* and of the preservation of the existing territorial, military and political balances if possible at a cost lowered through arms control measures. The other, that of the Nine and the neutrals, is based on the notion of peaceful change, of encouraging communications, reconciliation and mutual transformation of societies, of creating new political realities such as the unity of Western Europe, as long as they do not jeopardise the peace of the continent.

But this brings us back to the ultimate problem of European security, as defined at the beginning of this paper, in terms of the contradictions between the three levels of the European system, the strategic, the diplomatic and the social, between the rigidity of the first, the limited mobility of the second and the deeper and more unpredictable evolution and revolutions of the third. The essential questions raised by the three negotiations we have briefly reviewed — the future of the American nuclear presence and political commitment in Europe; their eventual partial or total replacement by a West European defence capability or, on the contrary, by a denuclearised Europe under a Soviet-American condominium; the nature of East-West *détente*, its *status quo*, its arms control-orientated or its dynamic, politically orientated character; the nature of relations between small European states and superpowers. All point to two basic dimensions: the place and role of Europe with respect to Soviet-American bilateral relations and the clashes between the dynamic, social transnational and national elements of the European scene and the stable territorial and strategic system.

True, the system itself may become less stable, mainly through the increasing uncertainties concerning American military presence and protection; but these are, themselves, less the direct result of military developments than their reflection through the transformation of American attitudes, due in no small measure to domestic evolution and to economic conflicts with Western Europe. In general, it remains true to say that the existing security system based on the balance of the two alliances led by the two superpowers and on the division of Germany and of Europe along ideological lines is still fulfilling its main function, that of avoiding a war between the two Germanys, two Europes, and two superpowers. A glance at other continents is enough to demonstrate its advantages from the point of view of peace and stability. But the costs, shortcomings and negative features of the system are more and more visible under the impact of national and social aspirations. Even for the avoidance of inter-state violence and threats thereof, the security which reigns in Central Europe exists much less elsewhere, in the North because of military imbalance, in the South because of political and national conflicts and domestic instabilities. The security which exists between alliances does not exist within them, as shown by the fate of Czechoslovakia and the fears of Romania or by the conflict between Greece and Turkey. The economic costs of the security system, as it is, are increasingly felt to be excessively high.

Finally, the political costs in terms of freezing not only borders but oppressive political and national situations are felt more and more to be intolerable, the more *détente* encourages a discounting of the threat of general war and a taking for granted of the advantages of the existing system. The domestic changes in Southern Europe and the Cyprus conflict are cases in point. Together, they may encourage a more general evolution which might challenge the bases of the existing security system and of the military balance themselves. To what extent, for instance, are they compatible with neutralist or pro-Soviet regimes in the whole Mediterranean, or with Communist participation in EEC or NATO governments?

The danger is that the aspirations to national independence or revolutionary change should bring Europe into an era of unpredictability from the point of view of violent conflict or, conversely, that the requirements of the East-West balance and of international security should serve as a justification for repressing popular movements and restoring unpopular regimes.

No conceivable alternative system would be free of these dilemmas, since the two pure models of the opposition between two symmetrical monolithic blocs or of the suppression of all alliances, inequalities and special links or conflicts between states in the name of collective security are out of the question. Since alliance structures, and social trends may diverge, two directions seem possible. The Soviet Union seems to advocate dismantling the alliance structures but keeping up the conflict between the two social systems, between a closely integrated 'socialist commonwealth' and capitalist imperialism. The prevailing Western approach would seem more in agreement both with historical experience and with popular aspirations: it consists in keeping the existing military balance and alliance structure (although, if possible, at lower costs) but increasing communications between and diversity within the two alliances and the two societies. But whichever of the existing and contradictory trends gets the upper hand, it is safe to predict that under any combination of systems Europe will more and more have to live with the difficult problem of reconciling stability and change, security and freedom.

14. THE MILITARY BALANCE BETWEEN EAST AND WEST IN EUROPE

Nino Pasti

Part 1 — General Considerations and Conventional Forces

Introduction

In order to give the general framework within which this paper must be considered, some points have to be clarified. Information concerning the number of armed forces is not readily available and not reliable, particularly as far as the Warsaw Pact is concerned. When one tries to deal with military budgets it is even more difficult. First one has to examine whether all defence expenditure is shown in the military budget, and this is not always the case. *The Military Balance, 1973-4*, published by the International Institute for Strategic Studies (IISS), stated that 'The Soviet defence budget, which has remained implausibly static at just under 18 billion roubles a year since 1969, excludes a number of items: "military R & D (Research and Development): stockpiling, civil defence, foreign military aid, as well as space and nuclear energy programmes"; and also frontier guards and other security troops'.[1] The *SIPRI Yearbook, 1973*, published by the Stockholm International Peace Research Institute (SIPRI), is not of the same opinion. It stated that 'The evidence showing that particular activities are financed outside the defence budget is not conclusive, and the upward adjustment made for these alleged omissions are highly speculative'.[2]

Incidentally, the same things happen in the United States. According to the *International Herald Tribune* of 24 May 1974, Senator John C. Stennis, Chairman of the Senate Armed Services Committee was not to be fooled:

> on 5 February he said that the sum of these two requests is $99.1 billion and that this sum compares to $80.2 billion which was appropriated for the Department of Defense last year for Fiscal Year 1974. When the Atomic Energy Commission's weapons programme is added to this sum, it breaks the $100 billion barrier.[3]

This means a 25 per cent increase on the initially declared military budget, an increase which is not very far from the 30 per cent increase in the Soviet military budget estimated by the IISS. Another official confirmation of American 'hidden' military costs came from Senator

189

Symington. During a Hearing before the American Senate on Soviet-American Strategic Policies held on 4 March 1974, he said 'The national debt is some $450 million . . . that is half of what we have spent on national defense in the last 12 years (about $878 billion) *and that does not count a lot of hidden expense that you* [Secretary of Defence Schlesinger] *and I know should properly go into military costs*'.[4]

Things are even worse when one tries to convert the military budget of the various nations into a common currency, normally the dollar, in order to have a common yardstick to make comparisons. While SIPRI and IISS are in agreement that the conversion of Warsaw Pact currencies to the dollar poses a special problem, the method adopted to deal with the problem is very far from being the same for the two institutes. The rate of exchange between dollar and rouble estimated by the IISS is considerably higher than SIPRI's. The IISS estimate is also much higher than what may be a well-informed American evaluation, namely that which has more than once been used in the *International Herald Tribune*. For example, on 19 December 1972 the newspaper stated: '[Soviet] Finance Minister Vasily F. Garbusov said that the defense expenditures in 1973 would remain unchanged at the level of the last few years, $21.5 billion'.[5] Because the declared Soviet military budget was actually something less than 18 billion roubles, the rate of exchange assumed was that one defence rouble was equivalent to 1.20-1.30 defence dollars. More recently the *International Herald Tribune* of 15-16 December 1973 stated that 'The Supreme Soviet . . . ostensibly cuts Soviet military spending next year from 17.9 billion roubles to 17.6 billion roubles; a reduction of over $400 million'.[6] Here again the assumed rate of exchange was 300 million roubles to 400 million, or one defence rouble to 1.20-1.30 defence dollars.

I do not propose to go into more details on this subject. I only desire to stress that all the figures subsequently given must be considered as orders of magnitude and not exact evaluations. If I raise some questions about the IISS data, which of course constitute my basic source of information, this does not mean that I do not greatly value the IISS estimates which are among the best and most complete available in spite of the fact that they cannot be absolutely accurate because of all the difficulties summarised above.

In the first part of this paper I attempt to evaluate the military forces in a general framework and, more specifically, conventional forces. In the second part nuclear forces are dealt with. The time period taken for conventional forces is 1963-74. The reason for choosing 1963 as the starting point is that the Cuban nuclear crisis of October 1962 may be considered the turning point between 'Cold War' and 'Coexistence' and the period under review thus covers 'coexistence' and 'cooperation'.

The Military Balance – East West Europe

Tables 1 and 2 represent NATO and Warsaw Pact military forces and military budgets, nation by nation and year by year. Table 3 is a more condensed presentation of the same data. Column 2 of Table 3 represents the armed forces of the European NATO nations without Canada and the United States and without the American troops presently deployed in Europe. It will be seen that from 1963 to 1974 the number of European troops has levelled off at around 3 million men. Recently the American Secretary of Defense confirmed this evaluation: 'The European members of the alliance maintain armed forces totalling over 3 million men'.[7]

Table 3 column 3 represents the armed forces of the Warsaw Pact excluding the Soviet Union and the Soviet forces presently deployed in Eastern Europe. From 1963 to 1974 the number of these forces has levelled off at around one million men.

An important conclusion can at once be drawn from comparison between columns 2 and 3 of Table 3: the European NATO nations have three times as many soldiers as the Warsaw Pact nations excluding the Soviet Union. Since it is a general military rule that an offensive, to be successful, requires that the aggressor have three times as many forces as the defence, the Warsaw Pact nations would thus be helpless against a European NATO attack without a substantial Soviet military reinforcement. Of course the Warsaw Pact nations have to pay something to the Soviet Union in terms of their own independence in order to get her military support. Hence the more the European nations try to increase their military power, the more the Warsaw Pact nations will be subjected to the control of the Soviet Union.

Tables 4 and 5 represent detailed figures concerning the NATO and Warsaw Pact nations for 1973-4. Table 6 summarises the same data. Columns 2 and 3 of Table 6 show that NATO Europe, compared with the Warsaw Pact nations apart from the Soviet Union, has three times the population, three times the armed forces, five to six times the Gross National Product, and six times the military budget. All this, viewed from the other side, may look seriously threatening.

Going back to Table 3, columns 4 and 5 provide a comparison of the defence budgets of the two sides. This may seem less convincing because of all the difficulties in converting the various currencies into dollars, particularly during the last three years when the dollar has not been linked to gold parity. But in any case the imbalance is so great as to render unimportant any and all possible distortions. An official American evaluation of the European NATO military budgets was given by Secretary of Defense Schlesinger on 9 April 1974 at a press conference in Federal Germany: 'The amount of money that is being spent on defence [has] increased among the Western European members of

191

Table1: NATO — Armed Forces (a.f.) (per 1000) and Military Budgets (m.b.) (million $)

Countries	1962-3		1963-4		1964-5		1965-6	
	a.f.	m.b.	a.f.	m.b.	a.f.	m.b.	a.f.	m.b.
NATO Europe								
Belgium	110	364	110	444	110	504	107	520
Denmark	46	180	49	225	52	238	51	239
Germany (F.R.G.)	353	3750	404	4607	430	5054	438	4372
Greece	160	170	160	167	162	210	160	181
Italy	450	1255	470	1510	480	1741	470	1984
Luxemburg	5	7	5	7	5	8	5	6
Netherlands	141	555	141	618	123	744	135	750
Norway	34	191	36	197	37	269	32	308
Portugal	80	158	102	176	108	172	148	205
Turkey	455	287	452	235	480	322	442	399
United Kingdom	415	4180	429	5140	425	5596	440	5937
NATO Europe w/o France	2249	11097	2358	13326	2418	14858	2428	14901
France	705	3531	636	4062	620	4270	557	4465
Total NATO Europe	2954	14628	2994	17388	3032	19128	2985	19366
Canada	124	1589	124	1480	120	1413	120	1438
United States	2815	52000	2700	52400	2690	50450	2660	52200
TOTAL NATO	5893	68217	5818	71268	5842	70991	5765	73004

Table 1: Continued

Countries	1966-7		1967-8		1968-9		1969-70	
	a.f.	m.b.	a.f.	m.b.	a.f.	m.b.	a.f.	m.b.
NATO Europe								
Belgium	107	520	102	451	99	501	102	519
Denmark	50	268	45	304	45	292	45	336
Germany (F.R.G.)	440	4335	460	4625	456	5108	465	5301
Greece	159	206	158	208	161	318	159	382
Italy	461	1982	496	2075	365*	1940*	420*	1930*
Luxemburg	2	10	1	4	1	7	1	8
Netherlands	129	750	130	816	128	898	124	940
Norway	34	298	35	303	35	320	38	344
Portugal	148	224	148	274	182	302	182	321
Turkey	450	377	480	439	514	472	483	510
United Kingdom	438	6081	429	6171	427	5460	405	5438
NATO Europe w/o France	2418	15051	2484	15670	2413	15608	2424	16029
France	522	4465	520	4879	505	6104	503	5586
Total NATO Europe	2940	19516	3004	20549	2918	21712	2927	21615
Canada	107	1461	103	1568	102	1589	98	1678
United States	3094	61000	3400	73000	3500	79576	3454	78475
TOTAL NATO	6141	81977	6507	95117	6520	102877	6479	101768

* Excluding 75,000 carabinieri and 30,000 other security forces.

Table 1:   Continued

Countries	1970-1		1971-2		1972-3		1973-4	
	a.f.	m.b.	a.f.	m.b.	a.f.	m.b.	a.f.	m.b.
NATO Europe								
Belgium	95	677	96	594	90	724	90	990
Denmark	44	365	40	410	43	438	40	568
Germany (F.R.G.)	466	5560	467	5961	467	7568	475	11083
Greece	159	420	159	338	157	495	160	580
Italy	489	2416	494	2651	514	3244	508	3964
Luxemburg	1	8	1	9	1	6	1	15
Netherlands	121	1075	116	1161	122	1562	112	2102
Norway	41	370	36	411	36	491	35	665
Portugal	185	356	218	398	218	459	204	425
Turkey	477	401	508	446	449	573	455	812
United Kingdom	390	5712	381	6108	372	6900	361	8673
NATO Europe w/o France	2468	17360	2516	18487	2469	22460	2441	29877
France	506	5874	501	5202	501	6241	504	8488
Total NATO Europe	2974	23234	3017	23689	2970	28701	2945	38365
Canada	93	1741	85	1687	84	1937	83	2141
United States	3161	71791	2699	78743	2391	83400	2253	85200
TOTAL NATO	6228	96766	5801	104119	5445	114038	5281	125706

Source: *The Military Balance.*

194

Table 2: Warsaw Pact — Armed Forces (a.f.) (per 1000) and Military Budget (m.b.) (million $)

Countries	1962-3 a.f.	m.b.	1963-4 a.f.	m.b.	1964-5 a.f.	m.b.	1965-6 a.f.	m.b.	1966-7 a.f.	m.b.	1967-8 a.f.	m.b.
Bulgaria	120	n.a.	135	256	150	n.a.	152	115	156	119	154	228
Czechoslovakia	185	n.a.	185	789	235	n.a.	235	715	220	754	225	1452
German Dem. Rep.	85	n.a.	116	65	106	n.a.	112	665	122	785	127	1063
Hungary	80	n.a.	99	277	104	n.a.	109	246	109	223	102	313
Poland	257	n.a.	257	911	272	n.a.	272	978	260	1052	270	1662
Romania	222	n.a.	227	342	222	n.a.	198	250	201	265	173	530
Total W.P. w/o USSR	949	(2500)*	1019	2640	1089	(2700)*	1083	2969	1068	3198	1051	5248
USSR	3600	33000	3300	34000	3300	34000	3150	40000	3165	35000	3220	34000
TOTAL Warsaw Pact	4549	35500	4319	36640	4389	36700	1233	42969	4233	38198	4271	39248

Countries	1968-9 a.f.	m.b.	1969-70 a.f.	m.b.	1970-1 a.f.	m.b.	1971-2 a.f.	m.b.	1972-3 a.f.	m.b.	1973-4 a.f.	m.b.
Bulgaria	153	228	154	234	149	279	148	279	146	279	152	301
Czechoslovakia	225	1538	230	1576	168	1635	185	1765	185	1875	190	1336
German Dem. Rep.	126	1715	137	1873	129	1990	126	2124	131	2240	132	2031
Hungary	102	370	97	457	101	511	103	511	103	558	103	695
Poland	274	1830	275	2080	242	2220	265	2220	274	2350	280	1799
Romania	173	551	193	574	181	745	160	798	179	725	170	528
Total W.P. w/o USSR	1053	6232	1086	6794	970	7380	987	7697	1018	8027	1027	6690
USSR	3220	50000	3300	53000	3305	51700	3375	55000	3375	77000	3425	85000
TOTAL Warsaw Pact	4273	56232	4386	59794	4275	59080	4362	62697	4393	85027	4452	91690

Source: *The Military Balance*

* Estimated by the author.
Note: Albania is not included because it has not collaborated in any way with the other members of the Warsaw Pact and has denounced the Pact in September 1968.

Table 3: NATO-Warsaw Pact Military Forces (per 1000) and Military Budgets (per million $)

	armed forces		military budgets		armed forces		military budgets		armed forces		military budgets	
	NATO w/o Canada & USA	WP w/o USSR	NATO w/o Canada & USA	WP w/o USSR	USA	USSR	USA	USSR	NATO total	WP total	NATO total	WP total
1962-3	2954	949	14628	(2500)*	2815	3600	52000	33000	5893	4549	68217	(35500)*
1963-4	2994	1019	17388	2640	2700	3300	52400	34000	5818	4319	71268	36640
1964-5	3032	1089	19128	(2700)*	2690	3300	50450	34000	5842	4389	70991	(36700)*
1965-6	2985	1083	19366	2969	2660	3150	52200	40000	5765	4233	73004	42969
1966-7	2940	1068	19516	3198	3094	3165	61000	35000	6141	4233	81977	38198
1967-8	3004	1051	20549	5248	3400	3220	73000	34000	6507	4271	95117	39248
1968-9	2918	1053	21712	6232	3500	3220	79576	50000	6250	4273	102877	56232
1969-70	2927	1086	21615	6794	3454	3300	78475	53000	6479	4386	101768	59794
1970-1	2974	970	23234	7380	3161	3305	71791	51700	6228	4275	96766	59080
1971-2	3017	987	23689	7697	2699	3375	78743	55000	5801	4362	104119	62697
1972-3	2970	1018	28701	8027	2391	3375	83400	77000	5445	4393	114038	85027
1973-4	2945	1027	38365	6690	2253	3425	85200	85000	5281	4452	125706	91690

* Estimated by the author

Source: *The Military Balance*

Table 4:   NATO 1973-4

Nations	Population (in 1000s)	Regular forces (in 1000s)	GNP (per billion $)	Defence budget (per million $)
Belgium	9800	90	35.5	990
Denmark	5020	40	20.3	568
Germany (F.R.G.)	60100	475	259.6	11083
Greece	8900	160	12.2	580
Italy	54400	508	118.1	3964
Luxemburg	345	1	1.3	15
Netherlands	13500	112	44.8	2102
Norway	4000	35	15.1	665
Portugal	9200	204	8.3	425
Turkey	37900	455	15.8	812
United Kingdom	56250	361	151.0	8673
NATO Europe w/o France	259415	2441	681.4	29877
France	52000	504	202.0	8488
Total NATO Europe	311415	2945	883.4	38365
Canada	22300	83	102.9	2141
USA	210900	2253	1151.8	85200
TOTAL NATO	544615	5281	2138.1	125706

Source: *The Military Balance*

Table 5:   Warsaw Pact 1973-4

	Population (in 1000s)	Regular forces (in 1000s)	GNP (per billion $)	Defence budget (per million $)
Bulgaria	8660	152	11.1	301
Czechoslovakia	14600	190	32.9	1336
German Dem Rep.	17000	132	35.3	2031
Hungary	10450	103	15.3	695
Poland	33725	280	44.5	1799
Romania	20900	170	26.5	528
Total WP w/o USSR	105335	1027	165.6	6690
USSR	250500	3425	439.0*	85000
Total Warsaw Pact	355835	4452	604.6*	91690

*   Estimate of Net Material Product which is lower than Gross National Product (GNP). Estimated GNP 1971 was $536 billion.

Source: *The Military Balance.*

Table 6:   NATO-Warsaw Pact 1973-4

	NATO w/o Canada & USA	WP w/o USSR	USA	USSR	Total NATO	Total Warsaw Pact
Population (X 1000)	311415	105335	210900	250500	544615	355835
Regular forces (X 1000)	2945	1027	2253	3425	5281	4452
GNP (X billion $)	883.4	165.6	1151.8	439.0*	2138.1	604.6*
Defence budgets (X million $)	38365	6690	85200	85000	125706	91690

*   USSR Net Material Product which is less than GNP.

Source: *The Military Balance.*

the Alliance by about 40 per cent in the last three years. [This] represents someting of the order of 12 per cent growth in real terms, so that defence expenditures in the aggregate have been rising even after the allowance for inflation'.[8]

The Military Balance: Central Europe

The military balance in Central Europe is of particular significance because of the Mutual Balanced Force Reduction (MBFR) talks going on between NATO and Warsaw Pact nations. According to an official American report, *U.S. Military Commitments to Europe*, dated 9 April 1974:

> The negotiations are focused on troop levels in the Central NATO region . . . NATO forces are substantial and are considered capable of giving a good account of themselves in a conventional encounter. But there are major disparities between NATO and Warsaw Pact forces in three areas: the Pact has more ground force personnel (925,000 to NATO's 777,000); it has more tanks (15,000 to 6,000); and it has its principal power, the Soviet Union, located much closer to the central European allies than the United States, giving the Soviets an added capability to reinforce the Central Region.[9]

The Warsaw Pact evaluation of the opposed forces in Central Europe is different. At a press briefing on 17 July 1974, on the occasion of the recession of the MBFR negotiations for the summer, Ambassador B. E. Quarles Van Uffold of the Netherlands, on behalf of the Western participants, said:

> The Eastern approach is different. Eastern participants proceed from the premise that the existing East-West ground-force ratio — which of course is highly favourable to them — should be preserved. Hence, they have proposed that all direct participants should from the outset reduce their forces by equal percentages. All types of forces, including air and nuclear forces, would be reduced.[10]

Because of this different approach the Warsaw Pact nations have dropped the 'balanced' and call the talks Mutual Force Reduction (MFR). The reason for this largely divergent evaluation between East and West may derive from the fact that the zone under consideration is limited and not clearly defined. *The Military Balance, 1973-1974* stated that:

> Central Europe was not defined in the communiqué agreed in the preparatory consultations, but to judge from the participants in the forthcoming negotiations and from reports of earlier discussions there has been a tacit understanding that, for the moment at least,

it is forces and armaments in Poland, Czechoslovakia, East Germany, West Germany, the Netherlands, Belgium and Luxemburg with which talks will be concerned. France will take no part in discussions and so her forces are presumably excluded (except, perhaps, under certain circumstances, the two divisions in Germany) as are any Soviet or NATO troops not stationed in the area described.[11]

France seems to be the element of disagreement. Geographically it is in the heart of Central Europe. It is located at the same distance as Poland from the boundary of the two Germanys. Politically France is still a full member of the Atlantic Alliance and its armed forces have the same commitments as the other armed forces of all the other NATO nations. The only difference concerning France is that it is no longer integrated into the allied commands. France, in addition, is a member of the Western European Union, an alliance which includes Federal Germany and provides for an armed force reciprocal support in case of aggression. Finally France and Federal Germany signed on 22 January 1963 a treaty still in existence with a chapter completely devoted to defence. Summing up, France and Federal Germany are associated by three treaties and thus all French forces have to be counted in calculations about the position in Central Europe in case of aggression against Federal Germany.

Table 7:   Ground Forces in Central Europe (in 1000s)

NATO		Warsaw Pact	
USA	190	Soviet Union	430
Great Britain	55	Czechoslovakia	150
Canada	3	East Germany	90
Belgium	65	Poland	201
Netherlands	72		
West Germany	334	Total	871
Total without France	719		
2 French Divisions in Germany	58		
Total with 2 French Divisions	777		
Total without France	719		
Total French ground forces	334		
Total with France	1053		
less US 190			
Canada 3	193		
Total without American forces	860	Source: *The Military Balance.*	

Table 7 represents the ground forces in Central Europe when only the two French Divisions stationed in Federal Germany are considered in line with the NATO evaluation and when all French forces are considered in line with the Warsaw Pact evaluation. In the first case the balance is NATO 777,000 and Warsaw Pact 871,000. In the second case the balance is NATO 1,053,000 and Warsaw Pact 871,000. It will be seen that when all the French forces are counted, there remains a good balance of ground forces in Central Europe even when and if all the Canadian and American were withdrawn from Europe. In such an eventuality the NATO forces would be 860,000 against the Warsaw Pact forces 871,000.

An official American evaluation of the balance of forces in Central Europe is given in the *Annual Defence Department Report, Financial Year 1975*, dated 4 March 1974:

We estimate that the forces which the Pact could launch against the Centre (that is the Federal Republic of Germany) with very little warning consist of:
- the 27 divisions deployed by the USSR in East Germany, Poland and Czechoslovakia;
- the 21 divisions deployed by East Germany, Czechoslovakia and Poland;
- about 2,800 aircraft of which the majority are primarily air-to-air fighters.

. . . To counter this immediate threat NATO has in the Central Region of Europe about 26 divisions and more than 2,700 aircraft in a roughly comparable area of Western Europe. The total includes 5 French divisions and 4 and one third US divisions.

. . . *Manpower in ground forces amounts to about 777,000 including French forces in Germany.* Around half of our tactical aircraft are fighter-bombers.

As a consequence of these deployments there is an approximate balance between the immediately available forces of NATO and the Warsaw Pact in the Central Region. The Pact has an advantage over NATO in the number of men in the ground forces. The Pact also has a large numerical superiority in tanks (about 15,500 to 6,000 for NATO) but NATO possesses important quantitative and qualitative advantages in tank destroyers, anti-tank weapons, trucks, logistic support, and — most important of all — modern fighter aircraft.

. . . With the war reserves that we propose to stockpile, we should be able to fight these forces longer than we believe that the Pact could sustain its attack.[12]

It is not clear why the number of NATO divisions includes five French divisions while the number of soldiers include only the two French divisions deployed in Germany.

Table 8:   Warsaw Pact Divisions and Tanks in Central Europe

Considering all divisions at full Soviet strength: 316 medium Tanks each Tank division and 188 medium Tanks each motorised division.

NATIONAL FORCES

Nations	Tr. Div.	Tanks	Mot. Div.	Tanks	Total Tanks	Tanks credited
East Germany	2	632	4	752	1384	2000
Poland	5	1580	7*	1316	2896	3400
Czechoslovakia	5	1580	3†	564	2144	3400
4 Cadre Div.s.					316	
Total number of tanks					6740	8800

SOVIET FORCES

East Germany	10	3160	10	1880	5040	?
Poland	2	632			632	?
Czechoslovakia	2	632	3	564	1196	?
Total number of tanks					6868	?

Grand Total number of Tanks with Warsaw Pact formations *at full strength*	13608
Grand Total number of Tanks estimated by NATO (Schlesinger)	15500

*   Poland has 1 airborne division.
†   Poland and Czechoslovakia have 2 cadre divisions each at less than ¼ of establishment.

Source: *The Military Balance.*

The Warsaw Pact's 'large numerical superiority' in tanks requires some comments. First, it is not clear how the NATO evaluators arrive at 15,500 tanks in Central Europe. If all the divisions were at full strength the maximum number of tanks in formations would be 13,608 (see Table 8). Very probably tanks in formations are only a fraction of this total. This difference between estimated and real numbers of tanks may be caused by the fact that the Soviets are replacing the old T54 and T55 tanks with more modern T62 and thus the Warsaw Pact has a considerable number of old tanks in reserve. It has also to be noted that, according to Trevor Cliffe:

Besides the tanks listed in Table 1 [5,450 NATO, 12,500 Warsaw Pact] NATO has a stockpile of approximately 5,000 tanks most of them main battle tanks of modern design in West Germany. These are partly intended as a reserve from which replacement would be drawn for the front-line damaged or destroyed in the battle but some are earmarked for the use of Americans and other reinforcement troops.[13]

In addition the Middle East War of 1973 showed the increasing vulnerability of tanks to highly mobile anti-tank missiles. About 5,000 tanks were poured into the battle by both sides and, according to the *SIPRI Yearbook, 1974,* 'over the three-week period of hostilities . . . tanks were lost at a rate of more than one every fifteen minutes'.[14] *The Military Balance, 1973-1974* specifies that 'This NATO numerical weakness in tanks . . . is offset to some extent by a superiority in anti-tank weapons, a field in which new missiles coming into service may increasingly give more strength to the defence'.[15] Finally, quality must be considered and not only quantity: 'NATO tanks are generally superior (even to the T62, now increasingly coming into service)'.[16] The T54 and T55 which still form the bulk of the Soviet allied forces were called by the Germans 'the 36-ton coffins' because when hit they burn immediately. We may therefore conclude that a more accurate qualitative and quantitative evaluation of tanks and anti-tank weapons on both sides would considerably reduce the actual or supposed Warsaw Pact advantage in numerical superiority.

The evaluation of the 'added capability to reinforce the Central region' that the Soviets are supposed to have because they are much closer to Central Europe than the United States has also been exaggerated. Sea movements have a far greater potentiality than road movements. During the Normandy landing in 1944 the Allies were able to move an enormous quantity of men and material by sea while the Germans were unable to move their forces by road. For a considerable period of time the Germans had more forces than the Allies within a range of 150-200 miles. But their reinforcements either never reached the battle or arrived too late and piecemeal. Another striking example is provided by the war in Vietnam. The United States was able to move millions of men and millions of tons by sea. It would have been impossible to fight such a wat at a distance of 10,000 miles if the supplies had had to be moved by road. Finally, one must note that the Soviet Union's forces are not concentrated along the borders of Poland, Czechoslovakia, and the German Democratic Republic, but are spread over vast territories, two-thirds being in Asia.

One last point must be clarified to avoid misunderstanding. Very often land power is measured by number of divisions. A Soviet division

Table 9:   USSR Land Power (army men X 1000)

	1962-3		1963-4		1964-5	
	a.m.	Div.	a.m.	Div.	a.m.	Div.
relation between army men (a.m.) and number of divisions	2500	160 15600	2000	150 13300	2200	140 15700

	1965-6		1966-7		1967-8	
relation between army men (a.m.) and number of divisions	2000	140 14300	2000	140 14300	2000	140 14300

	1968-9		1969-70		1970-1	
relation between army men (a.m.) and number of divisions	2000	140 14300	2000	148 13500	2000	157 12800

	1971-2		1972-3		1973-4	
relation between army men (a.m.) and number of divisions	2000	160 12500	2000	164 12200	2000	164 12200

USA Land Power

1973-4	Army men	801500	Divisions	14
	relation between army men and number of divisions			57200

The Annual Defense Department Report FY 1975, March 1974, states: 'The land force structure is expressed here in terms of Division Force equivalents because that concept provides a good standard of measure for land force capabilities. In the army (active and reserve) it encompasses the division itself plus two support increments (S/v) totalling about **48,000** men'. (p. 98)

Source: *The Military Balance.*

has very little in common with an American division. Table 9 represents the relationship between men and numbers of divisions. The Soviet Union with 2,000,000 men have 164 divisions with an average of 12,200 men per division. The United States with 801,500 men have 14 divisions with an average of 57,200 men per division. These averages include the manpower necessary to operate higher commands and ground organisations on both sides. A more exact evaluation of the American division is given by the *Annual Defense Department Report, FY 1975*: 'An Army force structure of 21 Division Force Equivalents (DFEs) would require more than one million men when deployed abroad for sustained combat'.[17] With 2,000,000 men the Soviet Union could build the equivalent of 42 American DFEs and not four times more. The main difference between a Soviet and an American DFE is represented by two 'Support Increments' which are included in the number of American divisions but not in the Soviet Union's. The Support Increments give the American division a far greater combat and staying power than the Soviet Union's. All this is not new. Winston Churchill wrote of the period of the Second World War: 'A Soviet division was equivalent to about a third of a British or United States division'.[18]

Function of the Soviet and American Forces Deployed in Europe

The function of the Soviet forces deployed in Europe was described by President Nixon in his *Foreign Policy Report to the Congress* of 9 February 1972: 'Soviet troops are not deployed in Europe just to match ours. They secure the Soviet hegemony over Eastern Europe; most importantly, perhaps, they embody the Soviet Union's permanent presence as a power in the European sphere'.[19]

The reason why the American forces are deployed in Europe was explained by Deputy Secretary of State Kenneth Rush to the House of Representatives on 10 July 1973 when he pleaded against any unilateral reduction:

It [Western Europe] is our most important market and our most important supplier. American firms have more than 28 billion dollars invested in Western Europe which earns American investors 3 billion dollars a year. *Make no mistake. Our prosperity and the prosperity of the entire world is deeply affected by Western Europe. That means American jobs, American dividends and American standard of living.*[20]

Kissinger stressed the same point with other words in his address *The Year of Europe* of 23 April 1973: 'The political, military and economic issues in Atlantic relations are linked by reality, not by our choice nor for the tactical purpose of trading one off against the other'.[21]

The forces of both the United States and the Soviet Union are deployed in Europe to protect their national interests and this is quite natural and understandable. But contrary to what is commonly believed, it is not necessarily true that the interests of the two nations are opposed and that they desire the withdrawal of the other's forces. This possibility is best illustrated by citing a series of newspaper reports of May 1971.

7 May 1971, International Herald Tribune: 'In the last session of the Congress which ended in December [1970] Senator Mansfield with a majority of the Senate's 100 members as co-sponsors put a resolution before the Chamber calling for a substantial withdrawal of American forces in Europe'.

8 May 1971, Le Monde: 'Le projet de lois [Mansfield] sera certainement adopté . . . La crise monétaire qui traverse l'Europe lui servira sans doute d'argument pour appuyer sa thèse . . . Le gouvernement maintien de sa côté que la participation militaire des Etats-Unis à l'Alliance Atlantique ne doit pas être réduite sans mesures réciproque de la part de l'Union Soviétique'.

8-9 May 1971, International Herald Tribune: 'U.S. Scientists say Pentagon exaggerated Soviet Threat'.

13 May 1971, International Herald Tribune: 'Despite White House opposition, an amendment requiring 50 per cent cuts in U.S. NATO forces by December 31 appeared today to have an excellent chance of Senate passage'. Ronald Ziegler, White House Press Secretary said that '*To unilaterally strip the forces would destroy the U.S. bargaining position*'. (Italics supplied.)

14 May 1971, International Herald Tribune: 'In 1964 . . . Eisenhower . . . said the six divisions in NATO could be cut to one'.

15-16 May 1971, The *International Herald Tribune* reported Leonid Brezhnev's speech in Tbilisi on 14 May when he said that the Soviet Union was ready to discuss a bilateral reduction of forces in Europe. The newspaper made the following comment: 'Some Western diplomats suggested that the Soviet leader, aware of Senator Mansfield's proposal, may be counting on a positive White House response to ease the pressure caused by Senator Mansfield'.

18 May 1971, Le Monde: 'Les controverses qui font rage en ce moment même aux Etats-Unis autour des propositions du senateur Mansfield ont probablement facilité l'évolution Soviétique'.

18 May 1971, The Daily American: 'The challenge to U.S. interests in Europe now is more political than military in a direct sense. *But U.S. forces levels are of major political and economic significance*'. (Italics supplied.)

21 May 1971, International Herald Tribune: '. . . it was the Kremlin which provided the key to Senator Mansfield's roll-call defeat. Leonid I. Brezhnev, the Soviet leader, held out the hope that mutual reduction of forces and armaments can be negotiated between NATO and the rival Warsaw Pact. A large number of Senators seized on that as a reason to stick with the present situation until they see what happens'.

22-23 May 1971, International Herald Tribune: 'Twenty-three Senators voted for the Mathias amendment which "requested" the President to negotiate reduction within a NATO-Warsaw Pact context and also within NATO. And 36 other Senators —with only one overlap, Mr Inouye — voted the Mansfield amendment . . . This means a full 58 Senators registered one degree or another of opposition to the *status quo*. Moreover, there is every reason to believe that 35 Senators (36 minus Inouye) who voted for the Mansfield amendment would have voted for the Mathias substitute had it been left until last. But the 35 rejected the Mathias amendment which their vote would have carried so that they could bring the Mansfield amendment to a final vote'.

American officials gave an immediate and warm reaction to Brezhnev's speech. On 14 May White House Press Secretary Ronald Ziegler said President Nixon welcomed the Brezhnev speech as a 'somewhat stronger indication' of the Soviet interest in force reduction. Mr Ziegler said: 'Now is not the time to unilaterally dismantle U.S. forces particularly in view of the possible prospect for negotiations'.[22] Also on 14 May Secretary of State Rogers warned the Crongress that a unilateral withdrawal of U.S. troops would eliminate the possibility of the Western Allies and the Communist Warsaw Pact negotiating a mutual and balanced reduction of forces in Central Europe'. As he put it: 'Obviously if we do it unilaterally we would kiss that issue goodbye'.[23]

On 18 May 1971, Charles Bray, State Department spokesman, in response to newsmen's questions regarding a meeting in Moscow of American Ambassador Jacob Bean and the Soviet Foreign Minister Andrei Gromyko, said that they discussed Brezhnev's proposal to explore the possibility of reducing forces and armaments in Europe: 'It appears more clearly now than it did that we [the United States and the Soviet Union] appear to have the same subject on our minds'.[24]

Summing up, without the timely Brezhnev intervention and the Gromyko confirmation of the Soviet readiness to negotiate a common force reduction, the Mansfield resolution had a very good chance of being carried. American forces in Europe would have had to be reduced by half by 31 December 1971. It is possible that, as stated by *The Washington Post*, 'the President doubtless would employ a veto if any significant shred of it reached his desk', but in any case the White House would have been under increased pressure to reduce unilaterally American forces in Europe.[25]

And this example of a considerable Soviet interest in the presence of American forces in Europe is not a unique example. *Strategic Survey, 1966* stated:

> There are some [in the Soviet Union] who feel that it [the American presence in Europe] can be a restraining and moderating influence upon the less responsible of her European allies, and those who hold these opinions are sufficiently influential for their views to be propagated in authoritative journals and newspapers .[26]

Finally, *Strategic Survey, 1972* stated: 'There even seemed a disposition [by the Soviet Union] to view the American presence in Europe as a safeguard against the growth of an undesired European Union'.[27]

We may thus conclude that the American and Soviet forces are deployed in Europe to protect their national interests, more than to defend their allies. Their national interests are not necessarily opposed to one another.

The Soviet-American Military Balance

Table 3, columns 6 and 7, represent the armed forces of the two superpowers. The first four years after the Cuban nuclear crisis show a decreasing trend. This is an indication that coexistence was considered by the two superpowers as the only way of living together. Another indication was that the United States changed their nuclear strategic doctrine from 'massive retaliation' to 'flexible response'. Massive retaliation meant a massive employment of strategic nuclear weapons against the Soviet Union in case of aggression. This doctrine was no longer acceptable after the Soviet Union acquired the capability to retaliate in kind. Flexible response implies countering any aggression with the minimum of forces necessary to stop the aggression without provoking nuclear escalation.

The decreasing trend in the level of American armed forces changed because of the war in Vietnam. From 1965-6 to 1968-9, the peak of the Vietnamese War, American armed forces increased by 840,000 men (plus almost 300,000 civilians). As the war declined and American forces disengaged, the total number decreased below the 1965-6 level. At the same time the United States' military doctrine was changed so that the Americans are now prepared to fight only one major and one minor war at the same time and not two major and one minor war, as previously envisaged. All this is a clear indication that the United States is reasonably sure that there is no danger of war both in the near and the more distant future. *The Department of Defense Military Threat Statement for Western Europe in 1974* contained this passage:

> While we do not consider aggression by the USSR likely in the present political climate, the fact remains that the Soviets have a vital interest in the present *status quo* in Central Europe and in retaining their hold on Eastern Europe. A crisis that could lead to conflict could arise if the political situation substantially changed in a way that threatened the USSR or its hegemony over Eastern Europe.[28]

In plain words, this means that a war in Europe may start only if NATO asssumes a political or militarily aggressive posture aimed at changing the present European situation. The Soviet Union's interest in preserving

208

the *status quo* is against any war in Europe.

Another indication that 'coexistence' has strong roots and is developing toward 'cooperation' is presented in Figure 1 which shows the number of treaties and other international agreements signed by the United States and the Soviet Union since 1933 when diplomatic relations were first established. During the period 1968-73 more agreements were signed than in all the previous thrity-five years and the increase was particularly strong between 1971 and 1973. President Johnson stated in his memoirs that 'the sum of our efforts was the conclusion of more significant agreements with Moscow in the years 1963-1969 than in the thirty years after we established diplomatic relations with the Soviet regime'.[29]

Because 'cooperation' is looming, President Nixon, on 16 April 1973, was able to ask for authority from the Congress to sell items from the strategic stockpile. Commenting on the President's request, Williams D. Clements, Deputy Secretary of Defense, said that 'the original thinking [about the stockpile] had to do with a five-year emergency, this was pulled down in the 1960s to a three-year emergency and the President and the Security Council are now thinking in terms of one-year emergency'.[30]

Figure 1: Treaties and other International Agreements concluded between the United States and the Soviet Union since diplomatic relations were first established in 1933

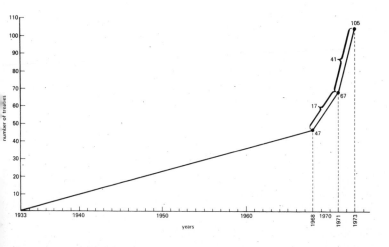

Source: Assistant Secretary of State for European Affairs, Arthur Hartman, 15 May 1974.

On the Soviet side – Table 3, column 7 – the number of troops decreased from 3,600,000 during 1962-3 to 3,150,000 during 1965-6.
After that year there was a moderate increase to 3,425,000 troops
during 1973-4. The reason for such an increase may be found in the
deployment of more Soviet forces on the Sino-Soviet border due to the
increased tension there. Table 10 represents the increased number of
Soviet divisions deployed on the Sino-Soviet border. It is interesting to
note that the total increase in the Soviet armed forces – Table 3,
column 7 – is far less than the increased deployment on the threatened
Asian border (Table 10). Joseph Luns, the Secretary-General of NATO,
stated in June 1974 that 'L'URSS a été capable de stationner aux
frontières de la Chine environ un milion d'hommes avec la logistique
nécessaire tout en maintenant en Europe, avec ses allies du Pact de
Varsovie, plus de deux milions d'hommes'.[31]

Table 10:   Soviet Divisions on Sino-Soviet Border Area

	1968	1969	1970	1971	1972	1973
Number of Divisions	15	21	30	33	44	45

Source: *The Military Balance.*

Table 11:   Soviet Military Budgets (billions of roubles)

	1962-3	1963-4	1964-5	1965-6	1966-7	1967-8
Billion roubles	n.a.	n.a.	13.289	12.8	13.4	14.5

	1968-9	1969-70	1970-1	1971-2	1972-3	1973-4
Billion roubles	16.7	17.7	17.9	17.854	17.9	n.a.

Source: *The Military Balance.*

Table 3, columns 8 and 9 represent the American and Soviet military
budgets. Table 11 represents the Soviet military budget in roubles. Because of the difficulties, elaborated above, in reaching an agreed evaluation of the 'real' defence expenditure on both sides and because of the
different views about the rate of exchange between defence rouble and
defence dollar, I will not dwell in detail on this subject.

The Military Balance: NATO-Warsaw Pact
Table 3, columns 10 and 11 represent the total number of troops of the
two alliances. NATO has always had, and still retains, a considerable

margin of superiority over the Warsaw Pact. Columns 12 and 13 represent the military budgets. The fact is that NATO has always devoted considerably more money to military budgets than the Warsaw Pact.

A more complete comparison between the two alliances is shown in Table 6, columns 6 and 7. NATO is stronger than the Warsaw Pact in population, in regular forces, in gross national Product and in the matter of defence budgets. Regular forces and military budgets represent the actual military power of a nation while population and gross national product give a good indication of the potential military power in case of mobilisation. NATO is stronger than the Warsaw Pact both in actual and potential military power. This same evaluation was given by President Nixon in his *Foreign Policy Report to the Congress* of 25 February 1971:

> The economic strength of the NATO nations, we found, make us considerably stronger in military potential than the Warsaw Pact. We and our allies collectively enjoy a three-fold advantage in gross national product, and a two-fold advantage in population. The actual balance of conventional military forces in Europe is much closer, however. NATO's active forces in peacetime are roughly comparable to those of the Warsaw Pact. Following mobilisation NATO is capable of maintaining forces larger than the Warsaw Pact. But geographic proximity and differences in domestic systems gives the Warsaw Pact the significant advantage of being able to mobilise its reserves and reinforce more rapidly than NATO.[32]

An American detailed evaluation of the opposed military capabilities in Europe was given during Hearings before the Senate on *The Consideration of Military Applications of Nuclear Technology* held on 22 May and 29 June 1973. During the Hearings a *Washington Post* article, dated 7 June 1973, was considered. The article stated:

> A new major Pentagon study challenges a common view that NATO armies would be routed by a massive ground attack ... that communist air forces would quickly gain superiority ... that Soviet submarines would prevent allies shipping from carrying supply across the Atlantic ... To defend against the most likely — though not the most severe — threat posed by the Warsaw Pact ground forces *requires less than we (NATO) have* ... Against the worst threat NATO appears to need about 8 to 14 more armoured division equivalents. But even here, officials say, analysis shows that the allies could hold for about 70 days with the outcome in serious doubt because allied air power and behind-the-line reserves may be able to stem a breakthrough.[33]

Melvin Price, Chairman of the Joint Committee on Atomic Energy, in a letter dated 7 June 1973, asked the Deputy Secretary of Defense, William P. Clements, whether this study showed that 'NATO has been overly pessimistic about their chances in a conflict with the Pact forces when only non-nuclear armament was involved'. Clement's answer, dated 22 June 1973, stated that 'within the limited scenarios explored to date, these in-process studies are consistent with the long-standing U.S. position that we retain together with our allies, a credible defence capability in NATO'.[34]

The Military Balance: NATO Europe-Warsaw Pact

When one considers a limited geographical area the comparison between the military forces deployed within that area is not convincing because the nations concerned may reinforce of withdraw their forces as they like. This is true not only in the Central region but in Europe as a whole particularly as far as American and Soviet forces are concerned. A different approach is desirable, namely to compare the NATO European forces, excluding all American forces and all the Warsaw Pact forces which may be available to fight a war in Europe, including all the available Soviet forces. With this approach the balance of forces is not debatable.

Table 5, column 2 shows that the total Warsaw Pact forces are 4,452,000. But we have to take into consideration that more than one million Soviet soldiers are deployed along the Sino-Soviet border (see Table 11), and that in case of a war in Europe these forces would not be available because they have to face a possible increased threat in Asia. The Soviet Strategic Rocket Forces constitute a separate service with its own manpower: a total of 350,000 men. These again are soldiers who would not be available for a conventional war in Europe because of the increased danger of nuclear escalation which would require increased readiness of the Soviet nuclear forces and because in any case the armaments and training of these forces make them unsuitable for use in a conventional war. If one takes into consideration these two bodies of forces, the remaining forces which can fight a conventional war in Europe are about 3 million, the same number as the NATO European forces. In other words, the NATO European conventional forces are in a state of reasonable equilibrium against all the Warsaw Pact conventional forces which may be available for a conventional war in Europe. And the balance is reached without any American forces.

My approach is based on the most generous assumptions about Soviet capability. The official NATO evaluation of the available forces of the Warsaw Pact is more conservative. NATO Secretary-General Luns, already quoted, considered that the Warsaw Pact has 2 million men available to fight a conventional war in Europe. Secretary of State

Kissinger is even more cautious. In a letter to Senator John C. Stennis, dated 1 June 1974, he stated that 'the Soviet forces deployed in Eastern Europe have increased by about 100,000 from 475,000 in 1972 to 575,000 now'.[35] Because the total Warsaw Pact forces without the Soviet's are about 1 million (see Table 3, column 3), the total Warsaw Pact forces available in Eastern Europe may be no more than about 1,600,000.

Conclusion

1. Neither the United States, nor the Soviet Union envisage any war in Europe in the near and distant future.
2. The American and Soviet forces are deployed in Europe to protect their national interests more than to defend their allies.
3. These national interests and the defence of their allies may or may not coincide.
4. The NATO European nations have sufficient conventional forces to face any and all possible Warsaw Pact acts of aggression without any help from American conventional forces.

Part II — Nuclear Weapons

Introduction — History: Nuclear Weapons and World Policy

At thirty minutes past noon on 15 July 1945 at Alamogordo, New Mexico, the 'Trinity' experiment was concluded. The first atomic explosion shook the desert and started to shake mankind. Never before had a single technological discovery had such tremendous importance. Unfortunately the first use of nuclear energy was in an evil direction: war. War took two forms: hot war — on the Japanese cities of Hiroshima and Nagasaki; and cold war between the United States and the Soviet Union. Before 15 July 1945, not only President Franklin Roosevelt who very often acted as a peacemaker between Winston Churchill and Joseph Stalin but also President Harry S. Truman showed a friendly disposition towards the Soviet Union. For example, during a press conference on 13 June 1945, Truman said:

> There has been a very pleasant yielding on the part of the Russians to some of the things in which we are interested, and I think if we keep our head and be patient, we will arrive at a conclusion because the Russians are just as anxious to get along with us as we are with them and I think they have showed it very conclusively in the last conversation.[36]

After 15 July, the tune changed completely. On 6 August 1945, announcing the use of the atom bomb on Hiroshima, President Truman said that 'If they [the Japanese] do not accept our terms, they may expect a rain of ruin from the air the like of which has never been seen on the earth'.[37] On the 9 August 1945 on a radio report to the American people on the Potsdam conference the President said:

> The new thing – the thing we had not known – the thing we have learned now and should never forget is this: that a society of self-governing men is more powerful, more enduring, more creative than any other kind of society, however disciplined, however centralised.[38]

These remarks were officially addressed to the Fascist nations but they applied also to the 'centralised and disciplined' Soviet society.

Truman was very explicit on this subject in his first speech after the Presidential election of 1948: 'Communism is based on the belief that man is so weak and inadequate that he is unable to govern himself and therefore requires the rule of a strong master'.[39] It is true that the 'rain of ruin from the air' was officially directed against Japan but it could devastate any other country who was not ready to accept American terms. Truman was very explicit on this subject. In his memoirs he wrote: 'Let there be no mistake about it, I regarded the bomb as a military weapon and never had any doubt that it should be used'. He added that Churchill was of exactly the same opinion.[40]

The United States monopoly of the atom bomb destroyed the balance of military power with the Soviet Union and caused the end of their wartime alliance and cooperation. On 1 March 1945 President Roosevelt reporting to the Congress on the Yalta conference said: 'Never before have the major allies been more closely united – not only on their war aims, but also on their peace aims. And they are determined to continue to be united with each other and with all peace-loving nations – so that the ideal of lasting peace will become a reality'.[41] One year later – 5 March 1946 – Churchill and Truman met at the Westminster College, Fulton, Missouri, to declare the Holy Crusade against Communism, the worst enemy of Christianity, the Holy Crusade of all the English-speaking people.

Churchill's speech represents the official starting point of the 'Cold War', but the real beginning took place at an earlier date. Lord Alanbrooke, Chief of the Imperial Staff and the closest military adviser of Winston Churchill, noted in his diary that on 23 July 1945 Churchill, after having examined a complete American report on the atomic explosion, expressed very openly his belief that the American possession of the bomb should be used to control Stalin.[42] Even more explicit on this subject was Douglas MacArthur, Supreme Allied Commander in the Pacific. During a conversation with Lord Alanbrooke on 2 November 1945 he expressed the opinion that the allies had to stockpile a thousand atom bombs in Great Britain so that with the new American bomber under construction it would be possible to combine in a joint atomic attack against the Soviet Union from both the East and the West.[43]

The British feared a strong world reaction against the use of the atom bombs on Hiroshima. Truman in his memoirs wrote:

> On August 8 1945, I received a message from Prime Minister Attlee, who suggested that we issue a joint statement that might serve to reassure the world.
>
> 'There is a widespread anxiety,' he observed, 'as to whether the new power will be used to serve or to destroy civilisation.' The economic effects of the discovery would probably not reveal themselves for some years, he pointed out, but its influence on international relations would be immediate. He urged, therefore, that we, as heads of the two governments, should without delay make a joint declaration on our intentions to utilise the existence of this great power 'not for our own ends, but as trustees for humanity in the interests of all peoples in order to promote peace and justice in the world'.[44]

Truman, while ostensibly agreeing with Attlee, also held this opinion:

> But until a practical and foolproof method of control could be found it was important to retain the advantage which the possession of the bomb had given us. In other words it was now more than ever necessary to guard and maintain the secrecy of the bomb.[45]

In effect the world reaction was very strong. A World Peace Council was formed and it issued various 'Appeals' demanding the absolute banning of atmoic weapons and declared that the government who first employed atomic weapons would be war criminals guilty of a crime against humanity. On 23 October 1950 Andri Vishinsky, the Soviet Foreign Minister, stated during a United Nations (UN) meeting that the 'Stockholm Appeal' was 'bolstered by the signature of five hundred million human beings'.[46]

In order to establish a 'practical and foolproof method of control' of atomic energy the United States on 14 June 1946 proposed to the UN a plan known as the Baruch Plan, after the man who presented it. The Baruch Plan envisaged the implementation of the control of the atomic energy step by step. The previous step had to be completed before the next step could start. The last step, after the United States was satisfied that all the controls were established and were working, was that 'existing bombs shall be disposed of pursuant to the terms of the treaty'. Another important feature of the Baruch Plan was the establishment of an International Atomic Development Authority that had to have managerial control or ownership of all dangerous activities, power to control,inspect and licence all other activities and had to promote the beneficial use of atomic energy. Baruch in his first address to the UN stated that 'we must provide immediate, swift and sure punishment of those who violate the agreements that are reached by the Nations'.[47] The International Authority, with such wide powers, would have been a form of World Government and contrary to the normal UN procedure in that no veto power would have been permitted to prevent punishment for violations.

On 19 June 1946, Andrei Gromyko, the Soviet delegate, presented to the UN a very simple Soviet proposal on three main points:

1. atomic weapons should be forbidden, and within three months all existing atomic weapons should be destroyed;
2. violation of the agreement would be a crime against mankind;
3. within six months legislation should be approved to punish violations.[48]

It may be interesting to note that the British were against the Baruch proposal to drop the veto, 'The veto was established not on the initiative of the Soviet Union but on the initiative of the United States of America, in particular of the late President Roosevelt and also the former Prime Minister of Great Britain Mr Churchill. The Soviet Union supported'.[49]

No agreement has ever been reached between the Soviet Union and the United States on the control of atomic energy. On 24 November 1961 the UN General Assembly, with 55 votes in favour, 20 against and 26 abstentions, approved a resolution presented by twelve Afro-Asian States and supported by the Soviet Union. The resolution stated that any use of nuclear weapons was a violation of the UN Charter and a crime against mankind and civilisation. It was the first time, to my knowledge, that the Soviet line prevailed at the United Nations.

Because at that time aircraft were the only delivery vehicles for atomic bombs, the Americans established a net of alliances with forty-two other nations in order to secure a chain of air bases from which their air force could hit every point of Soviet territory. The Atlantic Alliance — NATO — was the most importance alliance built under the protection of the United States nuclear monopoly. A short and comprehensive definition of the Alliance was given by President Truman in his memoirs: 'An offensive-defensive alliance to maintain the peace in the North Atlantic area but without automatic provision for war'.[50]

The American nuclear monopoly which was to protect NATO lasted only a few days. The Alliance was signed on 4 April 1949 but it entered into effect on 24 August 1949 upon the deposit in Washington of the final instruments of ratification. On 29 August 1949 the Soviet Union exploded its first atom bomb.

The consequences of the Soviet explosion were completely different on the two sides of the Atlantic. For the United States there was no practical change in its nuclear monopoly because the Soviet Union had no air bases from which to reach American territory with a sufficient number of atomic bombs. The NATO European nations, on the contrary, because of their territorial contiguity with the Communist States, were under the threat of a possible nuclear attack from the Soviet Union. In other words the European NATO nations within days of their alliance with the United States became the nuclear hostages of the Soviet Union. This situation reached an explosive level during the Korean War. At the end of November 1950 President Truman said at a press conference that 'there has always been active consideration of its [the atomic bomb's] use',[51] in order to improve a military situation badly shaken by the Chinese intervention. The European reaction was completely negative. Truman wrote in his memoirs: 'In London, one hundred Labour MPs signed a letter to Prime Minister Attlee to protest the possibility of the use of the atomic bomb . . . No one who read the account of this debate (subsequently held in the House of Commons) could possibly escape the fact that the British were seriously worried'.[52] Attlee made a hasty visit to Washington and in the press communiqué issued on 8 December it was announced that 'the President stated that it was his hope that world conditions would never call for the use of the atomic bomb'.[53] The Europeans could accept the American strategy of 'massive retaliation', i.e. complete atomic destruction of the Soviet Union, only in case of an actual grave threat against their own territories. For 'massive retaliation' could trigger the atomic destruction of the European NATO nations by the Soviet Union and this was not acceptable to the Europeans as a means of defending zones politically and/or geographically far from Europe. During the Korean War (and after) no atomic bomb was used and the Soviets said that 'L'aide désinteressée d l'Union Soviétique, sa puissance économique et militaire, sa volonté de tenir les engagements pris en vertu du traité d'alliance avec la Chine [1950] furent la raison essentielle que empêcha les Etats-Unis d'attaquer la Chine et d'utiliser les armes nucléaires en Korée'.[54]

On 31 January 1950 the United States in a public statement announced the decision to build the 'so-called hydrogen or super bomb'. The first full American test took place on 1 November 1952. The first Soviet H-bomb test occurred on 23 August 1953.

The most serious shock to the Atlantic Alliance was produced by the Sputnik, the first Soviet Satellite launched on 4 October 1957, followed by the Big Sputnik launched one month later, weighing 1,120 pounds. These satellites demonstrated in the most striking way that the Soviet Union had achieved the technological capability of producing missiles with sufficient power and accuracy to deliver a nuclear warhead on any place in the United States. The nuclear encirclement was not only broken, but the Soviet Union had acquired a considerable lead in nuclear and space technology.

The Sputniks caused considerable dismay within NATO. A meeting of the heads of government was held in Paris in December 1957 and in the press communiqué issued after the meeting it was stated:

> NATO has decided to establish stocks of nuclear warheads which will be readily available for the defence of the Alliance in case of need.
> In view of the present Soviet policies in the field of new weapons the Council has also decided that Intermediate Ballistic Missiles (IRBMs) will have to be put at the disposal of the Supreme Allied Commander Europe.[55]

Following that decision, IRBMs were deployed in Great Britain, Italy and Turkey and the so-called 'tactical nuclear weapons' were stockpiled in Europe. In the present writer's view, the decision to deploy nuclear weapons in Europe was wise because at that time it was the only means to re-establish the balance of power between the two sides, which was, or was believed to be tilting in favour of the Soviet Union. The present writer is still of the same opinion today, believing that a reasonable balance of nuclear power is essential in order to avoid any dangerous action by the country which believes itself to be stronger or by the country which fears it may become even weaker. I had a role in the negotiations for the deployment of the Jupiters in Italy, in my capacity of Vice-Chief of Staff of the Italian Air Force, and I prepared and signed on 28 March 1959 the Military Memorandum on their deployment and use after an agreement was reached between the US and Italian Governments.

The period between 1957 and 1962 was a transition period from the 'Cold War' to 'coexistence' with alternating phases of *détente* and of crises. Soviet superiority in space and in the nuclear sphere had other important aspects. On 13 September 1959 the first vehicle landed on the moon. When Nikita Khrushchev arrived in New York for a UN meeting he presented President Eisenhower with a copy of the Soviet flag that the day before was placed on the moon. A very significant gift! On 12 April 1961 Yuri Gagarin was the first man in space. On 30 October 1961 came the explosion of a Soviet nuclear bomb of 58 MT (one megaton [MT] is the equivalent of one million tons of conventional explosive) which remains the most powerful bomb so far tested.

The United States was in the climate of the 'missile gap' while the Soviet Union was in the climate of many 'firsts' and this may explain the Cuban nuclear crisis. In April 1961 a group of Cuban exiles, trained and armed by the United States, tried a landing on the island at the Bay of Pigs, in order to overthrow Fidel Castro. The landing was a failure. During the second part of 1962 Khrushchev began to deploy aircraft and IRBMs on the island with the declared aim of defending the Fidel Castro regime against possible American aggression. Politically Khrushchev had many good reasons to believe that the United States would try other actions against Castro's government. There was already a long history of American interventions in foreign countries to avoid a Communist takeover or to overthrow a Communist government. In a recent book Victor Marchetti and John D. Marks state: 'Referring to the CIA's coup in Iran and Guatemala he [Allan Dulles, the CIA's Director] wrote: "Where there begins to be evidence that a country is slipping and Communist takeover is threatened . . . we can't await an engraved invitation to come and give aid" '.[56] The United States was also involved in the Philippines, Indonesia and the Middle East. Finally, we learn that the 'CIA kept many of the Bay of Pigs veterans under contract paying a regular salary for more than a decade'.[57] It is interesting to note that the book is the first book the US Government ever went to court to censor before publication. Thus we may assume that all information given in the book was officially checked. Militarily, Khrushchev's action in Cuba was of the same kind as that taken by the United States with their establishment of a chain of air bases surrounding the Soviet Union and with their deployment of IRBMs and tactical nuclear weapons in Europe. Psychologically, however, the Soviet nuclear weapons in Europe. Psychologically, however, the proximity of the Soviet nuclear base in Cuba to American territory was a challenge which demanded a firm answer by the United States. Kennedy's reaction was the two most powerful nations in the world recognised that to fight one another was the equivalent of reciprocal suicide. Because they could not fight, they were forced to coexist. The 'massive retaliation' strategy was no longer credible and was replaced by 'flexible response' which means facing any aggression without provoking nuclear escalation. October 1962 is the dividing line between the 'Cold War' and 'Peaceful Coexistence'. Senate Majority Leader Mansfield in a statement to the Senate on 25 July 1973 said:

> But even more significant than evaluating the strength of Western Europe and appreciating the strong flow between East and West, is the great number of events since 1963 that manifest as well as contribute to lessening of tension between East and West. *I have selected 82 events I consider significant since 1963.*[58]

Peaceful coexistence improved year by year and so did the relations between the United States and the Soviet Union. A more stabilised nuclear balance led to 'cooperation' and to the first serious attempt at limiting strategic nuclear weapons. In his *Foreign Policy Report to the Congress* of 9 February 1972 President Nixon stated that 'it was possible that for the first time strategic considerations *freed the USSR from some of its own fears*, and might permit serious arms limitation at no disadvantage to either side'.[59] Table 12 represents American and Soviet missile strength from 1959 to 1973. The first round of Strategic Arms Limitation Talks — SALT 1 — was concluded on 26 May 1972. Two basic agreements were signed. One limited Anti-Ballistic Missiles (ABMs) to two 'deployment areas' with a total of 100 ABMs in each area. The other agreement provided that during the five-year term of the agreement the number of strategic missiles should be limited to 2,424 launchers for the Soviet Union including up to 950 Submarine Launched Ballistic Missiles (SLBMs) and 1,710 launchers for the United States including 710 SLBMs. The second round of SALT — SALT II — was less conclusive. The two ABM 'deployment areas' were reduced to one, with a total of 100 ABMs for each country.

Strategic Nuclear Weapons

Having outlined the general framework within which nuclear problems have to be considered, I will now try to deal with the two main families of these weapons: strategic and tactical nuclear weapons. A new sub-family, the mininukes, will be considered in an appendix.

Two definitions are essential for the understanding of strategic nuclear problems: first strike and second strike.

First strike is the capability of one nation to destroy another nation without risking a disastrous retaliation. Before the Soviet Union was able to build ICBMs the United States had a first strike capability *vis-à-vis* the Soviet Union, and was in a dominant military position.

Second strike is the capability to absorb an enemy nuclear surprise attack and still be able to retaliate and cause catastrophic destruction of the enemy. In order to reach a second strike level a nation must have sufficient warheads and delivery vehicles and these must be diversified so as to make a disarming strike impossible. While the land-based delivery vehicles — ICBMs — when in silos are easily located and may well be destroyed by a surprise enemy attack, the SLBMs and airborne aircraft cannot be destroyed because they cannot be located with sufficient accuracy. For this reason SLBMs and aircraft play a very important role in the second strike capability. Today the United States and the Soviet Union both have a second strike capability which is very stable because they both possess many times more nuclear weapons than the number necessary completely to destroy the other country after having suffered a surprise nuclear attack.

A second strike capability thus constitutes a deterrent against any enemy nuclear attack. It follows that every action which is or is perceived to be aimed at achieving a first strike capability promotes deterrence and stability. A counterforce strategy would be destabilising

220

because it would be aimed at destroying enemy nuclear weapons before they are launched and thus at disarming the enemy. An effective counterforce strategy would require vast numbers of weapons and great accuracy.

With this background it is easier to understand the real meaning of the new American nuclear doctrine. Toward the end of 1973 James R. Schlesinger, American Secretary of Defense, suggested a new form of strategic nuclear balance between the United States and the Soviet Union. He spoke of essential equivalence, true equality and total equality, without giving any more precise definition of what he intended in terms of quantity and quality of weapons. Kissinger's reaction to the proposed new balance was less than enthusiastic. At a news conference in Washington on 27 December 1973 he said:

> I agree with the phrase 'total equality', but like all slogans, it does not supply its own answer. And I am certain that my good friend Dr Schlesinger would agree that once you have enunciated that doctrine you still have to give it content in terms of what it is that you want to have equal. Is it the numbers, is it throw-weight, is it warheads, is it everything? How do you compare superiority in bombers to superiority in missiles? These are the rough questions that have to be answered.[60]

On 10 January 1974, Schlesinger made a public announcement that the Americans had changed their targeting doctrine for their ICBMs to include taking out Soviet missile silos in the light of the fact that the Soviet Union might gain by 1980 a counterforce capability greater than that of the United States. The reasons for the new targeting doctrine and for the quest for improved accuracy were more fully explained during a hearing in the Senate on 4 March 1974 and in the *Annual Defense Department Report FY 1975*:

> During the past year alone, the Soviets have tested four new ICBMs and have developed their first new MRV [Multiple Re-entry Vehicle] submarine-launched missile. The new ICBMs are of special interest, three of the four have been flown with MIRV [Multiple Independently-targetable Re-entry Vehicle] and all of them are being designed for increased accuracy . . . This throw-weight combined with increased accuracy and MIRVs could give the Soviets in the order of 7,000 one-to-two megaton warheads in their ICBM force alone. They would then possess one-sided counterforce capability against the United States ICBM force. This is not permissible from our point of view.[61]

It is true that the Soviets have under development a considerable number of new strategic weapon systems, but the Americans are not behind in this race. Their new weapon systems, presently in different stages of development, include a larger ICBM to be launched from Minuteman slios, a mobile ICBM, the Trident SLBM programme, a smaller missile-launcher submarine, air-and-sea launched strategic cruise missiles and the B1 strategic bomber.

In any case the new targeting doctrine is not really a new doctrine. McNamara in his *Statement on the FY 1965-1969 Defense Program and 1965 Defense Budget*, issued on 27 January 1964, stated:

> It is quite likely that the Soviet Union, in an attack upon the U.S. and NATO would not fire all of its strategic weapons in a 'salvo launch'. Regardless of whether the Soviet struck first at our cities or first at our military installations or at both simultaneously, it is probable that the launching of their bombers and missiles would extend over a sufficient period of time for us to receive the first blow, to strike back not only at Soviet cities, if that be our choice, but also at the elements of their forces that had not yet been launched. To achieve this capability we must have a force considerably larger than that which must be needed simply to destroy Soviet cities.
>
> Believers in the 'overkill' theory, however, argue that the U.S. would have already been gravely damaged by the initial attack, that it would be very difficult to destroy the enemy's residual forces and that, in any event, we could not know which of their missiles had not been fired and which were the 'empty holes'. Therefore they conclude that we should not even try to destroy the enemy's residual forces. Certainly the U.S. would be greatly damaged by the initial wave of nuclear attacks . . . But it is one thing to recognise the facts of life; it is quite another thing to throw up one's hands and not even make the attempt to save what we can of our Nation and Society.[62]

In 1965 McNamara's belief in the effectiveness of counterforce was already faltering, for he said that the possibility that a Soviet attack on American urban centres would be withheld for one hour or more after an attack on US military targets was 'an unlikely contingency'.[63] In 1967 McNamara stated: 'Feasible improvements in missile accuracy and re-entry vehicles could greatly increase the efficiency of our offensive forces against Soviet hard targets. However, the effectiveness of offensive forces in the damage limiting role *is sensitive to the timing of a nuclear exchange*'.[64] Finally in 1968, the last year of his assignment as Secretary of Defense, he expressed this view:

> Having wrestled with this problem for the last seven years I am convinced that our forces must be sufficiently large to possess an

'assured destruction' capability. By this I mean an ability to inflict at all times and under all foreseeable conditions an unacceptable degree of damage upon any single aggressor or combination of aggressors — even after absorbing a surprise attack. One can add many refinements to this basic concept, but the fundamental principle involved is simply this: it is the clear and present ability to destroy the attacker as a viable 20th-century nation and an unwavering will to use these forces in retaliation to a nuclear attack upon ourself or our allies that provides the deterrent and not the ability partially to limit damage to ourselves.[65]

Another reason given by Schlesinger to justify the new targeting doctrine is the possibility of reaching greater flexibility. Flexibility has always been a feature of American nuclear strategy. McNamara in 1965 stated: 'In the event of general nuclear war, attacks might be directed against military targets only, against cities only, against both types of target, either simultaneously or with a delay. They might be selective in terms of specific targets or they might be general'.[66]

Finally during the Hearing in the Senate on 4 March 1974 Schlesinger gave another justification for his new doctrine, namely the dramatic increase of the Soviet forces and the consequent change in the strategic balance: 'Their [Soviet] force structure has changed dramatically since 1969 so that the strategic balance in the last five years is not what it was for the period from 1949 to 1966'.[67]

Tables 12 and 13 give two different assessments of the evolution of the American and Soviet strategic forces from 1959 to 1973 and from 1966 to 1974. It is interesting to note that in 1964 when McNamara stressed the importance of a counterforce strategy in the damage limiting role, the Soviet Union appears to have had only 200 ICBMs and 120 SLBMs. If the counterforce strategy was able to destroy all the 200 Soviet ICBMs — and this might have been possible with the 843 ICBMs the United States had at that time — the Soviet Union would have been left with 120 SLBMs. The 120 SLBMs would not have been sufficient to destroy the 200 major American urban areas which was deemed necessary to a second strike capability. According to McNamara, 'beyond the 200 largest urban areas the amount of population and industrial capacity located in each additional increment of 200 cities falls off at a rapidly declining rate and smaller and smaller percentages of the total population and industrial capacity would be destroyed in the event such areas were subject to attack'.[68]

On the other hand, the United States, if it had employed all its 843 ICBMs in a counterforce strike, would still have had 416 SLBMs — more than double what was necessary for destroying the 200 major Soviet urban areas. In 1964, then, the counterforce strategy in a damage limiting role could have worked. By 1968, when McNamara

Table 12:   Soviet-US Strategic Missile Strength

		1959	1960	1961	1962	1963	1964	1965	1966
USA	ICBM	none	18	63	294	424	843	854	904
	SLBM	none	32	96	144	224	416	496	592
Soviet	ICBM	some	35	50	75	100	200	270	300
Union	SLBM	none	none	some	some	100	120	120	125

		1967	1968	1969	1970	1971	1972	1973
USA	ICBM	1054	1054	1054	1054	1054	1054	1054
	SLBM	656	656	656	656	656	656	656
Soviet	ICBM	460	800	1050	1300	1510	1527	1527
Union	SLBM	130	130	160	280	440	650	628

ICBM = Intercontinental ballistic missile.
SLBM = Submarine launched ballistic missile.
Soviet ICBMs include those deployed within IRBM/MRBM fields.
Soviet SLBMs include surface-launched ballistic and cruise missiles.

Source: *The Military Balance.*

Table 13:   US and Soviet Strategic Nuclear Forces, 1966-74

			Estimated number deployed mid-year				
			1966	1968	1970	1972	1974
1.	Delivery vehicles						
	Strategic bombers:	USA	708	646	517	525	496
		USSR	155	150	140	140	140
	Strategic submarines:	USA	37	41	41	41	41
		USSR	-	2	14	28	42
	Long-range submarine-launched ballistic missiles (SLBMs):	USA	592	656	656	656	656
		USSR	-	32	224	444	636
	Intercontinental land-based ballistic missles (ICBMs):	USA	934	1054	1054	1054	1054
		USSR	338	902	1498	1527	1567
	Total Delivery vehicles (bombers and missiles):	USA	2334	2354	2227	2235	2206
		USSR	493	1084	1862	2111	2343
2.	Missile warheads†:	USA	1526	1710	1874	4146	5966
		USSR	338	934	1722	1971	2203

*   For the USA, number operational
†   Independently targetable nuclear warheads on ICBMs and SLBMs.

Source: *SIPRI Yearbook 1974.*

224

was belittling the counterforce strategy, it would probably have been impossible for the United States to destroy the 800 Soviet ICBMs with the 1,054 American ICBMs. What would have been left on the Soviet side, after such an American counterforce strike, would have been more than sufficient completely to destroy the United States. Finally, we may note that the present and the foreseeable future balance of strategic forces seems to be more and more against a counterforce strategy because of the considerable number of SLBMs which cannot of course be destroyed by any surprise attack.

When we examine nuclear problems, however, we have to remember that nuclear weapons are not merely military weapons in the sense that they may be used; they are also political-psychological means of presure which are effective only when they are not used. As Kissinger puts it, 'the perception is more important in many respects than the reality'.[69] Schlesinger was more explicit when at the Senate Hearing of 4 March 1974 he said: 'I believe that it is necessary for our strategic forces to continue to be locked into the defence of Europe, in the minds of the Europeans and of the Soviet Union'.[70] I do not know whether the Europeans are convinced that Schlesinger's new doctrine provides a better 'locking' but I have no doubt that it will produce a considerable reaction in the Soviet Union. The military on both sides — including the US Secretary of Defense — try to counter supposed future enemy actions with present stronger counteractions. They do not take into consideration that the crux of the problem is effectiveness and sufficiency and not 'pacing' as argued by Schlesinger in the Hearing of 4 March 1974:

> With regard to the sizing issue I believe that we must pace ourselves by the Soviet programme. It has only been in recent years that one could say that the Soviet programme has become potentially the pacing item in what is referred to as the arms race. In the past years many observers have suggested that it was the United States which was pacing.[71]

In my opinion it does not matter very much who is 'pacing' whom because such a military philosophy leads inevitably to the nuclear arms race. A convincing example of this kind of military thinking was given before the Senate by Admiral Zumwald, who was for four years Chief of Naval Operation until his retirement on 1 July 1974: 'In view of the increasing vulnerability of land based missiles and the increase of Soviet warheads' size and accuracy, we cannot risk letting the Polaris system become vulnerable through *as-yet-unforeseen* Russian technological development'.[72]

While Schlesinger was projecting the Soviet strategic capability into the distant future and implementing plans to counter 'the worst case' and Zumwald was urging us to face an 'as-yet-unforeseen' Soviet technological development, politicians were more sober and realistic in their evaluations. For example, Representative Harrington said on 9 July 1974: 'In sum, the breadth and intensity of U.S. strategic arms development are such that assumptions of an eventual Soviet "superiority" are both premature and tenuous at best'.[73] Kissinger in a news conference in Brussels on 26 June 1974 said:

> This numerical [Soviet] advantage in missiles is substantially made up if you add to it the 450 long-range bombers we possess, and, if you look at it from the strategic point of view and not from the negotiating point of view, you will have to add to it also the fact that we possess weapons deployed elsewhere that would also be used in a general nuclear way.[74]

Senator Symington at a Hearing, held on 22 May 1973 and on 29 June 1973 said:

> The grand total [of nuclear weapons] stockpiled — abroad, with the fleet, and in this country — is several billion tons. In other words, all we dropped during World War II is around one twenty-fifth of one per cent of what we have available in case there is another war and nuclear weapons are used in a general fashion.[75]

It is appropriate to sum up this part of the argument with three quotations from the political leaders on both sides because they represent, in my opinion, the basic terms of the strategic equation:

> President Nixon, in his *Foreign Policy Report to the Congress*, 3 May 1973: 'To focus one's own policy to gaining advantages at the other's expense can only aggravate tension and precipitate counteraction'.[76]
> Secretary of State Kissinger at the *Pacem in Terris* meeting, 8 October 1973: 'Once sufficiency is reached additional increments of power do not translate into usable political strength and attempts to achieve tactical gains could lead to cataclysm'.[77]
> Secretary-General of the Soviet Communist Party Brezhnev's toast during the White House dinner of 18 June 1973: 'What is also required is to overcome the inertia of the "Cold War" and its after-effect in international affairs and in the minds of men'.[78]

Europe, without the United States, has no possibility of building a second strike nuclear capability in the near or more distant future. The French nuclear forces have a total explosive power of about 21 megatons, which does not constitute a deterrent *vis-à-vis* the Soviet Union and/or the United States. Nor are the French future prospects brighter. According to Kissinger's evaluation, 'After the French finish their nuclear programme in 1980, they will have as many weapons as we have in one Poseidon'.[79] Even if the 64 British megatons and the 21 French megatons are considered together they are no match for the nuclear power of the United States and/or the Soviet Union.

Europe needs today and will continue into the distant future to need the American strategic umbrella against an eventual Soviet nuclear threat. Of course the European politicians have to judge both the probability of a Soviet nuclear threat, and the credibility that the United States nuclear umbrella will be used to protect Europe. *And these two points are crucial for the future of the Atlantic Alliance.*

Tactical Nuclear Weapons

Nearly two decades after the decision to deploy tactical nuclear weapons in Europe — 1957 — NATO has not yet reached an agreement concerning their eventual use. This is a very convincing indication of the wide differences of opinion on this subject. President Nixon, in his *Foreign Policy Report to the Congress* of 3 May 1973, said:

If we maintain the high level of conventional defense that is our goal, we still must examine our nuclear doctrine. Where, in what way and for what objective should we use tactical nuclear weapons? How do independent national nuclear forces affect Alliance decisions? Do we require different institutions to examine such overriding issues within the Alliance?[80]

Nixon's question concerning the 'independent national nuclear forces' was clearly referring to the French forces which are exclusively national and not to the British ones which are closely integrated into the allied plans. On this subject things are moving. The French President, Giscard d'Estaing, in his first press conference on 25 July 1974, stated:

Nos grands choix stratégiques ont été faits en 1960, en réalité il-y-a donc douze ans dans un monde trés différent, un monde dans lequel la décolonization pour ce qui est de la France n'était même pas achevée. Donc à l'heure actuelle le problème de la défense est un problème qui doit être examiné à fond.[81]

Reverting to tactical nuclear weapons, the uncertainty about their use derived, at least in part, from the fact that no clear definition has ever been given of the distinction between strategic and tactical nuclear weapons. In principle, strategic weapons are aimed at Soviet or American territories while tactical weapons are aimed at European territories excluding the Soviet Union. This definition is not really accepted

227

either by the Soviet Union or by the United States because there are, in Europe and in the adjacent seas, air bases and carriers from which aircraft could reach the Soviet Union with nuclear weapons. The Soviets ask that these weapons and aircraft be included in the strategic equation while the Americans are opposed to this because they maintain that they are exclusively for the defence of Europe. This is the problem of the Forward Based Systems (FBS) which have been such a difficulty in the SALT II discussions.

If one considers that there are more than 7,000 tactical nuclear weapons deployed in the NATO territories and about half that number on the Warsaw Pact side, that many of these weapons have a yield many times greater than those of the Hiroshima and Nagasaki bombs and that the great majority of these bombs will be used against European territories, one is driven to the conclusion that they will cause the complete destruction of Europe if and when they are used. Tactical nuclear weapons were deployed in Europe following the NATO decision of December 1957 to balance a real or supposed Soviet Union lead in space/nuclear technology. Today the nuclear balance is assured without the need for nuclear weapons to be deployed in Europe. Why, then, are they still there in such enormous numbers? Schlesinger, discussing NATO strategy with the Senate on 4 April 1974 gave three major reasons:

> First, maintaining nuclear capability is essential to deterrence as long as the Warsaw Pact maintains roughly comparable theatre nuclear capabilities . . . Second, should deterrence fail, our tactical nuclear capabilities provide a source of nuclear options for defense other than the use of strategic forces. Third, in keeping with the flexible response strategy, we do not rule out the use of nuclear weapons by the United States and its allies if necessary to contain and halt major conventional aggression.[82]

Schlesinger's three reasons are not, in my opinion, convincing. A rejoinder to his first reason is to point out that the Warsaw Pact has half the number of tactical nuclear weapons possessed by NATO in Europe, NATO having started its deployment in Europe many years before the Warsaw Pact. His second and third reasons are very dangerous because they stress the possibility of a nuclear war in Europe with considerable employment of tactical nuclear weapons and while this may be accepted by the United States, it cannot be accepted by the European States. As Senator Symington put it during Hearings on 22 May 1973 and 29 June 1973: 'The United States may consider a nuclear war in Europe as tactical but to the Europeans it could well be a strategic nuclear war'.[83] In addition, it has to be considered that the use of tactical nuclear weapons in Europe has a limited deterrent effect, if any, on the Soviet

Union, which is not threatened by the tactical nuclear weapons because these are not aimed at its territory. Only if and when the coupling between the use of a very few tactical nuclear weapons in Europe and the use of strategic nuclear weapons on the Soviet Union is clear and automatic, would the use of tactical nuclear weapons have a deterrent effect on the Soviet Union. But, as General Goodpaster, the Supreme Allied Commander in Europe, put it during Congressional Hearings: 'I do not think that any of them [the European countries] believe that coupling is automatic. I think they will understand that our President retains the prerogative of decision as to whether to proceed to higher escalation steps'.[84] The coupling, understandably, is a prerogative of the President of the United States and I do not believe that he will take a decision which will cause 50 to 100 million casualties in the United States and 50 to 100 million casuatlies in the Soviet Union, to prevent the overrunning of Europe which would in any case result in its complete destruction. Without the automatic coupling, which is impossible and unbelievable, the use of tactical nuclear weapons in Europe thus has no deterrent effect on the Soviet Union. Senator Pastore at the same Hearings was very explicit:

> They [the Soviets] are not afraid of the bombs that are going to fall on Rome or Berlin or the bombs that are going to fall on Nürnberg. They are not worried about that. They are worried about the bombs that are going to fall on them. There is your deterrent.[85]

Schlesinger was also clear on this point, even if he was not so explicit. Asked by Senator Fulbright if he could visualise the circumstances that would result in a limited war, Schlesinger answered,

> One circumstance I can think of is the possibility of the overrunning of Western Europe. This would be a major defeat for the NATO alliance and for the United States. *I do not know what we would do under these circumstances in terms of the strategic forces*, but I believe that it is necessary for our strategic forces to continue to be locked into the defense of Europe in the minds of the Europeans and of the Soviet Union.[86]

Of course the overrunning of Western Europe by conventional means would be 'a major defeat' for the United States, but there is a considerable difference between a major defeat and the total destruction of the United States in a strategic nuclear war. Incidentally, the Warsaw Pact nations have no chance of overrunning Western Europe because their conventional forces are weaker than those of NATO, as I have earlier demonstrated. But even supposing that it was possible that Western Europe could be overrun, the United States' strategic weapons would be locked into the defence of Europe *only in our minds*. On the other hand, tactical nuclear weapons would be used in great quantity even if and when the European nations were against such use. General Goodpaster during the Hearings of 22 May 1973 and 29 June 1973 said: 'the agreement within NATO requires that there should be internal consultations *in the event time permits consultation*, but the decision itself rests with the nuclear power; that is the United States in this case'.[87] Asked by Senator Symington how many of the 7,000 tactical weapons in Europe would be available if some NATO nations did not concur with the decision for their use, General Goodpaster's answer was:

> In the circumstances that you describe, once the decision of the NATO power was given to me in response to my request and if the situation still required the use of these weapons, I would direct their use. *All 7,000 would be available for such use.*[88]

We may thus conclude:
1. Tactical nuclear weapons have no appreciable deterrent effect on the Soviet Union;
2. if employed they would produce the destruction of Europe;
3. the decision concerning their use is an American decision;
4. *the only rational decision the European nations can reach is their removal from Europe.*

This removal could be accomplished in the following three stages:
— first step: NATO destroys 3,500 tactical nuclear weapons in order to balance the quantitative level with that of the Warsaw Pact;
— second step: both sides convene a 'minor European SALT' to reduce and destroy 500 to 600 Soviet I-MRBM and 300 to 400 NATO Pershings;
— third step: both sides destroy the remaining tactical nuclear weapons and thus remove the most serious threat against Europe.

Appendix

Mininukes

Mininukes are the smallest members of the nuclear family. They have a yield of one kt or less and they have reduced or non-existent collateral damage. They are 'clean'. Married with very accurate delivery vehicles, they might provide 'surgical strikes' against any target without the serious collateral damage which is produced by the other nuclear weapons.

Opinions concerning the use of mininukes cover a wide range. First, there are the scientists who have built a new military doctrine around the mininukes. They would be used in great number against the advancing enemy units and in their rear but within a very limited depth, say round fifty miles. This posture would require a limited number of soldiers and, being wholly defensive, would be more in consonance with *détente* and cooperation than the present doctrine. Secondly, there are the military who are happy to have as many mininukes as possible, but in addition to the existing tactical nuclear weapons and with no change in the present doctrine which envisages the use of weapons of a large yield deep inside enemy territories. Third, there are the politicians who are against the introduction of mininukes into the NATO inventory because they fear that their relatively small yield and the absence of collateral damage may blur the distinction between conventional and nuclear weapons. They hold that it is of paramount importance to maintain an absolute 'firebreak' between the two kinds of explosive because if the Pandora's Box of nuclear weapons should be opened escalation would be almost inevitable.

Notes

1. The International Institute for Strategic Studies (IISS), *The Military Balance 1973-1974* (London, 1973), p. 8.
2. Stockholm International Peace Research Institute (SIPRI), *World Armaments and Disarmament: SIPRI Yearbook, 1973* (Stockholm, New York and London, 1973), p. 228.
3. *International Herald Tribune*, 24 May 1974.
4. 'US-USSR Strategic Policy', *Hearings before the Subcommittee on Arms Control, International Law and Organisation of the Committee on Foreign Relations*: United States Senate, Ninety-third Congress, 4 March 1974 (US Government Printing Office, Washington, D.C., 1974), p. 28. Italics supplied.
5. *International Herald Tribune*, 19 December 1972.
6. *Ibid.*, 15-16 December 1973.
7. *Ibid.*, 3 June 1973.
8. *Daily Wireless File*, United States Information Service, Embassy of the United States of America, Rome, 22 April 1974, p. 7.
9. 'US Military Commitment to Europe', *Report of the ad-hoc Subcommittee of the Committee on Armed Services*, House of Representatives, Ninety-third Congress, Second Session (US Government Printing Office, Washington, D.C., 1974), p. 20.
10. *Daily Wireless File*, 18 July 1974, p. 1.
11. IISS, *op. cit.*, p. 92.
12. Secretary of Defense James R. Schlesinger, *Annual Defense Department Report FY 1975* (US Government Printing Office, Washington, D.C.,), pp. 87-91. Italics supplied.
13. Trevor Cliffe, *Military Technology and European Balance* (IISS Adelphi Paper, no. 89, 1972), p. 26.
14. SIPRI, *op. cit.*, p. 5.
15. IISS, *op. cit.*, p. 99.
16. *Ibid.*
17. Schlesinger, *op. cit.*, p. 98.
18. Winston Churchill, *The Second World War: Closing the Ring*, Vol. V (London, 1952), p. 251.

19. *Weekly Compilation of Presidential Documents*, VIII (1972). (Published every Monday by the Office of the Federal Register of National Archives and Record Service Administration, Washington, D.C.)
20. *Daily Wireless File,* 11 July, 1974, p. 9. Italics supplied.
21. *Ibid.*, 24 April 1973, p. 3.
22. *Ibid.*, 17 May 1971, p. 1.
23. *Ibid.*
24. *Ibid.*, 19 May 1971, p. 1.
25. *The Washington Post,* 14 May 1971.
26. IISS, *Strategic Survey 1966* (London, 1967), p. 18.
27. IISS, *Strategic Survey 1972* (London, 1973), p. 6.
28. *Congressional Record* Extension Remarks, 11 April 1974, E 2319.
29. Lyndon B. Johnson, *The Vantage Point: Perspectives of the Presidency, 1963-1969* (New York, Chicago and San Francisco, 1969), p. 476.
30. *Daily Wireless File,* 17 April 1973, p. 10.
31. *Le Monde,* 5 June 1974.
32. *Weekly Compilation of Presidential Documents*, VII (1971).
33. *Washington Post*, 7 June 1973.
34. 'Military Application of Nuclear Technology', *Hearings Before the Sub-committee on Military Applications of the Joint Committee on Atomic Energy,* Congress of the United States (US Government Printing Office, Washington, D.C., 1973), p. 74.
35. *Daily Wireless File,* 6 June 1974, p. 9.
36. *Public Papers of the Presidents of the United States: Harry S. Truman, 1945* (US Government Printing Office, Washington, D.C., 1961), p. 123.
37. *Ibid.*, p. 199.
38. *Ibid.*, p. 213.
39. Harry S. Truman, *Memoirs* (2 vols, Independence, Missouri, 1955), II, p. 263.
40. *Ibid.*, I, p. 462.
41. *The Public Papers and Addresses of Franklin D. Roosevelt, 1944-45: Victory and Threshold of Peace* (New York, 1950), p. 537.
42. Arthur Bryant, *Triumph in the West 1943-1946: Based on the Diaries and Autobiographical Notes of Field Marshal the Viscount Alanbrooke* (London, 1959), pp. 477-8.
43. *Ibid.*, pp. 510-11.
44. Truman, *op. cit.*, I, p. 574.
45. *Ibid.*, I, p. 575.
46. *Documents on Disarmament 1945-1959* (2 vols., US Department of State, 1960, Washington, D.C.), I, p. 250.
47. *Ibid.*, I, p. 8.
48. *Ibid.*, I, p. 17.
49. *Ibid.*, I, p. 77.
50. Truman, *op. cit.*, II, p. 287.
51. *Ibid.*, II, p. 450.
52. *Ibid.*, II, p. 451.
53. *Ibid.*, II, p. 469.
54. *La Politique étrangère de l'URSS* (Moscow, 1966), p. 131.
55. *NATO Facts and Figures* (NATO Information Service, Brussels, 1969), p. 329.
56. Victor Marchetti and John D. Marks, *The CIA and the Cult of Intelligence* (New York, 1974), p. 26.
57. *Ibid.*, p. 122.

58. *Daily Wireless File*, 26 July 1973, p. 6.
59. *Weekly Compilation of Presidential Documents*, VIII (1972). Italics supplied.
60. *Daily Wireless File*, 28 December 1973.
61. Schlesinger, *op. cit.*, pp. 5-6.
62. *Statement of Secretary of Defense Robert S. McNamara before the House Armed Service Committee on the 1965-69 Defense Program and 1965 Defense Budget*, 27 January 1964. Italics supplied.
63. *Statement of Secretary of Defense Robert S. McNamara before the House Armed Service Committee on FY 1966-70 Defense Program and 1966 Defense Budget*, 18 February 1965.
64. *Statement of Secretary of Defense Robert S. McNamara before the Senate Subcommittee on Department of Defense Appropriation on FY 1967-71 Defense Program and 1966 Defense Budget*. Italics supplied.
65. *Statement by Secretary of Defense Robert S. McNamara on FY 1969-73 Defense Program and 1969 Defense Budget*, 22 January 1968.
66. McNamara, *FY 1966-70 Defense Program*.
67. 'US-USSR Strategic Policy', *loc cit.*, p. 12. Italics supplied.
68. McNamara, *FY 1966-70 Defense Program*.
69. *Daily Wireless File*, 25 June 1974.
70. 'US-USSR Strategic Policy', p. 12.
71. *Ibid.*, p. 7.
72. *Congressional Record*, Senate, 11 July 1974, S 12204.
73. *Ibid.*, House, 9 July 1974, H 6284.
74. *Daily Wireless File*, 27 June 1974.
75. 'Military Application of Nuclear Technology', p. 3.
76. *Weekly Compilation of Presidential Documents*, IX (1973).
77. *Daily Wireless File*, 9 October 1973.
78. *Ibid.*, 19 June 1973.
79. *Newsweek*, 22 July 1974.
80. *Weekly Compilation of Presidential Documents*, IX (1973).
81. *Le Monde*, 27 July 1974.
82. *Daily Wireless File*, 8 April 1974.
83. 'Military Applications of Nuclear Technology', p. 34.
84. *Ibid.*, p. 120.
85. *Ibid.*, p. 61.
86. 'US-USSR Strategic Policy', p. 12. Italics supplied.
87. *Ibid.*, p. 66. Italics supplied.
88. *Ibid.* Italics supplied.

15. CONSULATIONS IN NATO DURING AND AFTER THE OCTOBER WAR

Thomas Blau

The conflicts within the Western Alliance during and as an aftermath of the October War of 1973 almost equalled the War itself in their drama, yet were consistent with the international trends of the last few years. With respect to the Soviet Union, the United States has continued to de-emphasise seriously differing interests and resulting tensions. But with respect to Western Europe, friendships founded in both sentiment and community of interests have been put under grievous strain. Hence it is not surprising to read:

> When Kissinger said of his failure to consult with the allies during the Middle East crisis that some of those consulted with cooperated least, Jobert retorted: 'Who does he mean, the Russians?'[1]

The United States, insisting that *détente* ('a relaxation of tensions between nations') exists between itself and the Soviet Union, ignored the Soviet failure to give warning of coming conflict between third parties, played down the massive arms shipments to the Soviet clients and delayed its shipments to its own clients. And when the United States responded to the Soviet build-up in the Mediterranean, the troop massing, and the so-called 'brutal note' with an alert of forces, this move, despite having been effective, was subjected to serious question by friend and foe, domestic and foreign, as to its intention, wisdom, and efficacy. Indeed, when the Soviet clients began to lose, the United States moved quickly to end the fighting in the hope of preserving the superpower *détente* and a similar tense balance among the client principals. The status of forces which resulted gave little encouragement, then or subsequently, to those seeking the goal of peace, although 'shuttle diplomacy' has accomplished the unprecedented. Whether the Geneva negotiations will result in positions actually being modified is another question.

Disarray within the West exposed problems long in the making. These were partly substantial, partly symbolic, and partly a smoke-screen. 'Consultation', or rather its lack, became a core issue. Whatever consultation is — it is rarely defined — it was lacking, especially for the Western Europeans. Although 'consultative processes are an alliance's surrogate for executive authority',[2] they are incongruent with the mode in which American foreign policy was conducted after 20 January 1969. The Nixon-Kissinger style involved emphasis on highly personalised relations among leaders; secrecy; and spectacular movements dedicated to keeping others off balance, particularly one's friends and supporters. Its successes *and* its failures, it can be argued, owe much to its perception, which was to some extent 'sold' to its adversaries, that adversary leaders have a community of understanding which excludes others, such as one's own people and one's own government. In its worst moments, the Nixon-Kissinger style involved speed in showing pique and slowness in thinking through complex problems. It often took a dramatic form such as the call for 'The Year of Europe'.[3] In sum, the Nixon-Kissinger style was not very consultative, which means that the Alliance was hard-pressed for signs of 'executive authority'. The difficulties within the Alliance, the ambiguities of *détente* with the Soviet Union, and the ambivalence with which the Europeans have greeted that *détente* became in the autumn of 1973 more than *malaises* murmured over by statesmen and in distinguished newspapers.

The Arab 'oil weapon', such as it was, had existed long before the outbreak of war on 6 October 1973. Its increased salience was heralded by the Sunday *New York Times* of 7 October 1973, which carried an analysis of Saudi interests in employing an oil embargo against the West to challenge Western sympathy for Israel.[4] The United States' European and Japanese allies were well aware of their particular vulnerability to the oil weapon. The 'percentage of petroleum [consumption] dependent on Arab petroleum' in 1973 was about 65 per cent for Western Europe, 50 per cent for Japan, and only 10 per cent for the USA.[5] European reaction to oil dependence led to events which caused Robert Pfaltzgraff to comment acerbically that, 'Arab leaders wielding the oil weapon gained a measure of influence over European policies comparable to "Finlandisation", or perhaps the influence that the Europeans themselves once wielded in the Middle East'.[6]

Soon after hostilities began, reports circulated that European leaders were discussing the possibility of a unified European policy and that foreign ministries were hesitating to blame either Israel or the Arab nations for instigating the conflict,[7] but on the morning of 7 October Secretary of State Kissinger telephoned the British Ambassador to the United States and asked him if the British Government would be prepared to support Israel in the event that Israeli security and survival were seriously threatened. The British Ambassador apparently responded that his government preferred to remain neutral.[8] Although this was denied by Sir Alec Douglas-Home, the Foreign Secretary,[9] Great Britain was also reported to have rejected an American request to sponsor a ceasefire resolution in the United Nations, allegedly because of lack of Egyptian interest, which would have rendered the resolution futile.

Tad Szulc has reported a series of altercations between Kissinger and the British over the use of Cyprus as a base for SR-71 reconnaisance missions. Prime Minister Edward Heath is said to have asked for a 'cover story' to protect Britain. Kissinger, allegedly, 'flew into a towering rage, denouncing the British as unworthy allies because of Heath's demand for a "cover story" '. SR-71 reconnaisance was abandoned and Kissinger stopped sending American intelligence to the British.[10]

On October 9, Turkey announced its neutrality despite Arab hopes for support, and Italy stated its posture of 'active equidistance' in relation to all belligerents.[11] Claiming that it was deferring any decision to resupply Israel, the United States revealed on 10 October that the Soviet Union was resupplying the Arabs (citing evidence of Soviet Antonov-22s, fifty-ton cargo planes, flying to Syria and Egypt), and on 11 October, ordered a second American helicopter carrier (transporting additional American Marines) into the Mediterranean.[12]

The details were sobering particularly for devotees of *détente*. *Aviation Week* reported that, between 4 and 11 October, forty-four resupply missions were flown into Syria from the Soviet Union, and another fourteen into Egypt. Eight more were en route to Syria with tactical missiles on the 11th, and twenty-two more were being prepared for departure. Besides the very large An-22, the Soviets flew An-12s (which also serves as a troop carrier), Il-62s, Il-18s, and Tu-154s.[13] A month earlier, two brigades of Soviet SCUD missiles, with a 180-mile range, were shipped to Egypt from the Black Sea. Positioned east of Cairo, they were reportedly armed with nuclear warheads.[14]

On 13 October the United States announced its intention to replace lost Israeli aircraft. The next day, the United States officially announced its airlift to Israel, followed by a Soviet decision to respond in kind to the American 'aggression'. On 15 October, the *New York Times* reported that the British Government had announced on the previous day an embargo on all arms and replacement parts sales to all the belligerents, including replacement parts needed by the Israeli Army for their British-made Centurion tanks. At the same time, Great Britain did not terminate the training of Egyptian helicopter pilots on British soil on the grounds that there was no connection between the Sinai fighting and British flight-training of Egyptians.[15] While the Conservative Government's policy was not received well in Great Britain, it is difficult to imagine that Harold Wilson, for example, would have risked the disaster of an oil cut-off, had he then been in office.

Federal Germany, however, furnished a marked contrast to the other allies by not commenting on the use of its American bases for the resupply of Israel for ten days. This was halted finally by a German newspaper report of American troops loading material on an Israeli ship flying the Israeli flag in Bremerhaven. This was too blatant to be ignored and Bonn demanded the cessation of arms shipments to Israel from Germany the next day.

Monday 15 October was also the day the Atlantic Council convened to discuss the Middle East War and to consider what the crisis meant for the Atlantic Alliance. The French and British representatives took the position that:

> The war is taking place within territories that are not covered by the Atlantic Alliance, and that America consequently can act with the understanding that Europe will not feel obliged to become involved.[16]

These positions of two of the United States' more prominent NATO allies terminated any possibility of even passive Alliance approval of the American airlift to Israel.

Unified action or even formal consultation among the European allies seemed to be as difficult for them as it was for the United States. As *L'Express* put it:

> The European ambassadors to Washington behaved as if the crisis didn't concern them. They didn't put into effect, between themselves, a single procedure for emergency contacts.[17]

During this period, the Soviet airlift of arms and supplies to the Arabs was growing. *Le Monde* reported on 14 October that the lights over Yugoslavia of Soviet planes were of an unnaturally high frequency, as Antonov-22s with military markings flew at night and civilian Aeroflot aircraft flew during the day.[18] The number of military flights increased thereafter, as reported in *Le Monde* on 17 October.[19] In addition, it was reported that British sales and deliveries of armaments to the Arabs were continuing after the officially announced embargo.[20]

The *New York Times* of 17 October reported that NATO Secretary-General Luns had stated that a threatened oil embargo and price rises 'would come very close to a hostile act'.[21] He had cause to comment. On 16 October Iran, Iraq, Saudi Arabia, Qatar, Abu-Dhabi and Kuwait jointly announced a 17 per cent price rise on crude oil, which came two days after the Saudi Minister of Oil reportedly told Western oil executives that crude production would be cut back 10 per cent immediately, and 5 per cent per month thereafter if the United States resupplied Israel.

Between 19 and 21 October, Libya, Saudi Arabia, Algeria, and four other Arab oil producers cut off oil exports to the United States and Holland. American resupply flights to Israel continued despite resistance from NATO allies over American flights through allied air space and landings on allied territory. Spain, Italy, France, Greece and Turkey prohibited Israeli-bound flights through their air space (while Greece and Turkey aired no complaint over Soviet flights through their air space en route to Arab countries). In addition Spain objected to American use of the Torrejan air base for tanker aircraft which were first used to refuel Israel-bound A-4 Skyhawks and F-4 Phantoms over the Mediterranean.[22] It is ironic that in July 1972 President Nixon stated on the subject of continued American aid to Greece and Turkey, 'without aid to Greece and Turkey you have no viable policy to save Israel'.[23]

On 22 October Egypt and Israel agreed to the first UN-approved ceasefire, as Colonel Ghadaffy, attempting as usual to clarify matters, threatened a Libyan oil embargo against Western Europe for supporting the UN truce.[24] This first ceasefire broke down within a day, 'as the Israelis had taken full advantage of the initial Egyption violation'.[25] On 24 October Egyptian President Sadat, in accepting the second ceasefire, asked that a joint American-Soviet emergency force (with UN approval) be sent to the Suez front. Secretary Kissinger announced that under no conditions should the United States and/or the Soviet Union move troops into the Middle East.

Unfortunately for Kissinger, Soviet Ambassador Dobrynin, on the night of the 24th, delivered the famous 'brutal note' in which he said to the President:

> I will say it straight, that if you find it impossible to act together with us in this matter, we should be faced with the necessity urgently to consider the questions of taking appropriate steps unilaterally. Israel cannot be allowed to get away with the violations.

Soviet troops in East Germany and Poland were on alert. It is difficult not to suspect Soviet 'orchestration' in the Sadat-Brezhnev moves.[26]

In order to dissuade the Soviet Union from moving troops into the Middle East, American troops and military bases went on a worldwide alert (Defcon 3) at 3 a.m. (Washington time) on 25 October. This corresponded to 8 a.m. Brussels time and the Atlantic Council reconvened at 9.30 a.m. in Brussels. The American representative to the Council did not, however, inform his colleagues of the alert, as he was not himself informed of the alert until approximately 12 p.m. Brussels time. By the time he informed the Council representatives of the alert, his colleagues were already aware of it thanks to press reports from Washington and elsewhere.[27] On the same day Federal Germany banned American resupply of Israel from German territory. Some divergence of attitude now emerged in Europe. As Herbert J. Coleman wrote:

Accusations that the U.S. acted unilaterally, putting the Alliance in jeopardy, centered in London and Bonn. But in the Brussels operational headquarters, the entire matter was treated as primarily an American concern based on the need for quick reaction.[28]

When the Americans put their three Air Force strike bases and Polaris base on alert, the British Foreign Secretary was criticised for allowing it without prior American consultations: 'Douglas-Home admitted that the government finally was informed "at an early period", but opposition party leader Harold Wilson harangued him for allowing Britain to become a junior partner of the United States'.[29]

The worldwide American military alert without prior consultation of NATO allies brought a number of other responses from European capitals. *Le Monde* on 21 and 27 October sharply criticised the unilateral action. On 28 October Chancellor Brandt sent a letter to Nixon criticising the United States for not informing its allies of American estimates of the war and the evidence justifying the American alert.[30]

26 October saw a triple barrage across the Atlantic, fired by the President, the Secretary of Defense, and the spokesman of the State Department.[31] The Europeans were not warned of the attacks in advance. The American officials were bitter at the lack of European cooperation. Secretary of Defense Schlesinger complained of European dissent:

> We maintain troops in Europe in order that they be closer to certain theaters of operations. If we cannot use them, we will have to consider putting them elsewhere.[32]

Germany received blunt 'exemplary' comment from the Secretary:

> We maintain our forces in Germany, to cite one example, because it provides us with enhanced readiness. The reactions of the Foreign Ministry of Germany raised some questions about whether they view readiness in the same way that we view readiness, and consequently we will have to reflect on that matter.[33]

The President was no more subtle: 'I can only say . . . that Europe . . . would have frozen to death this winter if there had been no settlement'.[34]

Reactions in Europe to the alert of American support of Israel were varied. Jean-Jacques Servan-Schreiber lamented that, 'engraved on the face of the universe by these three weeks of October 1973, have been the impotence, the silence, the absence of Europe' in the affairs of the war and its resolution.[35] Jean-François Revel, in a column entitled 'The Bankruptcy of Europe', defended American policy:

> Instead of pretending to be offended because they were not, or

nearly not, consulted, the Europeans, on the contrary, should be grateful to Dr Kissinger for his charitable discretion. For, if he had consulted them, they would have been quite embarassed. To the extent that they were, they didn't know what to say. Far from being an affront, the Secretary of State's restraint is an example of tact. It would have been odd on his part to ask of us our solutions. And if he had had to wait . . . one can imagine where the carnage would be today.[36]

The Times, London, implicitly approved of the American unilateral decision to put its forces on alert without consulting the NATO allies because of the necessity to act quickly in the crisis.[37]

The (Manchester) Guardian view was an apologia that must have received many approving murmurs in European foreign ministries. Its editorial argued that the United States, in calling the alert, gave no information to, nor consulted with, its allies and thereby gave the alliance no chance to prepare itself in the event of any reprisals against any alliance member. *The Guardian* view claimed that the United States had mistaken European attitudes and interests in the Middle East as equivalent to American interests, although, 'Europeans would not let Israel disappear'. *The Guardian* presented no evidence for this bold assertion, which seems to have been the prudent course. It is, however, difficult to reconcile the assertion with its understanding of the Alliance:

> If the alliance is to be preserved the allies must first restate the principle that NATO exists for its members' mutual defence and not for the support of U.S. policy, whatever it may be, in other parts of the world.

Europeans, claimed *The Guardian*, 'do not see the conflict as a threat to the security of any NATO country'. As for the problem of 26 October, which transcended the issue of Israel, 'the projected or suspected movement of Soviet troops to the Middle East', this 'would not be recognised, automatically, if at all, as a similar threat [to the Cuban Missile Crisis] to NATO's integrity'.[38] Whereas the territory of the United States, a NATO member, was threatened by the Cuban missiles, this was not the case in October 1973, and thus European support was not obligated by Alliance membership and not forthcoming. Of course, European 'support' was hardly a major issue in 1962, while its lack eleven years later certainly was. This strict territorial interpretation also contradicted the major official NATO statement on consultation, that of 'the Three Wise Men', who declared that, 'NATO should not forget that the influence and interests of its members are not confined to the area covered by the Treaty, and that common interests of the Atlantic Community can be seriously affected by developments outside the

Treaty area'.[39]

On both issues, the airlift and the alert, the Europeans were critical of both the substance of the American position and of the failure to consult in advance. It is not clear, however, that European leaders demonstrated superior diplomacy in the ensuing weeks and months. On 6 November the EEC issued a Middle East declaration that called for more for the Arabs than Sadat was getting in the process of shuttle diplomacy, undercutting both him and Kissinger. As Kissinger put it mildly to the Pilgrims' Dinner in London weeks later, 'He would like "the United States to be given an opportunity to express its concerns before final decisions are taken affecting its interests" '.[40] It is difficult to understand what *European* interests were served, except perhaps that of appearing *plus arabiste que le colonel Ghadaffy*; they certainly were more so than President Sadat. Indeed, 'it succeeded simultaneously in alienating from the European Community both Egypt and Israel'.[41]

The Europeans did not deal gracefully with member nations' problems, despite declarations of a military 'European' interest which now diverged from that of the United States. At the same conference, 'the Foreign Ministers, after more than two hours behind closed doors, failed to respond to Dutch and West German calls for "Community solidarity" when it came to the specific issue of insuring the free flow of oil through the EEC'. For 'Britain and France want to avoid at all costs giving the impression that they are willing to come to the aid of their Dutch partners, who are already threatened by the Arab boycott'.[42] The Dutch had been designated for embargo and requested, at the end of October, oil help should the need arise. Faced with their allies' reluctance, the Dutch brandished their natural gas weapon, causing the French to take a more 'European' point of view.

Disputes and incidents continued until the discernible movement generated by shuttle diplomacy, the governmental changes of the spring, which included, of course, the departure of Jobert, and the Ottawa Declaration. Jobert and his government were particularly difficult for the United States, especially in the reported private overtures to the Syrians which attempted to undermine shuttle diplomacy. The French, however, presented only the extreme case of European attempts to establish special bilateral relations with oil producers by offering not only military and technological goods, but ideological support as well.

The French were recalcitrant in particular about the Washington Energy Conference of February. Two good reasons, from the French point of view, were Kissinger's clear leadership, and that recalcitrance provided an opportunity publicly to 'defend' Arab interests by decrying meetings that did not include the producers. With mixed results for their interests, the French were to carry through their positions into

241

isolation from the other Europeans by the end of the Washington Conference.

It appeared that the closer anyone came to defining plausible 'European' positions, the more these positions seemed to represent Arab interests at least as well as those of Europe. The interests of the United States ran a poor third. A month after the Energy Conference, Kissinger reacted:

> In terms of substance, there has been . . . too much of a tendency to seek European identity in opposition to the United States . . . when the definition of European identity on the part of some countries is the differentiation from, and in some cases opposition to, the United States.[43]

The sometimes frantic European search for Arab favour implied public hostility towards the United States. There seems, moreover, to be little evidence that the Arabs expected such zeal until the European leadership, in the manner of Dr Frankenstein, created their own monster. There seems to have been a distinct failure of intelligence in the West, both in the gathering of information on Arab aims and cohesion, and its interpretation. Apparently, the embargo became a threat when the West announced that it was threatened.

In 1970 Harlan Cleveland wrote thus of consultation in NATO:

> A member government should not, without adequate advance consultation, adopt firm policies or make major political pronouncements on matters which significantly affect the Alliance or any of its members, unless circumstances make such prior consultation obviously and demonstrably impossible.[44]

But consultation, conveniently, has vague and various meanings. These include the exchange of information, as in notification; the solicitation of non-binding advice; and to the brutal jargon of contemporary Washington, the collection of critical 'sign-offs', whereby officials give formalistic assent to policies, frequently under some kind of coercion, so that they cannot criticise those policies later. But the ideal version of consultation involves continual and routine participation in an active administrative process. The success of the Nuclear Planning Group (NPG) in NATO,[45] in which vital matters are subject to continual and productive policy formulation, demonstrates the feasibility of serious consultation, if only to provide the symbolic gratification which alleviates the pressure for proliferation within the Alliance.

The NPG shows that nations with competing claims to being 'most' affected by a policy area can create administrative structures which satisfy the friendly competitors. Such consultation seems inevitably to create new cooperative sections of smaller powers which can be 'difficult' for the major power in the alliance.[46] Such sub-grouping can occur, however, only if previously unrecognised conditions and interests become tangible. It is in the only slightly longer run interest of the major power that these conditions and interests become visible and open to analysis and discussion, that is to more consultation.

Rarely will these new issues and understandings emerge suddenly; thus, rarely will they be lacking in consultation from others. The benefits, then, flow both ways from the process of steady, unspectacular communication. The major activity of the NPG is scholarly, the writing of papers which involve research, analysis, synthesis, collegial criticism, and re-writing. The *ordinariness* of this process is a political advantage to all because it produces and requires time.

Time was not much in evidence in the events of October 1973. The claim of American leaders that they had to act quickly may be open to some criticism, but it is difficult to disprove. It is true that Kissinger could have been as polite as John Kennedy was eleven years before, and sent Dean Rusk or Averill Harriman to Paris to 'consult'. It will be remembered, however, that it was Jobert's spiritual father who asked Dean Acheson if he was asking or telling, and accepted the answer gracefully.

Despite their complaints, the Europeans were better off, perhaps, by *not* being asked. The responsibility of commenting would have been immense. If they had been consulted, in the sense of being asked about the resupply, they would have had to make an explicit choice between losing the oil or acquiescing in the destruction of Israel. The Americans, however, could have told the Europeans what they were doing and why, lessening European perceptions of American unpredictability. As for the alert, if the Europeans had been asked about it they might have said, yes. This would have rendered more plausible their suggestion that the alert made them targets. Either way in the case of the alert, the Europeans may well have been fortunate that there was no time to consult.

What made consultations particularly difficult was the lack of a vigorous, ongoing process, for which the United States deserved its rich share of the blame. Not only has the Alliance become poor at communication, but the Middle East itself was a difficult subject to communicate about because of problems of definition. Former NATO Secretary-General Manlio Brosio stated:

> From the geographical point of view there still exist illogical and even absurd situations which unjustifiably reduce consultation if it is kept within the area of direct responsibility of the Alliance. It seems completely irrational that the Atlantic Council should discuss in

depth questions relating to the politics and defence of the Mediterranean but cannot do the same for North Africa or the Middle East on the shores of the same sea — as if politics and defence were not related to the whole Mediterranean basin, both the sea and the contiguous countries.[47]

The question of geography raises a standard and essential issue for NATO about the limits of responsibility; where does a crisis have to occur before it is a threat to Western Europe? Certainly the Middle East involves the vital interests of Western Europe. Certainly the penetration of the sea-lanes and oil-lanes around the Middle East by the Soviet Union, however much we may argue about its extent, is a cause for concern to Western Europe.

What is important about the October War is that the superpowers treated it as *their* crisis. Indeed, Kissinger used the European leaders' own argument in dismissing them from the major decisions by saying that Western Europe was a regional power, but that the United States had global responsibilities. A client's crisis became one for the patron superpower. Perhaps it is just this view of October 1973 which suggests the strongest argument against the West European stance and for support of the American position, for it is the global balance between the superpowers that keeps the peace in Europe. The forces in being on the continent are effective only as part of the whole structure of superpower deterrence, not in and of themselves. (With respect to the Middle East, more examination than it has received is due to Israel's strategic contributions to American and West European interests.[48])

This of course is a debatable contention, particularly so when coming from an American. And while the alert should be analysed separately from the resupply, the resupply may have created intense feelings in a short period, making it very difficult for the Europeans to regard the alert with cool objectivity. It must be a short step for a nation to perceive an ally so clumsy as almost to get the nation's fuel cut off at the onset of winter, to perceiving that ally a little more literally ending the world. What is most striking, finally, about the West's diplomatic fiascos of October and after is that they happened at all, because although the parties perceived different interests and pursued them, the individual pursuits did not seem significantly to affect anyone else's. The maximising solution for the entire Alliance may well have been the events that occurred. For example, the cost to the United States of difficulties in the staging of the resupply may have been less than the cost in oil to Western Europe had the latter not been difficult.

The allies should have been able to behave in much the way they did without threatening to wreck the Alliance. The problem remains as to why so much rancour was created. It is easy to find problems in the substantive differences of the past in the military, monetary, and trade spheres, but such differences are surely the very stuff of alliances. The problem lies more directly in the failure of consultation *in the past*, and this has come about partly because of the personalism and excessive dramatics in much of the conduct of recent international relations. Combined with what many perceive as the American acceptance of strategic inferiority at SALT and the loss of American conventional military dominance in the Mediterranean, the effect is, inevitably, a weakening of the transatlantic ties.

Successful consultation cannot exist in the midst of distrust and well-known divergences of view. I believe, however, that divergences of view between Alliance nations are overestimated, since most of the set of views in most of the countries can be found in most of the others. The important divergences are between goals, held throughout the West, of only partial and sometime compatibility. These goals ought to be more compatible, but that is a matter for hard thought and frank discussion. It is not given by their nature.

Sanity and humanity have demanded continual search for alternatives to brinkmanship, but without endangering vital interests which the Soviet leadership would prefer not to tolerate. At the same time, in their eagerness for *détente*, Western leaders, scholars, and intellectuals have invented a dichotomy between diplomacy and force, alleging that the presence of one is the absence of the other. The consequence is not only the crippling of Western diplomacy but its paralysis in the face of those who not accept this dichotomy, such as the Soviets and the Egyptians. Americans can recognise this fallacy in Willy Brandt: Europeans are astute when it is practised by Henry Kissinger.

Now that all concerned are involved in discussions about Mutual Balanced Force Reduction (MBFR) — lately being apotheosised by many into a new incarnation, lacking the 'B' — the prospects for its recognition may be good. More importantly, it is in this area that the Soviet Union is playing a potentially tutelary role by embracing explicitly 'force' and 'diplomacy'. For years the West has tried to 'teach' the Soviets about subjects such as strategic theory and the model of a modern major power. Let the West be more humble for a change, for it has something to learn and the Soviets have much to teach.[49]

Notes

1. James O. Goldsborough, 'France, the European Crisis, and the Alliance', *Foreign Affairs*, LII (1974), p. 548.
2. Thomas Weigele, 'Nuclear Consultation Processes in NATO', *Orbis*, XV (1972), p. 462.
3. Henry A. Kissinger, '1973: The Year of Europe', *Current Foreign Policy*, US Department of State, Bureau of Public Affairs, 23 April 1973.

4. *New York Times*, 7 October 1973.
5. *BP Statistical Review of the World Oil Industry, 1972* (London, 1973).
6. Robert Pfaltzgraff, 'The Middle East Crisis: Implications for the European-American Relationship', paper prepared for the Annual Meeting of the American Political Science Association, Chicago, Illinois, September 1974.
7. *New York Times*, 8 October 1973.
8. *L'Express*, 5-11 November 1973.
9. Z., 'The Year of Europe?', *Foreign Affairs*, LII (1974), p. 237.
10. Tad Szulc, 'Is He Indispensable? Answers to the Kissinger Riddle', *New York Magazine*, 1 July 1971.
11. *New York Times*, 10 October 1973.
12. *Ibid.*, 12 October 1973.
13. 'Soviet Aid Sparks Arab Gains', *Aviation Week and Space Technology*, 15 October 1973.
14. Cecil Brownlow, 'Soviets Poise Three-Front Global Threat', *ibid.*, November 1973.
15. *New York Times*, 15 October 1973.
16. *L'Express*, 5-11 November 1973.
17. *Ibid.*, 22-28 October 1973.
18. *Le Monde*, 14 October 1973.
19. *Ibid.*, 17 October 1973.
20. *Ibid.*
21. *New York Times*, 17 October 1973.
22. *Ibid.*, 25 October 1973.
23. *Ibid.*
24. *Ibid.*, 23 October 1973.
25. Marvin and Bernard Kalb, *Kissinger* (Boston, 1974), p. 473.
26. 'Mideast Cease-Fire Spurs New Tensions', *Aviation Week and Space Technology*, 29 October 1973.
27. *L'Express*, 5-11 November 1973.
28. Herbert J. Coleman, 'U.S. Forces on Alert as NATO Politicians Fume', *Aviation Week and Space Technology*, 5 November 1973.
29. *Ibid.*
30. *New York Times*, 30 October 1973.
31. See *Department of State Bulletin*, 19 November 1973.
32. *Ibid.*
33. *Ibid.*
34. *Ibid.*
35. *L'Express*, 5-11 November 1973.
36. *Ibid.*
37. *The Times* (London), 29 October 1973.
38. 'The Alliance Under Strain', *Manchester Guardian Weekly*, 3 November 1973.
39. 'Report of the Committee of Three on Non-Military Co-operation in NATO', *NATO Facts and Figures* (Brussels, 1971).
40. Hella Pick, 'Kissinger Tries to Restore Trust', *Manchester Guardian Weekly*, 22 December 1973.
41. Pfaltzgraff, *op. cit.*, p. 13.
42. R. Norton-Taylor, 'EEC Tries to Appease Arabs', *Manchester Guardian Weekly*, 10 November 1973.
43. Press Conference of Secretary Kissinger on the Atlantic Alliance, SALT, and the Soviet Union, 21 March 1974, Department of State, Bureau of Public Affairs, Washington, D.C.
44. Harlan Cleveland, *NATO: The Transatlantic Bargain* (New York, 1970),

p. 15.

45. Weigele, *loc. cit.*, pp. 462-87.

46. *Ibid.*, p. 483.

47. Manlio Brosio, 'Consultation and the Atlantic Alliance', *Survival*, XVI (1974), p. 119.

48. One attempt is Alan Dowty, 'Does the United States Have a "Real" Interest in Supporting Israel?', in Morton Kaplan (ed.), *Great Issues of International Politics* (Chicago, 1970), pp. 312-22.

49. Steven Rhodes, M.A. candidate in International Relations at the University of Colorado, has been very helpful in providing the author with a chronology of the events referred to in this study. The author is also grateful to the Development Foundation of the University of Colorado for aid which enabled him to take part in the US State Department's Scholar-Diplomat Seminar in February 1974.

16. ARMS CONTROL IN THE MEDITERRANEAN AND EUROPEAN SECURITY

Ciro E. Zoppo

Introduction[1]

There is virtually no systematic analysis of the feasibility of or the prospects for arms control in the Mediterranean. The dearth of analysis is equalled by the determination of most European governments and those of the United States and the Soviet Union to exclude consideration of Mediterranean problems from their deliberations on Europe.

At the consultations that led to the Conference of Security and Cooperation in Europe in 1973, the Mediterranean did appear on the agenda, but to no avail. Yugoslavia and Malta, backed by Austria, stressed vigorously the interdependence between European security and conflict in the Middle East. They warned that without security in the Mediterranean, there can be no security in Europe. This concern is shared, in varying degrees, by Mediterranean states like France, Italy, Spain, Turkey, and Cyprus. Concern has been voiced as well by Algeria and Tunisia — whose diplomats went to Helsinki to give visible support to Yugoslavia's position. There was, however, no consensus on the matter among Mediterranean countries and the majority of participating states, including the United States and the Soviet Union, decided against including the Mediterranean as a subject for negotiations.

Military forces in the Mediterranean as a topic for serious discussion has been excluded with equal determination from the consultations on Mutual and Balanced Force Reductions (MBFR). There, the discussions are limited, by agreement, to forces on the central front. The original NATO position that only Central Europe should be discussed has been adopted by the Soviet Union. As a consequence, Mediterranean countries have been given a special status, which allows them to be present and to contribute and circulate working documents. Italy, Turkey, and Greece participate in MBFR on this basis. The flank countries in the north of Europe also have a consultative status. Most important, future reductions will not take place in these countries. France, with important Mediterranean interests, is not participating. The possibility that after dealing with the problem of troop reductions in Central Europe, reduction of forces in other zones of Europe could be discussed has been hardly broached. Hence it seems unlikely that at either negotiations will the Mediterranean be the subject of serious discussions.

Apparently, preliminary agreement has been reached between the United States and the Soviet Union, at Vladivostock, not to negotiate on forward-based systems in the negotiations for SALT II. This eliminates arms control in the Mediterranean from the talks on strategic arms limitations as well.

A host of complex issues make it prudent to restrict the initial discussions on Europe's security to the fulcrum of *détente* in Europe. With equal logic, it can be rationalised that considerations of Mediterranean arms control should be excluded from negotiations on strategic arms negotiations.

Yet it may be argued that because of the Arab-Israeli conflict and the recurrent Cyprus situation, and the dramatic impact of oil politics on world economics, the Mediterranean harbours the only currently recognisable threat to the security of Europe; and a worrisome avenue to potential escalation to nuclear war. This judgement is shared by many in Western scholarship and even by Soviet experts. For example, it was singled out in the Soviet paper on the future of European security presented at the Varna Conference as early as October 1972.

A modicum of political realism is sufficient to define *détente* as a condition that includes conflicting interests. *Détente* is a dynamic mixture of international rivalry and of judicious cooperation to avoid nuclear war and, secondly, to channel adversary instincts into less destructive political competition. Arms control can aid this process if properly designed. It is, therefore, possible that some forms of arms control could extend the *détente* to the Mediterranean, reducing the threat to European security that is created by inadvertent escalation to nuclear war.

Some would contend that without prior political settlement of the Middle East conflict, little can be done to reduce this threat to European security. I would not dispute that effective arms control must be a corollary to deterrence and not its substitute. It must function in both the conventional and the nuclear spheres of security without impairing either. Arms control, moreover, does not mean a reduction in the capability to guarantee the security of allies or nations friendly to either superpower. Arms control is more than limitations, reduction, or prevention of armaments. It is also the structuring of military forces and of the political incentives of nations so as to promote legitimate defence, deter the outbreak of warfare, and prevent the escalation of conflict to nuclear war. However, it can be a part of the process leading to political settlement, and need not await the resolution of conflict.

In the Mediterranean, if arms control is to reduce the frequency of local conflict and the potential for military violence, it must relate positively to the legitimate interests of the United States and the Soviet Union, and respect the local balance of power. European security, as well, must not be adversely affected. What follows is an attempt to assess how much and in what ways arms control in the Mediterranean might reduce, if not eliminate, the threat of escalation to general war and diminish the intensity of local conflict when it occurs, even in the absence of a negotiated peace settlement between Israel and its Arab neighbours, or a resolution of the Cyprus dilemma. The ultimate sanction of the feasibility of arms control in the Mediterranean, in this analysis, will be its political acceptability.

The Threat from the South

In Europe, the approaching strategic parity between the United States and the Soviet Union has led to a diplomatic search for ways to strengthen *détente*. Hardly a European political leader, East or West, fears the immediate future, although some malaise is discernible among West European defence experts in connection with some of the strategic outcomes of SALT I and the negotiations of SALT II.

In the Mediterranean region, by contrast, the future remains uncertain, even menacing. No sooner was the ceasefire between the Israelis and Arabs achieved by the exceptional diplomacy of the American Secretary of State than the Cyprus conflict exploded into a Turkish invasion of the island. Soviet influence in Egypt has been undermined by the events of the summer of 1972 and October 1973 to the point that Soviet control over Egyptian military initiatives has become highly contingent. Lebanon is in crisis. At the doorstep of Europe, a few hundred kilometres from the borders of the Soviet Union and the maritime frontiers of major European nations, the superpowers are engaged in a naval arms competition and in intense political rivalry — with their success seemingly as dependent on their willingness to transfer sophisticated weaponry to local belligerents as it is on adroit diplomacy. The energy crisis has compounded this arms transfer dilemma by introducing additional national actors (like Great Britain and France) and more incentives to transfer weapons to the Middle East.

The classical ingredients for miscalculation are all present: intense local conflict, uncertain control of military actions of local allies by the superpowers (as the Cyprus conflict has shown once more), mobile and powerful Soviet and American naval forces facing each other in the Mediterranean without a clear military and political boundary between them. To these factors must be added the portentous changes in conventional war technology, like precision-guided munitions, that are in the offing.

The United States and the Soviet Union are obviously concerned about their political influence in the Arab east. For the Soviet Union, control of this region would represent an important achievement in her bid for world leadership. For the United States the denial of such control will be an important way to contain her superpower rival. Since the Yom Kippur or October War of 1973, there has been a dramatic shift in the relations between the United States, Syria, and Egypt, but the situation remains fluid. Experience has shown that the objectives sought by the United States — eliminating military conflict from the area, maintaining access to Arab oil, limiting Soviet influence, improving relations with the Arabs, and guaranteeing the security of Israel — have often been conflicting, and the resulting dilemmas remain basically unresolved. Kissinger's conflict diplomacy has achieved results unimaginable before 1973, but the basic interests at issue remain to be resolved.

The Soviet Union, too, faces problematic choices in its policies toward the area. Soviet relations with Arab countries are characterised by as much friction as cooperation and by often unpredictable or hard-to-control Arab initiatives. The Soviet miscalculations about the Arab-Israeli dispute that led to the Six Day War of 1967 and the Egyptian policies that resulted in the withdrawal of the Soviet military advisers from Egypt in July 1972 are illustrative. The new round of fighting in October 1973 and another nearly decisive Egyptian defeat have confronted the Soviet Union, once again, with grave political and military risks. The American strategic alert and the tension that arose between the United States and its European allies during the critical phase of the 1973 October War make clear that the United States is also not immune.

The United States and the Soviet Union are, therefore, keenly aware of the risks of nuclear war. They have negotiated a number of arms control agreements designed to diminish the chances of inadvertent escalation and have taken steps to prevent nuclear mishaps that could lead to wrong perceptions of intentions. On 30 September 1971 the United States and the Soviet Union formally agreed to notify each other immediately if a nuclear weapon got out of control, by accident or a madman's design. They have committed themselves to immediate notification if either side suddenly found its early warning systems jammed or if radar showed unidentified and potentially hostile objects approaching. The superpowers have also signed an agreement to improve the direct communications link — the hotline — between Moscow and Washington by relying on satellites, and they have reached an understanding on how to avoid incidents with their warships and aircraft. At the June 1973 Washington Summit they also signed an Agreement on the Prevention of Nuclear War. In Article One, the United States and the Soviet Union agree 'that an objective of their policies is to remove the danger of nuclear war and of the use of nuclear weapons'. They pledge to act in a manner that would prevent the development of situations capable of causing a dangerous exacerbation of their relations so as to avoid military confrontations that could lead to the outbreak of nuclear war between them and between either the Soviet Union or the United States and other countries.

These accords demonstrate the Soviet and American realisation that miscalculation resulting from incomplete or false information is a very real threat to decision-makers in time of acute international crisis. But what is ambiguous and hard to predict often moves history decisively. The situation in the Mediterranean remains volatile. Confusing signals are easily generated, as was painfully demonstrated by the attack on an American communications ship by the Israelis during the Six Day War, and more recently by the response of the United States Government to the Soviet decision to place originally three, later seven, airborne divisions on alert during the Yom Kippur War.

At the very outset of the Six Day War, it is true, the Soviets promptly got on the hotline to Washington to declare that they would not intervene directly with their troops if the United States also abstained from military intervention. And Washington was in touch with the Soviets immediately upon learning of the impending Arab attacks in 1973. But what if American ships in the Mediterranean had been hit by fire, suspected of being Egyptian or Soviet, or clearly Soviet — hotline messages notwithstanding? Moreover, for the United States this problem is intensified by having to coordinate actions with its many allies. France, Great Britain, Federal Germany, Italy, Turkey, Greece, and also Spain (which hosts American naval and air bases) have policies toward the Arab-Israeli conflict at variance with those of the United States, in particular with respect to the contingency use of military force in the Mediterranean. The dearth of consultation on American military actions during the most recent developments in the Middle East crisis may have increased these difficulties. The change of regimes in Lisbon and Athens is likely to further constrain American freedom of action in the Mediterranean. In particular, Greece's dramatic waithdrawal from the NATO military organisation portends further changes in the relations of the United States with its allies in the Mediterranean.

The very stability alleged to exist in the strategic balance may make the superpowers more willing to risk conventional conflict during a confrontation. This may have been a calculation prompting both the Soviet decision to consider a possible military intervention in Egypt, and the American strategic alert that this Soviet decision precipitated. In fact Soviet behaviour, precisely because it came but a few months after solemn and formally negotiated pledges of *détente*, could be viewed as all the more provocative or reckless, or as evidence of a belief that parity lessens the risks involved in local intervention. It remains to be seen whether a naval balance of power between the Soviet Union and the United States, leading to mutual deterrence, can be achieved and mutually recognised before yet another military conflict between the Arabs and the Israelis or another Cyprus crisis spreads to envelop NATO. These eventualities remain very real. With the end of American military involvement in Indochina, and the reduction of political tensions in Europe, the *détente* is being tested in the Mediterranean. It is there it may ultimately fail or succeed.

The 1973 American-Soviet Agreement on the Prevention of Nuclear War was tested within three months of signature at the outset of the October War. It came dangerously close to being found wanting. The Soviet Union not only knew of the impending war and had not alerted anyone of this threat but had contributed to its outbreak by substantial shipment of ammunition and the latest anti-tank and anti-aircraft missiles to Egypt and Syria in the weeks immediately preceding hostilities. Once the Egyptians and Syrians had attacked, the Soviets increased seaborne supplies and within four days they had mounted a massive airlift of military resupply to the Arab belligerents. Within twenty-four hours there came a steep increase in the number of Soviet warships in the Mediterranean and soon Leonid Brezhnev was inciting other Arab States to join the war. Before the fighting stopped on the Egyptian front, the Soviets had alerted several airborne divisions for the declared purpose of unilateral intervention in the conflict, after their insistence that a joint Soviet-American peacekeeping force be sent to the Middle East was rejected by the United States and had reportedly landed nuclear weapons in Port Said.[2] A direct Soviet intervention, it has been noted, could only trigger an American counteraction, possibly spiralling to nuclear war. Kissinger has characterised these events as 'a murderously dangerous situation, much worse, much more dangerous than the 1970 Jordan crisis'.[3] Can we have both *détente* and war? Certainly, the Soviet Union held this belief during the initial period of the Middle East war. There is some evidence that it may still flirt with this notion,[4] though Soviet behaviour in the Cyprus conflict is in low profile. Another trial like the October 1973 one could be catastrophic.

Neither Israelis nor Arabs nor Greeks nor Turks would have their interests served by repeated confrontations between Soviets and Americans in the Mediterranean. Escalation to nuclear conflict would benefit no one. Arms control mechanisms that reduce the likelihood of inadvertent escalation to nuclear war, without undermining the political commitments of the superpowers, should be welcomed in Europe too.

The *détente* tenor of relations between the Soviet Union and the United States coupled with the changing political relations between the superpowers and the countries of the Middle East may make it possible seriously to explore the possibility of arms control in the Mediterranean. Such arms control could be modest at first and gradual. It could be undertaken without compromising Soviet and American political commitments to promote a peaceful settlement in the Middle East conflicts, according to values congenial to Soviet and American policies, and acceptable to Israel and her Arab neighbours.

Arms Control in the Mediterranean

Among the arms control measures proposed which directly affect Soviet and American military forces in the Mediterranean have been the elimination of bases, nuclear free zones, and the withdrawal of naval forces. There have also been Soviet attempts to include in the SALT II negotiations, forward-based systems in Europe and the carrier-borne American and NATO aircraft capable of nuclear delivery and stationed in seas peripheral to Europe, although the Ford-Brezhnev meetings in Vladivostock have reportedly shelved active consideration of the Soviet proposal.

The Non-Proliferation Treaty and various early attempts to limit arms transfers to local combatants are also relevent. I am concerned here, however, only with arms control measures that relate to inadvertent escalation between the superpowers. Unless or until Israel or its Arab enemies acquire a nuclear military capability, measures relating to naval arms control are of more immediate concern, when approached in relation with land-based air power. In fact, the anticipation of local nuclear capabilities (an Israeli one being most imminent) increases the importance of analysing the impact of naval arms control in the region.

In this connection, there has been a mild disposition on the part of the Soviet Union and the United States to consider arms control in the Mediterranean. The US Government has been less interested than the Soviet one, if we take Soviet declarations as representing genuine interest. In 1973, the former Defense Secretary Laird revealed that plans were being pursued for future policy meetings between American and Soviet defence ministers on board ship in the Mediterranean. During the year top officials shared shipboard visits to discuss ways of averting incidents at sea, and other unspecified topics. It is not known if these included mutual force reductions in the area.

Soviet interest is of longer standing. Noteworthy are several statements made by Brezhnev, the first in 1971, the most recent in July 1974. In his report to the Twenty-fourth Communist Party Congress on 30 March 1971, he stated:

Our country is prepared to participate, together with other powers that are permanent members of the Security Council, in the creation of international guarantees of a political settlement in the Near East. After this is achieved, it would be possible, in our view, to consider further steps aimed at military *détente* in this whole area, in particular steps aimed at transforming the Mediterranean into a sea of peace and friendly cooperation.[5]

On 12 June, of the same year, Brezhnev amplified his original proposal by stating that the Soviet Union was prepared to resolve the problem of an American and Soviet naval presence in the Mediterranean 'on an equal footing'. He went on to say that this included the willingness of the Soviet Union to discuss the mutual reduction of fleets 'plying the seas for long periods at great distances from their shores';[6] an implicit suggestion of spheres of influence determined by distance from superpower homelands.

Since that time Soviet commentaries on the Mediterranean situation have often referred to these proposals and have amplified them as well. A theme in these commentaries has been the extension of the equal strategic principle adopted for American and Soviet strategic arms to the field of general purpose naval forces, as a means of relaxing tensions in international affairs. The Soviet Union has also proposed the establishment of a nuclear free zone in the Middle East and the Mediterranean, first advanced formally in May 1963, in connection with the stationing of US Polaris submarines in the Mediterranean. The proposal was shelved and resurfaced in June 1971 when a Soviet broadcast reiterated the desirability of the establishment of this nuclear free zone. The commentaries stressed that warships in the Mediterranean had nuclear weapons aboard and that a nuclear free zone would greatly reduce the danger that countries in the Middle East and the Mediterranean would be 'dragged into great international military disputes'. The formal proposal was rejected by the United States. However, both countries have vigorously promoted the Non-Proliferation Treaty and if all the local countries ratify the agreement, and a way is found to remove nuclear weapons from the respective fleets, one would achieve such denuclearisation.[7]

On 21 July 1974, in his speech before the Polish Parliament in Warsaw, Brezhnev returned to Mediterranean arms control. Reporting on the recent American-Soviet summit meeting he emphasised that the Soviet Union would have liked more results. He said:

We also consider it useful to agree on the removal from the Mediterranean of all Soviet and American nuclear-weapons-carrying ships and submarines . . . Let us hope that the time will come when agreements on these questions will become possible.[8]

Taken seriously, these proposals imply two kinds of naval arms control for the Mediterranean: measures designed to minimise accidents and misperceptions between Soviet and American ships,[9] and measures to limit the respective naval forces at some kind of functional parity, or possibly redeploying the Soviet squadron and the Sixth Fleet out of the Mediterranean.

Prudential Arms Control

It was noted above that a protocol placing restrictions on the manoeuvres of Soviet and American warships to avert collisions and/or provocative behaviour by aircraft and ships tracking each other was signed in Moscow during President Nixon's visit in May of 1972. A second protocol was added in May 1973, which deals with the manoeuvring of military vessels in the vicinity of merchant ships. Ships and aircraft of the United States and the Soviet Union are prohibited from making simulated attacks against American or Soviet merchantmen. They are also prohibited from dropping dummy mines in the path of ships.

These are useful measures. One can also imagine corollary agreements to improve ship-to-ship communications in case accidents occur anyway, especially under ambiguous circumstances. The implementation of these agreements comes as a welcome change after many years of daring games of nerves between American and Soviet warships in the Mediterranean and elsewhere.

Other modest arms control measures, separately or jointly negotiated, would be agreements to limit ship-operating days and to limit the number of naval exercises each year. The first would apply only to American and Soviet ships. The latter would be between NATO (including the Sixth Fleet) and the Warsaw Pact, limiting all naval manoeuvres and exercises. Such an agreement might limit their number, provide for mutual on-board observers, and require prior notification. Easy to verify, these agreements could reduce unnecessary political tensions and give useful advance warning of changed political intentions.

The greatest danger exists, of course, during crises such as the Jordanian Civil War of 1970, the 1967 Six Day War, the 1973 October War, and the 1974 Cyprus conflict. Under similar conditions, incidents resulting from precautionary manoeuvres are still possible. Such mishaps may be misunderstood as deployment to attack opposing naval forces. If they are nuclear weapon incidents, risks would take a quantum jump.[10] The chart on US-Soviet naval deployment in the eastern Mediterranean during the 1970 Jordanian crisis leaves little doubt about the promiscuity of contending naval forces in crisis situations. During the October War the Sixth Fleet did not deploy as far east, the easternmost penetration of significant American naval activity being off Crete;

Figure 1: The US and Soviet Fleets (submarines not shown) during the peak period of September and October 1970

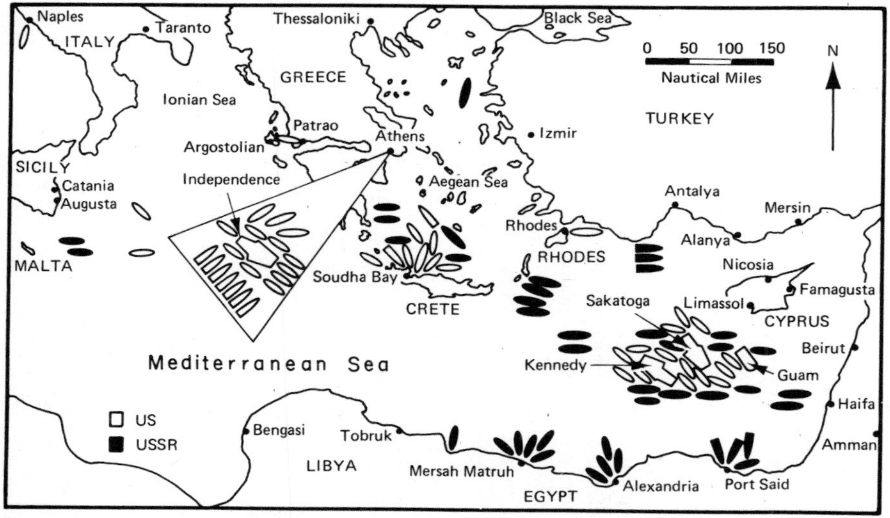

Source: *US Naval Institute Proceedings*, 98:2/828, February 1972.

but the Sixth Fleet commander, Admiral Murphy, did note the very close proximity of American and Soviet warships in the Mediterranean.[11] To this clutter of warships must be added an average of 2,000 commercial ships a day plying the seas between Gibraltar and the Bosphorus. An indication of the increased naval traffic in the Mediterranean may be surmised from the sharp increase in the Soviet Navy's ship-operating days there. In 1965, they amounted to 4,000. In 1972, there were 19,000,[12] and they seem to be yet increasing.

Of interest is the system of command and control for tactical nuclear weapons. Only one person, the US President, can grant authority to fire nuclear weapons controlled by American forces. This authority is, moreover, subject to physical restraints and administrative safeguards. Administrative procedures include psychiatric screening of military personnel with access to nuclear weapons, the no-lone zone rule, and the two-man requirement. Among physical restraints are double-keyed locks, altitude and acceleration locks, and permissive action links. Except for tight disciplinary control, Soviet safegaurds have not been publicised.[13]

Nevertheless, when one considers the many levels through which command authority must be delegated and the communication problems and misunderstandings that might arise in tense crises, the possible fragility of the system cannot be dismissed.[14]

Fred C. Iklé has observed:

> It is often fallacious to assume independence for the probabilities of mishaps which, in combination, could produce a major accident. The possibilities for statistical interdependence of such probabilities is illustrated by the delay in U.S. military communications that occurred during the *Pueblo* seizure. Admiral Sharp, in explaining the delays in communications, pointed to the heavy overload of communications traffic in his headquarters because of the war in Vietnam. It is, of course, precisely during an acute crisis that the safety of nuclear arms — of all nuclear powers — becomes of greatest concern. And in a crisis, some of the safeguards considered to be independent might become jointly degraded.[15]

Conditions similar to these that might lead to accidental war have obtained on several occasions in the past few years in the Mediterranean. Local political conditions make it foolhardy to predict they will not occur again. Thus, even modest arms control measures that could reduce the probability of unintended mishap, or the effects of unauthorised acts, are worth pursuing. Arms control in this sense can hardly be objected to by the most hell-bent of naval commanders. Its primary objective is to ensure that command and control is not degraded and that combat is the consequence of a deliberate decision to engage the enemy — taken at the highest levels of government. Even conceding the necessity for reconnaissance, one may wonder at the rationales that have moved, in the past, the Soviet and American navies to engage in risky and provocative manoeuvres.

The purposeful effects of Soviet-American agreements to avert collisions and restrict provocative military behaviour at sea and in the air could be expanded by complementary understandings on operational deployments, on manoeuvres, and on adversary communications, *in situ*, during a crisis. Agreements to give advance notification of manoeuvres, mutually agreed reductions on ship-operating days, and the exchange of observers are illustrations.

Measures already negotiated, and germane ones that might be, can be implemented in the Mediterranean without fanfare. If, however, the Soviet Union and the United States desired to project intentions of *détente* into the Mediterranean, publicised and official declarations are required.

The United States and the Soviet Union might sign a protocol that specifically applies to the Mediterranean their Agreement on the Prevention of Nuclear War of June 1973 which in essence provides that each side attaches major importance to preventing the development of situations capable of causing dangerous exacerbations of their relations and will do their utmost to avoid military confrontation and to prevent the outbreak of nuclear war.[16]

This kind of approach would create, of course, political implications beyond arms control. It might be seen as emasculating American commitments to Italy, Greece, Turkey and Israel and as undercutting Soviet policy objectives in the Arab world. Indeed, it would emphasise the determination of the superpowers to avoid falling victims to wilful or inadvertent catalytic actions by local belligerents and would reassert the shared Soviet-American interest in avoiding the risk of escalation to nuclear war that might arise out of conflicts or crises in the Middle East and the Mediterranean.

The arms control benefits of this suggestion may seem remote were it not for the accelerated tempo of potential nuclear proliferation, following the Indian nuclear explosion of July 1974. Evidently, a transfer of nuclear technology from France to Iran is under way. And the United States by its agreement to provide nuclear aid to Egypt (and concomitantly to Israel) will, itself, help create the preconditions for possible proliferation in the Middle East. Rumours of deals between India and Iraq for exchanging assured oil supply for explosive nuclear technology are even more ominous. The position taken by the Soviet Union on the rationales presented by India for its nuclear explosive technology programme show how political considerations can mute arms control policies.

Sharing these arms control interests in regard to escalation does not presume, nor require, common Soviet and American political goals in the region, nor should it cause uneasiness about a superpower 'condominium'. Timely diplomatic reassurances to respective friendly governments in the Middle East and Europe would explain the independence of political support to client states from the requirements of arms control in the Mediterranean. The Agreement on the Prevention of Nuclear War cited above incorporates a clause in its Article Six stipulating that the signatories' obligations towards their allies and other countries are not impaired by the treaty.

Whether the arms control measures in the Mediterranean, here discussed, should be undertaken quietly or with publicity, by concerted but unilateral acts, or as a result of formal agreements is a matter of policy choice and not an imperative of arms control.

The measures outlined would help to reduce the possibilities of misperceptions and miscalculations where they could occur more easily. Notwithstanding some awesome experience, the rules of confrontation remain vague and the danger of crisis escalation real. Taken together, these measures could help clarify 'the rules of the game' without undercutting deterrence or weakening political commitments to respective allies and friends. In contrast to the days of the Concert of Europe, this century, before the advent of nuclear weapons, and even up to the 1962 Cuban Missile Crisis, was not very encouraging with respect to the modalities governing international military conflict. The enormity of the consequences attending nuclear war makes imperative the development of clearly understood 'rules' of confrontation. This requirement applies to military intervention with conventional forces in third areas as well. Some rules, it has been suggested, already exist for naval intervention. I will discuss this hypothesis later. At this point, I would note only that the arms control measures discussed above would facilitate the development of prudential rules for avoiding unwanted escalation.

As dramatic as these actions might seem, when measured against the memory of the superpower military behaviour in the Mediterranean just a few years ago, they do not constitute a radical shift from the current arms control policies of the Soviet Union and the United States, and would not change substantially American and Soviet policies in the Mediterranean.

Substantial Arms Control

The second category of measures, namely to limit, restructure, reduce, or withdraw Soviet and American military forces from the Mediterranean to demilitarise this sea — or to limit the transfer and the resupply of arms to local belligerents — would signal, instead, a major change in policies. Their political, military, and arms control implications would be complex and significant. The prospects for negotiating these substantial measures are quite uncertain.

Although arms control of this type involves primarily the national weapons stockpiles and the naval forces of the United States and the Soviet Union in the Mediterranean, they would require, at minimum, extensive and prior consultations with NATO. Their possible impact on the strategic balance, because of the air and underwater systems that are part of and are associated with these fleets, would also relate them to issues of European security.

The United States would have to make explicit that no degradation of the American commitment to the defence of Europe would result from any agreements. If functional and symbolic symmetry of reduction or redeployment is feasible, this political requirement would be less problematic.

Although the implications for arms control, for military doctrine, and for political relationships in the Mediterranean of these measures are major, there is a further distinction that can be usefully made, because of the difference in their political impact. In discussing these measures it might be useful to consider those that would limit, reduce, or restructure the naval forces of each side separately from the more radical proposal to withdraw forces from the Mediterranean. The measures involving denuclearisation are probably closer in their characteristics to those involving withdrawal, but can also be treated in the restructuring approach.

Whether arms control measures fall in a category of restricting and restructuring forces or withdrawing them, it is difficult to assess them without relating them to the military and political objectives that brought them to the Mediterranean. Setting aside for the moment their strategic utility and, just as criticial, their NATO and Warsaw Pact roles, the American and Soviet fleets in the Mediterranean represent a capability to intervene in local conflict, primarily in the Middle East and the Maghreb. It is this implicit political intention and the physical capability to intervene, taken together, that create the major danger of superpower confrontation in the event of a clash of local interests; and consequently a threat to the security of Europe. The accidental war problem, discussed above, can be negotiated so as to be averted without major policy changes. Inadvertent escalation from involvement in local conflict would require curtailing the military capabilities of both sides to intervene.

Therefore, an important issue is to what extent the Soviet Union and the United States possess a viable intervention capability, And more importantly, whether they would exercise it in the face of the opponent's military forces in the area. The answer involves imponderables of the first magnitude. To say that the willingness of either power to confront the other will depend on their perception of the national interest, the likelihood of a favourable military outcome, the judgement of the other power's determination to resist, or the degree of confidence either may have that engagement will not result in escalation to general war is merely to state the factors that operate in such a situation. It is possible to say, however, that currently the US Sixth Fleet and the Soviet Squadron have the potential to militarily neutralise each other. And this might lead the Soviet Union and the United States to inaction; that is to crisis manoeuvring to prevent rather than undertake intervention. American intervention would seem likely only if Israel's national survival were at stake or in the event of a major political shift through revolutionary changes in a key Arab country. As for the Soviets, a threat to the political or national integrity of Egypt or Syria would have to be at hand, before they would seriously consider intervening. Some would take a different view and see the continued use of naval intervention forces.[17]

This apparent stalemate seems likely to be continued rather than weakened with the passage of time. The gradual and constant build-up of Soviet naval forces and the reported construction of Soviet aircraft carriers in the Black Sea strengthens this supposition.

Soviet ships permanently on station in the Mediterranean are a dramatic indicator of the changes affecting the United States' freedom of manoeuvre in the Middle East and the Mediterranean. The inhibitions on American actions are well illustrated by the behaviour of the Sixth Fleet during the initial phase of the Six Day War and the October War. In 1967, most of the US Fleet was in the western Mediterranean when the crisis broke. It immediately observed three important restrictions: no premature departures from scheduled port visits; deliberate and visible retention of its amphibious forces in the central Mediterranean, at Malta; and, purposeful retention of American naval forces south of Crete and well clear of the area of action. Soviet naval forces were in the eastern Mediterranean, being reinforced through the Straits, with some units on the way to Egyptian ports. In 1973, similar inhibitions were observed.

The operational capability of the Soviet Mediterranean fleet is curtailed by Turkish control of the Straits, the ease with which the Suez Canal can be blocked, and Great Britain's control of Gibralter. An even more serious drawback is the Soviet fleet's seeming lack of air cover. The Soviet Navy has as yet no carriers and there are no Soviet airfields near the shores of the Mediterranean. Soviet naval doctrine has sought to surmount this difficulty by creating an operational doctrine that emphasises missile-carrying submarines and missile-carrying aircraft. This would permit Soviet naval units and aircraft to attack American carriers without entering the zone of anti-submarine and air defences of the carrier force. In the future, there will be Soviet aircraft carriers, like the *Kiev* under construction in Black Sea shipyards. The carrier-based aircraft of the Sixth Fleet — two carriers with about eighty strike aircraft apiece — is a formidable force. Its effectiveness is contingent, however. The potential availability of land-based Soviet aircraft and the existence of Soviet submarines in the area may hobble the offensive use of the carrier's craft. The number of aircraft available to strike at Soviet ships will depend on how many aircraft will be necessary to defend the carrier system itself against air and submarine attacks, the strength of inhibitions against using aircraft with a nuclear mission in a conventional mode, the distance between the contending fleets, the types and number of land-based aircraft available to each side, and above all on the political constraints operating at the time of engagement.

The Sixth Fleet was stationed in the Mediterranean in the 1950s to complement Strategic Air Command (SAC), and presumably still has a nuclear mission. Consequently, the strategic mission of the Soviet Squadron is to deal with this nuclear threat posed by the aircraft carriers of the Sixth Fleet. But it should be clear that nuclear war and large scale conventional warfare in the Mediterranean are, under present circumstances, unlikely contingencies and offer questionable justification for an operational doctrine for either the Soviet Mediterranean Squadron or the Sixth Fleet.

It is more reasonable to assume that the likely contingencies in which the Soviet and American naval presence will play an important role will not only be ambiguous but sufficiently limited, from a military viewpoint, to preclude extensive engagements. The Soviet and American naval forces in the Mediterranean therefore create capabilities more likely to threaten or inhibit possible interventions than to engage in combat to carry them out. This seems clear from the experience of the October War when the fleets played a role second to air power in raising the possibility of intervention with troops and in the emergency resupply of Egypt and Syria and of Israel.

In the past, the utility of the Sixth Fleet went beyond its NATO nuclear role. It was political as well as conventional in the military sense. One need only recall the freedom of action of the United States at the time of the Lebanese crisis to realise the telling changes that have taken place in the Mediterranean region. With the Soviet Squadron in these waters, the capabilities for intervention are more symmetrical. The landing of marines in Lebanon in 1958 or a similar operation to aid Israel is more problematic. In 1958 there were no Soviet fleet units in the Mediterranean. Turkey gave unqualified support to American policy in the Middle East. The staging area for the American troops who landed in Lebanon was in Turkey. The Americans proceeded on the assumption that Turkish territory was available for their use and were not disappointed. They had no overflight problems in Turkey or any other Mediterranean country, including France.

Would such unencumbered American intervention be possible in present circumstances? Putting aside whether any Arab government is likely to request American aid, the answer must be a qualified no. Turkish territory, except for the Jordanian crisis, has not been available as a staging area, if for no other reason that that the American and Turkish positions diverge on what policy should be towards Israel and the Arabs. The Turks and other allies have drawn the distinction between contingencies affecting NATO and those in the Middle East. Using Italian facilities in a situation not explicitly affecting NATO would also be contingent. France, seeking to forge an independent Mediterranean role, might be even less likely to cooperate. And Greece has abandoned NATO. Constraints on American actions in the Mediterranean could become severe. Only Portuguese territory, the Azores, was made available to the United States for resupply during the October War, and the changes that have occurred in the political governance of that country now mean that these facilities will not again be available for use in a comparable crisis.

In addition to the purely military constraints operating on the freedom of action of the Soviet Squadron, there exist political constraints similar to those operating against the United States. Soviet actions surrounding the September 1970 Jordanian-Syrian crisis highlight the analogous dilemma confronting Soviet leaders. Official Soviet reaction expressed alarm at the movements of the Sixth Fleet in the eastern Mediterranean and its possible military intervention into Jordan. Ships of the Soviet Squadron engaged in close and constant surveillance of the American task forces during the crisis. But no effort was made to interfere with the Sixth Fleet's movements. The Soviet Union was careful to provide no signals that it intended to frustrate by force the deployment of American warships.

The political constraints operating on Soviet freedom of action in case of internal strife within Arab countries could also be great enough to dissuade them from intervention, as would be the possible difficulty of obtaining overflight rights for the Soviet Air Force from Yugoslavia, Turkey, or Iran.

Advancing technology may add more mutual restraints. Countership and shore bombardment will rely increasingly on cruise missiles. The advent of precision-guided munitions (PGMs) will make apparent the vulnerability of sea transport and of carrier task forces and troopships, particularly in interventions. It will no longer be desirable to cluster forces on land or sea. The close support role of carrier aviation may be

264

waning and could decline even more in the future.

The technology of conventional warfare is now on the threshold of significant breakthroughs that should bring about dramatic changes in military doctrine. For the first time since the beginning of the Second World War, weapons technology may make the conventional defence dominant over the offence. The PGMs for anti-tank, anti-aircraft, and anti-ship use, laser-guided and man-portable, are the most prominent of these technologies. Others are the rapidly improving technologies of reconnaissance and control.[18]

The full implications of these developments remain to be determined. But if the new technologies can create the conditions for preferring defence over attack, they will reshape more than military doctrine. By challenging military relationships, in the conventional area of security, between major and lesser powers, and by affecting regional military balances and the operational structure of alliances, they may have important political consequences.

Intervention capabilities must be reassessed. If coastal gunboat navies become a feasible and effective defence for small countries, the structure and doctrines of American, Soviet and other major navies may have to be radically altered. Compelling arguments can be made to re-examine the role of air power as well. The meaning of the new technologies of surveillance and control for arms control can be also profitably explored.

If prudence prevails, future landings in the Mediterranean area may become politically unfeasible and militarily difficult. Checkmated Soviet and American naval forces in the Mediterranean would seem to have a dubious future as instruments for intervention. These developments may have increased genuine incentives to limit the growth of Soviet and US naval forces in the Mediterranean and created the possibility for more than prudential arms control.

Complicating factors that generate contrary incentives are the very active American-Soviet naval arms competition in the conventional and strategic sectors and the relation they are seen to have. An additional consideration is the independent status of the Soviet Squadron and the Sixth Fleet. Although both have combat missions supporting Warsaw Pact and NATO plans, they are not formally part of these forces — facilitating independent arms control negotiations between Moscow and Washington. Obviously, limiting, more so reducing, these forces cannot be considered without reference to NATO and Warsaw Pact navies. Nor can meaningful arms reduction be achieved without full consultation with allies. Arms control agreements in this area need not complicate negotiations on arms control in Central Europe in a formal negotiatory sense. In terms of military security and alliance cohesion, it is obvious, however, that they are intrinsically related to Europe, and to the global naval balance.

Of critical importance to the future of surface fleets in the Mediterranean and to any arms control considerations is the role of air power. The Mediterranean is virtually landlocked. Distances from shore to shore are substantial but within the range of land-based air power. Soviet ships in the Mediterranean are vulnerable to the combined US and NATO land-based and carrier air power.

By 1979, the Soviet Union could have several aircraft carriers of the KURIL-class, the first of which is now approaching operational status in the Black Sea. It will probably be deployed to the Mediterranean.[19] The Soviet air threat to the US Sixth Fleet already exists, however, in the shape of land-based bombers like the Tu-16 Badgers and Tu-20 Bears, which are based in the western part of the Soviet Union and can with one refuelling reach out thousands of miles to encompass the Mediterranean. Another Soviet aircraft, the BACKFIRE, now undergoing major development, would eliminate the need for refuelling to reach targets in the Mediterranean.

The vulnerabilities of carrier task forces due to land-based air power would take a quantum jump if nuclear weapons were used, even sparingly. The use of nuclear weapons against sea targets would obviously breach the nuclear threshold. But it would be a lesser escalation than would the use of nuclear weapons on land, because of the isolated nature of the targets and the near absence of collateral damage; thus, the international political repercussions would probably be less than if nuclear weapons were used in land war.[20]

It may be that reflection upon the role of air power will generate additional incentives for considering possible arms control in the Mediterranean.

An extended discussion of the relationship of Mediterranean arms control to strategic deterrence and SALT would unduly expand the scope of this analysis. Therefore, only the most salient issues will be considered. Even without further agreement at SALT II, research and development of weapons and force postures will continue to be shaped by the Soviet-American negotiations on the limitations of strategic arms. Inevitably, deterrent doctrine is being re-examined and will seek new definitions. No radical qualitative changes in the technologies of strategic forces seem in the offing, but concomitant changes in accuracy and vulnerability and Multiple Independent Re-entry Vehicles (MIRV) technology on both the American and Soviet sides will demand a re-statement of doctrine. The renewed American emphasis on flexible options has alerted Europeans (and Japanese and Israelis) to the importance of the options and constraints that SALT is creating in security policies. The political cushion provided by American strategic superiority has manifestly eroded, and the political realities in which American deterrence must operate are profoundly different from the 1960s.[21]

One outcome of SALT I is the added impetus given to research in weapon systems like MIRV. SALT I has spurred the refinement of Soviet and American MIRVs. And it is unlikely that SALT II will introduce qualitative curbs in this area. The freezing of ABMs may help to perpetuate the emerging vulnerability of land-based systems. For this reason, it has created additional incentives to strengthen the naval components of the strategic deterrent forces of both sides. Moreover, the growth of Soviet strategic naval forces is practically guaranteed by the 1972 Interim Agreement so that at the very least strategic naval parity is virtually assured to the Soviets. SALT I and probably SALT II (notwithstanding the test-ban understandings and the Vladivostok agreement) promise to have marginal impact on the technological aspects of the arms competition between the Soviet Union and the United States. However, in general there is no major concern about destabilising technological breakthroughs in the years immediately ahead. The issue of increased accuracy for ICBMs remains moot, but is directly relevant to Secretary Schlesinger's flexible options policy.[22]

Also relevant to substantial measures of naval arms control in the Mediterranean is the refinement of nuclear submarine technology. By the late 1970s, when the Trident submarine and its long-range missiles become operational,[23] targets now assigned to nuclear submarines in the Mediterranean will be covered by submarines cruising the Atlantic and the Indian Ocean. Even now, Poseidon and Polaris A-3 have practically doubled the SLBM ranges. These increased ranges and the ABM Treaty combine to reduce the special value of the Mediterranean for strategic deterrence and could diminish objections to arms control based on considerations of strategic requirements.

SALT has aborted the arms competition in ABM systems. It has set some ceilings on offensive forces. Presently projected ratios between Soviet and American offensive and defensive strategic systems will be maintained by agreement. With some necessary adjustments to guarantee neither side a first strike capability, eventual codification of strategic parity could result.

On the American side, Admiral Zumwalt has testified that the credibility of general purpose naval forces in the Mediterranean is tied directly to the kind of strategic posture that can be maintained under the SALT agreements.[24] On the Soviet side, Admiral Gorshkov has justified the Soviet naval presence in the Mediterranean as a deterrent to an attack on the Soviet Union by the aircraft and missile submarines of the American naval forces in the Mediterranean.[25] From the Soviet viewpoint, because American carrier aircraft in the Mediterranean can reach targets in the Soviet Union and are capable of nuclear delivery, they are part of the American strategic threat. (Land-based forward systems in NATO are viewed similarly by the Soviets.) The Soviet Union would prefer, therefore, to treat them as a subject for negotiation in SALT II.

Early in the SALT negotiations, the Soviet Union introduced the contention that SALT should seek to limit not only those offensive weapons which the West had habitually regarded as 'intercontinental' but also any other system with which one superpower could deliver nuclear weapons on the territory of the other. American strike aircraft on West European bases and on carriers in the Mediterranean would thus be included. Arguing on the premise that it is intention, rather than capability, that is pertinent, the United States insisted that these forward-based systems (FBSs) be counted as part of the American contributions to the tactical capability of NATO. In SALT I, this view was allowed to prevail.[26] Technically, NATO forward-based systems are intended for tactical use. Politically, West Europeans see them as a way to couple the American commitment.

Modern technology and nuclear weapons have made definitions for purposes of arms control negotiation more complex than ever. If FBSs were redeployed to the United States, could they be flown back in time to be of use? Criteria of range, yield, targeting, and organisation are all pertinent. The most salient definition of strategic weapons is in fact whether they can strike the homeland; but this criterion is not necessarily useful for FBSs. More critical for these systems is how they relate to other weapon systems in the local balance of each side, and what is the political context in which they operate. The Soviets have apparently agreed not to push for negotiations on FBSs in SALT II, as part of the recent Vladivostok preliminary agreements with the United States, in December 1974. Whether this means that negotiations for force reductions or limitations in the Mediterranean would be more, or less, difficult is a moot question that can be answered only by attempts to negotiate by the United States or the Soviet Union.

European Security and Arms Control in the Mediterranean

Arms control objectives in the Mediterranean must be congruent with the European goal of keeping arms competition from reimposing Cold War politics in Europe. There are strong Western European inhibitions against the removal of any American military strength from Europe. This would seem to hold for the Mediterranean — though it may be less so for the naval vessels of the superpowers. Ian Smart has pointed out that there would be strong Western European objections to any significant reduction of dual-capable FBSs. We are reminded by him that the fundamental issue is 'less one of the value of particular weapon systems than one of the relative importance which the United States seems to be giving to alliance relationships, on the one hand, and to the super-power relationship, on the other.[27]

I have identified the most important considerations that must operate in assessments of the feasibility of limiting or restructuring naval forces in the Mediterranean by mutual Soviet-American agreement. I have also broached relevant political factors. The latter are more malleable when limitations or restructuring alone are considered; such as denuclearising the Soviet and American naval forces in the Mediterranean. If reductions of forces necessitate operational restructuring of Soviet and American naval forces or their redeployment from the Mediterranean, political aspects would increase, however, to decisive importance.

Reductions that lead to sizeable or complete redeployments are unlikely under present conditions but illustrate the serious issues of arms control in the Mediterranean. American willingness to negotiate some form of denuclearisation in the Middle East could lead to Soviet consolidation of its military 'parity' in the naval sphere. Denuclearising the Mediterranean would remove US Polaris boats, and mutual withdrawal of surface warships would put American carrier-based air power at sea in the Atlantic, several days from a Mediterranean contingency. Soviet fleets would be withdrawn to the Black Sea, where they would be handicapped by Turkish control of the Straits. Units could be withdrawn to the Persian Gulf, to be reintroduced through the Suez Canal. But there they lack the necessary base facilities.

Such handicaps might be compensated by the fact that the reintroduction of warships, by either side, into the Mediterranean would constitute a powerful political signal of intention. Hence, an agreement would be strongly inhibitory; the deterrent gap, created by such agreement, could be compensated for by means of land-based air power, although political constraints could be powerful on their use. This signalling of intentions is an important arms control consideration.

A withdrawal by agreement, however, could alter significantly the military balance of power in the Mediterranean. It would be interpreted as a powerful signal of changed Soviet and American political intentions. The issues are, therefore, essentially political. The impact of a withdrawal agreement on the relations of the United States with its NATO allies and Spain, and even the changed American relations with Egypt, are paramount. American and Soviet withdrawals from the Mediterranean would directly affect Israel — the American withdrawal more critically.

French naval policy on the Mediterranean is now unclear. But during the tenure of the Pompidou Government, a policy, relevant to the issue at hand, was advocated by France, and it elicited a response from other Mediterranean countries, which reveals the attitudes that might prevail if serious efforts are undertaken to achieve naval arms control in the Mediterranean.

In terms of the political acceptability to Mediterranean countries of a withdrawal from the Mediterranean of Soviet and American ships, France, under the Pompidou Government, had been expounding the advantages of non-alignment to Lebanon, Morocco, Tunisia, and Algeria, as well as to Spain, Italy, and Libya. France defined the security of the Mediterranean as a more active French role at the same time that the United States and the Soviet Union 'withdrew' their naval presences. At the time, France argued for common efforts with the Arab countries of the Maghreb, Spain, Italy, and Greece, to avoid 'excessive external influence in the Mediterranean region'.

France also endorsed a previous Spanish suggestion that both Soviet and American fleets be withdrawn from the Mediterranean. Except for Italy, whose position coincided with that of Turkey and Greece (before withdrawal from NATO), and was defined in primarily NATO terms, all other Mediterranean countries have at that time and subsequently promoted or endorsed the withdrawal of Soviet and American ships from the Mediterranean, with various degrees of commitment. Lebanon, Syria, Algeria, Tunisia, Libya, and Egypt, at one time or another since 1968, have stated support for the withdrawal of all foreign naval forces from the Mediterranean. In essence, these have been similar to the 'zone of peace' resolution proposed by India and supported by Iran, for the Indian Ocean. The qualifications they have voiced in their proposals are important and worth indicating.

Mediterranean and European countries have defined their policies for the Mediterranean almost exclusively in terms of the Middle East confrontation; and, in the case of France and Spain, with special attention to their relations with the Maghreb countries and other Arab countries of the Mediterranean littoral.

Although in the aftermath of the Six Day War France's Mediterranean policy has been viewed favourably by most of the Arab states, French aspirations to leadership have been rejected. Arab leaders support the denuclearisation or withdrawal of the US and Soviet Mediterranean fleets, but have not seen such action as creating a power vacuum to be filled by France. On the contrary, Algeria and Tunisia, for example, have specifically rejected French expectations that the French Navy would replace the American and Soviet naval presence. Even so, France's Mediterranean policy has been viewed positively by most of the Arab states of the Mediterranean, but regarded almost exclusively in terms of the Arab-Israeli confrontation.

The importance attached to the Mediterranean in French security and foreign policies was made apparent by the attention given it by the leading members of the Pompidou Government. The then French Defence Minister, Michel Debré, in a policy speech before the Institute des Hautes Etudes de Defense Nationale, in June 1970, devoted a good deal of attention to the Mediterranean. He conceded that the situation in the Mediterranean might require France to take action in concert with other nations, and that the Mediterranean had changed from 'a European sea' to one that was also African, American, and Soviet. But then he stressed that this change, by modifying the basis of French security, demanded a new and active approach for the defence of French national interest. France, he argued, must promote common efforts with the Arab countries of the Maghreb, Spain, Italy, and the countries of the Eastern Mediterranean to avoid 'excessive external influence' in the Mediterranean region.

The late President Pompidou was at once more specific and equally forceful in his definitions of France's future role. He noted the importance of the conventional navy and its mission. The French Navy, he pointed out, is important in maintaining the prestige and the political influence of France in the Mediterranean.

More concretely, the French Navy in the Mediterranean was reorganised as an autonomous operational command. A squadron of about twenty-five ships, including several conventional submarines, the aircraft carrier *Arromanches*, destroyers, anti-submarine forces, minesweepers, and support vessels, have also been given additional capability from land-based air power.

In terms of a call for the naval withdrawal of the United States and the Soviet Union from the Mediterranean, and their reactions to French initiatives during the previous French Government, the Arab states may be grouped into two categories: Syria, Lebanon, Egypt, and Libya; and Tunisia, Algeria, and Morocco.

As far back as February 1968, the Egyptian press gave support to the withdrawal of all foreign naval forces from the Mediterranean, although it then qualified the circumstances for the withdrawal of Soviet forces. This support of the French position may have been merely declaratory, given Egyptian dependence on Soviet military assistance. The visit of the Egyptian Foreign Minister to Paris in 1971 did not result in any statements on French Mediterranean policy. Nevertheless, the prior concurrence with French policy may have future implications of some significance, because of the changes that have occurred in Egypt's relations with the United States, following July 1972.

Lebanon's position has been understandably cautious. Its security and internal integrity have been sustained traditionally by the Western military presence in the Eastern Mediterranean. Withdrawal of the Sixth Fleet would further and severely undermine this Western presence, already undercut by the increasing vulnerability of American naval forces in the eastern Mediterranean caused by the increase in Soviet military capability in that area. At the same time, France has expressed its willingness to shoulder this responsibility. Pro-Western Lebanese would be likely to support an assertive French Mediterranean posture.

The Libyan Government is not on record as favouring French Mediterranean policy. On the other hand, Libya's policy to eliminate foreign bases, while encouraging Malta to do the same (and more recently its underwriting of Malta's planned expansion of maritime service facilities), is congruent with the thrust of this French Mediterranean policy.

The Arab countries of the Western Mediterranean have been more forthright and generally favourable towards the basic French position. Among the reasons is that France articulated its own plans primarily in terms of the actions of these countries and Italy and Spain. Algeria has been the most forceful in proposing the withdrawal of the navies of non-Mediterranean powers. Tunisia and Morocco have been more cautious because of concern about their relations with the United States. President Boumedienne was actually among the first to call for a withdrawal of all non-Mediterranean naval forces. And Algeria remains strongly disposed toward neutralising the Mediterranean from superpower naval presence. It is too early to draw conclusions about what policy France will follow under the Giscard Government. It would seem, however, that the ambitious Pompidou policies will not be renewed in the immediate future.

Italy and Greece have not agreed with these positions, although recent changes in their domestic politics may have qualified their outlook. The same can be said of Portugal, for similar reasons. Italy is party to a bilateral treaty with the United States that grants special access and facilities to the Sixth Fleet. In 1973, she opened additional facilities to the US Navy on the island of Maddalena in the Mediterranean. Before the fall of the military junta in 1974, Greece had agreed, contingently, to make Piraeus the Sixth Fleet's 'home port'. Spain is about to renegotiate its base agreements with the United States, extending privileges to American naval and air units on Spanish territory. The change of government in Greece may change the outlook of Greece toward the Sixth Fleet. Certainly, the withdrawal of Greece from NATO may make her more sympathetic to a reciprocal American and Soviet naval withdrawal from the Mediterranean. Unlike American policy in previous crises, the Sixth Fleet did not bar the Turkish landings in Cyprus in 1974.

Although relations between Turkey and the United States have been strained, Turkish leaders have seemingly cast a jaundiced eye on the Soviet Squadron. For example, in 1973, Turkish Defence Minister Izmen told the National Assembly that Soviet ships in the Mediterranean were a threat and created the 'impression that the *détente* and negotiation atmosphere started between NATO and Warsaw Pact countries clashes with events'.[28] After the Greek withdrawal from the military structure of NATO, when asked in August 1974 whether Turkey would provide port facilities for the US Sixth Fleet if such facilities in Greece were denied to the United States, Prime Minister Ecevit replied 'we should be able to compensate for any weakness that ensues as a result of Greek withdrawal'.[29]

The altered political context in which Soviet and American naval forces must operate in the Mediterranean portends possibly radical changes in the constraints on the Soviet Squadron and the US Sixth Fleet. For the immediate future, however, there are few incentives for substantial naval arms control in the Mediterranean. For the NATO flank countries in the Mediterranean, the Sixth Fleet is the primary instrument of American support. Withdrawal of the American naval presence would leave these countries in the shadow of overwhelming Soviet land forces and air power, even if reciprocally the Soviet Squadron were withdrawn.

The fact is that there is no way of measuring military capabilities without taking into account political aspects. Even this brief survey of the positions taken by Mediterranean countries on the withdrawal of American and Soviet naval forces suffices to underscore this point. It should be observed, moreover, that arms control is not a decisive element in the policy considerations of the Mediterranean countries. The same may be said of Western Europe in general. Western European countries will be apprehensive about any Soviet-American agreements in the Mediterranean with respect to the FBSs of the US Sixth Fleet.

It must be concluded that the prudential arms control measures analysed could be implemented in the Mediterranean with little difficulty and mutual benefit by agreement between the United States and the Soviet Union and would have positive impact on European security. By contrast, the substantial measures discussed, while technically feasible, are politically problematic for the Atlantic Alliance in particular.

A compromise might be restructuring Soviet and American naval forces in the Mediterranean so as to denuclearise them and limit their number. Adequate surveillance technology to verify compliance is available. The Soviet Union seems prepared to negotiate on a 'withdrawal from the Mediterranean of all Soviet and American surface ships and submarines with nuclear weapons aboard'.[30] And such a measure might undercut the incentives for proliferation at the doorstep of Europe.

Notes

1. This study was originally written under the auspices of the California Arms Control and Foreign Policy Seminar.

2. There may be curious antecedents to the Soviet demand for a joint force. It has been reported that the original Soviet proposal for what became the 1973 Nixon-Brezhnev agreement to prevent nuclear war contained a clause that could have committed the United States to intervene jointly with the Soviet Union anywhere in the world if there was a danger of conflict. The United States rejected this concept but because it represented Soviet views advanced in negotiations for over a year, American officials considered it necessary to give the Soviet Government a secret note clearly stating the American interpretation of this document; namely, that the agreement imposes only an obligation to consult to prevent the outbreak of war. Flora Lewis, 'Soviet Bid for Police Role with the U.S. is Reported', *New York Times*, 22 July 1973.

3. As reported in Marvin and Bernard Kalb, 'Twenty Days in October', *New York Times Magazine*, 6 June 1974.

4. See, for example, Y. Primakov, 'The Fourth Arab-Israeli War', *Problemy Mia I Sotsialisyma*, 12 November 1973.

5. *Pravda*, 31 March 1971.

6. *Ibid.*, 13 June 1971.

7. It is of interest that during the October War the United States was able to monitor, for several days, the progress of a Soviet ship carrying radioactive materials, as it headed toward Egyptian ports, by means of reconnaissance aircraft.

8. *Pravda*, 22 July 1974.

9. In recent years there have been more than a hundred reported incidents at sea involving American and Soviet warships. Soviet and American military aircraft continually overfly each other's ships to photograph armaments and follow their movements. Mishaps, like collisions and firings, have occurred.

10. The most destructive conventional weapon is the 10,000 lb. bomb. Small nuclear weapons with yields below 40 tons of TNT equivalent have been reported.

11. Paul Hofman, '6th Fleet Still on Alert in Mediterranean', *New York Times*, 9 November 1973.

12. Barry M. Blechman, *The Changing Soviet Navy* (Washington, D.C., 1973).

13. Tight discipline is not a reassuringly adequate measure even when subordinate officers retain control. In fact, military discipline can itself contribute to the outbreak of accidental war. John R. Raser, 'The Failure of Fail-Safe', *Society*, VI (1968-9), p. 23.

14. The report of the Congressional Subcommittee of the Armed Services Committee investigating the Defense Department's worldwide communications in connection with the *Liberty* incident suggests that, in the event of a limited war, American military communications might be seriously disrupted at a time when central control of nuclear weapons would be most crucial. Survivability studies have also demonstrated that the overseas portion of the Defense Communications System would be vulnerable in the event of nuclear attack. We have it on good authority that the President cannot now communicate with submerged nuclear missile submarines. Polaris and Poseidon submarines now must approach the surface with their antennae in order to communicate with US command centres. One of the problems is that some messages never get delivered. Fred C. Iklé, *Can Nuclear*

Deterrence Last Out the Century?, California Arms Control and Foreign Policy Seminar, January 1973, p. 25.

15. *Ibid.*, p. 26.
16. See especially, Articles I, II, and IV. US Department of State, *The Washington Summit: General Secretary Brezhnev's Visit to the United States*, June 18-25, 1973, p. 30.
17. Two at least would disagree with the thrust of these remarks and the analysis that follows in the paper. McConnell and Kelley argue the absence of this dilemma. They maintain that 'experience shows no across-the-board paralysis of action, but also no anarchic test of superpower wills'. On the contrary, these experts see the emergence of 'rules' of intervention to discipline behaviour and expectations. The 'rules' permit the United States and the Soviet Union both the right of intervention and the right of deterring intervention, 'subject to limitations of context'. In each case of conflict between clients, the balance between competing superpower wills is struck such that defensive interventions are reluctantly allowed, offensive interventuons discouraged. The object is to avert decisive defeat and restore the balance, not to assist the client to victory. James McConnell and Anne Kelley, 'Super-Power Naval Diplomacy: Lessons of the Indo-Pakistani Crisis 1971', *Survival*, XV (1973), pp. 289-95. The problem, as I see it, is how to operationalise this doctrine of intervention, so that it is unambiguous.
18. For a precise if brief review of these technologies, see Albert Wohlstetter, 'Threats and Promises of Peace: Europe and America in the New Era', *Orbis*, XVII (1973-4), pp. 1107-44.
19. Report of the Secretary of Defense, James R. Schlesinger, to Congress on the Fiscal Year 1975: *Defense Budget and FY 1975-1979 Defense Program*, 11 March 1974.
20. Alfred Goldberg, *Land-Based versus Sea-Based Air: The Role and Impact of the Carrier* (Santa Monica, California, 1970).
21. For an analysis of the strategic and political impact of the SALT negotiations, see Edward Luttwak, 'The Strategic Balance', *The Washington Papers* I (1972-3).
22. Controversy between proponents of a flexible options policy and of a mutual assured destruction policy is waging in the United States. I will not discuss this here, but a useful overview of the debate is found in the various papers discussed at the California Arms Control and Foreign Policy Seminar's Conference in June 1974 on Arms Competition and Strategic Doctrine: Graham T. Allison, 'Questions About the Arms Race: Who's Racing Whom? A Bureacratic Perspective'; Donald G. Brennan, 'Alternatives to MADness'; Sidney D. Drell, 'SALT: Technological Impact on Progress and Prospects'; Nathan Leites, 'Once More About What We Should Not Do Even in the Worst Case: The Assured Destruction Attack'; William Schneider, Jr., 'The U.S. Strategic Defense Posture in Arms Limitation Environment'; Albert Wohlstetter, 'Legends of the Strategic Arms Race Part I: The Driving Engine'; Herbert F. York, 'The Present Nuclear Strategy and Some Alternatives to it'.
23. *Defense Budget and FY 1975-1979 Defense Program*, p. 59. Operating fire range of Polaris A-2 is 1,500 nautical miles, of Polaris A-3 and Poseidon is 2,500 n.m., of Trident I is 4,500 n.m. and of Trident II is 6,000 n.m. International Institute for Strategic Studies, *The Military Balance 1974-1975* (London, 1974), p. 3.
24. *The Military Implications of the Treaty of the Limitations of Anti-Ballistic Missile Systems and the Interim Agreement on Limitations of*

Strategic Offensive Arms, Hearings of the Committee on Armed Services, US Senate (Washington, D.C., June-July 1972 and 1974).

25. Admiral Gorshkov, *Morshoi Sbornik*, March 1972, pp. 31-2. See also Admiral Novikov, *Sotsialisticheskaia industria*, 29 July 1973; Admiral Oleynik, *Sel'skaia zhizn*, 29 July 1973; General Ogarkov, *Red Star*, 10 July 1973.

26. Ian Smart, 'Perspectives from Europe', in Mason Willrich and J. B. Rhinelander (eds.), *SALT: The Moscow Agreements and Beyond* (New York, 1974), pp. 192-3.

27. *Ibid.*

28. *The Pulse*, October 1973.

29. *New York Times*, 23 August 1974.

30. TASS, Moscow, 30 August 1974.

17. THE BRITISH INDEPENDENT NUCLEAR DETERRENT AND THE FUTURE OF EUROPEAN SECURITY

David Carlton

The time is rapidly approaching when the British Government, possibly in association with one or more of its allies, will have to take decisions of a potentially momentous character on the subject of the British independent nuclear deterrent. Indeed, despite the current tendency of some commentators to write about the previous phases of the British experience as a major nuclear weapons power as if they constituted a chapter drawing towards an inevitable close, the period 1975-7 could prove to be an infinitely more important turning point even than 1947-48 when the Attlee Government decided to manufacture nuclear weapons or 1962 when the Macmillan Government opted to purchase the Polaris missile system from the United States under the terms of the Nassau Agreement.[1] In recent years of course the British capability has been much derided, not least in Great Britain, as an unnecessary and rather pathetic attempt to duplicate on a small scale the American umbrella. This, taken together with London's policy, in sharp contrast to that of Paris, of assigning strategic submarines to NATO duties, has ensured that the British deterrent has not been taken particularly seriously either in Washington or in Western Europe. But if decisions should presently be taken which enable Great Britain to retain or enhance a serious nuclear capability into the last two decades of the present century, the possible implications for the security of Western Europe can hardly be exaggerated, particularly if one does not rule out either an evolution in Western Europe towards a pooling of sovereignty or a recrudescence of American isolationism. It is thus the purpose of this study to explore the technical feasibility and the political likelihood of Great Britain having such a serious nuclear capability.

The question at once arises how a serious nuclear capability is to be defined? For the purposes of this study, it is taken to imply at the minimum a British ability, on the same basis as in the past, to inflict massive *second strike* damage on the Soviet Union. For it is difficult to see how the capacity to inflict a surprise but not disarming massive *first strike* on the Soviets could ever be a particularly credible option for a medium power! Nor are we here concerned with the retention by Great Britain until the end of the century of the capacity to exert nuclear blackmail against, say, Uganda, or even to engage in an evenly balanced nuclear conflict with another medium power, say the future Iran — although it may well be desirable that such a capacity should be maintained *faute de mieux*.

What, then, is the present British position *vis-à-vis* the Soviet Union? Foreigners at least can be forgiven for asking whether Great Britain has not already lost the means of delivering a *second strike* retaliation to a Soviet pre-emptive blow. For has not Harold Wilson, the British Prime Minister, long derided the 'so-called independent, so-called deterrent' and have not all British political parties for the last decade largely avoided controversy on the former burning issue of whether or not Great Britain should unilaterally forego nuclear forces by stressing that these have been assigned to NATO and thus implied that there is no longer an issue to debate? Yet the simple truth remains that Great Britain does possess, and, at any rate for the rest of the 1970s, will retain the capacity to inflict unacceptable *second strike* damage on the Soviet Union. For British nuclear weapons have not been *irrevocably* committed to NATO. And, as for Harold Wilson's scorn about the non-British *origin* of the Polaris missiles, it does not of course mean he cannot order independent *use* of them, any more than a European who buys an American raincoat will expect it to protect him against rain only in the United States. Talk about the so-called 'so-called independent, so-called deterrent' is thus mere sleight of hand.

What, then, is the precise character of the present British second strike nuclear capability *vis-à-vis* the Soviet Union? It consists essentially of the sixty-four A-3 Polaris missiles purchased from the United States under the Nassau Agreement, negotiated by Harold Macmillan and John F. Kennedy in 1962. These missiles are carried in four British-built strategic submarines, between one and three of which are at sea at any one time. Each of the sixty-four missiles has up to three warheads of 300 kilotons each and a maximum range of 2,880 miles.[2]

There is virtual unanimity among British commentators that if Great Britain does have a credible nuclear capability *vis-à-vis* the Soviet Union — and this assumption is much contested on political rather than purely technical grounds — it must rest solely on this Polaris fleet after withdrawal from its present NATO assignment. There has not been for many years any pretensions to a 'triad' doctrine, that is the possibility of a serious and successful assault on the Soviet Union by a combination of manned bombers, land-based ballistic missiles and submarine-based ballistic missiles. There appears to be no longer much serious interest among the British even in the strategic nuclear role *vis-à-vis* the Soviets of manned aircraft such as Vulcans and Phantoms; and they have of course no land-based strategic missiles at all. This is in sharp contrast to both the American 'triad' doctrine and the rather less plausible French aspirations in the same direction. But, in the absence of either large-scale Soviet Anti-Ballistic Missile (ABM) deployment or a major Soviet breakthrough in Anti-Submarine Warfare (ASW) techniques, this one-sided reliance on SLBMs is not at present a serious weakness, though it may mean that in the long run that France may conceivably have a significantly more credible deterrent. On this point Ian Smart has written:

> The former French Minister of the Armed Services, M. Messmer, advanced the ingenious argument in 1967 that the SSBS [*sol-sol ballistique stratégique*, i.e., land-based ballistic missile] force would be an essential adjunct to French ballistic-missile submarines because, although an enemy might destroy patrolling submarines in a clandestine and untraceable manner, it would have to show its hand clearly in order to attack land-based missiles (*L'Express* [Paris], 11 December 1967). He did not explain what would happen if the hypothetical enemy, in showing its hand, also succeeded in destroying all the SSBS missiles in their silos.[3]

It may be argued, however, in reply to Smart, that if the Soviets in attempting to destroy one or more of the patrolling submarines in a 'clandestine and untraceable manner' were accidentally exposed in so doing, the French SSBS force, if kept on a launch-on-warning basis, might just be successfully launched before the arrival of the Soviet pre-emptive strike. Thus if the Soviets achieved a breakthrough in ASW techniques and felt able to attempt the silent elimination of the French and/or British patrolling strategic submarines, they might be taking a somewhat greater risk in the French case than the British and might thus be deterred from attempting the first but not the second.

The present British nuclear capability has another much more severe weakness. It is almost impossible to believe that in its present form it could be used other than in an all-out 'spasm' attack; and only a little more plausible to see such use other than in a *second strike* retaliation to a *nuclear* attack. This lack of flexibility arises from the fact that the whole British deterrent force is located in a mere four vessels. Moreover, only in exceptional circumstances, that is if the hypothetical crisis with the Soviet Union had escalated over a period and if none of the British strategic submarines was on a long refit, might it be possible that all four submarines could be simultaneously on patrol as the tension came to a head. But the odds are that the Soviets would only attempt a final showdown with the British when one or more submarine would be a totally vulnerable target either at the Gareloch base in Scotland or wherever a refit was in process. But whether all or only one of the British strategic submarines were at sea would probably make not more than a marginal difference to the policy-makers in London. Even in the best case they could scarcely embark on limited and sophisticated use of strategic strikes as mere demonstrations of resolve. For the chances are that a submarine used for this purpose would give away its position and thus face instant elimination by Soviet attack submarines. It is of course difficult to be sure how many strategic submarines the British would need to be able to engage on more or less equal terms with the Soviets in a duel of limited 'teaching strikes'. They certainly would not need as many as the sixty-two which the Soviets are entitled to possess under the terms of SALT, but it is equally clear that four are totally insufficient to enable the threat of limited strikes to seem a convincing policy option and thus to carry much credibility as a deterrent. Hence the only threat which the British can plausibly make is one involving an all-out massive strike in certain extremities.

Paradoxically, precisely because they have no plausible alternative nuclear strategy, the British (and French) can expect their threats to act in this way to carry more weight than similar threats made by the superpowers against one another. As James Schlesinger, US Secretary of Defense, put it on 19 January 1974:

> We must be in a position in which the President of the United States, if he's called on to use strategic forces, has an option other than the option that I have referred to, which concentrates on cities and which therefore carries in its wake the notion of inevitable destruction of American cities.

> That is not an option lightly implemented. In fact one can say that these kinds of strategies, are strategies historically that have [been] embraced in two sets of circumstances. One set of circumstances is when a nation, such as the United States in the 1950s or indeed during the early 1960s, was in a position of such preponderance in terms of its forces . . . that it could well threaten a potential opponent with that kind of all-out strike, and the relative damage in the event of such an exchange would be such that no potential foe would care to test those circumstances.

> *The other set of circumstances in which the threat of all-out retaliation against cities seems to be appealing — doctrinally appealing — is when a nation possesses a relatively small and weak nuclear capability*, in which its deterrence depends upon the convincing of its potential foes that it has the will and the determination under any circumstances, no matter [if] involving its own destruction to wreak devastation on a potential opponent.

> The United States is no longer in the first position in which it has preponderance of nuclear forces that prevailed into the later 1960s. It is certainly not in the position of the *second category of power*

with a relatively weak nuclear force that [it] must threaten to employ immediately and entirely. It has a large and sophisticated establishment that permits the application of pressure while maintaining intra-war deterrence to protect its own cities and consequently, is in a position to maintain a credible threat of the application of force for the foreseeable future, because of the relative sophistication of its force in a period in which there is another power that has roughly equivalent forces.4

The question next arises how extreme the contingency would have to be for a medium nuclear power to resort to an all-out 'spasm' strike, and, no less important, carry any degree of conviction if threatened so to do. At one extreme, it is surely clear that no medium power would seem not to be engaging in absurd bluff if it threatened a 'spasm' response in the event of a superpower attack upon an ally. At the other extreme such a threat would seem most plausible if a superpower was contemplating subjecting the medium nuclear power itself to all-out nuclear attack. Less certain is the credibility of the threat of a spasm response in the event of a superpower launching only a limited nuclear 'teaching strike' on, say, one or two targets in the heartland of a medium nuclear power or, alternatively, carrying out an irresistable conventional conquest of the medium power. In the last case, the medium power would be threatening nothing less than an all-out nuclear *first strike* against a superpower — something which must surely be on the extreme margins of credibility except perhaps in circumstances where the policy-making elite of the medium power was singularly resolute and united.

If the foregoing analysis has merit, the conclusion would seem to follow that, whatever the technical merits of her Polaris fleet, Great Britain's security prospects *vis-à-vis* the Soviet Union would not be particularly enviable if the American nuclear guarantee were withdrawn. For with a mere four submarines she could not hope to take over the American role as nuclear guarantors of the non-nuclear European NATO members. And it might not be too easy to avoid the impression that there was an element of bluff in threatening all-out nuclear war as a means of guaranteeing even her own physical safety. Nor, from the British military standpoint, does this constitute the only or even the main cause for alarm. For doubtfully credible for some purposes as the independent British deterrent would be if the American went isolationist at once, the outlook if that occurs in the future is even more gloomy in view of the prospective obsolescence of the present Polaris fleet.

There are in fact three principal grounds for doubting the long-term *physical* capacity of the British to inflict unacceptable damage on the

Soviet Union. First, there is the possibility that a significant Soviet ABM system may in due time emerge. Secondly, much may depend on whether the Soviet Union will achieve any significant breakthrough in ASW techniques. Thirdly, there are doubts about whether or not the Americans will be prepared to continue to service the present British missiles and/or provide a new generation of missiles as and when that became necessary. We shall consider each of these possible threats in turn.

First, and least immediately ominous, is the threat of a major Soviet ABM deployment. The SALT Agreements of 1972, together with subsequent amplifications, have undoubtedly been of great significance to the British. For as long as the present superpower limitations on ABM apply, the British could expect, other things being equal, to retain the physical means of destroying most Soviet population centres with the possible exception of Moscow itself. But the ABM Treaty is not permanent and may indeed be unilaterally abrogated as early as 1977 when an American review is promised. Moreover, as China grows in nuclear strength, the superpowers might even be tempted to amend their present ABM deal by agreement so as to permit the creation of significant ABM defences which would be designed to be tolerably effective against medium nuclear powers but not in any way so effective as to destroy their own mutual assured destruction (MAD) relationship. Given the relatively small number of British missiles and the fact that their warheads have not been MIRVed, such a *pari passu* increase in superpower ABM capabilities could thus decisively undermine whatever credibility the independent British deterrent might have in Moscow's eyes. There is, moreover, a precedent in arms control history for the provision for such an escalation by powers in the first tier whose mutual equilibrium is satisfactory but whose relationship to powers of lesser rank is threatened with destabilisation. In 1930 a so-called escalator clause was written into the London Naval Treaty, whereby the United States, Great Britain and Japan agreed to an upward revision of numbers of cruisers, destroyers and submarines if the French and the Italians, who refused to be parties to the Treaty, seemed likely so to expand their fleets as to become a threat to the leading naval powers.[5] It is thus possible that in the foreseeable future the Soviets could deploy a significant ABM force either unilaterally or in agreement with the United States. If so, the British would be faced with great problems, for this would be a move which certainly could not be countered by a comparable limited ABM deployment, there being absolutely no lobby in Great Britain, however hawkish, which believes that that would be technically feasible.

The second major threat to the British independent deterrent lies in the possibility of a significant Soviet breakthrough in ASW techniques.

Here one has a very real parallel with the earlier history of ABM except that so far the superpowers have made no serious moves towards limitation. Possibly the absence of any search for agreement on ASW in SALT is evidence that neither superpower at present takes seriously the possibility of a breakthrough so destabilising as to threaten MAD.[6] On the other hand, feverish research is no doubt proceeding and may well in time produce results which will make the tracking of strategic submarines at least a good deal easier than it now is. When that begins to become clear, we may expect that the superpowers will then begin to take seriously the need to protect MAD. But because of the problem of verification, this is unlikely to take the form of a limitation on research or on the improvement of attack submarines. It is much more likely to involve the agreed creation of zones in the oceans into which the entry of attack submarines would be limited or forbidden.[7] In such a case, with each superpower having its present number of strategic submarines, MAD could probably be preserved. But the tiny British fleet of between one and four strategic submarines on patrol might at a quite early date become dangerously exposed to total surprise elimination, particularly if cooperation between London and Washington had also meanwhile ceased. This, then, obviously constitutes a major threat to the future of the British deterrent, though its imminence must be a matter for speculation.

A third and possibly most deadly threat to the future of the British deterrent is the prospective obsolescence of the existing technical equipment even on the assumption of no significant ABM or ASW improvements on the part of the superpowers. Of the three decisive components — submarines, missiles and warheads — only the last poses no obvious problems if the character of the superpower nuclear balance remains static during the next two decades. But even the difficulties associated with the first — submarines — could be overcome with little difficulty if other things were equal. For although the present four submarines will require periodic refits, they are expected to remain viable until 1986-90 when their hulls will become worn out. And even after that, complete replacement ought not to be so expensive an exercise as to be unthinkable. The decisive problems, then, concern the sixty-four Polaris missiles.

These missiles are regularly maintained by the Americans under the terms of the Nassau Agreement and would soon cease to be of value if these support facilities were withdrawn. The official British view is that such a development is unthinkable. For example, on 27 February 1973, Lord Carrington, then Secretary of State for Defence, when giving evidence to the Defence and External Affairs Sub-Committee of the House of Commons Expenditure Committee, was asked this question by Dr David Owen (Labour): 'Would it be a fair interpretation of the Polaris sales agreement . . . that you have received assurances about the support facilities for Polaris through the normal life cycle of the system?' Carrington replied: 'Yes. The Polaris sales agreement is irrevocable and the Americans are obliged to do so.'[8] But whether such an obligation will *in practice* be binding upon the Americans over decades is a matter for legitimate doubt. For the United States has by now largely abandoned the Polaris system and gone over to MIRVed Poseidon. True, ten American submarines will continue to carry Polaris A-3 missiles until 1978 and a reducing number will do so for some years after that,[9] but by 1982 the Americans may have abandoned Polaris altogether. Therefore the crucial question for the British is whether the Americans, if and when they completely abandon their Polaris system, will be prepared, probably at considerable cost, to maintain support facilities solely for the benefit of Great Britain. It must surely be expected that, in such circumstances, the Americans would press the British either to abandon the independent option or, alternatively, to move over to Poseidon or some still more advanced missile system.[10] And the Americans would be in a position to exert such pressures that the British would be unlikely in practice to insist on attempting to hold Washington to the letter of the Nassau Agreement. Apart from other obvious areas for exerting leverage, such as trade or financial support for the pound sterling, the Americans might well be able, even within the strict terms of the Nassau Agreement, to render the efficient operation of an independent nuclear system difficult in the extreme.[11] We may thus conclude that if the Americans so decide, the British independent capability *vis-à-vis* the Soviet Union may not last much beyond 1980 — and that if it is to be enabled to continue, agreement on the acquisition of a new generation of missiles will probably have to be reached in the fairly near future.

In these circumstances a major review of the whole direction of British policy on nuclear weapons is surely desirable and inevitable. There are indeed a large number of options which will need at least to be examined even if some of them on close scrutiny will have to be dismissed as impractical. Here a possibly modest selection of seven such options will be listed in ascending order of ambitiousness.

First would be a clear decision to abandon the independent strategic deterrent by renegotiating the Nassau Agreement with a view to handing back the existing Polaris missiles to the United States. Such for a time was declaratory policy of the Labour Party in opposition before 1964. It was not, however, taken seriously when Labour was in office between 1964 and 1970, although George Ball, US Under-Secretary of State, apparently came to London in 1967 to ascertain that this was indeed the case. There have long been powerful arguments for this course of action from both the American and British points of view.

There have always been Americans, among whom Ball has been numbered, who have seen risks in promoting a British independent capability. First, such a policy is an encouragement to other medium powers to acquire nuclear weapons and thus refuse to accede to the American-sponsored Non-Proliferation Treaty. Secondly, the chance must always exist, as many British politicians have openly acknowledged, that the British capability might be used in a catalytic fashion in circumstances where the British might be determined either actually to force or to threaten to force the Americans against their will into a nuclear conflict with the Soviets. On the other hand, the existence of an independent nuclear capability in Western Europe may also be of some value to the Americans in that it would add to the complications facing any Soviet decision makers contemplating major aggression in Europe and may thereby serve to shore up deterrence. From the British point of view many divergent and sometimes contradictory arguments have been advanced over the last quarter of a century in favour of some form of 'unilateralism'.[12] Certainly such arguments have by no means always derived solely from ethical commitments to pacifism or nuclear pacifism or from a belief that the Soviets could in no circumstances constitute a military threat. For example, Denis Healey argued shortly before becoming Secretary of State for Defence:

> . . . so long as the Prime Minister insists that you cannot trust the Americans to come to your help in a crisis and that therefore you must have atomic weapons in order to trigger off the American Strategic Air Command against the will of the American Government, he is strengthening and accelerating that very trend in the United States to reduce America's liabilities in Europe which is the excuse for his position.[13]

And it is perhaps this internationalist argument for a form of British 'unilateralism' and for the promotion of an essentially bipolar East-West nuclear balance which may be said to have most evidently weakened by the events of recent years. For until the Americans began to fail in Vietnam, there was no significant movement in the United States towards neo-isolationism and no prominent personalities to compare with Eugene McCarthey, George McGovern and Mike Mansfield. And hence it was perhaps understandable, if mistakem, for some in Great Britain to assume that the Americans would be no less resolute than the Soviets in defending the integrity of their sphere of Europe and to contend therefore that neo-Gaullist arguments for an independent nuclear force were based on absurdly pessimistic assumptions.[14] Today it seems no less absurdly optimistic to take it for granted that the American physical presence in Western Europe will be as permanent as the Soviet presence in Eastern Europe. Moreover, the emergence of strategic nuclear parity between the superpowers, as even John Foster Dulles foresaw, must inevitably somewhat reduce the credibility of the American guarantee even if this is not formally withdrawn and even if American forces remain in Europe. In these changed circumstances, therefore, it would be surprising if even a Labour Government actually went so far as to divest itself of nuclear weapons as a deliberate act of policy, especially as Harold Wilson and his colleagues did not do so a decade ago when the American presence and guarantee could be almost implicitly relied upon.

A *second* possibility is that the British may simply drift. This is in fact by no means unlikely, particularly if there should be a long period of Labour Government. For whereas the majority in the Cabinet and in the Parliamentary Labour Party will not be sufficiently 'unilateralist' to press for the renegotiation of the Nassau Agreement, few will probably wish to risk the unpopularity with the bulk of the Labour Party's activists which would certainly flow from any major policy change designed to ensure a prolongation of the independent deterrent beyond the point at which the present system became obsolete or lost American support facilities.[15] In this scenario, therefore, Great Britain will simply fade away as a major nuclear power.

Thirdly, the British Government could approach the Americans and ask for specific and public pledges that they would sustain the British Polaris missiles until at least 1990 whatever their intentions for their own Polaris system. This course might well prove rather costly for the Americans but considerations of honour might nevertheless lead an American President to give the desired promise. The question would then be whether a future President, possibly of an isolationist or even anti-European disposition, would be bound by a renewed pledge dating from the mid-1970s any more than he would be by the terms of the original Nassau Agreement of 1962. The answer may be that while plainly nothing can be absolutely guaranteed, a renewed pledge would at least to some degree decrease the chances of American derogation from the Agreement. The British could also effect a further slight improvement in their chances of having a viable independent deterrent in 1990 by taking steps to build one or more additional strategic submarines. This would extend the span of time over which the units in the submarine fleet became obsolete. But, more important, such a move would enable Great Britain to have at least two submarines on patrol at any one time. As the possibility of a Soviet ASW breakthrough grew, the British might even seek to add considerably to the number of her submarines and simply spread her sixty-four missiles among them rather more thinly.

Fourthly, the British could approach the Americans and ask to be allowed to purchase a new generation of missiles to replace Polaris A-3.

If the date of purchase were to be rather soon, Poseidon might be appropriate but it would probably make most sense for the British to skip a generation and acquire the Trident system in, say, 1980. This might be a rather attractive option for both Washington and London. It would presumably enable the Americans to honour the spirit of the Nassau Agreement without having to maintain Polaris servicing facilities indefinitely. For the British, too, a more up-to-date system would have self-evident attractions. There may, however, be two possible difficulties for London. First, the Americans might ask for a much more realistic financial contribution than the British made to Polaris — and the latter are not likely for as far ahead as can be foreseen to be in a position to add greatly to their present astonishing balance of payments deficit. Secondly, there might well be great political difficulties in a period when the whole British population was being asked to take a cut in real living standards. Indeed, it is difficult to see how Labour Ministers could even begin to argue for this course — although they have often surprised us in the past; Attlee, for example, having a good claim to having been the political father of British nuclear weapons. For the Americans, too, there might be a major difficulty: the attitude of the Soviet Union and the effects on the continued progress of SALT. At one time the Soviet Union was surprisingly indifferent to the existence of the British independent deterrent. But this has now apparently changed. For on 17 May 1972, at the time of the SALT Agreement on limiting strategic submarines, the Soviets made the unilateral declaration that

> if during the effectiveness of the Agreement, US allies in NATO should increase the number of their modern submarines to exceed the numbers of submarines they would have operational or under construction on the date of the signature of the Agreement, the Soviet Union will have the right to a corresponding increase in the number of its submarines.[16]

It might of course be argued that a Poseidon/Trident deal between Washington and London need not be strictly incompatible with this Soviet proclamation provided that the number of British strategic submarines remained at four. But, as has already been argued, it is probably not in the British interest to be limited to four submarines. And, in any case, the Soviets might well object equally to the proposed deal in missiles. The Americans, it is true, have never formally acknowledged their acceptance of the Soviet unilateral statement on submarines. And they might be quite unwilling to be dictated to on a missile deal. Moreover, SALT may in any case collapse — to the possible advantage of the British from this point of view but equally possibly to their disadvantage in the matter of ABMs. But there must be some chance that SALT will continue and that in that context the Americans will see the suggested British missile deal as a bargaining chip and thus as something expendable in return for Soviet compliance on some other issue more central to American interests. We thus again are compelled to see that much may rest on whether the British can persuade the Americans that they have a real interest, above and beyond the letter of an Agreement signed more than a decade ago, in prolonging the British independent deterrent. But this is a question to which we will return.

Fifthly, the British might have the option of a go-it-alone course if the Americans were uncooperative both in maintaining the Polaris system and in supplying a replacement. This could only take the form of attempting to prolong the life of the Polaris system without American help. For the construction by Great Britain alone of a new generation of independently-produced missiles is certainly out of the question. The House of Commons Expenditure Committee, in its Report for the 1972-3 Session, did not in fact rule out the possibility of Great Britain developing its own facilities to maintain Polaris. But it noted ominously: 'we have no estimate of the likely cost'.[17] On the other hand, if the cost should be relatively modest, the political difficulties, particularly for a Labour Government, would probably be much less than those which would surely arise out of a new public agreement with a foreign state.

Sixthly, the British might abandon the quest for further deals with the Americans but turn instead towards the French and/or other Western Europeans. Briefly, it may be asserted that the European version of the option is inextricably linked with the evolution of the European Economic Community towards some kine of superstate, which, if feasible at all, must lie rather far in the future. The French option is, on the other hand, much more immediately practical provided that the political will existed in Paris, and still more so, in London. Cooperation in constructing nuclear weapons systems need not of course imply close political harmony. The latter would only be essential if cooperation in construction was intended to be followed by joint targeting, mixed manning or shared decision making. Nor should too much be made of the difficulties involved in Franco-British cooperation arising out of constraints on the British under the terms of the NPT or the Partial Nuclear Test Ban Treaty or the American McMahon Act. For it seems questionable whether the British really are prevented, as some have argued, from passing on nuclear know-how to the French (or ultimately to a Western European superstate) but in any case there is provision for withdrawal from the NPT or the Partial Nuclear Test Ban Treaty; and the McMahon restrictions might well be either unimportant in practice, or be overridden with the tacit agreement of the Americans whose attitude might be benevolent, or be simply disregarded with the sort of bland aplomb with which the Indians apparently treated the Canadians in 1974.[18] The principal difficulty about the Anglo-French option, then, is the want of political will. No doubt this, on the British side is attributable to the belief that such cooperation would probably at least at first produce a less sophisticated and more expensive system than might be on offer from the Americans. Hence even the recent Conservative Government, despite some hints of interest by Edward Heath before 1970, showed no inclination to discuss these matters with the French even as a bargaining counter in the British EEC entry negotiations. For example, Carrington told the Defence and External Affairs Sub-Committee of the House of Commons Expenditure Committee on 27 February 1973:

> Might I say a word about Anglo-French nuclear collaboration. Leaving aside whether anyone would think it desirable . . . or whether the USA would like it, there seem to me to be two factors which make it impossible at the present time for there to be any Anglo-French nuclear cooperation. The first factor is the present French defence policy, which entirely relies upon national sovereignty and is not prepared to share the decisions about defence with anybody. Consequently, any real collaboration with the French would be impossible. It would not be possible to target or to share areas or anything of the kind that you might have, because the French would not be prepared to do it . . . The second issue which makes it impossible is that, as so much of the information is derived from American sources which we have pledged not to reveal to third parties without the agreement of the Americans unless the Americans were prepared to accept that Anglo-French nuclear collaboration or some kind of tripartite system was in the interests of the Western Alliance generally, then this could not come about. I do not think that in either of these two cases are these criteria met. Consequently, even if we think it is a good idea it is a long way off.[19]

One cannot doubt, however, that, even without any changes of attitude in Paris, these difficulties would seem less weighty to many in London if Washington brought collaboration to an end.

Finally, we may note the most ambitious option which the British could contemplate. This would of course involve the Americans but would go far beyond the mere purchase of a new missile system — in short a super-Nassau Agreement. The House of Commons Expenditure Committee was evidently not unaware of the possibility although, in its 1972-1973 Report, it mentioned it only in this rather oblique fashion:

> The remaining 10 American Polaris submarines are not suitable for conversion and will reach the end of their active life between 1979

(20 years for the first) and 1988 (25 years for the last). No decision has yet been made but it is possible that these 10 submarines will be phased out earlier than their full lifespan. This is particularly likely if the U.S. starts to build any new submarines since the SALT agreement fixed an overall limit of 44 on the number of U.S. submarines, only 3 more than now. The phasing out of the U.S. Polaris Fleet would mean that Polaris support facilities would if they were to be maintained at all have to be maintained solely for the benefit of the Royal Navy, but it would also mean that surplus missiles, equipment *and even submarines* would be available for purchase.[20]

If the British could obtain at no great cost ten submarines to add to their present four, together with additional missiles and possibly also promises of appropriate support facilities, they would have for at least a decade a force *vis-à-vis* the Soviet Union which would be far more credible than the present version as a means of deterring conventional aggression against British territory and even possibly the territory of other members of the EEC. For with so many strategic submarines at sea the British could threaten to wage limited strategic nuclear war on a scale which might be in practical terms equal to that of the Soviet Union — always assuming no major ASW or ABM breakthrough. Moreover, such an enlarged force might well give the British a major bargaining chip if she wished to sponsor the early creation of a Western European sovereign superstate, since only in this way, in the event of a recrudescence of American isolationism, could the populations of the non-British areas of Western Europe be totally assured of the full protection afforded by this nuclear force. Why should not the Americans agree to such a super-Nassau? There is of course one obvious difficulty: SALT might be wrecked in the light of the previously-mentioned Soviet objections to any increase, among the United States' NATO allies, in independently controlled strategic submarines. On the other hand, all in Washington can see that the credibility of their nuclear guarantee of Western Europe has been wearing thinner since the Soviets attained effective strategic parity; and, in addition, few of the American internationalists can be wholly certain that a neo-isolationist administration will not in the long run emerge.

It is with further reflections on this theme that this essay may best be concluded, since American goodwill is essential to many of the aforementioned options for prolonging British nuclear independence. Of course Schlesinger may be hopeful that his new doctrine of 1973-4 has for a time solved the problem of the credibility of the American guarantee of Western Europe. Certainly the emphasis on limited strikes on the Soviet heartland is far more defensible than the pretence that tactical nuclear warfare in Central Europe is a serious option, and all the more plausible because Soviet military targets and not population centres are singled out for 'teaching strikes'.[21] Yet the fact that Schlesinger needed to change the American doctrine at all is itself eloquent proof that there are fundamental problems of credibility about extended deterrence and it would be surprising if Schlesinger and many others do not have doubts whether the present doctrine is wholly adequate for a long term future. For the fact is that after more than a decade of feverish debate the Americans have even now not found a strategic posture which entirely and beyond argument overcomes the ineradicable asymmetry which distinguishes the Soviet commitment to maintain its Eastern European sphere from the American commitment to the West Europeans, namely distance and hence the adversary's perception of what constitutes the United States' fundamental national interest. The Channel has often provided Great Britain with a similar problem of credibility. In 1914, for example, despite rhetorical commitments, the British had a serious option about whether or not to defend Belgium and the Germans knew that this was so. Again, in 1936 the British did not insist on the Germans abandoning the remilitarisation of the Rhineland – even though many Britishers had sought to reassure their European friends that their Locarno commitments were of a different order to their obligations to the Abyssinians whom they had betrayed some months earlier, namely that in the Locarno case, they were based on *real* national interests. Today, in an ominous parallel, many Americans tell the Western Europeans that the guarantee to them is of a different order to those recently found wanting in Indochina because Western Europe is a *real* American interest. But the very existence of the Atlantic, like the Channel in earlier times, means that in a desperate crisis there is bound to be a serious debate in Washington about whether it is worth putting American cities at risk for the sake of Hamburg or London. If we were living in an era dominated by internationalist ideological fervour such as that which Harry S. Truman, John Foster Dulles and Lyndon B. Johnson personified, the Western Europeans could feel reasonably confident that the outcome of the debate would be in favour of such risks being taken. But in the present climate the issue is much more open. Whatever the climate, however, a debate would be inevitable. By contrast, no parallel debate is conceivable in Moscow about the worthwhile character of risking the Soviet homeland for the sake of preventing Warsaw and Prague from being overrun by NATO forces. The Soviet response would assuredly be automatic. No doubt there would be a debate if the cities in question were Havana or Cairo; and, if, as some suppose, Soviet ideological fervour is also in decline, the outcome might even be one of non-intervention. But that is scant consolation for the Western Europeans.

Is it, then, too unreasonable to foresee at least the possibility that an

American President will emerge who will accept that the only solution which guarantees Western European security while simultaneously reducing the risks that the Americans will otherwise eventually face either humiliation or a domestically unacceptable degree of destruction is to ensure that the British, and through them ultimately the Western Europeans, have their own adequate nuclear means of deterring aggression and thus overcoming the present credibility gap?[22]

Notes

1. For studies of the earlier history of British nuclear weapons policy see Margaret Gowing, *Independence and Deterrence: Britain and Atomic Energy 1945-52* (London, 1974); Andrew J. Pierre, *Nuclear Politics: The British Experience with an Independent Strategic Force, 1939-1970* (London, 1972); Richard N. Rosecrance, *Defence of the Realm* (New York, 1968); William P. Snyder, *The Politics of British Defence Policy, 1945-62* (London, 1964); and A. J. R. Groom, *British Thinking about Nuclear Weapons* (London, 1974).

2. House of Commons, *Nuclear Weapon Programme: Twelfth Report from the Expenditure Committee, 1972-1973* (London, 1973), p. 1.

3. Ian Smart, *Future Conditional: The Prospects for Anglo-French Nuclear Co-operation* (The International Institute for Strategic Studies [IISS] Adelphi Paper, no. 78, London, 1971), p. 5, n. 7.

4. Extracts from Press Conference, 10 January 1974, reproduced in *Survival*, XVI (1974), p. 89.

5. See David Carlton, *MacDonald versus Henderson: The Foreign Policy of the Second Labour Government* (London, 1970), ch. 6. For other comparisons of SALT with interwar naval arms control diplomacy see Hedley Bull, 'Strategic Arms Limitation: The Precedent of the Washington and London Naval Treaties' in Morton A. Kaplan, *SALT: Problems and Prospects* (Morristown, New Jersey, 1973), pp. 26-52; and Donald C. Watt, 'Historical Light on SALT: Parallels with Inter-War Naval Arms Control', *Round Table*, LXII (1972), pp. 29-36.

6. This lack of any sense of urgency about dealing with ASW is evidently shared by some commentators who have generally held alarmist views on other aspects of the arms race, especially ABM. See for example B. T. Feld and G. W. Rathjens, 'ASW, Arms Control and the Sea-Based Deterrent' in Kosta Tsipis, Anne H. Cahn and Bernard T. Feld (eds.), *The Future of the Sea-Based Deterrent* (Cambridge, Massachusetts and London, 1973), pp. 121-47.

7. See various essays in *ibid*. See also Kosta Tsipis, 'Anti-Submarine Warfare and Missile Submarines' in David Carlton and Carlo Schaerf, *The Dynamics of the Arms Race* (London, 1975), pp. 36-46.

8. House of Commons, *op. cit.*, p. 31.

9. IISS, *The Military Balance 1974-1975* (London, 1974), p. 3.

10. One possible way out of the dilemma has been advanced by Richard L. Garwin. He suggested in a memorandum, dated 2 May 1973, and presented to the Defence and External Affairs Sub-Committee of the House of Commons Expenditure Committee, that:

    it is highly probable that the longevity of . . . Polaris missiles can be very much extended by storage at somewhat reduced temperature say 40°F in a large refrigerator warehouse such as is used for food. Under these circumstances, the question of a replacement for a Polaris missile need not be addressed at this time.

House of Commons, *op. cit.*, p. 41. Whether or not this theory has much merit is unclear.

11. In this connection particular importance might attach to American aid to the British in the matter of communications and navigation aids such as satellites or submarine beacons. For hints on this aspect see Smart, *op. cit.*, p. 7.

12. See Hedley Bull, 'The Many Sides of British Unilateralism', *The Reporter*, 11 March 1961. See also Groom, *op. cit.*

13. Denis Healey, *A Labour Britain and the World* (Fabian Tract, no. 352, London, 1964), pp. 13-14.

14. The present writer, for example, made a plea in 1968 for a renegotiation of the Nassau Agreement on internationalist grounds. David Carlton, 'Labour and the Nuclear Deterrent', *Socialist Commentary*, March 1968. See also his paper, delivered to a Pugwash Symposium in July 1968, arguing that the United States ought to deploy ABM systems in order to create conditions of essential nuclear bipolarity at the superpower level and that the United States ought simultaneously to adopt the doctrine of Limited Strategic Nuclear War as a means of defending Western Europe: 'Anti-Ballistic Missile Deployment and the Doctrine of Limited Nuclear War' in C. F. Barnaby and A. Boserup (eds.), *Implications of Anti-Ballistic Missile Systems* (London and Toronto, 1969), pp. 126-38. A form of Limited Strategic Nuclear War has indeed meanwhile been adopted as an American doctrine but it may be argued that this shift, however welcome, is in itself insufficient to neutralise the vastly enhanced power of the neo-Gaullist case deriving from the American failure in Indochina and the rise of neo-isolationism in the United States. The present writer is, therefore, no longer convinced of the practical utility of a policy of seeking nuclear bipolarity.

15. Evidence of the feelings of Labour Party activists came in June 1974 when strongly-worded protests were made after the Labour Government announced the completion of a series of British nuclear tests in the Nevada Desert. The views of the mass of Labour *voters* were no doubt very different.

16. House of Commons, *op. cit.*, p. xii.

17. *Ibid.*, p. xiii.

18. On the problems posed by the NPT, the Partial Nuclear Test Ban Treaty and the McMahon Act see Smart, *op. cit.*, pp. 31-8. See also United Nations Association (Great Britain), Disarmament Committee, *Anglo-French Nuclear Sharing: A Strategic Conundrum* (London, 1973).

19. House of Commons, *op. cit.*, pp. 28-9.

20. *Ibid.*, p. xii. Italics supplied. See also evidence by François Duchêne, *ibid.*, pp. 4-5.

21. Such strikes against military targets would not of course be intended, as Schlesinger has made abundantly clear, to be of a disarming character. But the case for choosing military sites rather than cities rests on the fact that this would obviously be the more humane course while nevertheless certain to cause a good deal of pain to the Soviet leaders. For the latter seem on occasion to resemble nobody more than the eighteenth-century Sergeant King, Frederick William I of Prussia, in their inordinate sensitivity about

and pride in their defence forces.

22. Since this essay was prepared a valuable study of many of the associated technical problems has been published. See Geoffrey Kemp, *Nuclear Forces for Medium Powers* (IISS Adelphi Papers, nos. 106 and 107, London, 1974).

The author has had the advantage of presenting versions of the present essay to a number of American audiences, namely the California Arms Control and Foreign Policy Seminar, Santa Monica; the Center for International Studies, Cornell University; and the University of Colorado. He wishes to thank those concerned for raising a number of valuable criticisms.

PART IV

PEACE TEACHING AND THE STUDY OF CONFLICT

18. PEACE EDUCATION: A SCEPTIC'S VIEW

Michael Nicholson

Education is a concept which has many meanings and is in many ways very ambiguous; peace is similarly ambiguous. The two together make for a maximum of ambiguity and so it will be necessary to decide what we are to discuss before discussing it. The general plan of this paper is that I shall first define my terms more closely, even if some ambiguity remains. I shall particularly concentrate on the concept of education. Then I shall rather briefly discuss the forms of education which I regard as useful, without, however, having a great deal of confidence in the effectiveness of any of them. Political systems of all countries appear to show a stubborn resistance to new ideas, particularly if they involve long term readjustments of society and indeed they show a curious inability to make, on anything like a rational basis, decisions over the long term as opposed to short term allocation of resources whether these resources are economic or otherwise.

Indeed the principal purpose of this paper is more to outline the framework and presuppositions which lies behind peace education and the categorisation of various attitudes towards it rather than to lay down a peace education programme as such. While everyone has his own individual ideas about what the programme should comprise, this is not a debate I want to go in to more than cursorily. The presuppositions appear to me to be more important.

To claim that peace is a good thing is rather like claiming that sin is a bad thing. However, peace, like sin, has its price and one has to decide what price one is willing to pay for peace in terms of other socially desirable objectives which may conflict with this. Justice, for example, is also important. In a very peaceful society, in the sense that there is no violence present in its overt form, there can be injustice in the distribution of both political and economic resources. Slave societies are often peaceful in this sense, but in this case an inhabitant might forego peace for justice or that other closely related ideal of individual liberty. Only if one is a complete pacifist is peace regarded as an ultimate ideal to which all others should be subordinate. The values implicit in this paper are that there is a price to pay for peace which might not always be worth paying. The paper will still have considerable relevance to those who do not share these values, however, and they can make adjustments to the argument as they become necessary.

However, while peace is not the value which I hold to be totally dominant in the pacifist sense, I regard it very highly, and view violence as a great evil even on a small scale, and even more on the large scale where the possibility that whole societies will be largely destroyed has been a serious possibility for almost the last quarter of a century. Thus our aim is to enable social change, sometimes of a very radical nature, to come about with the minimum of violence. I take two postulates as being given and I shall not argue for them in this paper. First (an ethical postulate) that social change of certain sorts is desirable in many, perhaps all, parts of the world and the second (an empirical postulate) that change can be brought about without at least some of the vast costs in violence and other forms of social unpleasantness which seem at the moment to be the frequent concomitant of change.

I shall first consider rather briefly the subject matter on which people are to be educated. There is a whole set of terms which describe the subject matter to be communicated under the heading of peace education. Presumably it is not only to be interpreted as education which itself makes people more peaceable but also anything which concerns the issues of peace and war. A lot of such teaching is in any case done under a variety of headings. One can list five (there may well be more) disciplines which overlap and would appear under the heading of peace education. They are Peace Research, Strategy, Conflict Analysis, War Studies and International Relations. The first two of these are prescriptive or policy disciplines whereas the last three are descriptive. By descriptive, I do not mean this to be taken in any narrow sense. Under conflict analysis comes a lot of theory but I am regarding a theory as something which ultimately describes how the world behaves, or might behave under various sets of circumstances, and I explicitly do not want to use descriptive in the rather narrow sense of the word.

A policy discipline or science is one which phrases its questions in such forms as 'If we are to obtain objective X what do we have to do?' It may be a search among the other disciplines would provide some answer; or it may be that the question in the present state of knowledge is unanswerable and it is then that the research comes in. The boundary between such policy sciences and the descriptive sciences is necessarily vague. Policy sciences imply some sort of predilection for certain sorts of answers but this is not the same as saying that people will cheat in order to get them. Indeed if one wants to get sensible answers to questions then one has to be extremely rigorous in making sure that the answers which come are the right ones, inasmuch as it is possible to tell. There are many areas where this ambiguous area between the prescriptive and the descriptive areas exists. Economics provides many clear cases. For example, the description of how the process of inflation starts or gathers momentum and the prescriptions about what to do become very closely interrelated and it is often hard to differentiate between a pure search for knowledge and a search for indications about the appropriate policy to adopt. Economics however lacks words like 'peace research' or 'strategy' to differentiate between the policy-orientated and the descriptive; which may or may not be a good thing.

Whatever may be the merits or otherwise of using a widened but overlapping vocabulary to describe activities, I shall assume that peace education is education concerning violent conflict at a social rather than an individual level; thus it is broader than the discussions of just international conflict and includes in its domain communal conflict. Further, that it would also include discussions of why groups do not fight when they might be expected to, why they integrate into larger communities, and so on. This then is putting it on a broad base, both in terms of subject matter and approach for I am now saying that peace teaching is the teaching about anything to do with peace, though, because of the inevitably value laden connotations of the word 'peace', it does have some value overtones just as the word 'strategy' does.

Having dealt abruptly with the possible content of peace education, I would like to discuss the concept of education as such in order to suggest a few more lines which should be followed. This discussion is slightly fuller than the last though in view of space still necessarily somewhat superficial.

First, let us clarify what we mean by education. Crudely, we mean that educating a person means making them aware of attributes of the world about which they were previously unaware, or else had some rather primitive notions. It may involve correcting false impressions but more usually it is the provision of new information rather than the correcting of existing but incorrect viewpoints. There is clearly the notion that in educating a person one is telling them something which is true or correct whatever these terms may mean. At least there is the supposition that the educator is acting in good faith and is not deliberately trying to mislead those whom he is educating. This is, of course, not always the case, but I shall be charitable and assume that educators educate in what they believe to be true.

Another point of clarification necessary before getting down to the more substantive part of the paper is who is going to educate? In stable political societies a threefold grouping is convenient: first, the decision makers who will actually have to act on any policies conceived; second the elites who can bring some pressure to bear on the decision makers, and in this I include the media, members of a legislature (who also have some decision making authority, though not often a very high one except in a formal sense); and finally there is the rest of the population who are not particularly influential but whose general attitudes and support is required if any significant switch in social policy is required.

The methods will be different for all three groups and this will be discussed a little later in the paper.

There is also the situation pertaining in unstable societies. I am particularly thinking of cases where there is some communal conflict such as in Ireland. Here, the individual citizen is frequently in a conflict situation and his or her attitudes and behaviour become important in a way that is not the case in the bulk of political decision making where the political process is often perceived (correctly) to be remote. The question of peace education becomes something rather different in this context and this is again something I shall return to, though briefly, later in the paper.

There are a number of categorisations of education which can fruitfully be made. These categorisations of which I single out four, I shall refer to as dimensions of education. Education in different situations and to different groups of people occupies different points on these dimensions and perhaps only rarely does it occupy a place at the extremes. In the case of at least two of the dimensions, the middle points are the most interesting ones.

The first dimension of education is the one which has education by rational argument at one end and education by emotive persuasion at the other. There can of course be a mixture of the two. Rational education can be regarded as the provision of information either of a theoretical or factual nature, of which the recipients were not aware. This information presumably then is intended to readjust their attitudes and ultimately their behaviour. Emotive persuasion involves the highlighting of knowledge that a person may already have and of bringing this knowledge into saliency and increasing his awareness of a problem. Thus, if the problem is one of homelessness, the education might in part be the provision of some statistics about the number of people homeless in, say, London and the nature of the family units who are homeless. This can create the intellectual awareness that a problem exists but it may still be a part of a rather abstract scheme of knowledge and have little emotional impact. However, a person who is fully aware of the statistics might begin to regard it as a matter of urgency if he meets a homeless family, or perhaps sees a film about them or reads a book about what it feels like to be down and out in a city. This, as much as figures, and unless he or she is a person of great imagination, might well cause people to act simply by realising at first hand just what homelessness means to the homeless. Both these things can be regarded as education even though the second may involve a relatively minor addition to knowledge in a more formal sense. Clearly the borderline between education in this second sense and propaganda is a tenuous one. I would define propaganda as the attempt to persuade people to believe or act in certain ways irrespective of whether the information provided is true or false (or in many cases meaningless). Education, however, is presumed to be the attempt to persuade people to believe in things or act on them which the educator believes are true inasmuch as they are statements about the behaviour of the world, or right moral attitudes in the case of moral exhortations. Thus education and propaganda overlap in the sense that the persuasive part of education and the true part of propaganda are the same thing. Clearly, therefore, I am not using propaganda in a necessarily pejorative sense, simply because some of it is wrong or goes, in my opinion, to stir up repugnant attitudes.

Another dimension of education involves as its end point the distinction between knowledge of how to act in various situations in order to achieve certain results, and knowledge which is known more or less for its own sake. I might, for example, be educated in British seventeenth-century poetry. This might conceivably have the effect of making me a nobler spirit and hence someone who in general might behave rather better in my social life, but by and large one would not justify the teaching of seventeenth-century poetry on the lines that society as a whole will be substantially improved by it. It is knowledge and experience for its own sake. In fact one could go as far as saying (as Keynes said only slightly differently when writing on economics) that the point of seeking social and political knowledge in order to solve problems is so that we can devote our lives to such things as poetry instead of having to spend our time making the world habitable. Poetry is perhaps the end rather than the beginning of social action. However, at the other end of this spectrum is knowledge of how to do things. If we want to build a boat, we must learn how to build boats and take advantage of other people's knowledge. If we want to have a revolution, we must learn about revolutions. That is, we acquire certain sorts of knowledge not for the sake of the knowledge itself but in order that we can do something with that knowledge. This particular spectrum has a most important middle point. In order to do something effectively we often require first understanding of the processes involved. Hence we have to learn, or discover, what the processes involved in the system we wish to alter are. Thus we initially learn, rather as we would if we were interested in knowledge for its own sake, and subsequently act. The balance of learning for the sake of learning and learning for the sake of acting is a blurred and hazy one. One frequently embarks on learning without any too clear idea of what the eventual outcome in the terms of actions will be. The same of course applies to teaching. One may teach potential actors without knowing quite how they will perform as actors when the situation arises.

300

A third dimension is that which has at one end education about matters of fact and at the other matters of doctrine or ideology. What is a matter of fact is, of course, a subject of endless philosphical discussion which it would be pointless at this stage to enter into. I shall adopt a simple-minded definition of this and regard something as a matter of fact if virtually everyone agrees that it is true or, if the matter in hand is still one about which one might have rational doubt, then the general procedures for determining its truth are known. About many facts all but a few specialists are ignorant but we accept their views on the truth or otherwise of certain propositions inasmuch as all competent specialists seem to agree. I recognise that there are many problems omitted in this simple-minded view of matters of fact but nevertheless it seems to be a helpful if simple way of going about things. An example of education on matters of fact would be education in physics or mathematics. To educate people in physics means to teach them things and ways of going about finding out things. The teacher has some knowledge which he imparts to the pupil and, at least in the earlier stages, there is little controversy about the truth of what is being taught. As one progresses and gets into the research area of physics, then clearly there are controversies, but the procedures for settling these are by and large known and accepted. Doctrinal education on the other hand is education about certain sets of doctrines which are not accepted by large numbers of people who would by intellect, general education and so on be perfectly able to accept them. A good case of this is religious education. Suppose a person is educated in the doctrines of the Catholic Church, for example. Thus the pupil is told that various things are true even though the truth of this would be disputed by many people. Now it is of course possible to maintain that all schemes of thought within which people are educated are doctrinal and that to a certain extent physics is a body of doctrine just as much as Catholic theology. The only difference is that whereas virtually everyone accepts as true those parts of physics which they can understand, a large number of people do not accept Catholic theology. Hence we have differences of degree only. However, these differences of degree are of sufficient magnitude for us to call them different sorts of procedure when represented at their extremes. However, they are useful points of comparison in order to take our bearings by when we want to examine what we mean by education in any sort of sense.

There is a mid-point on this dimension which is of critical importance. These are questions over which there is doubt, that is, there are many propositions about which we do not know whether they are true or false even though further information might establish much higher probabilities of the truth or otherwise of some statement. Of no feature of the world can we be completely certain, though there are quite a number (such as the earth is a sphere) about which we are fairly certain. Now there are not many assertions about social behaviour which we can make without some considerable degree of doubt, at least when these are generalisations about behaviour rather than individual facts such as the population of Great Britain. Explanations of behaviour consist of relating individual and specific instances of something to a more general class of events and are only valid explanations if these generalisations are true. However, as we can have only moderate confidence in our generalisations, it follows that we can have only moderate confidence (at best) in the validity of our explanations. If we make propositions about deterrence, we implicitly adopt a theory of deterrence and about this theory there is considerable doubt, in all directions, about whether the implied generalisations are true or false.

I think that this is in practice an important point in the discussion of all social behaviour including the behaviour of states and other social groupings which have access to violent means. We seem to have an inbuilt desire for certainty and hence we are frequently tempted to make propositions with a degree of confidence that the evidence does not in fact warrant. It is important to realise that virtually nothing (other than particular facts) can be asserted about social behaviour without there being a considerable degree of doubt about the validity of the generalisations involved. It becomes an important part of peace education, as well as of other forms of education about social behaviour, to make this clear.

The final dimension I would like to consider is that of learning as an act of knowing and learning as a process where one becomes familiar with various forms of conduct which require practice in order to carry them out properly. At one end one might learn about the industrial set-up of Italy, that is, the industries which are carried out in Italy, their relative importance, the market in which the various goods are sold and so on. At the other extreme one thinks in terms of learning how to play the piano or learn a language. It is relatively easy to learn how to read music and to learn the list of what the various signs and symbols mean. It could, I suspect, be learnt within the period of a day. To learn how to play the piano, however, even at a lowish standard requires a great deal of practice. One may know what is wanted or what one aims to achieve, but the process of learning how to achieve it is a lengthy and arduous one. Somewhat similar factors apply in learning a language. It is not simply a matter of learning a vocabulary and a set of grammatical rules (though this itself is a big job), it is also a question of learning by doing and cannot be done in any other way. Thus one might very well know what to do in the sense of having the information but not be able to do it because of insufficient practice.

There is a final characteristic of education worthy of mention which is more to do with the method than the actual education itself. This is the degree to which the education is asymmetric between teacher and pupil. Most education has some degree of asymmetry in it, though the more advanced it gets, the more likely it is to be a mutual learning process. It is common enough, for example, for a doctoral student to know more than his supervisors about his area. While it is fashionable to decry notions of asymmetry, it is usually there and a teacher is a teacher because he or she knows more about the subject taught. Even if the teacher views his role as catalytic in the sense of directing the students' attentions to ways of discovery, this is still a different role from that of pupil and still implies an asymmetry (it normally implies a salary as well).

I have devoted a high proportion of my paper to the discussion of the nature of education because of the high degree of ambiguity which is involved. I think this ambiguity is a concomitant of all education but particularly in the social sciences where the relationship of knowledge to policy and action is often a close one. It therefore becomes more necessary to see just what is meant by the whole notion of education as a process of altering people's ideas and attitudes in order to ensure the legitimacy of one's actions. If one is talking about a policy science in a political community then one is talking politics which is the art, philosophy and science of choice within political societies. This involves considerable responsibility, and an important element of responsibility is clarity.

I shall now proceed briefly to discuss the relevance of the different dimensions of education in the different constituencies people operate in. Different emphases are appropriate in a university-based education as distinct from education directed towards the general public. I shall briefly look at the different dimensions and relate them to the various constituencies, spending more time on university education than the rest.

In my view, the purpose of a university education is to educate people in matters of facts and matters of doubt but not in matters of doctrine except in the sense that different doctrines are examined, so to speak, from the outside. This is not the view of anyone holding a stern doctrinal view but on this issue I take an essentially liberal stance. Those responsible for offering such an education should further pay particular care to analyse different points of view and the procedures for such an analysis. It is, however, not just the purpose of a university to teach people to think nice thoughts but also to teach them to be effective citizens. Hence there has to be some understanding of problems which will involve them in action at some stage or at least be useful to them if they choose to embark on a course of action.

The actual nature of the subjects to be taught in a university course is not my main aim in this paper. I am more concerned with the basis on which education is constructed rather than the subject matter beyond the rather general definition which was given at the beginning.

The basic views I hold concerning a university-based education can be grouped under four headings. These headings are basic presuppositions of what I would regard as a proper form of education in a university setting, given the basic nature of the type of problem we are dealing with, namely problems of peace and war.

First, it is important to separate out value statements from factual statements and furthermore make as explicit as possible the values involved in any particular piece of work. Any student should furthermore be warned against the dangers of mixing fact and value and should be trained to recognise implicit as well as explicit value statements. Emotive attempts are thereby not barred. Indeed, they are proper in the sense that one needs to experience emotive persuasion to be aware of what it is. Nor am I using 'emotive' in a necessarily pejorative sense. An incapacity to appreciate more than a narrow range of issues at an emotional level is part of our human make-up and it is proper to expand it. To repeat, however, it is important at the university level to make people understand the difference between emotive and rational argument. This proposition that values and facts should be clearly separated looks more innocuous than it really is. As stated, few people would disagree with it. What I am more concerned to emphasise is that there are basic underlying value positions about whether or not existing societies should exist in their present form, whether war is sometimes desirable or not, to what extent the State should be (as distinct from is) the prime factor in international contacts and so on. This is not to say that all problems should become submerged in a search for values but that there should nevertheless be an awareness of the problem of the value base of any area of theory and explanation, and this value base can be missed by the unwary.

Secondly, all generalisations (and hence all explanations which rely on generalisations which in my view they necessarily do) are subject to doubt and in social affairs this degree of doubt is usually large. Thus all conclusions are open to perpetual scrutiny and re-examination.

Thirdly, the problem of why wars occur is a researchable problem and our knowledge about such behaviour can be expected to increase over time. It is hopefully possible to have a theory of conflict behaviour which has a parallel status to a theory of economics and of the economics which might be developed in the future. There is commonly an implicit assumption that we can do research on particular topics and improve knowledge from that point of view, and of course do research on ongoing problems expanding our knowledge of events as the events themselves evolve. However, I am arguing that we can hope that

304

our knowledge of the principles which govern human behaviour will increase and that hence our explanations will improve through an improvement of theory and not just of the facts involved in some particular instance. Clearly this is a controversial issue and this is not the point to elaborate on the particular view of the philosophy of the social sciences from which this assertion is derived.

The final point to be aware of is that changes occur in the system, both in the character of the actors involved and their behaviour *vis-à-vis* each other. There exists no coherent theory of social change at the moment in which we can predict such changes in behaviour with any confidence (or indeed predict them very much at all). Clearly any observer of the international scene quickly becomes aware of it as a changing scene. However, we still have some inbuilt habits of thinking that what is, for evermore shall be so.

In attempting to educate a decision making group or group close to decision making groups like a foreign office or indeed other elites one is in a rather different position. One is dealing with people who are essentially experts and they have to be very anxious to expand their expertise and also confident that the educator has something relevant to tell them before there is any point in even starting at all. Once started it seems that all the dimensions of education are relevant including the emotive end of the fact-emotive dimension. A problem which is almost inevitable in decision making is that issues are reduced to technical issues and their implications in human terms are forgotten. Hence it is sometimes worth bringing these to people's attention.

Of one is dealing with reasonably sophisticated people, as one hopes in this case one is, then they are surely not going to be carried away in some sense illegitimately by emotive arguments. One fears more that the emotion of convention will be a more powerful factor in inhibiting imaginative change and hence some heterodox emotion may well not come amiss. The major thing that can be done in such circumstances is again to suggest options which would not otherwise be thought of. However, it seems normal that whenever decision making groups call in consultants, they do so to have their predilections confirmed, not refuted.

As far as the general public is concerned there is very little that can be said with this analysis of education that could not be said without it. Emotive arguments are clearly legitimate. The general public is bombarded with emotive arguments the whole time and one must at times combat emotion with emotion. However, this is not the full story. By and large there is a tendency, even in a pluralist society, for orthodoxy to get a better hearing than heterodoxy. The mere provision of facts, which, though not concealed, are nevertheless not widely published is important and can influence people. This must be done through the media — newspapers, television and so on — and hence it is via the media that one must go to the public. I am not arguing that societies like that, say, in Great Britain, are too bad in this respect. There are opportunities for the expression of heterodox views though there are also powerful pressures to play safe. The effectiveness of the various classes of argument may leave much to be desired, but I think this is within the area of a psychologist of mass learning rather than within the scope of this rather formalist analysis of education.

The final constituency towards which peace education might be directed are those who are within some conflict situation such as Ulster or Cyprus and where the individual is actually caught up directly and as a possible participant in the conflict. The problem here is very different, in that one is involved with people who are actually forced to act in some sort of way and it is a matter of teaching them how to act more effectively. Furthermore, one is not involved in the provision of information for a debate or anything of the sort; unless one is interested in peace at any price, and it is likely that the people involved are not, then one might also become identified with groups in order to help them more effectively achieve their aims. The learning by practice and of the fourth dimension of education becomes significant for it is often important that people should behave in ways which do not come naturally in situations of high tension. It is presumptuous of me to say very much about this sort of topic as I have not been personally involved in such a situation, and writing and thoughts of people who have been are much more relevant. The purpose of this paragraph is really to note the existence of a class of problems in education which seems to me substantially different from the more background forms of education which are appropriate to the other groups of people.

This paper has dealt with some of the conceptual bases of education and, in particular, peace education. It is thus a very abstract piece of work and is intended to be so. I hope, however, that the categories I have discussed will be of some use as boxes to fit things into.

I said at the beginning that I was sceptical of the value of peace education in that reason seems to play little part in the organisation of political societies. However, no matter how forlornly, I think it important that something should be done, and that a climate of opinion should exists and be encouraged in which facts and values are in constant debate. In particular all possibilities, including the heterodox, should be brought forward and debated. It is clear that the future of the human race viewed over a period of two or three hundred years is precarious. Consequently to amble on from year to year, if not day to day, is a strategy which might be locally acceptable but in the long run will be disastrous. Hence, any idea, however superficially absurd, deserves some degree of serious examination in order to differentiate between the absurd and the unusual, between which a confusion frequently exists.

19. AN EDUCATIONAL STRATEGY FOR ARMS CONTROL

John H. Barton

Those interested in arms control often think of themselves as partisans of an exotic speciality that is essentially unintelligible to the public. Their educational efforts, at least in the United States, tend therefore to emphasise the full education of a small arms control elite and the occasional propagandisation of the public on the horrors of war or the evils of the military establishment. This essay suggests an explanation for this emphasis, shows that it can no longer be successful and attempts to suggest an alternative strategy of broader education. Detailed analysis is limited to the United States, the nation whose arms control politics are more familiar to the author, but conclusions will also be suggested on the basis of a cursory summary of contrasts with Europe and with developing nations. The possibilities of arms control education in the Soviet Union and China are crucial but are not explored here.

To explain the current arms control attitudes, one must go back to the arms control framework of the late 1950s and early 1960s. For the American public, disarmament was considered unrealistic and was believed to smack of communism. Arms control was not intellectually separated from disarmament. All were somewhat suspect, and raised the question 'How can you trust the Communists?'. For this reason, coupled with the relatively primitive state of unilateral reconnaissance technology and the hangovers of public belief in a nuclear secret, inspection emerged as a particularly crucial negotiating problem. But even more, the whole idea of negotiating in the armament area drew fire. Thus in 1961 when Congress passed the act which created the US Arms Control and Disarmament Agency, it not only insisted on taking the word 'Peace' out of the proposed title; it also imposed extra severe security clearance requirements and a duty that all agreements in the arms control area be submitted to Congress. The fear of disarmament negotiations and of those associated with them was clear.

In the face of these public attitudes, arms controllers made four crucial decisions. The first was to seek limited agreements only. Each step was rationalised as all that was available and as a small step towards something bigger — but no one even displayed a map showing where the steps were going. This step was fateful — for example, the partial nuclear test-ban separated from a cut-off on military production of nuclear materials antagonised France and contributed to its departure from arms control negotiations. The limited steps decision also tended to imply that arms control would be a superpower issue and would ignore the United Nations framework. This limited approach, epitomised by the American rejection of the Soviet initiatives of May 1955, certainly depended heavily on perceptions of international politics. It also had a domestic basis in the public opposition to negotiation with the Soviet Union.

The second decision, which flowed from the first and from Soviet concerns about on-site inspection, was to yield on on-site inspections, and depend almost entirely on unilateral intelligence capability. This decision influenced future arms control politics, because arms control would in a sense become an expertise reserved to those with access to intelligence data. Those who are outside the government have less credibility on arms control matters than those within. The system came full circle in the case of those Soviet nuclear tests which vented in technical violation of the Partial Test Ban — the government's control over technical data becomes a way to help forestall public outcry. Another interesting twist is suggested by the no-first-use proposals, which have never been considered seriously in the United States with the primary objection being the verification problem.

The third decision was that the recipients of arms control thinking should be the elite strategic thinkers within the government. Like the previous decision this was a response (possibly correct!) to easy temptation. The Secretary of Defense was sympathetic to ways to reduce arms costs. The arms controllers could make a persuasive argument that certain arms control agreements would be mutually beneficial to the United States and the Soviet Union — in the jargon, the agreements would be non-zero-sum games. The elite strategic thinkers were the only ones responsive to this argument — therefore arms controllers emphasised contacts with them and avoided the problems of public opposition.

The public was dealt with through a fourth decision — to allow arms control to rest politically on the shoulders of something else. Thus, the Antarctic Treaty of 1959 was an interim territorial arrangement, coupled with arms control. The Hot-line was a form of crisis management. The Outer Space Treaty combined arms control with astronaut safety and a general ordering of outerspace law.

The unusual case is the Partial Test Ban. It is difficult to look at the history of that treaty's ratification and not to say that an attempt was made to draw political support from a budding environmental movement responding to the fall-out question. However, Gallup polls for May 1957 showed 63 per cent who supported an agreement to stop nuclear tests and only 52 per cent who believed that the fall-out

309

problem was real. The latter figure, incidentally, was even lower for those with more education. Perhaps public opinion had changed by 1963. Or perhaps the Treaty's brokers hitched their cart to the wrong horse, which could help to explain the difficulty of obtaining Senate ratification. The ratification process shows a further impact of public opinion. Apparently enough Senators would be swayed by Joint Chiefs support that Kennedy offered several commitments to obtain that support. These included a promise to continue underground testing, a promise to maintain systems to detect Soviet testing, and a promise to maintain a stand-by atmospheric testing capability.

Thus, a pattern had been set with three critical domestic aspects. First, treaties could be emasculated by domestic side-arrangements. Second, the arms controller would seek to co-opt defence experts as the prime recipients of his studies. Third, little serious effort would be made to inform the public.

Over the next ten years, the arms controller's approach did not change but public opinion did. Presumably in response to the Vietnam War, but probably aided by many other factors, public opinion shifted towards favouring peace and *détente per se*. Arms procurements received less support in Congress (although Congress's position may be swinging back very recently). Arms control became an asset instead of a liability. Thus when President Nixon brought home the SALT I package in 1972, he chose as his chief selling point *détente* instead of the subtleties of deterrence theory or the virtues of a bipolar world. He was even able to secure the passage of weapons systems through Congress by arguing that they would be bargaining chips. Arms control helped weapons rather than vice versa. And these procurements may have been in addition to those derived from the political bargains within the executive branch to obtain military support for new arms control agreements. Thus, the superpowers arms control negotiations became a way to manage the arms race and to extract arms from a somewhat reluctant Congress. The arms controllers were co-opted by the very officials they had sought to co-opt.

The possibility of making arms control agreements has been limited along with the effectiveness of the agreements once made. It is in part because the public, and Congress — and even foreign leaders — were inadequately informed about the concepts of deterrence theory that Senator Henry Jackson was able to succeed with his parity argument. (Even if one accepts the suggestion that President Nixon supported Jackson's efforts, explanation of Nixon's actions still requires an assumption that many Senators and much of the public would be moved by simple numerical disparity.) The upshot is that numerical parity has become required for future agreements, whether or not such parity is required by a reasonable theory of extended deterrence.

This restriction on agreement content was shown in a different way in the 1974 Moscow Summit. An agreement restricting counterforce targeting would almost certainly have been to the joint benefit of the United States and the Soviet Union (although one can argue that it would be opposed to West European interests). Even under the other limitations placed on arms control agreements, such a restriction would have been theoretically possible, by means of controls on missile testing or substantial reductions in the land-based missile force. Although there may have been analogous Soviet difficulties, it seems likely, judging from Secretary Kissinger's remarks, that the President felt unable to overrule Secretary Schlesinger, who wanted to develop such capabilities. Perhaps Nixon could have done so had he not been counting impeachment votes; he would probably never have done so without public support on the issue.

Generalising, under current arms control politics, it is *impossible* to negotiate any reductions of any forces which nearly anyone wants to keep for nearly any reason. There are two independent supports for the conclusion. One is the bargaining chip logic; the other is the ratification debate on military veto logic. The first of these is the classical argument — already stated forty-five years ago by Salvador de Madariaga — that nations will be so concerned about relative force levels under arms control that the negotiations will increase absolute force levels. The problem was and is acquisition of weapons for bargaining chips. There is more hope now — Madariaga was writing in an era before nuclear weapons and deterrence theory, which do provide a rationale for decreasing force levels. Moreover, public attitudes towards arms have changed substantially. If one tries to solve the bargaining chip problem, the direct approach is to change the mode of international negotiation. But the history just described suggests a second reason why arms reduction fails — arms are procured in order to obtain military support for the arms control agreement — thus Kennedy's commitments in 1963 or the B-1 and Trident in 1972. Or, as with the counterforce capability in 1974, military opposition vetos the agreement beforehand. There is no easy change in the mode of international negotiation that avoids this problem. Instead, one must find a court of last resort in which the military pressure can be overcome. The only practical ways are through public opinion and expertise independent of the military.

I hope I have argued persuasively that arms control must now turn from its elitist orientation and view its audience much more broadly. This implies a need for public education. Without public opinion, the military veto cannot be overcome in the United States and probably not in Europe either. For the public education to be responsible and for the decision maker to be able to decide rationally between conflicting public and military positions, the need is for independent expertise. This expertise already exists in the strategic weapons area. It emerged within the Government in the time of MacNamara and outside the Government during the 1969 Anti-Ballistic Missile debate. But there are still many issues for which new independent expertise is needed — and these needs also affect educational strategy.

The reason is that arms control itself is changing. The decisions taken in the 1950s may now be obsolete and the body of knowledge on which arms control relies is nearly exhausted. The arms controllers of the 1950s thought of a Soviet-American nuclear war as the most serious threat. That threat is no longer nearly so serious, and other wars have become much more likely. Many of the wars that have killed people recently have taken place in developing nations. The wars most likely to escalate to the nuclear level have taken place in the Middle East. And the future spectre is of a world in which nuclear and major conventional capabilities have spread to many nations, tied together by alliances and guarantees. Some of these nations can be counted on to be politically or economically aggressive. Few will share common understandings of the exact force relationships of one to another. Most will accept a *Realpolitik* ideal but few will have the diplomatic tradition to exercise *Realpolitik* wisely. This is a recipe for World War III.

It is now possible to suggest specific areas in which arms control education is needed. That needed for elites, namely international affairs decision makers and those who advise such decision makers, will first be discussed. It is these elites who are educated in graduate-level university programmes and to whom one must look for balanced judgements on military and political issues that would otherwise be neglected. Then, public education, meaning that which ought to be available to any interested adult, will be discussed. It can be acquired through non-specialist university programmes, TV, or journalists trained in specialised programmes.

American experience makes it quite clear that education in deterrence theory is still needed at the elite level. Ignorance here was found in Congress as well as among laymen, and has been crucial to the success of the military veto. The change of arms control emphasis implies a need to include military affairs generally — too many leaders are too impressed by relatively naive comparisons of conventional forces. European understanding of force capability evidently, for example, restricts the availability of some arms control agreements, and, although this need may be stronger at the public level than at the elite level, the weakness of aircraft carriers could usefully be more widely understood. The new military technologies need also to be more widely understood; it would be a tragedy if they offered an arms control potential that was lost through simple military inertia.

The list of areas for elite education can be expanded to face the contemporary problems which are often ignored in favour of the problems defined by the choices made in the 1950s. Examples are the way that small-step arms control agreements might be cumulated and the interactions between arms control and international organisation restructured. These problems typically require additional research: the political scientists do not have available ready-made theories or even ready-made debates.

Finally, these are elite-orientated problems that are related specifically to the non-superpower arms control mentioned above. For the shambles of the diplomacy of the Non-Proliferation Treaty (NPT) demonstrate that a far deeper understanding of developing nation incentives and interests is needed. A deeper understanding on the part of the leaders of the developing nations is needed of how balance-of-power diplomacy works and of what its limitations are.

These are the sort of subjects which should be the point of emphasis in university specialist programmes and in the institutes devoted to specialists. The possibility is shown by the number of courses already in operation. Judging from the present author's Stanford experience, interest levels are only moderate (particularly in some of the more subtle areas as opposed to deterrence theory), but a few students become intensely interested and relatively few specialists are needed. A programme to provide short courses for journalists and decision makers is ideally combined with such a university programme.

Publics need some of all of the above. The areas where particular detail is needed probably include the counter-initiative aspects of deterrence theory and the non-superpower aspects of arms control. The first of these has been crucial in SALT; the second will be central to the issues of the future. The failure of the NPT really was a surprise to the American public. Finally, the public clearly needs a chance to learn more about the domestic politics of arms control and the way in which arms control is frustrated in its current political mode. These subjects should not be too difficult to convey to the public, which does, after all, often have substantial insight into such areas as football tactics or Second World War strategy. The obvious medium in developed nations is TV, in the hands of politicians themselves or of broadcasting journalists. Similar education is also needed in the developing nations, particularly in those which are rapidly acquiring weapons. It may be necessary to make sure that the developing nation elites participate in many discussions with developed nation elites. These contacts are desirable in themselves – and the developing nation elites will, it is hoped, disseminate their own knowledge within their own nations.

313

20. TOLERANCE OF AMBIGUITY IN INTERPERSONAL BARGAINING

Lillian Davis

Introduction

This study is an attempt to analyse the psychological factors and personality characteristics of negotiators, as distinct from the political forces which probably only partially determine international policy. The personality variable under observation is the negotiator's tolerance of ambiguity (TOA) — how does it affect the outcome of the negotiations and how does information (INFO) in the bargaining environment influence the effects of TOA?

Ambiguity in Bargaining

People who engage in bargaining are interdependent, or mutually tied, at some level(s). In an economic sense, interdependency exists when relevant parties all perceive that their utilities are partially controlled by each other. The innate ambiguity existing in an interdependency might best be shown by comparing single actor decision-making to negotiated decisions-making. In the first case, the single actor need only survey available options and select the one assessed as most suitable. When bargaining is used for decision-making, on the other hand, the parties' strategic interaction induces ambiguity: person A's decisions are dependent upon what person B thinks, which in turn depends on what person B thinks person A thinks, and so on. The parties' choices are dependent upon expectations about the others' choices.

A sports analogy might also be illustrative. Negotiating is more like playing tennis than golf. In a golf game, the opponent (the course) is constant; in tennis, the opponent is always changing. An aspiring golfer might play the same course again and again until it is mastered. A tennis player may practice with the same opponent, but if the stakes are raised, a good tennis player will expect the unexpected.[1]

The same sort of ambiguity exists in bargaining strategic interaction. Negotiators interact with some ignorance of each other's value systems and strategy options if only because such facts are inherently unknowable or incommunicable.[2] Further, gamesmanship in bargaining often entails purposely manipulating ambiguity in the process. The inevita-

314

bility of compromises in bargaining encourages participants to bluff and to be secretive. Because the negotiation process is believed to be an ambiguous exercise, TOA should be a significant personality variable in a negotiator's psychological make-up.

Tolerance of Ambiguity

Before relating the specific manifestations of TOA to bargaining behaviour, a composite sketch of gradations of the personality variable might be useful. Low TOA has been defined as the tendency to perceive ambiguous situations as sources of threat and high TOA as the tendency to perceive ambiguous situations as desirable or preferable.[3] An ambiguous situation is one which is perceived to be too complex to be structured or categorised; thus ambiguity is called 'subjective uncertainty'.[4]

Ambiguity implies some degree of behavioural conflict: that different aspects of a situation evoke discordant reactions or else that a particular reaction is called forth by one aspect and inhibited by another. The ambiguous situation is contrasted to those seen as clear, distinct, and conclusive and which generally evoke appropriate and/or unconstrained learned behaviours.[5]

People with low TOA strongly prefer familiarity, symmetry, definiteness, and regularity.[6] They also express needs for clarity, righteousness, seriousness, routine, high standards, moral strictness, determination, hard work, authority, decisiveness, conventionality, and conformity. People with high TOA tend to demand less clarity, less routine, and so on in their relationships.[7]

These different preferences are probably manifested in interpersonal conflicts. For instance, a person with low TOA would be expected to make total acceptance/rejection evaluations of possible solutions; whereas a person with high TOA would tend to look for advantages and disadvantages coexisting in some solutions. Similarly, lower TOA persons likely make rigid, premature evaluations of the opponent's intentions, while higher TOA persons are likely to make more flexible, tentative evaluations of the bargaining relationship.

Because different TOA predispositions are probably triggered by elements in interpersonal conflict and because bargaining is an essentially ambiguous process, the behaviours associated with high and low TOA would seem significantly to affect negotiated decisions.

An Experimental Investigation

An experiment was designed to test five sets of hypotheses about the relationship between TOA and bargaining.[8] The following discussion will include only two of these sets. The first section below will provide a brief rationale for the hypotheses, the second section is a description of the methodology, the third section is a summary of the results of the statistical tests, and the concluding discussion deals with possible interpretations of the data.

1. *Rationale*

(i)   TOA and Pay-offs: The first bargaining variable of interest was pay-offs, that is, was high or low TOA associated with winning or losing? In this study, pay-offs were reward measures. They represented rewards like wage increases and productivity contracts in labour negotiations; ransom money and returned family members in kidnapping negotiations; privacy and attention in marital bargaining. Economists assign utilities to pay-offs according to how much the recipient is believed to value the reward.

Regardless of whether negotiations are primarily cooperative or competitive, people with low TOA were expected to receive a smaller pay-off than people with high TOA. In cooperative situations, people with high TOA are expected to perceive the advantages of collaboration and to devise settlement terms by which each party can maximise returns. People with low TOA are expected to interpret a conflict as a win/lose situation, and the resultant polarisation would tend to prevent an equal split of the joint pay-off.

Even in a highly competitive situation in which each party seeks to minimise the other's pay-off or to maximise the difference between the two pay-offs, low TOA was expected to be a handicap. Apparently these people have severe difficulty thinking clearly and communicating in psychologically threatening situations. They probably become so compulsively defensive that they can be victimised by more relaxed tolerant aggressors. (However, if a person's stubbornness or rigidity forces an opponent to concede to avoid a stalemate, a person with low TOA would be predicted to win more than the person with high TOA who is believed to be more flexible.) The low TOA person's handicaps are mainly intense emotional and avoidance tendencies which might supersede the initial objectives in the bargaining situation.

The relationship between the negotiators' pay-offs (equal, close, divergent) is also critical, as it can be used as an indicator of a power balance at the point of settlement. For instance, if a joint pay-off were 500 and one person won 450, there would be evidence that an asymmetric power structure was created or restored in the process. On the other hand, if each person won 250, the settlement would reflect a balance of power.

In conflicts between persons with significantly different TOA predispositions, a balanced settlement was not expected to occur. Past

316

research suggests that conflicts are most intense between persons with very high and very low TOA.[9] Since they tend to perceive situations differently, and since they usually solve problems with distinctly different logic patterns, their communication is impaired. The normally 'easy-going' high TOA person probably becomes frustrated in negotiations with a person who clings stubbornly to two-valued orientations (black-white, either-or). Therefore, an asymmetric power balance and widely divergent pay-offs were expected in matches between high and low TOA bargainers.

Pay-offs were expected to be less divergent in matches between two persons with low TOA. Although these people were expected to be rigid and perhaps hostile, the participants would tend to similarly perceive the conflict and would have less difficulty accepting each other's dichotomous thought and speech patterns. In conflicts between two persons with high TOA, pay-offs were expected to be even less divergent. The participants not only would have the advantage of similar problem-solving patterns, but would also be more likely to pursue mutually rewarding settlements.

The hypotheses derived from the above rationale were:

Pay-offs: $\epsilon(H) > \epsilon(L)$

Pay-off Differences: $\epsilon(HH) < \epsilon(LL) < \epsilon(HL)$

(ii) Information: In order to isolate the effects of the personality variable as much as possible another independent variable, information, was manipulated. The kind of information of interest is data about each other's value systems, priorities, or utilities. It has been suggested that incomplete information in a bargaining situation creates dilemmas concerning goals and communication.[10] The bargainer with incomplete information is uncertain about the level of pay-off to be expected, about when and how much the other person should be trusted, and about when and much to be honest. The effects of uncertainty were measured by comparing the case in which one bargainer in each pair lacked utility information with the case in which both bargainers had complete utility information.

(iii) INFO and Pay-offs: Many negotiators probably prepare with the assumption that the more information they can accumulate, the more they will increase their bargaining strength. As Thomas Schelling has pointed out, however, an asymmetric information distribution may be a handicap to the person with more information.[11] If irrational behaviour forces the informed opponent to concede in order to avoid a stalemate, credibility is enhanced if information is actually lacking. In other words, irrational demands are more threatening if they are made by one with truly incomplete information about the situation.

317

Others' observations of bargaining behaviour supports the prediction that people with less information might win more:

(a)   large initial demands improve the probability of success;
(b)   losers make the largest concessions;
(c)   losers tend to make the first compromise;
(d)   a very high initial demand tends to lead to success rather than failure or deadlock[12]

Schelling's rationale for the 'strength-in-ignorance' proposition suggests that the person with more information (and more reasonable aspirations) might well behave like a loser, namely make smaller initial demands, larger concessions, the first compromise, and lower initial demands than a rival with less information.

When both bargainers have extensive and symmetrical utility information, a victory-defeat outcome is less likely. Under these conditions bargainers usually debate a relatively small range of solutions; and neither bargainer can legitimately force the other to a losing position. Although there are cultural differences, Americans with complete utility information are unlikely to accept a losing pay-off or to expect a winning pay-off if an equitable one is perceived.

Pay-off discrepancies are much more likely with asymmetric information as discussed earlier. The hypotheses derived from the rationale above were:

Pay-offs: $\epsilon(\text{C in CI}) < \epsilon(\text{I in CI})$
Pay-off Differences: $\epsilon(\text{CC}) < \epsilon(\text{CI})$

2. *Methodology*

A personality instrument measuring TOA was administered to 400 undergraduate business majors. The 90 subjects with the highest scores (high TOA) and the 90 subjects with the lowest scores (low TOA) were selected for the study, and grouped in three kinds of pairs or dyads:

high — high
low   — low
high — low

They participated in a two-hour simulation in which information was manipulated so that half bargained with symmetric 'complete' information (CC) and the other half with asymmetric information (CI):

	CC	CI
H-H		
L-L		
H-L		

There were 30 subjects in each of the experimental cells.

The experimental task was based upon a labour dispute in which a union had made unacceptable demands on five issues (wages, vacations, union security, seniority, and contract length). The selected subjects were assigned the union representative role or the management representative role to negotiate a new contract.

In the incomplete INFO conditions, the subjects could only infer the utilities or priorities assigned to the five issues. In the complete INFO condition, however, the subjects received a table showing precisely how much the constituencies valued the five issues.

This table was used as a game scoring plan also, and the subjects were paid according to how well they accomplished their constituency's objectives. For instance, settling on a 40c wage increase resulted in the union representative winning $1.44 and the company representative winning $.36. Each settlement point on each of the five issues resulted in a specified pay-off for the subjects, but those with incomplete information did not know the scoring plan (i.e., the assigned utilities). Each pair split a joint pay-off of $5.05 according to points accumulated with the terms of the contract.

A linear models method of statistical analysis was used to test the hypotheses. Similar to analysis of variance, this method generates predicted values by experimental treatment. Models were tested subsequently for significant differences with F values as the decision rule.

3. Results

(i) TOA Effects on Pay-off Differences: Hyp: In H-L dyads, the difference between the pay-offs will be greater than in L-L dyads. In the latter, differences in the pay-offs will be greater than in H-H dyads.

Using the points scored by the subjects with the terms of their contracts, the difference (Δ) between the pay-offs in each dyad was measured. For example, if the company negotiator scored 363 points and the union negotiator scored 142 points, the value of interest was 221.

The data supported the predicted relationships among the group means, and the probability associated with the F value was less than 0.001. In the H-L dyads the predicted difference between the bargainers' pay-off (rounded to the nearest cent) was $0.68; in the L-L dyads the predicted difference was $0.57; and in the H-H dyads the

319

predicted difference was $0.25.

Table 1:   TOA Effects on Pay-Off Differences

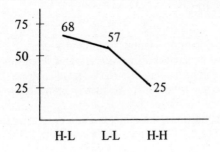

(ii)   TOA Effects on Pay-Offs: Hyp: bargainers with high (H) TOA
will win more than bargainers with low (L) TOA.

To determine if the H TOA bargainers scored more points than the
L TOA bargainers, a test for significant differences was made only in
the H-L dyads (N = 60).

Although the sample size was small, the data clearly did not support
the hypothesis. The predicted score for an H TOA bargainer was $2.45
and the predicted score for an L TOA bargainer was $2.50. This result
is especially interesting because of the highly discrepant scores in the
H-L TOA dyads. Apparently there were just as many L TOA as H TOA
'big winners'.

(iii)   INFO Effects on Pay-Off Differences: Hyp: in CI dyads, the
differences between the pay-offs will be greater than in the CC dyads.

The difference between points scored within each dyad was compared across INFO conditions, and note was made of the TOA score
of the subject with complete INFO in the CI dyads. The difference in
the CI dyads was predicted to be greater than the difference in CC
dyads.

Statistically significant differences (F = 25.8, p < 0.001) supported
the hypothesis. With CC the predicted difference was only $0.21. With
asymmetric INFO, the predicted difference was considerably larger:
when an H TOA person had the complete INFO, the predicted difference was $0.72, and when an L TOA person had the complete INFO,
the predicted difference was $0.87.

320

Table 2:   INFO Effects on Pay-Off Differences

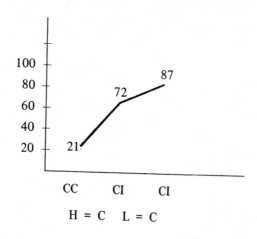

(iv)   INFO Effects on Pay-Offs: Hyp: in CU dyads, bargainers with
I INFO will win more than bargainers with C INFO.

Significant differences in experimental treatments were observed
(F = 35.1, p < 0.001) and the predicted relationship was supported.
The mean pay-off for a subject with complete INFO in CI was $2.28;
the mean pay-off for a subject with incomplete INFO was considerably
higher, $2.78.

Table 3:   INFO Effects on Pay-Offs

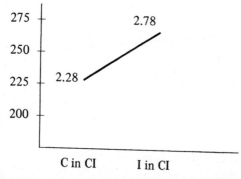

(v)   Two Attribute Model: Hyp: in LL dyads, the points difference
of the HH dyads will be less than the points difference of the LL dyads
and the points difference of the latter will be less than the points difference of the A dyads; in CI dyads, the points difference of the HH

dyads will be greater than the points difference of the A dyads in CC but less than the points difference of the LL dyads in CI and the points difference of the latter will be less than the points difference of the A dyads in CI.

$$\epsilon(HH,CC) < \epsilon(LL,CC) < \epsilon(A,CC) < \epsilon(HH,CI) < \epsilon(LL,CI) < \epsilon(A,CI)$$

This type of model controls for the effects of INFO condition while observing the effects of TOA on bargaining behaviour. This is the central hypotheses in the study because the basic question concerned the interaction of TOA and INFO in bargaining situations.

The data showed that within the H-L TOA dyads INFO conditions produced considerable effects. With CC the predicted difference between the subjects' pay-offs was only $0.22. When the H TOA bargainer had incomplete INFO, however, the difference was $0.75, and when the L TOA bargainer had incomplete INFO, the difference was almost twice as much, $1.42. Again the H-H dyads had less differences within dyads, but the effects of INFO were clear. With CC the mean pay-off difference was $0.15 and with CI it was $0.32.

The differences between information effects in the L-L TOA case were again obvious: with CC the predicted difference was $0.25 and with CI the mean was almost four times as great, $0.93.

The test for interaction was also significant (F = 18.8, p < 0.001), showing that the effects of TOA were different under different information conditions.

Table 4:   TOA and INFO Effects on Pay-Off Differences

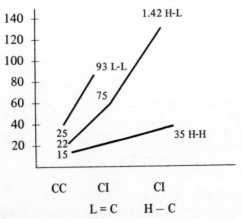

4. *Discussion*

One unexpected result was that the data provided no evidence that winning or losing is associated with H or L TOA. This is especially interesting because the pay-off measure is the study's closest indicator of bargaining skill or competence.

However, the TOA composition within a dyad (i.e., who is matched with whom) did affect the pay-off measure. The H-H dyads tended to split the joint pay-off equally, regardless of INFO condition. This may be a result of a basically cooperative nature, a less aggressive nature, similar problem-solving tendencies and/or facilitated communication in these matches.

The L-L dyads had much greater pay-off discrepancies. With CC the difference was relatively low ($0.25), but with asymmetric INFO it was much higher than the differences observed in the H-H dyads. Less willingness to cooperate, more hostility, more rigidity, or less ability to respond to cues about an equitable settlement from the informed partner are possible explanations of this pattern.

When an H TOA bargainer was matched with an L TOA bargainer there were clear winners and losers only when information was asymmetric. Apparently when the L TOA bargainer had additional INFO, there was a stronger tendency toward a mutually-satisfying pay-off split (75) than when the L TOA bargainer had incomplete INFO. The data provide evidence that a fifty-fifty split or collaboration is least likely to occur in a match between an H TOA bargainer with complete INFO and an L TOA bargainer with incomplete INFO.

The support for the Schelling hypothesis that incomplete information may be an advantage with regard to pay-offs is interesting. One explanation not discussed by Schelling is that bargainers with more information become unrealistically confident and are not prepared to counter irrational demands with similar strategies. Probably a reasonable prescriptive implication, if this situation is a factor, is that negotiators should not flaunt additional information but rather use it subtly and to strategic advantage.

Generally what the data showed is that people with high or low TOA should not avoid bargaining or should not be eliminated from a list of potential representatives in a bargaining situation. Neither predisposition seems related to winning or losing. Further, when information is relatively complete and symmetrical the mutual pay-offs are likely to be similar.

In cases of asymmetric INFO, however, pay-offs might be highly divergent, especially when the person with low TOA has less information. A mediator or third party who has a vested interest in a mutually satisfying division of rewards may try to equalise the available utility information by keeping the low TOA negotiator as informed as possible.

323

Most people have some idea of their tolerance for ambiguous situations. A third party cannot only ask the negotiators about their tolerance, but can also observe extreme predispositions in their behaviour. Such tendencies as dichotomous (black/white) evaluations, extreme attention to detail, and blocking of complex or unstructured input are good indicators of low TOA. Tendencies to avoid clear evaluations of solutions, lack of attention to detail, and fascination with seemingly unrelated information probably indicate high TOA. If these differential behaviours seem to be preventing communication or blocking a settlement, a third party might manipulate information in ways suggested by these data to facilitate conflict management.

Notes

1. For this analogy I am indebted to Professor F. S. Brandt, Professor of Management, University of Texas at Austin.
2. T. C. Schelling, 'Uncertainty, Brinkmanship and Chicken' in K. Archibald (ed.), *Strategic Interaction and Conflict* (University of California Institute of International Studies, 1966), pp. 74-87.
3. S. Budner, 'Intolerance of Ambiguity as a Personality Variable', *Journal of Personality*, XXX (1962), pp. 29-50.
4. V. Hamilton, 'Perceptual and Personality Dynamics in Reaction to Ambiguity', *British Journal of Psychology*, XLVIII (1957), pp. 200-15.
5. D. E. Berlyne, 'Uncertainty and Conflict: A Point of Contact between Information Theory and Behavior Theory Concepts', *Psychological Review*, LXIV (1957), pp. 329-39.
6. E. Frenkl-Brunswick, 'Intolerance of Ambiguity as an Emotional and Perceptual Personality Variable', *Journal of Personality*, XVIII (1949), pp. 108-43.
7. W. Eckhardt and A. G. Newcombe, 'Militarism, Personality, and other Social Attitudes', *Journal of Conflict Resolution*, XIII (1969), pp. 210-19.
8. Lillian Davis, 'An Experimental Investigation of Tolerance of Ambiguity and Information in Interpersonal Bargaining', unpublished Doctoral Dissertation for the University of Texas at Austin. (In progress.)
9. See, for example, B. D. Slack and J. O. Cook, 'Authoritarian Behaviour in a Conflict Situation', *Journal of Personality and Social Psychology*, XXV (1973), pp. 130-6; and R. J. Meeker, G. H. Shure, and W. H. Moore, Jr., 'Real Time Computer Studies of Bargaining Behavior: The Effects of Threat Upon Bargaining', *AFIPS Conference Proceedings* (Spring Joint Computer Conferences, XXV, 1964), pp. 115-23.
10. H. H. Kelley, 'A Classroom Study of the Dilemmas in Interpersonal Negotiations', in Archibald, *op. cit.*, pp. 49-73.
11. T. C. Schelling, 'Bargaining, Communication, and Limited War', *Journal of Conflict Resolution*, I (1957), pp. 19-36.
12. A. Harras, *The Negotiating Game* (New York, 1970).

CONTRIBUTORS

JOHN H. BARTON (US) is Associate Professor of Law at the Stanford Law School. He is a member of the Stanford Arms Control and Disarmament Group and is preparing a book analysing the effectiveness of arms control.

J. BOWYER BELL (US) is Senior Research Associate at the Institute of War and Peace Studies, Columbia University. He has written six books and thirty articles on war, revolution and political violence. He holds a Ph.D. degree from Duke University and has been awarded at various times a Fulbright Fellowship; a Guggenheim Fellowship; and a Ford Foundation Grant.

THOMAS BLAU (US) is Assistant Professor of Political Science and Social Science at the University of Colorado. He was formerly in the US Department of Defense and Assistant Director of the Chicago Arms Control and Foreign Policy Seminar. He was awarded a Ph.D. by Chicago University.

GASTON BOUTHOUL (French) is the President and Founder of the Institut Français de Polémologie and currently Director of Research. He is the author of many widely translated works on philosophy, sociology and polemology.

DAVID CARLTON (British) (Co-Editor) is Senior Lecturer in Diplomatic History at the Polytechnic of North London. He is the author of *MacDonald versus Henderson: The Foreign Policy of the Second Labour Government* (Macmillan, London, 1970) and of numerous articles on problems of international politics in the twentieth century. He is Co-Editor of the previous volume in this series, *The Dynamics of the Arms Race* (Croom Helm, London, 1975).

LILLIAN J. DAVIS (US) is engaged in personnel management for the Information Records Division of International Business Machines, Indiana. She is registered as a Ph.D. candidate at the University of Texas at Austin, her dissertation to be entitled 'An Experimental Investigation of Tolerance of Ambiguity in Interpersonal Bargaining'.

LLOYD J. DUMAS (US) is Associate Professor of Industrial and Management Engineering at Columbia University. Awarded a Ph.D. in Economics from Columbia in 1972, he has also taught at the City University of New York. He has contributed to Seymour Melman (ed.), *The Defense Economy* (Praeger, 1970).

BERNARD T. FELD (US) is Professor of Physics at Massachusetts Institute of Technology. He has also been visiting Professor of Theoretical Physics at Imperial College, London, and, since 1973, Secretary-General of the Pugwash Conferences on Science and World Affairs. He has written widely on problems of arms control. He has recently acted as joint editor of two volumes on the arms race: *Impact of New Technologies on the Arms Race* (MIT Press, 1972); and *The Future of the Sea-Based Deterrent* (MIT Press, 1973).

ROBERT FRANK (US) is a student of International Relations at Brandeis University, Massachusetts, and at the Institute of European Studies, University of London. He has also studied Semitic Languages at the Hebrew University, Jerusalem.

VICTOR GILINSKY (US) is Head of The Department of Physical Sciences at the Rand Corporation, Santa Monica. He was formerly Assistant Director for Policy and Program Review at the US Atomic Energy Commission, Washington, D.C. He is especially interested in peaceful nuclear energy and in the possibility of nuclear weapons proliferation.

PIERRE HASSNER (French) is engaged on research under the auspices of the Centre d'Etude des Relations Internationales at the Foundation Nationale des Sciences Politiques, Paris. He is also Professor of Politics, Johns Hopkins University, Bologna. He has written extensively on problems of European security. His most recent work is *Europe in the Age of Negotiation* (The Washington Papers, 1973).

DANIEL HERADSTVEIT (Norwegian) is Deputy Director of the Norwegian Institute of International Affairs. His publications include *Nahost — Guerrillas* (Berlin Verlag, 1973) and *Arab and Israeli Elite Perceptions* (Humanities Press, 1974).

BRIAN M. JENKINS (US) is a staff member of the Rand Corporation, Santa Monica. He has specialised in the study of conspiracy and revolution and has published extensively on these themes. He acquired a notable expertise on the Vietnam conflict, winning the US Department of the Army's highest award for Outstanding Civilian Service following his work for the Long Range Planning Task Group based in Saigon.

J. HENK LEURDIJK (The Netherlands) teaches international relations at the University of Amsterdam. He specialises in general theories of international politics, in strategic analysis, and in problems of arms control and disarmament.

MICHAEL NICHOLSON (British) is Director of the Richardson Institute for Conflict and Peace Research, London. He was formerly a staff member of the Centre for the Analysis of Conflict, University College, London and Senior Research Fellow at the University of Lancaster. He is author of *Conflict Analysis* (English University Press, 1971) and *Oligopoly and Conflcit: A Dynamic Approach* (Liverpool University Press, 1972).

NINO PASTI (Italian) is a retired Italian Air Force General. He was at various times Italian Military Representative to the Allied Command Europe; Vice-Chief of Staff of the Italian Air Force; Italian Member of the NATO Military Committee; and Deputy Supreme Allied Commander Europe for Nuclear Affairs.

STEVEN J. ROSEN (US) is Assistant Professor of Politics at Brandeis University, Massachusetts, specialising in the political economy of international conflict. He will shortly take up an appointment as Senior Research Fellow at the Australian National University, Canberra. He is author of *The Logic of International Relationships* (Winthrop, 1974) and of several articles on conflict.

CARLO SCHAERF (Italian) (Co-Editor) is Professor of Physics at the University of Rome. He was formerly a Research Associate at Stanford University and on the Staff of the Italian Atomic Energy Commission. With Professor Eduardo Amaldi he founded in 1966 The International School on Disarmament and Research on Conflicts (ISODARCO). He was appointed Director of ISODARCO in 1970. He is Co-Editor of the previous volume in this series, *The Dynamics of the Arms Race* (Croom Helm, London, 1975).

GEORGE SLIWOWSKI (Polish) is Professor of Criminal Law at the Nicholas Copernicus University at Torun, Poland. In 1973-4 he was Vice-Dean of the International Institute of Higher Studies in Criminal Sciences at Syracuse, Italy. He has written several monographs and 200 articles in a variety of languages.

THOMAS STONIER (US) is Professor of Science and Society, University of Bradford, Great Britain. He was formerly Professor of Biology and Director of the Peace Studies Program, Manhattan College, New York. He is author of *Nuclear Disaster* (Penguin, 1964).

327

HERBERT YORK (US) is based at the University of California, San Diego, where he has been Chancellor and Dean. He was one of the nuclear scientists who developed the Atomic Bomb. He subsequently served in the US Department of Defense under both Presidents Eisenhower and Kennedy. His most recent work is: *Race to Oblivion: A Participant's View of the Arms Race* (Simon and Shuster, New York, 1970).

CIRO E. ZOPPO (US) teaches International Relations at the University of California, Los Angeles. He is Executive Director of the California Arms Control and Foreign Policy Seminar and a Consultant at the Rand Corporation, Santa Monica. He is author of many studies on arms control and on Mediterranean politics.

LIST OF COURSE PARTICIPANTS

Urbino, Italy, 12-24 August 1974

Name	*Nationality*	*Present Address*
AEBI Alfred	Swiss	Mädergutstrasse 37, Berne, Switzerland
AITKEN Martin P.	British	63 Holbrook Road, Cambridge Great Britain
ANNEQUIN Jean Louis	French	12 Rue Fabre d'Eglantine, 75012 Paris, France
BARNABY Frank	British	Sveavägen 166, S-11346 Stockholm, Sweden
BARTON John	US	University of California, Arms Control and Disarmament Group, Stanford, California 94305, United States
BELL J. Bowyer	US	Columbia University Institute of War and Peace Studies, 420 West 118th Street, New York, NY 10027, United States
BISCARETTI Emanuele	Italian	Via Alberto da Giussano 26 20145 Milano, Italy
BLAU Thomas	US	850 20th Street, 503, Boulder, Colorado 80302, United States
BRUNI Alessio	Italian	Via Mantellini 8F, 50016 S. Domenico di Fiesole, Firenze, Italy
CALOGERO Francesco	Italian	Via Sant'Alberto Magno 1, Roma, Italy
CARDAMONE Carmine	US	1415 N. 3rd Avenue, Tucson, Arizona, United States
CARLTON David	British	28 Westminster Mansions, Great Smith Street, London SW1, Great Britain

CHAMMAH Albert	US	7201 Fred Morse Drive, Austin, Texas 78723 United States
CREMER Pierre	Belgian	Ave Paul Deschanel 9, 1030 Brussels, Belgium
DAVIS Lillian	US	5914 Highland Hills Drive, Austin, Texas, United States
DUMAS Lloyd	US	150 Glenwood Ave, Yonkers, New York, United States
FABIYI Edwin Oluwafemi	Nigerian	25 Bode Thomas Street, Palm Grove, Lagos, Nigeria
FELD Bernard T.	US	60 Great Russell Street, London, Great Britain
FONTANA GIUSTI Luigi	Italian	Capo Ufficio XIV, Direz. Gen. Affari Politici, Ministero AA.EE., Roma, Italy
FOURIE Deon	South African	University of South Africa, Pretoria, South Africa
GEERAERTS Gustaaf	Belgian	Lange Haagstraat 35, Brussels, Belgium
GELY Chantal	French	20 Avenue A. Briand, 39000 Louis-le-Saunier, France
GILINSKY Victor	US	369 Sumac Lane, Santa Monica, California, 90402 United States
GIOVANNINI POSA M. Grazia	Italian	Viale Castro Pretoria, 116, Roma, Italy
GROSSJOHANN Klaus Wimar	West German	Handstrasse 2, 53 Bonn – Oberkassel, Federal German Republic
GUSMAROLI Franca	Italian	Via Aubrey 2, Roma, Italy
HASSNER Pierre	French	28 Rue du Ranelagh, Paris XVI, France
HERADSTVEIT Daniel	Norwegian	Gabelsgt 47B, Oslo-2, Norway
HOEFNAGELS Marja J.R.	Dutch	Avenue de la Sauvagine 7, 1170 Brussels, Belgium
IMBER Mark Frederick	British	109 Taybridge Road, Battersea, London SW 11, Great Britain
JACCHIA Enrico	Italian	Piazza dell'Orologio 7, Roma, Italy

JENKINS Brian	US	RAND Corporation, 1700 Main Street, Santa Monica, California 90406, United States
JOHNSON Douglas K.	US	43 Hamilton Drive, Glasgow, Great Britain
JÖNSSON Christer	Swedish	Sunnanväg 2B, 5-222 26 Lund, Sweden
LEURDIJK J. Henk	Dutch	Lepelaarlaan 6, Kortenhoef The Netherlands
MORGENTHAU Hans	US	19 East 80th Street, New York, NY 10021, United States
NAKAI Yoko	Japanese	3-27-806, Shibuya-4-chome, Shibuya-ku, Tokyo, Japan
NICHOLSON Michael	British	21 Fitzwarren Gardens, London N 19, Great Britain
PASTI Nino	Italian	Via Due Ponti 221, Roma, Italy
PINO Christopher	US	4865 West Clarence, New York, NY 14031, United States
POTTER Jeff	US	Kohlbrennerstrasse 16, 8 Munich 81, Federal German Republic
PRICE Robert D.	British	25 Rugby Close, St Peter's Court, Broadstairs, Kent Great Britain
RHODES Steven	US	704 Spruce Street, Boulder, Colorado, United States
ROSEN Steven	US	4505 Stearns Hill Road, Waltham, Mass., United States
ROSSI Sergio	Italian	Via Cerulli 43, Roma, Italy
SANDOLE Dennis	US	Landstrasse 101, Escherheimer, 6 Frankfurt a.Main, Federal German Republic
SCHAERF Carlo	Italian	Instituto di Fiscia, Università degli Studi di Roma, Roma, Italy
SCHÜTZ Hans J.	Austrian	Heischberg 2/6, D-23 Kroushagen/Kiel, Federal German Republic

SIMEONE Robert	US	5455 Olive Avenue, Long Beach, California, United States
SJOBERG Hans	Swedish	Toresundsvagen 2, S-12540 Alvsjo, Sweden
SLIWOWSKI George	Polish	Nicholas Copernicus University, Institute of Criminal Law, Torun, Poland
SORIANO Ronald	US	6231 Hokett Way, San Jose, California, United States
STONIER Tom	US	University of Bradford, Bradford, Great Britain
TESHOME Kebede	Ethiopian	Box 5670, Addis Ababa, Ethiopia
VAKSMAN Fabian	Israeli	Beit Student N. 12, Kiryat-Shmuel, Jerusalem, Israel
VETSCHERA Heinz	Austrian	Helenestrasse 124, A-2500 Baden, Austria
WONG Yiu Chung	Chinese (Hong Kong)	Rm 610, Block 9, Valley Road, Estate Hung Hom, Hong Kong
YORK Herbert F.	US	6110 Camino de la Costa, La Jolla, California, United States
ZIAI Iradj	Iranian	148 Avenue, Arya-Mehr Machad, Iran
ZIERMAN Katherine A.	US	76 Thurlow Park Road, London SE 21 Great Britain
ZOPPO Ciro E.	US	12451 Deerbrook Lane, Los Angeles, California United States

NB. Two authors of papers were unable to attend the course, namely Gaston Bouthoul and Robert Frank.